Representations of Gender, Democracy and Identity Politics in Relation to South Asia

Naari Series on Women Studies No. – 2

Representations of Gender, Democracy and Identity Politics in Relation to South Asia

Edited by

Renuka Sharma

Sri Satguru Publications
A Division of
Indian Books Centre
Delhi - 110007

Published by:
Sri Satguru Publications
Indological and Oriental Publishers
A Division of
Indian Books Centre
40/5, Shakti Nagar,
Delhi-110007
(INDIA)

First Edition : Delhi, 1996

ISBN 81-7030-503-9

Printed in India

Published by Sunil Gupta for Sri Satguru Publications, a division of Indian Books Centre, 40/5, Shakti Nagar, Delhi and Printed at D.K. Fine Art Press, Delhi-100 052.

For my grandmother
Indrani

Acknowledgements

The subject matter for this book evolved over a period of time between 1985 and 1995. Over this decade of time there were numerous influences and changes within the field of international feminism. As a diaspora feminist I became aware that there was a lot in contemporary western feminism that did not approximate the placement of non western women in the global context. To thank those that inspired this book in direct and indirect ways is an impossible task. However, the spirit of my grandmother's achievements at the turn of the century in speaking sanskrit, the language of a patriarch brahmanical tradition echos through this work. This acted as a reminder for me of the central importance of the role and function of the language of power structures towards achieving equity and representation.

I would like to thank the constant inspiration from women friends deeply engaged in the development of perspectives that could inform and develop an awareness of difference. Smt Vishalakshi writer and poet provided endless hours of debate, discussion and material on the meanings of Indian, in particular Kannada mythology and the possible interpretations of these for the feminist movement. Also Edith Kelvin friend and travel companion though parts of South India whose clinical work in the area of contemporary psychoanalysis shed light on the interpretation and distinction of religious phenomena from other subjective states.

Numerous other contexts provided ideas for thought such as the Women's sections within the American Philosophical Association and the American Academy of Religion. Within Australia the support from the Women in

Asia Conference Committee and the National Centre for South Asian Studies provided the final inspiration for the book. The establishment of the South Asian Women's Studies Group in 1993 in consultation with the Committee for South Asian Women (USA) was a by product of some of the research and networking conducted for this book. At the final stages of research, the book had mushroomed to 500 pages. Due to this ground swell of articles flooding in, certain emergent categories were identified, i.e. history of the women's movement; themes related to religious, legal, organizational aspects as well as secularism, trade union movements and unique regional perspectives. The emergence of these categories lead to the international conference Women, Power and Cultural Deference. Negotiating Gender in South Asia in conjunction with the XI International Feminist Bookfair. This conference consolidated perspectives as well as reveal the intensity of newly emerging phenomena such as fundamentalism and the related issues of freedom of speech; the evaluation of personal laws towards greater human rights and the tensions against them. This heterogeneity of perspectives certainly challenges a unitary notion of feminism. I would like to thank Susan Hawthorne, Renata Klein and Jane Sloane in helping make the conference possible as well as provide insight to the developments in contemporary western feminism, the subject of the sixth International Feminist Bookfair.

The field of diaspora Asian Feminism is certainly finally developing. The establishment of the Immigrant Women's coalition in Melbourne in 1993 was a mile stone towards the recognition of difference. Melba Marginson co-ordinator, centre for Philippines Concerns provides constant discussion on the development of the women's movement in the Philippines; Pranee Rice on the developmental issues in relation to women and health; Prasuna Reddy for her personal intuitiveness in the development of health issues for women of Asian origins; KumKum Sangari, Gitiara Nasreen, Sara Ahmed and Margie Maistry who in long distance communications provided engagement on critical issues. Foong Ling Koong for the persistent cross Pacific editorial assistance. Last but not least my friend and husband Purushottama Bilimoria, for persisting with discussions well into the night.

This book was completed while on sabbatical. Institutional support from Loyola Marymount University, was kindly offered by Professor Chris Chapple. The facilities offered by Professor Robert Goldman and the staff at the Center for South Asian Studies, Berkeley provided collegiate support. The material in this book was presented at numerous forums as well as used in critical discussions with students. The full text of the book was also the subject of fruitful discussions at The University of Santa Barbara. Last but not least the manuscript traveled to Beijing where the support of women friends who have been part of the decade long communications on the subject provided the necessary determination to see the book to a finish.

Contents

Contributors

Flavia Agnes. Advocate and activist who has helped establish the first free legal aid centre, Majlis for consultation by women in Bombay. She has been actively involved in the women's movement in the last two decades. She has written extensively on issues of domestic violence. Feminist jurisprudence, minority rights and property rights of married women. Her recent books include: My Story . . . Our Story of Rebuilding Broken Lives (1984); Journey to Justice-Procedures to be Followed in Rape Cases (1990); Give Us This day our Daily Bread. Laws and Procedures on Maintenance. (1992).

Sara Ahmed. Centre for Women's Studies and Sociology at Lancaster University. Has published in the areas of psychoanalysis and culture and her post doctoral work Post-Colonia Encounters is to published soon as a book.

Barbara Watson Andaya. Was born in Sydney and was educated at the University of Sydney and the University of Hawaii. She received her Phd from Cornel University in Southeast Asian History and is currently associate professor of Asian Studies in the School of Hawaiian, Asian, and Pacific Studies at the University of Hawaii. Her research interests are concerned primarily with the western Indonesia-Malay archipelago in the early modern period. Her most recent publication is To Live as Brothers. Southeast Sumatra in the Seventeenth and Eighteenth Centuries. (Honolulu 1993).

Videsha Bagchi, born in Sydney, Australia is currently completing postgraduate studies in Sociology at Latrobe University. She has written on the sociology of Indian families in a monograph, 'The Hindu Family as a Matriarchy' with particular reference to Bengal and is currently working on Kierkeguard's Theory of Cultures threw artistic and literary examples.

Aparna Basu. Secretary General, All India Women's Conference. Professor of History. University of Delhi. India.

Gillian Castellino. Belongs to the Goan-Indian diaspora community on which she is currently completing postgraduate studies in relation to diaspora identity at Deakin University. She has worked with the Times of India and in other areas of media.

Shivani Banerjee Chakravorty is the Director of the Office of Women's Research, at the University of Hawaii and teaches in the women's studies program. her Phd theses was on 'Twentieth Century American Women's Fiction' and her post doctoral work was on 'The Girl Child and Gender Construction in 19th and Early 20th Century Bengali Women's Literature' She has also worked as Co-ordinator at the Centre for South Asian Studies, University of Hawaii.

Vinitha Jayasinghe. Founder Director of the Women's Bureau of Sri Lanka, established by the President of Sri Lanka. Also served on the UN Committee on Elimination of All Forms of Discrimination Against women from 1981-1986. First woman Commissioner of Probation and Child Care Services in Sri Lanka. Later to become the first woman State Secretary in the Ministry of Women's Affairs.

Bernadette Joseph, is currently a postgraduate at Monash University. Her main area of interest is the relationship between gender, state and religion towards the construction of identity in Bangladesh, in particular the impact of christianity.

Nalini Kasynathan. Works as a project officer, in relation to South Asia, with Community Aid Abroad, in Melbourne. She has travelled extensively in South Asia towards the development of aid programs for Community Aid Abroad.

Ratna Kapur is an activist, advocate and researcher who has practiced in the Supreme Court of India and works on women's issues and has written and published widely on women and the law.

Lashvinder Kaur. Completed media studies at Swinburne University. Currently works in journalism and media in Malaysia and has a strong ongoing interest in Asian, especially south Asian women and education.

Madhu Kishwar. Founder of Manushi Trust, a Delhi based organization committed for working for social justice and equity in India with a special focus on women' rights. The most visible part of this organization's activity is the publication Manushi-a journal about women society, founded in 1978.

Helen Lay is a postgraduate at Monash University currently completing work in the area of the trade union movement in the Asia Pacific Region. She has had experience of field work in the area of grassroots trade unions in India.

Gitiara Nasreen. Born in Bogra, Bangladesh. Graduated from University of Dhaka. Has organised and participated in numerous workshops and colloquia on gender issues at the University of Hawaii and the University of Dhaka. Founding member of 'Nari Nirmiti,' a study group which publishes a feminist magazine in Bengali, The Rupantor.

Indira Parikh. Professor in Organizational Behaviour at the Indian Institute of Management, Vastrapur, Ahmedabad. She has conducted workshops with women in management for a number of years and is recognised as an expert in her field. her book 'Inner Dialogue' has received wide readership. She is founder-member and the Executive director of the Indian Society for Individual and Social Development. Her interests are related to organizational structure and the role and identity of men and women managers. she has worked as a consultant in many countries and has authored numerous papers and books.

Santi Rozario is a member of the Faculty at the Department of Sociology and Anthropology at University of Newcastle, NSW. Her recent work includes Purity and Communal Boundaries. Allen and Unwin, Australia. 1992.

Seemanthini Niranjana. Teaches at the Department of Sociology at Goa University. She has just completed a dissertation in the area of Women's Studies.

Tanika Sarkar. is a lecturer in history at St. Stephen's College Delhi. She was a Research Fellow at the Nehru Memorial Museum and Library in 1994. Her publications include a monograph, Bengal 1928-1934: the Politics of Protest as well as a large number of articles in books and journals on political literature, religious conflict, gender and class struggles. Her present interest lies in exploring the connected themes of law, family and religion in 19th Century Bengal. Her most recent work is titled 'Women and the Hindu Right'. Kali. Delhi 1995.

Nayana Shah. Research Associate at the Centre for Educational Innovation. Indian Institute of Management, Ahmedabad.

Renuka Sharma. Has worked within India, in the area of health provision for women with various NGO's and established the South Asian Women's Studies and Support Group in the diaspora as well as provide consultancy for a wide range of Immigrant Women's Groups. She has published in the areas of feminist studies especially Asian Gender studies, psychoanalysis and health issues for women. She currently teaches Asian Gender Studies at Monash University.

Olga Valladares wrote a weekly local column with the Times of India and has been a journalist for the past thirty five years, having completed a masters in sociology from the University of Bombay. She has a long-standing interest in the historical developments in Goa.

Fareeha Zafar was educated at the universities of Lahore and London. She has been involved in both activism and academics in Pakistan and is founding member of the Women's Action Forum (WAF) in Lahore. At present she is Assistant Professor, Department of Geography. University of the Punjab-Lahore and has been nominated as Director, Centre of Excellence for Women's Studies at the same university.

Introduction

The essays collected here represent a variety of contemporary writings about gender, culture and society in South Asia, pertinenent in the present context of a growing sectarian fundamentalism. The authors are all participants in debates about feminist epistemology; the growing grassroots democratic movements; the challenges and pitfalls of globalization; women's intellectual property rights as well as the articulation of alternative strategies for current legal and social problems. This then is what I feel is the Other Revolution, a chipping away of hegemonic, monolithic traditional and or western perspectives.

In returning to an examination of identity politics hinging on an examination of race, gender and nationalisms needed analysis of and democratic strategies may emerge for the reframing of difference be that in the form of constitutional laws, family laws, nation-states and the implications of these changes for the lives of women as subjects but also as agents of change. In moving away from the nihilism of choice reflected in the first 40 years of identity politics, this return I believe, reflects the dissatisfaction with staid dichotomies to the space occupied by the middle ground. Here, where the issues are not so clearly demarcated, the phenomenon of different lived experiences points to the need for not exclușivisms but generative options to issues faced by grassroots non-governmental organizations on the debates broadly around human rights.

This collection began with a dissatisfaction with existing perspectives within the history of feminisms. Over the period of time of working with the perspectives in this volume, post identity politics have emerged. Yet the return to identity politics often reflects an incompleteness of the original analysis as redefinitions continue to emerge to remind us of the lost aporias of various kinds. Thus it seems fair to say that the trajectories of identity and post identity politics mingle, co-inform and are not discontinuous strategies of analysis. Stratagems of knowledge co-inform i.e. the groundedness of citizenship and nationalisms debates on geographical identities exists with other kinds of needs such as to transform narrow boundaries towards global 'hybrid' ideologies. This also leads to the deconstruction of traditional epistemes as well as the creation of new liberating epistemes; a reaching back as well as a reaching forth. No essential structures can be prescribed. Thus no hegemonic constructs are prescribed, no attempt is made to create a fetish of difference; only reflections on gender, aspects of democracy and identity can be glimpsed in this collection of essays.

The works included here allow for a number of different themes, viewpoints, methodologies to emerge. Five main thematic sections have been arbitrarily constructed however, the articles may be read also in a regional and geographical historical sequence as outlined later in the first chapter. This historical introduction hopes to elucidate geographical timelines in contrast to the thematic organization of the chapters presented in the general introduction. The hope is that the two frameworks provide different perspectives that compliment each other and provide referents of another sort to the same material.

The initial section focuses on the history of action and formation of the feminist movements in this region. Basu addresses some of the historical aspects of the women's movement in India at inception. Although the movement can be thought to be ahistorical and predates the founding of the All India Women's Conference, this nonetheless was a decisive point in time for both the nationalist and current women's movement. Likewise Zafar highlights developments in post-partition Pakistan. The issues of constitution and personal laws are brought into sharp focus on the subject of gender and Islamic Laws. Jayasinghe and Nasreen address more contemporary changes on women's issues in relation to Sri Lanka and Bangladesh. The presence of the UN in relation to Sri Lanka and the increasing incidence of the use of the veil in Bangladesh at the present time act as a signifier of other global changes.

The second section examines thematic issues in relation to law, religion, secularism, organizations and organizational change. These themes point to the relevance of activist concerns in nonwestern contexts to the articulation of feminist methodologies. This section intersects with the previous section highlighting the different sorts of processes present at any one historical point of time. Time then can be viewed from any one of thc these contexts or together to allow for a very different reading of history, place and context. Textualisation of events plays with linear referents to produce complexities that deny simple causal explanations. Feminist epistemology and methodology while placing gender centerstage has implications for a number of other disciplines, such as cultural studies, a genre while promising much remains elusive and runs the risk of essentializing difference as well as for more traditional disciplines, such as history.

However, feminist epistemology devoid of non western representations remains class and region bound. Andaya in examining *The Changing Religious Role of Women in Premodern South East Asia*, allows for a premodern tradition to emerge into foreground as well the impact of the diaspora South Asian religions on Southeast Asia. Limited historical research on the pre-nineteenth century makes this work exceptional in the attempt to reexamine herstory from a broader perspective than the hitherto anthropological frameworks have allowed for. The interplay between religion, ritual and sexuality during this time period perhaps lead to a diminished sense of authority and power by women in traditional settings but this was certainly not a static or a generalizable norm. In the general paucity of literature on premodern traditions, this paper acts as a signpost to what further examinations of premodern traditions may bring to the area of identity politics and beyond.

Kapur's work on legal literacy again re-affirms the theme of activism by academics. In taking the ivory tower of a historically patriarchal institution, such as law, to the grassroots women's communities in a pertinent and relevant way reveals this as a possible strategy of empowerment. In an issues sensitive approach to legal literacy, three examples of workshop situations are discussed. Firstly, within the purview of a developmental aid organization in the bastis; followed by a workshop within the frames of a governmental organization and finally within a feminist organization. The analysis of context proves as necessary as analysis of process; each organization with widely different goals and structures towards literacy indicating a need for a, 'flexible approach to legal literacy.' The continuum between the understanding of rights both within and without the court structures, literacy, and the issues of traditional law and court processes are addressed in a pragmatic framework. This overall scheme of literacy takes away some of the felt nihilism within the feminist circles in relation to the monolithic nature of the debate on personal laws at the present times. Although many of the articles in this book touch on the issues to do with personal laws, law as a separate field to other disciplines within the social sciences as a potential legal and power discourse on identity and culture has been slow to emerge.

Agnes discusses the theoretical framework that emerged from her engagement during and following the Bombay riots. She provides a much needed historical appraisal of the place of the women's movement as distinct to the increasingly communal nationalist frameworks in India at the present times. The distinctions between the fundamentalist call for a uniform civil law and the feminist review of family laws stem from different epistemological directions, yet the appropriation of a call for universalization of family laws by the BJP in this instance against the minority Muslim population, fueled into dire consequences for the minority Muslim party and called into question Hindu secularity. The institution of Hindu notions of conjugality lead into an opposition of a group with significantly different ideals of marriage. Following the Shah Bano case the ease of political pointscoring by fundamentalist parties on issues of cultural and political difference, has implications for the Indian feminist movements' recognition of difference within its own ranks. The role of the women's wing of the Hindu fundamentalist parties and their implication in the zeal against minority groups adds further distinction to the rank and file membership of the movement in general as the admixture of feminist and communal ideologies provides various interpretations of family laws. This present debate on the universalization of communal laws will face the test of communal difference. Agnes provides a work of importance, the methodology of action research is a heroic example of the possible forms of intervention by the feminist movement in current debates and areas of strife. Furthermore, a 'critique' from within the movement and a placement of the Indian feminist movements within the broad social and cultural context gives an insight to the integral organicity of a movement constantly reformulating itself in the context of current challenges, as well as reinscripting the notion of secular from gender and caste perspectives of difference.

SEWA the focus of the next article is now a well recognized name in the context of trade unions, microeconomics, women's advocacy and empowerment groups as well as an innovator in relation to International Labour Relations Laws. Lay examines the rise of a women's institution from humble grassroots origins of information, formation and education. The recognition of unemployed women as a formal sector with a move towards the implementation of a self-managed women's bank and changes implemented in the ILO laws, speaks of a process of synchronous change at many levels. In contrast to other trade unions such as in the jute industry of the Textile Labour Association (TLA), traditional bastions of male trade-uniounsisms, SEWA's innovations are indicative of a process of change that is complex, gender and class focused. The 'success' has implications for the traditional hierarchies of male tradeunions both in India and elsewhere. Already there are the beginnings of tradeunions along gender lines inspired by SEWA outside India. In terms of a feminist inspired episteme of change as occasioned by this organization, the interplay between activism and theory is remarkable.

The last article in this section is a reflection on the

nature of organizational structures and the role-identity of women working within these structures. As seen in the previous article it is not (any longer) the submission to an ideological paradigm but the construction of structures that better reflect the needs of women in their working lives. Parikh and Shah have conducted numerous workshop and consultancies to women working in organizations. The move from afflictive to managerial roles creates challenges and confusions. While SEWA acts as a model of empowerment, work in the professional governmental and nongovernmental sector isn't necessarily so. Traditional definitions of identity, filial piety and duty may be restrictive and fall short of empowerment. Avoidance strategies at a personal level lead to continuation of models of conformity and a vacillation between ideals, aspirations and emotional restrictions. The internalization of martyrdom and the 'reproduction of mothering' results in the replication of models of disempowerment for the girl child. Indian feminists in declaring the nineties the decade of the girl child, pay heed to the impact of 'double colonization' by imperial and patriarchal societies on the girl child, the carrier of ideals for the future. The current literature on female infanticide draws attention to the misogynist litany against women, internalized and transgenerationally transmitted which forms a double injunction against empowerment. The fallout from psychological disabilities within South Asia but also in the diaspora with the added injunction of migration stress on the 'Woman at Risk' is increasingly addressed by women's self-help groups, support networks and crisis intervention centers. While it may not be fashionable to speak of individual subjectivity in relation to mental health in the postmodern enlightenment about socio-historical constructions of subjectivity, Shah and Parik's work is pioneering in the breadth of consultations with women in the workplace. The sensitive richness of this work drawing from the lives of women reflects multiplicity of identities and boundaries which opens up new space for self-definition by women, as well as new methodologies and perspectives for the women's movements.

The issues of grassroots activism and its relation to

feminist epistemology remains centerstage during this section. If thinking at the 'coal face' is to be trusted then it is often the option best informed of the collective social processes of our times. Moving with this 'other revolution' towards the next century promises much hope for the revisioning of mainstream western feminist hegemony on the construction of knowledge structures about 'all' women. The plethora of Non Governmental Organizations present at the Women's Conference and the United Nations Conference in Beijng, gives voice and also needed analysis of new forms of collectives emerging. While the lure of hopeless idealization of a global sisterhood is at one level to be resisted as this could in itself reflect a parallel process to the transnational powers of globalization, at another level analysis may reveal grassroots empowerment model such as SEWA, offering epistemic shifts of many kinds for the next century. While this analysis can lead to a kind of optimism it can also reveal the rapid bureaucratism of the NGO movement along corporate lines, funded by transnational conscious money. The critique of aid philosophy is essential to an understanding of citizenship structures in a rapidly globalizating world industry with necessary analysis of the tensions between citizenship, globalization, fragile national economies and human rights abuse in a post cold war environment. Continued analysis of the role of the women's movement in constructing the future may be essential such that women's groups are not yet again the handmaidens of the post cold war patriarchal structures, or of elite women's movements located entirely in the global north. Reworking of strategies for the processes of information analysis by grassroots non-western ngos, in order to implement and interact with structural adjustments at local and global level then becomes a pressing concern for the future of the movement.

The third section is a inclusion of work focussing on specific geographic regions. There can, as discussed above, be no one correct position of representation as the varieties of experiences introduced by the processes of human geography, class, caste and gender are far too complex for simple formulaic explanations and general norms of interpretation. Much feminist scholarship still needs to be encouraged on non-western feminisms articulating difference. This section could never be inclusive or complete but only an indicator of the possible kinds of woven identities possible. The section draws on the local geographical representations of gender. Themes of the midwife, wife, girlchild, education and the issues unique to the Christian religious minority, the Cudds within India and the diaspora gives form to the heterogeneity of the nation-states of the region and its history.

Rosario places the midwife in village Bangladesh, in a border zone both empowered and essential yet viewed as disempowered and polluted by the nature of the work of childbirth. Such a reading of the transitional space occupied by such a pivotal figure in the structure of a society reflects on the contradictions present in any attempt at gender and culture analysis. The context and site of the women's body is thus the location of collective symbolic and textual definitions of norms in the ordinary world of mundane action but is also symbolic of the realm of the sacred. The biological reproductive and sexual functions are interpreted in terms of folk culture, religion and text. The world of folk religion appears to be prescriptive in the protection against malign influences such as bhut, prets, churels, and lesser deities (bhairava) who may cause madness, miscarriages as well as death. The body is also the context of spiritual elevation such as the tantric traditions whereby the naked female form and menstrual blood etc are seem as the gateway, and may be used in rituals towards mystic elevation. On the other hand strict brahmanic laws govern the notions of purity and permission and to espousal of the priestly traditions. These mix of premodern and modern thematic structures on the notion of the female body and its utility adhere to certain patterns. The local healer (vaid) or dai may be the repository of these traditions both inculcating and instructing in the ways of the old but also a barrier in the ways of the new order of technology and advancement.

The dai and other healers become as powerful as the Brahmin priest in the hierarchy of real and numinous power structures. The body of the women is thus the site of the sacred as well as a site of possible contamination from premodern times but also in modern times a cause celebre for the freedom movements attempts against British rule. At the present time this domain is again subject to reinscription with the rise of the present fundamentalist movements with the recruitment of women towards traditional practices of worship rather than self agency and educated decision making processes in this arena of reproduction.

Sarkar gives a historical account of the development of conjugality. The influence of the colonial period on trade relations and the economic prospects of the colonized invariably affected the formation of the domestic space. The nationalist agenda in nineteenth century Bengal developed the domestic space along the lines of family values and duty setting up complex interrelatedness between the home space and the nation space. Women seen as culture carriers and guardians of the home space; as transmitters of family values subject to religious laws reflects ultimately on to the production of sons (masculinity) imbued with a proper reverence for the nation space, Bharat Mata (Mother India). This delineation of gender roles in a historical context undermines a purely cultural or biological construction of gender roles. The strength of the resistance movement in the face of colonial oppression led to the conscription of family values and gender based role definitions. This deification is somewhat at odds with the notion of women's liberation and education in the context of an increasing global, capitalist-colonizing economy of the present times with implications for a growing middle class economy with different family values. The links between culture, oppression and global economy being inextricably linked.

Chakravorty gives a cultural account of the development of the notion of the specialness/separateness of the girl child. The implications of this work are enormous as India now prepares for the decade of the girl child. Recently, Indian feminists declared the nineties to be the decade of the girl child. The Vienna Declaration re-issued the rights of the child especially those of the girl child'. The long term aim of this is the incorporation of the Convention on the Rights of the Child in national action plans worldwide thus reducing infant mortality, malnutrition, and female illiteracy rates and improving access to safe drinking water and education. Also highlighting the need for protection against infanticidal practices, child labor, prostitution, pornography and sexual abuse as well as modification of cultural practices that cause harm and violate the rights of the girl child. These statements of intent were amplified at the Cairo Conference on Population and Development.

'Since in all societies discrimination on the basis of sex often starts at the earliest stages of life, greater equality for the girl child is a necessary first step in ensuring that women realize their full potential and become equal partners in development. In a number of countries, the practice of prenatal sex selection, higher rates of mortality among very young girls, and lower rates of school enrollment for girl children as compared with boys, suggests that 'son preference' is curtailing the access of girl children to food, education and health care. This is often compounded by the increasing use of technologies to determine foetal sex, resulting in abortion of female fetuses. Investments made in the girl child's health, nutrition and education from infancy to adolescence are critical'.

The triple objectives towards action are, of reducing the loss at or prior to birth to strengthen the status of the girl child and to improve the welfare of the child especially 'health, nutrition and education. However, similar public health measures and public medical campaigns over a century show in fact the same levels, if not worse incidence in some parts of the practice of infanticide. The adaptation of modern technology such as amniocentesis highlights the persistence and maintenance of value systems on the notion of the girl child. Structural analysis of the process and of the socioeconomic concomitants of the subjugation of women will take wide reaching concerted analysis. The value of the girl child will need to be seen in a broader context then towards a future geared only towards mothering and child rearing. The examination of gender stereotypes often buttressed by religion and mythology will need to be interpreted in the context of the special needs of the girl child, and adolescents, Other contentious issues such as consent to marriage, minimum age at marriage with the provision of viable alternatives such as employment and educational opportunities remains a challenge for the twenty first century.

The next article by Kaur in this section explores the links between education and women's rights in Kerala, a state with a matrilineal system of culture and land inheritance, influenced by Marxist ideals on land reform and education. In Valldares we see the development of traditional and nontraditional structures in relation to identity. Goa until 1977 was the colony of Portugal. Since 1977 the issues of citizenship takes on multiple nuances in the 'home state' and its diaspora. The Cudds a christian community framed its support networks differently to other groups. This issue of alliance to identity of a particular geographical location is reflected in Castellino's work on the diaspora from this region. The original geographic location and transmission of culture produces variations of identity yet again. The notion of a state producing a nonresident diaspora state (NRIS) is an interesting one. The location of diaspora agency in relation to the notion of state has always been accepted in terms of the flow of funding from the first world located ex-third world nationals as in the case the funding for terrorisms and extremisms of various kinds is well established e.g. Sikh and Tamil first/third world located aid funding, however the transport of ideas in relation to identity, formation of nation as state and other cultural phenomenon are less well explored. This was the subject of a panel on the history of feminisms in south Asia at Beijing organized by SAWSSGG (South Asian Women's Studies and Support Group) highlighting the difficulties in definition of nationality, for those located in the first and third world feminist space simultaneously.

The final section, Self Representation and identity Politics, examines the issues related to difference and the sociocultural constructions of difference. Contemporary philosophy's concern with 'other' kinds of writing questions the notions of marginality and identity as well as the power structures that construct and maintain these distinctions.

Genevieve Lloyd in 'Being in Time. Selves and Narrators in Philosophy and Literature,' highlights western philosophy's relationship to the 'maleness of reason.' Within western feminisms, literature, culture and alterity are current concerns. The enterprise of deconstructionisms while laying bare some of the commonly held humanistic, western, phallocentric perceptions does not attempt an understanding of 'orientalism' under its various guises relation to gender and class. The construction of knowledge in about the context and lives of 'Third/Other' world women suffers some serious epistemological setbacks.

The construction of the notion of Woman is problematic. Ahistorical frameworks elude the complexity of factors in the current framing of the subcontinental feminist movements. The origins of the movement within nationalist insurgencies, cultural placement of women in religious structures within changing third world economies are potentially productive of ways of knowing that point to an alternative metaphysics of reason.

Sangari and Vaid point to the difficulties in the construction of feminist cultural knowledge. Gender difference in relation to class, colonianlity and culture can be analyzed through various disciplines. However the various analysis of these disciplines is part of the construction of that realm between experience and theory. An ethics of experience may lead to the development of knowledge given the trajectories of history, class, caste and culture.

Subaltern deconstruction as popularized by the works of the subaltern group and the works of Spivak cast light on the construction of the subaltern women. However in the absence of real examination of the women's movement the subaltern group displays a peculiar lacunae with respect to feminist epistemology and the realm of experience of women in relation to issues such as personal law and the concomitant inequities.

Issues directly relevant to the lives of women such as infanticide, violence, communalism, dowry, sati, land ownership, sexuality raise ethical issues of massive proportions. A reexamination of the works of women activists and freedom fighters such as Pundita Ramabai reveals a contradictory language and ethic of action which was generative of enormous social change yet excluded from representation within mainstream resistance movements.

Colonial and precolonial representations of the lives of women by women is an interesting interplay of caste, class, culture, language and time period. The pre-sixteenth century poets such as Akkhamadevi and Atukuri Molla apart from providing social commentary used particular linguistic styles in the interpretation of texts such as the Ramayana etc.

As western feminisms moves away from a monolithic self imago, other ways of knowing are acknowledged. The examination of the problematic of the current tenants of the Indian feminist epistemologies draws from a number of sources to formulate the suggestion that the future of Indian philosophy will have to include an account of not only the few women writing in sanskrit but also women's activities and writings in other spheres.

In concentration on the understanding of the other, the notion of empathy remains a problematic. While Bhabha writes of hybridity and ambivalence as the emergent norms of the postcolonial state the act of the representation of difference remains a problematic. If postcolonial writings borrow metaphors from psychoanalysis then empathy remains loosely defined both in psychoanalysis and cultural studies. In the first article in this section, 'The Politics of Subjectivity' if the subjective space of the other one is to be understood and defined in relation to one self then, history and culture need to be resited into subjectivity. Difference provides a closure to empathy, an incommensurability to the other on the horizon of understanding. Emergent childhood subjectivity is defined in relation to the other, the mother as culture carrier. The pivotal location of the mirror stage, a eurocentric notion of reflection of emergent selfhood presumes a western history and culture, suigenris. Whereas in the black mirror of history, I dimly perceive myself. In the dark shiny surface of black, non white renaissance, there can only be a cultural located other and a cultural self. The reflection remains shadowy, refracted, undefined, emergent-potential. This raises a number of questions about empathy as an epistemological tool.

Historically, the term arose and was popularized by

usage within the field of aesthetics. This notion was then extended to the fields of religion, anthropology, comparative and cross-cultural studies and philosophy. Within psychoanalysis the notion was initially raised in relation to psychoanalytic technique, but it has recently re-emerged largely due to the proponents of Self psychology in the past thirty years. Specific issues raised in the study of empathy are, as follows:

The problem of accurately perceiving another; Whether the experiences of another can be comprehended on the basis of purely intra-psychic theories as distinct to the relational and interpersonal elements; whether empathy is a free-standing *a priori* category of experience, or a developmental process in the interaction of the subject with the temporal environment; whether the mode of perception involved in empathy is the same as that in altruistic defence mechanisms, and this raises issues about the misuse of this perception; what are the precise roles of affect and cognition in this mode of perception? What is the relationship to other mental acts such as introspection, countertransference, hybridity and ambivalence; what are the roles and function of empathy within theory and clinical practice of psychoanalysis, and cultural studies.

Although empathy like other psychoanalytic terms, is frequently cited within the literature, it is often unclearly articulated in relation to existing terminology. Whereas psychoanalytic descriptions are based on an understanding of psychic processes common to all humans, the phenomenological empathic stance seems to foster an exploration of the uniqueness and difference of the other in a relational setting. This notion of unconcealment differs from psychoanalytic descriptions of empathy aimed at discovering similarities. A reformulation of the concept of empathy, presents a novel hermeneutics of empathy in the context of current cultural analysis.

In proposing mental representation as a basis for empathy, I am suggesting that empathy occurs as a separate mental act within the subject and this is episodic in that it allows for the inclusion of objective reality as well as subjective states. As such it can be regarded as a separate category of experience which has epistemological ramifications as well as implications for clinical applications. As an epistemological act it is a means of knowing the other-object, person, event, cultural artifact, and text. It was this original intentionality that led to its adoption in aesthetics, which idea perhaps goes back to the 18th century German philosopher, Emmanuel Kant, for whom the *a priori* forms of intuition (space and time) and categories of understanding (unity/plurality, cause/effect, possibility/impossibility, etc) combine with sense-data to give synthetic knowledge. The experience of the 'sublime' suggests the possibility of being a free-standing aesthetic category, and it shares some of the characteristics of empathy. Epistemologically, empathy remains an attempt to define the *noemata* in the horizon of understanding in which the other is appropriated in the subjective reality of oneself, i.e., in the process of, "double representation".

Furthermore, my contention as I have argued, is that this process occurs by means of double representation: a representation of self, be that in the form of memory, experience, part object, imagination or linguistic trace, with a collateral representation of the other. On the basis of congruence, deductions are made about similarities to oneself and on the basis of noncongruence an openness allowed for the difference. Similarities can be understood on the basis of analogies, about common psychic phenomena such as defined by principles of psychoanalysis, and differences acknowledged by an ontological openness to the unconcealment of the other's self in the present moment.

Thus it is possible that the metaphors of psychoanalysis allow for the emergence of understanding on the basis of psychic similarities, and these may include an analysis of transference or an understanding of continuous traits. A phenomenological openness allows for the possibility of difference to emerge and discontinuities in the other's experience in relation to oneself. As it is in the nature of mental acts to be transient, unlike mechanical objects, the appraisal of the other by this means is constantly in a state of flux influenced by other mental acts as well as changes in the perceiver and the perceived. Thus, as a clinical tool empathy provides data about long-standing transferential aspects of the other, but also provides traces or the immediate reality of the other. The understanding of the other based on similarities with self is in keeping with the classical Western philosophical notion of self as a discrete continuous phenomenon.

However, recent trends in Western philosophy's attempt at a 'deconstruction' of this notion questions the continuous nature of self. In discussing the 'identity of difference and difference of identity', Mark C Taylor states that 'philosophy begins and ends with the question of the other. The question is not a question, it is a complex of questions.' Without wishing to enter into a discussion on the philosophical basis of the notion of self, it is perhaps important to locate the problem of empathy within this larger discourse as one question about the larger problem of the means of knowing the other person, culture or text. Having thus addressed this problem of empathy within a larger discourse of self, it is important to be aware that definitions of empathy have been, by and large, unsatisfactory. Psychoanalytic analogies or attempts at understanding the problem of empathy have been beset by problems of semantic and epistemological difficulties. New analogies of this process are provided by developmental studies of the interaction between mother and child, psychological studies examining the development of empathy and moral reasoning, and phenomenological explorations of the experience. The future horizons of empathy clearly lie in this direction, although much more work and careful thinking remains to be done in this area before the frontier is likely to open any further. In using psychoanalytic concepts in framing subjectivity, often careful analysis of the dangers of derivative analysis from historical disciplines such as psychoanalysis is not heeded to, thus risking the colonization of psychic spaces by postmodern/ postcolonial analysis.

This last section raises epistemological issues about the representation of subjectivity. The first article, 'The Politics of Subjectivity' addresses this issue in the context of India. Niranjana, in' Of Gender and Difference' provides a framework for the cultural renegotiation of the representations of the body and gender, opening up the analysis to history and culture. Joseph offers a meditation on difference beyond polarity representations to the lived world of linga worship. This is contrasted to penis envy in a cultural entronde that raises questions about labelling the difference, the incomprehensible with the linguistic meaningful in a gesture of appropriation. Bagchi offers a sociological critique of Gandhian nationalism towards the construction of women and the conflict between austerity and adornment by hair and jewelry. Gandhi's symbolic gesture of stripping his wife's hair and jewelry has implications for nationalisms constructions of femininity. Ahmed provides the necessary critique of the dependence of western critical theory on psychoanalysis. The power vacuum of history as it seizes in the language of psychoanalysis although opening up the language of liminal spaces, and concepts of hybrid living need reflect on the origins of psychoanalytic language. The birth into language as marked by the mirror stage marks the passage in to a Lacanian framework of meanings. The unconscious in the Lacanian, structuralist schema is contrasted with Althusser and a move towards individualism, ethnomethodology and autobiography. The distance between I and the notion of a subject resonates with hidden meanings. The phantasy of I opens up authorship of otherness, otherness predicated by language, linguistic signification and predication. This tension between I and otherness, this dialectic echoes the dialectic of empathy, other as self in contrast to Ricoeur's hemermentetic of 'Self as Other'. The 'Other of the Black Mirror' as self; self as black historicism or black renaissance, would indeed lead to reworking of the base concepts of psychoanalysis of generalizing from self to other-towards understanding self in the light cast by the 'other's' history. This resisting of self within noneurocentric history, raises questions about the liberal use of psychoanalysis within the domain of cultural studies and in the studies of cultural difference. While the tenants of psychoanalysis are predicated on notions of cultural similitude, it may then be that that cultural difference forms a basis for and provides location for incommesrability; with black historicism and renaissance in contrast to the culturally loaded predicates of psychoanalysis. The final section completes with two accounts of activisms by activist-researchers.

Section I
Theory, Praxis and History

History of Feminism in South Asia

Renuka Sharma

The history of feminism in South Asia is as diverse as the geographic region itself. Its history, culture and religions tend to constitute and contexualise the disparate feminist movements' trajectories over time. There are certain themes which are similar across the regional boundaries and others which are unique to location. Historically, certain issues remain constant and yet new ones appear on the horizon. In order not to construct a monolithic view of feminist movements it is important to emphasise this heterodox complexity of the regions with a multiplicity of movements concerned with the emancipation of women. In this entry I will present brief accounts of the main regions with particular attention to the indigenous cultures as shaped by periods of invasion and migration over millennia. This necessarily includes the three hundred years or so of colonization. At the present time the issue of growing national religious fundamentalism highlights the birth of the mordernist feminist movements within nationalist struggles for independence, and the consequences for the movements of the intertwining of ideologies. Implications of this are seen in the growing self critique engaged within the movements in recent times. Attention will be given to a few historical figures such as Begum Rokkhya and Pandita Ramabai as figures who condensed into their struggles many positions. It would be remiss not to mention the present concerted efforts towards the reform of constitutional and personal laws across the regions. Feminist efforts to provide a symbolic horizon of the 'enlightenment' ideals of justice, equality and access to human rights while seen to be retrogressive by postmodernist theorists, offer new readings of these very concepts, as the emergence of an experiential ethics of action in the face of a growing sectarian extremism, has not been witnessed to this degree and nature before.

Pakistan

The nation state of Pakistan was created in 1947 as a Muslim majority state amidst complex political strategies. The social, economic and political status of women can only be understood in the context of these changes as well as the Islamic laws of present and past times. Zafar (1995) examines the complex threads of these developments leading to the present inequities. The constitution of Pakistan was an outcome of an alliance of rich landlords and the military creating a relatively autocratic patriarchal rule. This patriarchal basis of the society is promoted by the clergy (ulema) on the authority of authenticated Islamic texts and further interpolated by the sectarian preachers (mullahs) of Islam.

The placement of women as religiously inferior, economically dependent, and politically naive carries with it assumptions about women within the private domain needing to be shielded (purdah) and defended by men (honour) and betrays a condensed set of assumptions of the nature of women. Zia (1994) examines the issues related to women's sexuality, fitna (chaos, disorder) in relation to sexual assault and the assumption of blame. The elaboration of the notion of sexuality is explored sensitively by Mernissi who examines the interwoven themes of religion, sexuality and Islamic text.

Paradoxically a secular state which has religious underpinnings appears to avow freedom of speech and gender equity. However constitutional and personal laws are framed in religious terms and are therefore open to religious interpretation. This paradox although present in the formation of the original secular state, has in recent times moved closer towards a theocratic state with a more overt reliance on religious law to bolster the Islamization of the state.

The Objectives Resolution passed in 1949 formed the basis of the Constitution developed initially in 1956. A collusion between the state and the injunctions of Islam recurs in the subsequent constitutional amendments enacted by Ayub Khan in 1962 and by Z. Bhutto in 1973, thereby further consolidating concessions to the ulema. The proliferation of Islamic structures under the autocratic rule of Zia-ul-Huq, such as the Qazi Courts and Federal Shariat Courts, allowed for intrusions in the field of family law as it pertains to the issue of women's rights to property, modesty dress laws (hejab) and the divorce and rape laws passed in 1980 (Hadood Ordinances). In the hierarchy of power structures and the constitution of individual rights, religious injunctions superced legal injunctions and are in turn superseded by concessions to the Islamic authority of the imam or religious leader. Thus in terms of a redress of the inequities faced by women, decision is deferred to the higher authority, leaving ambiguous the fundamental issues of human rights and gender equity.

The intersection of class with culture is also one that affects women. Women of a more elite, urban-educated background may not conform as rigidly to dress laws, but conversely be portrayed as 'western, liberal and loose'. Thus the cultural depiction of woman may fall into categories of traditional, religious, good, submissive and abiding of a patriarchal order as against western, liberal and thus deserving of sexual assault. This dichotomization reduces the heterogeneity of lived experiences and the possible construction of laws concerned with the real lives of women. The infamous rape laws established by General Zia (Hadood), reflect this juncture of patriarchal state laws bolstered by religious ideology. This is also highlighted by the Shariat Bill which allows all laws to be examined in the light of religious ordinances.

The Hadood Ordinances codify criminal laws related to property, prohibition, Zina (crimes of rape, adultery, abduction, fornication.) Central to the construction of this thesis is the notion of female sexuality as one that puts masculinity at risk of chaos (fitna). In the pre Hudood era rape was punishable as a crime. However, in the post-

Hudood era confession and the provision of witnesses are seen as the onus of the victim in the case of rape. In this instance rape is equated with adultery. Proof of the event, in the form of four male witnesses, is to be provided by the victim. This reduction of a number of categories of personal law leaves the law open to religious interpretation with dire consequences for women. The intersection of state and religion was used by the dictatorial regime of Zia-ul-Huq to bolster his political ambitions in uniting the diverse political parties under the banner of religious interpretation of law with relation to women. The identification of the body of a nation-state with the body of a woman leads to the framing of patriarchal laws aimed at the protection of the honour of the state-woman by Islamic patriarchy against the intrusions of honour by modernity and any immoral behaviour by women (fitna). This reading of the dangerousness of women serves a political partiarchy in maintaining sovereignty in the public sphere and inscripting the lives and 'honour' of 'invisible' women.

Progressive legislation such as the Muslim Family Laws Ordinance passed in 1961 was subsequently counteracted by the Shariat Laws and the Hadood Ordinances in 1979 together with the Law of Evidence (which equates the evidence of a women is half that of a man) and the Laws of Qisas and Diyat. This was accompanied by the introduction of religiously sanctioned punishments such as stoning and death for misdemeanors according to these new religiously laced legislature.

The formal origins of the women's movement began within the Muslim Women's League. This was a branch of the nationalist Muslim League which was instrumental in assisting the partition of India and the establishment of Pakistan as a separate state. A parliamentary women's division was established by General Zia with the preparation of the Report on the Status of Women, subsequently released by Benazir Bhutto who in her second term in office established a women's bank, ministry for development of women, various committees and literacy programs for women. However these gestures are often seen as tokenism in the face of the autocratic systematic disempowerment of women, levels of illiteracy, and limited representation in parliament. The Hudood Ordinances introduced by General Zia galvanised women activists towards the formation of the Women's Action Front (WAF), and subsequently affiliation with the international group, Women Living Under Muslim Law. The slow and persistent examination of Islamic texts on the position of women in the religious scriptures holds potential for the revision of personal laws. The heterogeneity of interpretations of the Quran (Divine Word of Allah) and Sunnah (exemplary deeds of the Prophet) provides the basis for the framing of personal laws at the present time; change may only be possible by feminist scholars working from within traditions as the backlash towards militant feminist groups is well documented.

Bangladesh

The resurgence of fundamentalism in Bangladesh has been highlighted in the western literature in relation to the anti-woman sentiments expressed about the subversive writer Taslima Nasreem. This public and polemical debate has been the subject of much speculation but can only be analysed in relation to the larger issue of the current rise of sectarian extremism in a global context of Islamic fundamentalism. The Bangaldeshi women's movement is part of a longer tradition of indigenous 'subaltern' or grassroots women's movement within the greater Bengal region, whose critiques are not couched in western feminist frames or discourses.

The sensitivity of responses from within the indigenous movements to the subject of the fatwa on Taslima Nasreem aims to disentangle the polemics of the discourse and recreate a more effective space within which both the debate and agitation about women's rights and role in the Bangladeshi society could continue. The empowerment issue concerns not merely one individual voice but a whole larger movement which feels particularly grieved about the turn of events following the death threat on Taslima's life. Her actions could appear to be a historical and outside of grassroots Muslim women's expressions, scholarship and support. That she did not work in tandem with the grassroots movements and took it upon herself to rally against the Muslim Shariat has somewhat alienated her from various supports and movements across gender, class and subreligious groups and a history of achievements within Bangladesh.

The cause taken up by secular Hindu intelligentsia and Hindu fundamentalist groups on this issue, reflects as much on the stance taken in response to Muslim extremism in India. The two need to be kept separate. It is feared that the fatwa, were it to be carried, could unwittingly lead to the death of that more systematic dissent by the indigenous women's groups. This paradox faced by the Bangladesh women's movement is poorly explored in the Indian and Western media who may project her as in isolated case of resistance to Muslim law. These issues were discussed by South Asian feminists at the International Conference on Women, Power and Cultural Difference: Negotiating Gender in South Asia resulting, in a historic document position statement taken by the women at the conference. (Melbourne Declaration. On Freedom of Speech for Freedom of Writers in Non-Western Countries. July 1994).

Gitiara Nasreen's analysis of the present situation of working women in Bangladesh is in the context of a new global market which leans heavily on the work of women in Third World countries as cheap labour has implications for the economic self-perception of the nation-state of Bangladesh which draws heavily on women's resources in relation to the garment and jute industries. In drawing a distinction between private and public spaces she examines the role that purdah has played in the transition to modern times of age-old customs. The unique fusion of Hindu and Muslim syncretic practices in Bangladesh places women as dependents within a cultural familial milieu. Generalizations about oppression do not take into account the distinctions afforded women through the portals of education and economic class structuring. Thus modern western dress is the dress of a large percentage of the urban, middle-class elite.

Historically, the emergence of Bangladesh was within the context of two hundred and fifty years of postcolonial rule (British and Pakistan). The postcolonial economy depended on external aid, which came with it western ideologies of gender, birth control methodology and medicines enshrined in a reproductive ideology often already obsolete in host countries.

The introjection of religion into the hitherto secular constitution in 1977, subsequently amended to institute Islam as the state religion in 1988 parallels this movement in other regional states, for instance Pakistan, and possibly also the growing movement calling for a theocratic state in India at the present times. The contradictions raised by the permissiveness of economic liberalization and at the same time a return to orthodox legal practises and cultural mores has far-reaching implications for the feminist movement. Nasreen argues that modified forms of the purdah (burkha), i.e. chaddor (sheet) symbolise upward mobility and agency in allowing movement with the confines of traditional space (purdah) into the workforce in larger numbers, hence bypassing the censor of misogyny, harassment and stigmatization. This view is supported by M. Rock who outlines the national shift from socialism towards privatization, following the achievement of independence in 1971 under the Mujibe regime (1972-75) and subsequent rule of general Zia (1975-81), President Ershad (1982-90) and the election of Begum Khaleda Zia in 1990. This change has been paralled by a steep rise and movement into the public sphere of large numbers of women entering the workforce for a variety of reasons.

The exploitation of women in this climate of rapid economic change has led to the preliminary organization of trade unions towards the implementation of minimum work rates and other work conditions. This counters the popular myth of subservience that is the dominant image portrayed within the western media. Haque provides an alternative history on the emancipation of women beginning in 1880 with the birth of Begum Rokeya Sakhawat Hossain, a pioneering educationalist. In 1880 there were no high profile Muslim women. The Report of the Indian Education commission indicated only 1500 girls at school; however by 1936 this figure had changed to 400,000 with numerous visible women activists, indicating the radical changes at work. In 1937 Muslim women contested for equal representation. This led to the election of two Muslim women to the legislature.

The achievements of Begum Rokeya began with the publication in 1904 of "The Innocent Bengali." This was the first publication by a Bengali Muslim woman and the first in a series of achievements, such as the establishment of the first Muslim girls school in Calcutta in 1911; first Muslim Women's Association, 'Anjuman-E-Khawateen' in 1916, books etc. Her activism led to a noticeable increase in numbers of women involved in education and by 1927 the number of girl children involved in primary education exceeded that the Hindu community. Since then a great number of woman activists have been part of the indigenous women's movement. Voting rights were achieved in 1950, a separate journal 'Begum' was established in 1947, the 'Begum Club,' a group of writers formed in 1953. This level of activism has been without adversity: women members of the Muslim Womens League were massacred in 1952 while protesting against the imposition of Urdu as the State language. However the activism continues with the formation of the Bangladesh Women Writers Association in 1973 to support women writers in the country. In 1991 Narigrantha Prabartana organised the first women's freedom fighters assembly which is commemorated every year to remember the courageous movements within Bangladesh, which will surely be tested by the rising tide of fundamentalism of our times.

Sri Lanka

Historically Sri Lanka is unique in the region for the emphasis that was placed on education for women. Kumari Jayawardena in 'Emancipation and Subordination of Women in Sri Lanka' places the origins of the women's movement within a historical framework. The highlights of this movement have been one of the highest rates of literacy for women in comparison to other nation in Asia as well as a strong 'elite' women's movement which produced the first woman prime minister in the world. However, it is precisely this structure of the womens movement that maintains a class distinction and in the absence of strong oppression, the movement retains connections to the religious and nationalist identity of the major groups without heed to some of the fundamental issues facing women of lesser privileged backgrounds in this country torn apart by fierce civil struggles.

Sri Lanka has close cultural links with India. Lanka plays a vital role in the epic tales of the Hindu tradition such as the Ramayana. The Lankan king Ravana was denounced for his role in the abduction of Sita from the mainland. In contemporary analysis the contrast between Sita and Suphanaka, sister of Ravana, shows how virtue for women was constituted by machievelian documents such as the Ramayana. Sita did not own land, was the ideal wife and after the abduction was rejected by Rama (the just ruler) for fear of possible contamination. Suphnaka, a more emancipated land owner having lived out her passions and anger at being replaced by Sita had her nose cut off as retribution. This brief analysis of the otherness of 'Lanka' in the Hindu tradition highlights the peculiar and complex role that the colonization by India has played on the past of Sri Lanka's history.

The ethnic rubric of the nation state is at the root of the civil and terrorist violence in the state today. The indigenous Singahlese population exists side-by-side with the Tamil, Burger Dutch etc. This heterodoxy is represented in the mixture of state religions. The predominant ones being Buddhism, Hinduism and Christianity. Buddhism introduced in the third century BC blended with the lives of the prosperous agrarian indigenous population and became part of the state ideology and religion. The origins of Buddhism in India as an anti-caste religion had implications for the status of women as distinct to that in Hinduism. Women in Sri Lanka were thus able to enter the monastic orders in pre-modern times as well as be present in the domestic sphere. The entry of women into religious orders had implications for the subsequent education of women and their participation in religious ritual. Popular religious culture thus moved away from the practice of sati, dowry, child marriages prevalent in India under this more egalitarian Buddhist, religion-political structure (Jayawardena 1986).

Continuing imperial and colonial influences was continued by the Portuguese settlers in 1505 for 150 years. This was succeeded by the Dutch for a further 150 years and was finally supplanted by the British between 1815-1948. Family law practices affecting the lives of women is a reflection of the complexity of these influences. The shift from agrarian practices which included polyandric provisions, possibilities for inheritance in 'binna' (contract) marriages as well as the more traditional dowry 'diga' towards a more western system occurred gradually under colonial rule.

Women's writings were present in early centuries as the products of monastic Sinhala and Sanskrit learning and the eighteenth century flowered into a school of women poets. By the early nineteenth century women were joining up with the largely middle-class anti-colonial resistance movements under nationalist religious banners, as elsewhere in this region. This class reification is a recurring theme which continues to the present day. In her incisive exposition Kumari Jayawardena gives reasons for this to occur. The Dutch co-ed parish schools, monastic traditions with its emphasis on education for women continued into the twentieth century and mingled with the works of the Christian missionaries towards this aim. The Morgan Report as early as 1869 recommended the establishment of girls schools and the provision of subsidies towards this. A complex system of private and public schools catered to the various socio-economic categories reifying the value systems of the English of schooling towards a Cambridge certificate.

Another added stimulus towards education came from the founders of the Theosophical movements, Annie Besant and Helena Blavatsky, both of whom lived and travelled in this region. Joining forces with the rich aristocratic Buddhist women a Women's Education Society was formed in the 1880's. This interplay between western theosophists with Sri Lanka left an indelible impression on the future of education for Buddhist women.

With this rich historical intentionality towards literacy it is little surprise that in the twentieth century Sri Lanka was one of the first countries to achieve women's suffrage in 1931. The Mallika Kulangana Samitiya (Womens Organization) wing of the Congress commenced work towards this in 1925. The Women's Franchise Union was formed in 1927 to continue the preparation of submissions. Following the achievement of the suffragettes petition in 1931 several subgroups formed including the Lanka Mahila Samiti, Women's Political Union, Tamil Women's Union. Subsequently in 1944 the All Ceylon Women's Conference (ACWC) was established.

Against this backdrop of achievement by elite women's groups the context of struggles by other classes centered on rights for unskilled workers in the tea, coffee plantations, share farm workers etc. The 'coolie' conditions of work left women open to exploitation of various sorts. Subsequent participation by women in labour and trade unions under the influence of A.E. Goonaesinha occurred under the aegises of the Ceylon Labour Party and later under the rubric of nationalist-socialist trade union movements.

Kumari Jayawardena, herself an outspoken activist and academic points to the influence to the present-day impasses in the women's movement in Sri Lanka as being based on the relative absence of hardship in the form of relative freedom of religious oppression of women, achievement of independence by negotiation processes rather than civil strife, the placement of and encouragement of liberal class-based education systems that enshrine rather than critique the patriarchal values on family and sexuality.

India

Thc spatc of writings on Indian feminism and on Indian women in general far surpasses in volume then that from other Asian nations. The reasons for this are never apparent but may relate to the works of the postcolonial writers with an already long history of writing in English and an even earlier philosophical tradition that drew attention to the plight of women in the Indian society.

However even in precolonial and colonial times descriptive accounts of India by the Schlegel brothers, Herder, Max Muller, Hegel and Walt Whitman are only a few examples of the early western fascinations with the Indian tradition. Likewise today the genre of western feminists, indologists and other sorts of scholars that proclaim a continuing interest is a phenomenon which can is some circumstances be described as continuing orientalism. In attempting to put in perspective some of the changes faced by the Indian women's movements I shall utilize the writings of women who have by and large sprung from the tradition in order to avoid the issue of insider-outsider authenticity prevalent in contemporary postcolonial discourse.

Tharu and Lalita, in making accessible to the English speaking world a collection of writings by women from 600 B.C. to the early twentieth century write 'against the grain of literary history.' In highlighting the plethora of writings by women in this time, contrary to the perceived western norm of paucity and disempowerment of women are indeed 'against the grain.' The social reform movements of the nineteenth century in placing itself against the rule of colonial powers redefined the notions of gender, class and caste reification in unprecedented ways to suit the context of the anti-colonial resistance struggles. Orientalist readings of the fall from a glorious Aryan Vedic past of braminical ascecitism to the ungovernable inchoate Indian populace carried within it a notion of certain colonial standards. The social reform movements in reinstating its position undertook widespread reforms aimed at improving and proving the worth of it's own attitudes to women, caste and orthodoxic practices worthy of these standards. Cast in this light the early make reformers, are viewed as the originators of the women's movement. Thus this modernist phase of reform is situated closely with the nationalist movement for which the lot of women became a cause celebre. However the women writing in the ancient period were also invoking gender ideals. The reasons put forth for much of this not surviving into present times may be related to the canonization of history in the language of male dominated Sanskrit texts rather then the oral regional dialects from various regions.

The Sanskrit texts, as registered in the IX World Sanskrit Conference (Melbourne 1994), in relation to women and sexuality are most often misogynous, but on closer readings of women writing in Sanskrit, issues related to concubinage, property and maintance rights of mistresses equal to that of wives, niyogas (begetting of children by sanctioned sexual permissiveness in the case of the absence of progeny, a sort of premodern surrogacy), prayers for the welfare of illegitimate children, the attitude and disposition towards secret lovers (jara) addresses some modern problems in a forthright manner. However, there is limited scholarship in this area available to an English readership.

The recent (1925) discovery of the pre aryan agrarian settlements to Harappa and Mohejodara highlights an indigenous people whose traditions mingled with the Aryan traditions. The Lokayata texts (texts prevalent among the common people) speak of an agrarian culture where social ease was enjoyed by the feminine principle as manifest in the local culture of the times. These feminine concepts and icons were incorporated into female goddesses in the popular vedic texts and later given voice in the bhakti traditions, which continue as themes in popular resistance movements (satyagrahya, non-violent devi inspired movements) and in present feminist consciousness.

Popular historical texts locate the formation and decline of the Hindu Aryan society during the first to the fourth century, leading into the period of Mughal invasion in the seventh and twelfth centuries. The bhakti cults arose during this early phase and were a form of mystical permissiveness and self-worth typified by the stories of Radha's love for Krishna. Subsequently the Vedic Aryan and indigenous traditions mingled culturally and contributed to the writing of the later religious texts in which female deities are added to the predominantly male Aryan pantheon of gods. The bhakti tradition may be seen as an early form of resistance to the traditional patriarchal forms of religion such as Vaishnavism practiced through the agency of male pandits whereas the bhakti cults allowed for the direct experience of god as lover.

The Mughal rule was generative of cultural forms of

diversity with the development of trade, industry and the textile industries during the 16th to the 18th century. Women in this time had access to land as peasants, continued the bhakti traditions. But the introduction of Mughal culture saw upper aristocratic women, although in purdah and segregated, engaged in intellectual pursuits ranging in activities from the leadership of empress Nur Jehan, the compositions of the 'tawaif' (courtesan), Umrao Jan and other courtly activities. During this time the rise of the anti-bramanical Buddhist traditions influenced women with its pantheon of goddesses and acceptance of women into religious, orders thereby providing access to traditions of Pali and Sanskrit learning.

The nineteenth and twentieth centuries were largely concerned with the travails of the formation of a nation-state. The modernist Indian women's movement began with the social reformers of the 19th century. These were mostly men such as Ram Mohan Roy, Tilak and Phule but also women such as Pandita Ramabai, a controversial woman who was progressive and seen as contradictory by her fellow freedom fighters in that she focused solely on the plight of women. The freedom movement subsequently coalesced around Gandhi towards the nationalist struggle and the mass mobalization of women towards independence in 1945. In 1975 many women activists regrouped and see this year as a watershed where there was a refocussing on women's issues by women involved in other spheres of life since independence such as trade unions etc. Coinciding with the International Women's year there was a state declaration of emergency with the institution of despotic rule by Mrs Indira Gandhi for a two year period. The post independence euphoria had worn off and the was a realization that the Nehruvian social economic post-independence experiments had not succeeded in many ways, but especially in relation to women's needs and rights.

The impact of partition remains a colossal under current. Forced repatriation of women across geographical borders and the plight of the mentally ill remain as yet largely undocumented. The 19th century saw a systematic framing of an ego-ideal for Indian women. Gandhi in fighting against the evils of Hinduism in the form of child marriage, discrimination of widows and the social status of women attempted to put in place a new ideal of woman that would help counteract imperial condescension of bramanicalism and the ruling British. The women's struggle was closely connected with the political freedom struggle. The active participation of women in the freedom movement has stayed embedded in the memory of the middle-classes. From the position of being the objects of social and religious reform to being active participants in the political and social processes during the ninteenth and twentieth century. Maria Mies describes these changes as happening under the banners of education, legislation and politics.

The modern women's movement was from the beginning defined in tertiarly opposition to men, the British and 'western women' which may account for the present womens movement having difficulties in facing the 'other' of nationalism and finding correspondences to western feminism. At the present time thee are echoes of this past wherein the fundamentalist reform movements such as the VHP and BJP, again promulgate literary ideals to define masculinity (Rama-like) as saviour of woman in the context of the 'other' of Islam. The difficulties faced by Muslim women on issues such as health, divorce (talaq) and education add to the complexity of the present cultural fabric. In the face of the current anti-Muslim sentiments expressed by Hindu extremists, any statements by the Indian feminist groups are unfortunately seized by right wing Hindu critics. The Muslim Intelligensia Meet organised by Dr Imtiaz Ahmed, of Delhi, following the anti-Muslim riots in 1984 is at present conducting meetings with women in order to obtain some consensus on issues from within this community of women.

South Asian Diaspora

The South Asian Diaspora is one of the largest in the world. Kotkin argues that this 'global tribe' may be the next diaspora to emerge as a great economic force. During the early nineties 20 million overseas Indians were one of the best educated and affluent migrant groups of the world. This phenomenon is a relatively recent one as there were only five million in the early sixties. Due to the diversity of the religions and ethnicities this creates a series of 'tribes within tribes,' as for instance the one million diaspora Sindhi's from the former state of Sind now known as part of Pakistan or the four million members of the Jain sects associated with the diamond industry. Other groups include the Muslim Ismalis and Gujerati trades people settled through Africa and now largely resettled in United Kingdom or the early Afghan and Sikh traders in Australia; the Sikh agrarian settlers in California; the hotel owners of USA; new large scale merchant bankers and realtors in New Jersey, as well as the immigrant scientists and computer technicians in Silicon Valley. At another level the contributions are also in the world of fusion music, fashion, and diaspora literature that retains a distinct South Asianness with the emphasis on the maintenance of tight knit family structures and cultural values.

Although the overall impression is one of achievement and communal structures a number of issues have sprung up given the changing patterns of migration and the vulnerabilities of gender and age experienced by and through the migration process. The marginal groups within this are often the first generation women who bear the brunt of resettlement, non recognition of qualifications and the raising of families in the absence of extended networks. The care of the aged is a contentious issue as often in the country of origin this is provided for by the extended family. In the new setting this is left to the limited resources of the nuclear family. Other disenfranchised groups include the elderly single women, second generation adolescents who experience the conflicts of interfacing with the new culture as well as the confines of the traditional values such as arranged marriages and entrenched patterns of authority within the family.

In recent years a number of networks have sprung up in order to redress some of these issues, provide support networks and mentor schemes for women and children with relation to issues that incur stigmatization within the close knit community groups. Organizations such as Apna Ghar (Chicago), Sakhi (NY), SAWSSG (South Asian Women's Study and Support Group-Australia), Southhall Black Sisters (UK) link in with academic networks of women to examine the difficulties experienced as well as provide a platform for the changing experiences of migration, identity formation and needs for the future.

Chandra. T. Mohanty examines some of these discourses on identity formation and displacement at an academic level as do Grewal and Kaplan. Bhatteracharjee looks at the complexity of settlement given the interweaving of religion, identity and migration stress at the more personal level of an Asian Women's shelter and the sorts of cultural issues that arise in relation to a culture in transition by migration processes. The language of feminist discourse in relation to the lived experiences of women's lives are generally framed in the language of western epistemology. This new genre of writing opens up spaces for reflection about the construction of social reality in new and unique ways and provides the most challenges for the future of feminism and postmodernist thought.

Diaspora Studies in relation to South Asia is not well researched for a variety of reasons but with the growing awareness of the scale and impact of globalization a number of streams are beginning to emerge. The flow and affiliations of a international Asian labour market is being explored in terms of the legislatures of the ILO (International Labour Organization.) Urbanization in the country of origin with a breakdown of agrarian communities leads to a rural urban drift with a new sort of international migration patterns. Changing economic and trade agreements such as the historic GATT in India has implications for the flow of money between Non Resident Indians (NRI's) and the construction of a future nation state. The exchange of social capital between NRI's and the state happens in many ways such as the context of arranged marriages. Analysis of matrimonial advertisements reveals the replacement of traditional notions of wealth such as caste, appearance by other concepts such as material wealth and education as marriageable commodities. The phenomenon of the 'green card' or imported spouse is well accepted but the implications of this in terms of sociological, psychological and economic prospects are poorly conceptualised.

Over time the issues confronting second, third and fourth generation expatriates are poorly understood. The migrant South Asian communities of South Africa, Trinidad, Fiji, Malaysia and Mauritius are often intermingled with that of the indigenous populations. The differences of ethnicity and racism faced by marginal indigenous and ethnic groups are often collapsed allowing for very little differentiation of the problems. The incidence of suicide among Fijian Indian women is one of the highest in the world. Inadequate analysis often reduces this to the punitive gender practices of the Indian Community rather than an understanding of the strictures of land ownership and education by the indigenous colonised dictatorship rule at the present time. In South Africa the Coalition of Black Women since the 1990's although allowing a sisterspace is dominated by a few and collapses categories of socio-historical difference. Likewise the banning of Lindsey Collen's book 'The Rape of Sita', in Mauritius speaks of a Hindu orthodoxy and religious fundamentalism among third-fourth generation Hindus which parallels that found in India today, highlighting the transmission of certain values unaffected by geographical distance (Kalapani-black waters across which the indentured Indian labourers were transported a century ago and following which were presumed to have lost standing of caste, culture and religion).

This brief analysis can only serve to highlight the complex woveness of gender, culture and its interplay with migratory factors with relation to the South Asian diaspora. In the next decade a number of important trends should become more apparent as the research and work in this area become available.

References

Ashcroft. B., Griffiths G., Tiffin. H., The Post-Colonial Studies Reader. Routledge. London. N.Y. 1995.

Bhattacharjee. A. The Habit of Ex-Nomination : Nation, Woman and the Indian Migrant Bourgeoisie. Public Culture. Bulletin of the Society for Transnational Cultural Studies. Volume 5, Number one. Fall 1992.

Bhabha. H.K., The Location of Culture. Routledge. London. N.Y. 1994.

Chattopadhyay. K. Indian Women's Battle for Freedom. Delhi. Abhinav Publications 1983.

Danielsen. D., Engle. K., After Identity. A Reader in Law and Culture. Routledge. London. N.Y. 1994.

Gitiara. N., (Ad)dressing Change. Working Women and the Resurgence of Purdah in Bangladesh. Naari Series on Women Studies. Sharma. R. (ed) Representations of Gender, Democracy and Identity Politics in Relation to South Asia. Indian Books Centre. Delhi. 1996.

Grewal. I., Kaplan. C., Scattered Hegemonies. Postmodernity and Transnational Feminist Practices. University of Minnesota Press. Minneapolis. London. 1994.

Gunew. S., Yeatman. A., Feminism and The Politics of Difference. Allen and Unwin. Sydney. 1993.

Haque. R.A. Muslim Women in Bengal : 1880-1937. Unpublished manuscript.

Jayawardena K. Jayaweera S. A Profile on Sri Lanka. A study of The Integration of Women in Development Planning Women's Education Centre Colombo. WEC Series No 13 May 1986.

Jayawardena K. Emancipation and Subordination of Women in Sri Lanka. In Feminism and Nationalism in The Third World. Zed Books. London. 1986.

Jasyasinghe The Impact of the Women's Decade for Women in Sri Lanka. Naari Series on Women Studies. Sharma. R. (ed) Representations of Gender, Democracy and Identity Politics in Relation to South Asia. Indian Book Centre. Delhi. 1996.

Joel Kotkin. Tribes. How Race, Religion and Identity Determine Success in The New Global Economy. Random House Incorporated, Inc. New York. 1993.

Mies. M. Indian Women and Patriarchy. Delhi : Concept 1980.

Mohanty. C.T., Russo. A., et al. Third World and the Politics of Feminism. Indiana University Press. Bloomington and Indianapolis. 1991.

Mernessi. F., Beyond The Veil : Male-Female Dynamics in Muslim Society, revised edition, (London : Al-Saqi Books, 1985)

Rock. M. South Asian Women in Export Orientated Production : The Garment Industry in Bangladesh. Naari Series on Women Studies. Sharma. R. (ed) Women, Power and Cultural Difference. Negotiating Gender in South Asia. Indian Books Centre. Delhi. 1997.

Ricoeur. P., Oneself as Another. University of Chicago Press. Chicago. London. 1992.

Sangari. K. Vaid. S., Recasting Woken. Essays in Colonial India. Kali For Women. 1989.

Sharma R., Understanding The Concept of Empathy and It's Foundations in Psychoanalysis. N.Y. Edwin Mellon Press. 1992.

Tharu. S., Lalita K., Women Writing in India. 600 B.C. To The Present. Volume 1 : 600 B.C. to the Early Twentieth Century. Volume Two : The Twentieth Century. Pandora Press Edition 1993.

Yasmin. S. The History of the Women's Movement in Pakistan. Naari Series on Women Studies. Sharma. R. (ed) Women, Power and Cultural Difference. Negotiating Gender in South Asia. Indian Books Centre. Delhi. 1997.

Zafar. F. Ideology, Gender and The State : The Pakistan Experience in Naari Series on Women Studies. Sharma. R. (ed) Representations of Gender, democracy and Identity Politics in Relation to South Asia. Indian Books Centre. Delhi. 1996.

Zia. A.S. Sex Crime in The Islamic Context. Rape, Class and Gender in Pakistan. ASR Publications. Lahore 1994.

Feminism and Nationalism in India 1917–47

Aparna Basu

Feminism incorporates a doctrine of equals rights for all women. It is an organized movement to attain rights and an ideology of social transformation with the aim of creating a world for women beyond simple social equality. It is broadly the ideology of women's liberation, since intrinsic to it is the belief that women suffer injustice because of their sex. In recent years the definition of feminism has gone beyond simply meaning movements for equality and emancipation, which agitate for equal rights and legal reforms to redress the prevailing discrimination against women. The word has now been expanded to mean an awareness of women's oppression and exploitation within the family, at work and in society, and the conscious action by women to change this. However, in the first phase of feminism in India (1917–47), with which this paper deals, the women's movement was primarily concerned with demanding equal political, social and economic rights for women and for the removal of all forms of discriminatory procedures against women. Although feminism was a middle-class ideology, it presupposed the idea of women as a distinct group, who despite their differences of class, caste, religion and ethnicity shared certain common physical and psychological characteristics and had certain common problems.

Nationalism is a broad concept which includes many values but is basically a belief that a group of people sharing a common territory, culture and history, often also a common language and religion, possess a national identity and are entitled to a nation state. With the people claiming nationhood in many countries, including India, there were differences of class, caste, and gender but despite these, they were able to launch a struggle that deliberately blurred these divisions and stressed the commonality of a national identity against the foreign enemy.

A national movement in India can be said to begin with the foundation of the Indian National Congress in 1885. The process of nation-building and the creation of a national identity was parallel; in fact, preceded by the growth of social reform movements, which focused on women's issues. Since the status of women in society was the popular barometer of 'civilization' many reformers agitated for legislation that would improve women's situation.

By the second decade of the nineteenth century, social reformers began deploring the condition of women. Under British rule, with its new agrarian and commercial relations and the introduction of English education, law courts and an expanding administrative structure, an urban intelligentsia began to emerge in Calcutta, Bombay and later Madras, which took up issues concerning women: The first man to publicly speak out against the injustices perpetrated on women was Raja Rammohan Roy who in the early nineteenth century, condemned *sati, kulin* (high-caste Brahmins) polygamy and spoke in favour of women's property rights. Roy held the condition of women as one of the factors responsible for the degraded state of Indian society. Following him, improving the position of women became the first tenet of the Indian social reform movement. Women's inferior status, enforced seclusion, early marriage, the prohibition of widow remarriage, lack of education, were facts documented by reformers throughout the country.

The reformers were influenced by Christian missionaries such as William Ward and Alexander Duff, East India Company's officers such as Charles Grant and James Mill, travellers such as Tavernier, Barbosa and Crawford who were all critical of the position of women in Indian society. The Indian intelligentsia, therefore, focussed its attention on women's issues and suffering. Inspired by Western Orientalists like Sir William Jones, H.T. Colebrook,

H. H. Wilson, Max Muller and others, they created the notion of a golden age in ancient India where women held a high position which subsequently declined. From a sense of humiliation as a subject people, they tended to glorify the past. Every measure of reform demanded for women was justified on the ground that it was sanctioned by religious texts.

There was a link between these reformers and British officials and non-officials as the former depended on the latter for enacting laws prohibiting *sati*, raising the age of marriage or permitting widow re-marriage, and measures to improve the status of women. The foreign government was perceived by the reformers as an ally in its fight against orthodoxy.

By the end of the nineteenth century, a few women from within the reform movement formed their own organizations. Swarnakumari Devi of the Tagore family in Calcutta started a Ladies Theosophical Society in 1882 and four years later the Sakhi Samiti 'so that women of respectable families should have the opportunity of mixing with each other and devoting themselves to the cause of social welfare'.[1] At the same time, Pandita Ramabai Saraswati formed the Arya Mahila Samaj in Poona and in 1889 she started a home-cum-school for widows in Bombay named Sharda Sadan. Women in Calcutta, Bombay and Madras and even in smaller towns like Poona and Ahmedabad formed associations whose members were drawn from among a small group of urban, educated families. These associations aimed at bringing women out of their homes and encouraging them to take an interest in public affairs outside their families. Some of these were practical social reform organizations, while others were discussion platforms for women.

From the very beginning membership of the Indian National Congress was open to women. At its first session, Allan Octavian Hume asked political reformers of all shades of opinion never to forget that 'unless the elevation of the female element of the nation proceeds *pari passu* (with an equal pace) with their work, all their labour for the political enfranchisement of the country will prove vain'.[2] The report of the 1889 session of the Indian National Congress in Bombay notes that 'no less than ten lady delegates graced the assembly'. Among them were Europeans, Christians, one Parsi, one orthodox Hindu and three Brahmas. Panita Ramabai Saraswati was one of the delegates.[3] In fact, the participation of women in this Congress appears to have been mainly Ramabai's doing. Charles Bradlaugh, a member of Parliament in Britain, suggested to her and many others that women delegates should join the Congress from this time on, so that their concerns should be represented when the Congress constituted free India's parliament.[4]

Though the women delegates were allowed to sit on the platform, they were not allowed to speak or vote.[5] According to some, women first spoke at the Congress sessions in 1890.[6] Another writer puts the date ten years later, when Kadambini Ganguli, the first woman graduate of Bengal, moved the customary vote of thanks to the President, Pherozeshah Mehta at the sixteenth Congress session in 1900 at Calcutta.[7] Sarala Debi Ghosal (Chaudurani, 1872–1946), daughter of Swarnakumari Debi, composed a song urging people of different provinces of the country to join the freedom struggle and trained a group of over 50 girls to sing this song in chorus at the Congress session in 1901. The proceedings of the Congress at Ahmedabad in 1902 commenced with the singing of the National Anthem by Vidya Gauri Nilkanth and Sharda Mehta, two sisters who were the first two women graduates of Gujarat.[8] Respectable girls singing in public was itself a new thing as singing before men was associated with courtesans.

Prostitution was one of the first issues concerning women to be referred to by the Congress, and what they had to say about it sheds some light on early nationalist attitudes to the question. At the 1888 session, the Congress resolved to cooperate with English 'well wishers' of India in their attempts for the 'total abrogation of laws and rules relating to the regulation of prostitution by the state in India', and this resolve was reiterated in 1892.[9]

First steps to regulate prostitution had been taken by the British in India from the turn of the eighteenth century to deal with venereal diseases which British soldiers were held to have caught from prostitutes they visited. In 1864, the Contagious Diseases Act was passed making registration and medical examination of prostitutes compulsory.

Missionaries, evangelicals and non-conformists in England opposed the Contagious Diseases Act (1864) on the ground that it was legalizing instead of eradicating prostitution. This argument was taken up in India in the 1870s but it was only one of the arguments against the Act. It was also argued by the nationalists that such action gave the police the power to harass all classes of Indian women indiscriminately. In 1895, a government Bill to expand the scope of the police over prostitutes was opposed by Surendranath Banerjee, a nationalist leader, on the ground that it threatened individual liberty by giving the police unchecked power.[10]

In the 1890s, the handling of plague operations by British soldiers in Poona was criticised by nationalists on the ground that women were being dragged out in public and inspected before being taken to hospitals. By the end of the nineteenth century, the issue of rape and racism were interlinked and this was used by the nationalists as a weapon against British rule. Cries for the protection of 'our' women from sexual attacks by British soldiers abounded, specially in Bengal. Sarala Debi Ghosal, a militant nationalist who edited *Bharati*, urged young men to become physically strong to defend their women from molestation by British soldiers.[11] Nationalists were using rape as an example of imperialist barbarism but they saw it as a violation of national honour rather than as an act of violence against women. This became evident when they kept silent in the case of the death of Phulmoni Debi, an 11-year-old child bride who died in 1893 when her adult husband raped her.

The partition of Bengal by Lord Curzon in 1905 infused a new spirit of patriotism and was the beginning of women's participation in the nationalist movement on a larger scale. The poet Rabindranath Tagore announced his plan for observing *rakhi-bandhan* (tying threads on wrists of brothers) on 'Partition Day' and women took part in it. Another rite observed by women on this day was *arandhan* or not lighting the stove for cooking. Protest meetings were held by women and about 500 of them watched the laying of the foundation stone of the Federation Hall at Calcutta on 16 October 1905, which was 'Partition Day'. Women organized *swadeshi melas* (fairs selling indigenously made goods) and opened shops which sold only indigenous goods. We read of women giving up use of foreign cloth and smashing their foreign bangles.[12]

Various revolutionary societies such as the Swadesh Bandhab, Anusilan and Dawn sprang up during these years in Bengal; the women helped circulate revolutionary leaflets and literature and maintain liaison between the groups. They contributed jewellery as well as money to these societies. Sister Nivedita (Margaret Noble), one of Swami Vivekananda's most ardent disciples, inspired many young men and women. When Vivekananda's brother, Bhupendranath Dutta, a revolutionary, was arrested, Sister Nivedita stood surety for him, a ladies' meeting was held in his honour, an address of honour signed by 200 women was presented to him and his mother, and contributions were made for his legal expenses. The Swadeshi movement was, however, largely confined to Bengal.

In Bengal, goddess-centred nationalist rhetoric gained new ground. In the revolutionary terrorist groups that started developing during the Swadeshi movement, anti-British feeling was imbued with a Hindu nationalism in which Kali, the goddess of strength, was repeatedly invoked to liberate Mother India and become a beacon for her nationalist sons. Worship of Kali, Durga and Chandi became incumbent for many young nationalists on the ground that the 'mother' would ease the path to national liberation. For many, the Mother Goddess was identified with Mother India and poems and songs were written about the motherland whose image was worshipped in temples. Hindu worship of Shakti (power) looked upon women as the embodiment of power, energy and action.

The harnessing of Shakti to nationalism was not only a way of making female power safer, of containing it, but also a way in which women could find a role in the nationalist struggle. As the rhetoric of nationalism grew mother-centred, more and more women began to get involved in nationalist activities. Sarojini Naidu in her presidential address to the Indian National Congress described India as a 'house', the Indian people as 'children' and 'members of a joint family' and the Indian woman as 'mother'. Women had to work hard to put the house in order.

Bhikaji Cama (1861–1936), popularly known as Madame Cama, was involved in the revolutionary movement in India and abroad. Among other activities she smuggled revolvers concealed in toys into India. In 1907 she attended the International Socialist Congress in Stuttgart, where she unfurled the Indian National Flag and persuaded the Congress to support Indian independence. In 1909, her group started a monthly journal *Bande Mataram* and published it from Geneva. She believed that nationalist movements all over the world were linked by their anti-imperialism. A staunch supporter of women's education, Madame Cama's views were that Indian liberation movements would fail without the support of Indian women. Statements to this effect were made by nationalists all over India. Women's education was necessary, it was argued, for women to fulfil their roles as wives and mothers: 'India needs nobly trained wives and mothers, wise and tender rulers of the household, educated teachers of the young'.[13] The power and strength of Indian mothers was asserted, rather than their weaknesses; education was a birthright, and those who denied it to their women robbed themselves and the nation, for Indian women were mothers of the nation. Education was not only a birthright, it was what sons inherited from their mothers. The place of Indian women in national life was as mothers, 'the hand that rocks the cradle rules the world'. As Sarojini Naidu said, women all over the world were united by the 'common divine quality of motherhood'.[14] Surendranath Banerjee echoed this sentiment when he appealed to all Indians 'to sink their differences and unite under the banner of (the) religion of motherhood'.[15]

In 1910 Sarala Debi Chaudhurani formed the *Bharat Stri Mandal* (Great Circle of Indian Women) with the object of bringing together women of all castes and creeds on the basis of their common interests in the moral and material progress of India.[16] Between 1910 and 1920 the number of women's organizations grew rapidly. Called by various names—Mahila Samitis, Women's Clubs, Ladies' Societies – they emerged in the cities and towns of British India and native states. In 1917 the Women's Indian Association was established by Annie Besant, Margaret Cousins and Dorothy Jinarajadasa to start new branches as well as affiliate societies already in existence. These Irish ex-suffragettes took up the issue of votes for women and when the Secretary of State for India, Lord Edwin Montagu came to India to discuss the demand for political reforms, the WIA organized a delegation of Indian women to meet the Montagu-Chelmsford Committee. A memorandum was presented, written in the main by Margaret Cousins, asking that when the franchise was widened, women should be given the right to vote under the same conditions as men. The Southborough Franchise Committee was initially reluctant to give the vote to women because it felt that this would be premature in a society which continued to enforce *purdah* and prohibit women's education. But because of the sustained campaign launched by women's organizations and the support given by the nationalists, it was finally left to the provincial legislatures to decide the matter. Madras was the first province to give voting right to women in 1920, followed by Bombay in 1921. Franchise was, of course, extremely limited and in the first elections held under the Montagu-Chelmsford Reforms, less than 1 per cent of the female population could exercise the right to vote. In the movement of votes for women, Indian women appealed to British suffragettes for support. A delegation of Indian women went to England which through newspapers and meetings campaigned for women's franchise. It met members of British Parliament and established links with women's groups in Britain. Thus feminists were building bridges across nations.

In 1927 the All India Women's Conference was established at the initiative of Margaret Cousins to take up the problem of women's education. Women from different parts of the country as well as from different religious groups attended the first session at Poona, which was a great success. The deliberations were in English and all who attended were educated; they also travelled at their own expense and came from well-to-do families. All India Women's Conference's initial concern was with education, but it soon took up issues such as child marriage, reform of Hindu law for providing right to divorce and property to women. These reforms were opposed vehemently by orthodox Hindus as posing serious threats to their religion but of course they challenged patriarchy also. Women's organizations carried on a sustained campaign for these reforms.[17]

While on the one hand, women's organizations were fighting for women's political and economic rights and trying to improve their status through education and social reform, the women's struggle entered a new phase with the arrival in 1917 of Mahatma Gandhi on the Indian political scene. He claimed that women were better than men in waging non-violent passive resistance because they had greater capacity for self-sacrifice and endurance, were less self-seeking and had more moral courage. With his experience of South Africa behind him, Gandhi was aware of the potentialities of women as passive resisters. As he experimented with his weapon of *satyagraha* in India, he realized that women could participate effectively in it. At first, Gandhi launched local agitations: in Champaran (Bihar) against indigo planters in 1917, in Kheda (Gujarat) for non-payment of revenue in 1918 and in the same year, the Ahmedabad textile workers strike in which he was brought in by Anasuya Sarabhai, the sister of the textile magnate, Ambalal Sarabhai.

The involvement of really large numbers of women in the nationalist movement began with the Khilafat and non-cooperation movements in the 1920s. Addressing public meetings in different parts of the country, Gandhi appealed to women to donate their jewellery for the national cause and to help him collect money for the Tilak Swaraj Fund. He compared British rule to *Ravana-rajya* and said that just as sita did not cooperate with ravana, so the Indians must not cooperate with the British.[18] He told the women of India that he expected great things from them and that he had enormous faith in their capacity to sacrifice and endure suffering. Sushila Mayar, a close disciple of Gandhi, recalls a meeting at Rohtak where the hall was filled to capacity with women in *lehangas* and rustic clothes, and Gandhi with outstretched hands received money and jewellery for the Tilak fund.[19] Women in different parts of the country were drawn to his magnetic personality, unique naturalness and transparent sincerity.

During the non-cooperation movement (1920–22) Basanti Devi accompanied her husband, Deshbandhu Chittaranjan Das, in his tours of Bengal and asked women to boycott foreign goods. Women volunteers sold *khadi* on the streets of Calcutta. Kasturba Gandhi, wife of Mahatma Gandhi, presided over the Gujarat Provincial Conference and appealed to women to take to spinning and weaving *khadi*. In Allahabad, Lahore, Bombay, Ahmedabad and various parts of India women held meetings advocating *swadeshi* and use of *khadi*. In the *satyagraha* in Borsad, a rural district of Gujarat in 1923–24, women turned out in such large numbers that Gandhi remarked he had never seen such huge gatherings of women. Women displayed greater courage than men when police confiscated their cows, buffaloes and other property.

In the Bardoli Satyagraha of 1928, women soon outnumbered men in political gatherings. Singing patriotic songs, they attended Sardar Patel's meetings. When the peasants refused to pay taxes to the government, the women supported them fully. Bardoli set a new example as this was the first time that simple, unsophisticated rural women participated in the freedom struggle, though most of them belonged to the dominant, well-off peasant groups.

In February 1930 Gandhi announced that he would launch a *satyagraha* by marching from Sabarmati Ashram in Ahmedabad to Dandi, a coastal village in Gujarat, and illegally manufacture salt there. In the Dandi March, originally no women had been included. Khurshedben Naoroji, grand-daughter of Dadabhai Naoroji, one of the founding fathers of the Congress, wrote angrily to Gandhi about the exclusion of women.[20] Margaret Cousins protested in *Stri Dharma*. Kamaladevi Chattopadhyaya went to meet

Gandhi and asked him to make a special appeal to women. On the last day of the Salt March, Sarojini Naidu joined it at Dandi and was the first woman to be arrested. Women all over the country broke the salt law, organized processions and meetings and picketed shops selling foreign cloth and liquor. This agitation marked a new level of participation of women in the nationalist movement. Women, young and old, rich and poor, came tumbling out in their hundreds and thousands, shaking off the traditional shackles that had held them so long.[21] Special women's organizations were set up to mobilize and coordinate women's processions, pickets, *prabhat pheris* (processions at dawn), and spinning. Women hawked *khadi* and engaged in publicity and propaganda. Over 80,000 persons were arrested during the Salt Satyagraha, more than 17,000 of whom were women.[22]

Thousands of women actively participated in the Quit India movement of 1942. As the news of the arrest of Gandhi and other Congress leaders spread, women spontaneously came out to hold demonstrations, organized strikes and courted imprisonment. Many went 'underground', helping parallel governments and leading 'illegal' activities in the course of which a few were killed.

While thousands of women joined the freedom movement in response to Gandhi's call, there were a few who could not accept his creed of non-violence and joined revolutionary or terrorist groups. These young girls had a streak of idealism in them and were highly emotional and impulsive. Their hatred for the British was intense and their plan was to make attempts on European lives as widely as possible. They believed in individual acts of heroism, not in building up a mass movement. They were inspired by patriotism, not feminist ideas. Most women joined the freedom movement, inspired by nationalism and wanted to see the end of foreign rule. An important factor was family influence. Women from families such as those of Gandhi, Nehru, C. R. Das, Jamnalal Bajaj, Lajpat Rai naturally wanted to participate. Where the atmosphere at home was nationalistic and fathers, husbands or brothers were active, so were usually the women.

Books played a part in inspiring the educated. Annie Besant's autobiography influenced Kamaladevi;[23] novels such as Saratchandra Chatterji's *Pather Dabi*, or Bankimchandra's *Anand Math* and *Debi Chaudharani* inspired Bengali revolutionaries.[24] Personalities were perhaps most important: Subhas Bose in Bengal, Sardar Patel in Gujarat, Jawaharlal Nehru, and, above all, Mahatma Gandhi. Gandhi inspired confidence in women. His use of religious symbols and simple language appealed to ordinary, unsophisticated women. His mode of struggle was such that women could easily participate. Gandhi's letters to his women followers reveal that he understood their strength, ambition and hopes. He asserted that women were true *satyagrahis* and without them he could do nothing. The biographies and autobiographies of women in the national movement reveal the tremendous impact of Gandhi on them. Initially, political awakening among women was confined to the cities, and largely to those who came from middle-class professional and business families. By the 1930s women from the working classes and peasantry were also involved. What did this political participation mean for women and what were its consequences?

Unfortunately, those who have written on women's participation in the nationalist movement have opted for one of two simplistic views. On the one hand, there is a widespread view that by their participation in political movement, Indian women helped their own struggle for liberation, that in India, feminism and nationalism were closely linked.[25] The merging of the women's movement with the Indian National movement, it is argued, helped the cause of women and prevented the development of man-woman hostility, which is a characteristic of Western feminist movements. Kamaladevi Chattopadhyaya holds the view that Indian women launched a struggle to fight not only for the country's freedom but also for their own freedom.[26] There is a view that women's participation in the Gandhian movement was in a sense an extension of their role within the family.[27] Women were traditionally supposed to sacrifice themselves, and participation in politics was internalised as a special form of sacrifice in an essentially religious process. The language, imagery and idiom of nationalist protest remained steeped in tradition and religion as self-conscious alternatives to alien Western norms. It is held by many scholars that while such traditional moorings permitted the political involvement of thousands of women, at the same time it inhibited the extension of radicalization to other spheres. Gandhi and Congress are condemned for manipulating women for political ends. These scholars ask whether the lack of man-women hostility is desirable? Was it absent because men accepted gender equality or because women recognized male supremacy but were happy with the removal of some of the excesses of the patriarchal system?

The interaction between feminism and nationalism was complex. The activities of women in local and national organizations, and the activities of thousands of women who joined the nationalist movement together made up the women's movement. The freedom movement did not lead to a separate autonomous women's movement since it was part of the anti-colonial movement but it did generate a sense of power among women who realized their own strength. While many women who picketed shops selling foreign cloth or liquor, who marched in processions or went to jail did not question patriarchal values, for others, political involvement did spur their feminism and commitment to improving women's status. On the other hand, if patriarchal values had been challenged, women's participation may not have been so widespread as women could not really come out into the public sphere without the consent of the men in the house.

In the period between 1919-47, charitable, philanthropic and social reform activities as well as taking part in the nationalist movement were the main aspects of the women's movement. The organizations for women tried to remain apolitical, but many of their members joined political parties, participated in the national movement and even went to jail. Sarojini Naidu, for instance, was involved both in the women's movement and the nationalist movement. She was a founder member of WIA and AIWC, and also a frequent member of the Congress Working

Committee and its President in 1925. She urged women to petition on issues which affected women's status but to remain apolitical in terms of party allegiance. Her concern for the status of women manifested itself in petitioning, urging more facilities for women's education, demanding legal changes in marriage laws, property rights and franchise. They represented urban, upper class, English-speaking women. The nationalist movement brought into its fold both women of this class as well as poor, illiterate rural and urban women. The political movement stressed the importance of *Swaraj* (self-rule). Women's organizations argued that uplift of women was necessary because women are the mothers of future generations. While women were urged to come out and work for the nation, there was no rejection of the traditional role of mother and wife. In fact, it was stressed that if they were educated and widened their horizons, women would be good wives and mothers. Women's organizations began by concentrating on issues of social reform to 'uplift' the status of women but with the rising tide of nationalism, the country's freedom was given priority. Caste, class, gender issues were not stressed in order to create solidarity against imperial rule.

The women's organizations had been pressing for the reform of marriage and inheritance laws and a common civil code but when the government in the 1940s appointed a committee under the chairmanship of Sir B. N. Rao to look into this matter, opinion among women was divided as to whether they should cooperate with this Committee, as the Congress had launched the Quit India movement in 1942 and most nationalist leaders were in jail. Some women opposed giving evidence before the Committee, whereas others argued that social equality was as important as political freedom. The former argued that the nation's freedom could never be against women's freedom.

Women's active role in the freedom struggle, their courage and organizational skills led the nationalists to grant women political equality. At its session in Karachi in 1931, the Indian National Congress declared that in independent India women would have complete political freedom and equality. The National Planning Committee appointed by the Congress in 1937 had a sub-committee on women which made quite radical recommendations regarding women's equal status that were accepted by the Congress. Yet the majority of men in the Congress and others involved in the freedom struggle subscribed to patriarchal values and resented any challenge to male authority within the family or outside.

Fighting for the country's freedom brought women out of their homes and made them politically conscious but it did not emancipate or improve the position or status of the vast majority. How else do we explain the fact that despite this long history of women's struggle, Indian women today are one of the most backward in the world with regard to literacy, female work participation and sex-ratio such that customs like dowry, child marriage, bride burning, still persist? Changing societal attitudes towards women and women's self-perception that are deeply rooted in our psyche and social structure is not an easy task. The Indian women's movement has a long way to go in its struggle for bringing about new values, a new morality and a new egalitarian relationship.

Notes

1. Usha Chakraborti, *Condition of Bengali Women around the Second Half of the Nineteenth Century* (Calcutta, 1963), p. 148.
2. J. Murdoch (com.), *Twelve Years of Indian Progress*, the resolutions of its Thirteenth Session (Madras, 1898), p. 36.
3. Meera Kosambi, 'Women's Emancipation and Equality: Pandita Ramabai's Contribution to Women's Cause', *Economic and Political Weekly*, vol. 23, no. 44, October 1988, p. WS-48.
4. Sita Ram Singh, *Nationalism and Social Reform in India: 1805-1920*, (Delhi, 1977), p. 206.
5. Ibid.
6. Pattabhi Sitaramayya, *History of the Indian National Congress*, vol. I, (Delhi, 1969), p. 114.
7. Ibid., p. 51.
8. B. B. Mazumbar and B. P. Masumbar, *Congress and Congressmen in the Pre-Gandhian Era, 1885-1917* (Calcutta, 1967), p. 128.
9. Kenneth Ballhatchet, *Race, Sex and Class under the Raj* (Delhi, 198), pp. 12-39.
10. Ibid., pp. 123-43.
11. Uma Chakravarti, 'Whatever Happened to the Vedic Dasi? Orientalism,

Nationalism and a Script for the Past', in Kumkum Sangari and Sudesh Vaid (eds), *Recasting Women*, (Delhi, 1989), p. 62.
12. Sumit Sarkar, *The Swadeshi Movement in Bengal*, (New Delhi, 1973), pp. 287-8.
13. Sarojini Naidu, *Speeches and Writings*, (Madras 1904), pp. 18-20.
14. Ibid., p. 100.
15. Surendranath Banerjee, *Speeches*, Calcutta, vol. I, p. 21.
16. Sita Ram Singh, op.cit., pp. 190-1.
17. Aparna Basu and Bharati Ray, *Women's Struggles: A History of the All India Women's Conference, 1927-87*, (New Delhi, 1991).
18. Aparna Basu, 'The Role of Women in the Indian Struggle for Freedom' in B. R. Nanda, ed. *Indian Women from Purdah to Modernity*, (New Delhi, 1976), pp. 20-1.
19. Ibid.
20. Ibid., p. 23
21. Kamaladevi Chattopadhyaya, Interview, NMML Oral History Section, pp. 72-3.
22. P. J. Thomas, *Indian Women Through the Ages* (Bombay, 1964), p. 331.
23. Kamaladevi Chattopadhyaya, op.cit., pp. 72-3.
24. Transcript of interview with Kamala Das Gupta, NMML Oral History Section.
25. Aparna Basu, 'The Role of Women in Freedom Movement', Lakshmi Menon, 'Women and the National Movement' in Devaki Jain, ed. *Indian Women* (New Delhi, 1975).
26. Kamaladevi Chattopadhyaya, 'The Women's Movement, Then and Now', in Devaki Jain, op. cit.
27. Gail, Minault (ed.), *The Extended Family: Women's Political Participation in India and Pakistan* (New Delhi, 1981).

Gender and Politics in Pakistan

Fareeha Zafar

Introduction

The distinctly low level of participation of women in affairs of the state and government and their invisibility in social public space can be understood as being a reflection of the several implications inherent in patriarchal structures and systems. Given the male-dominated and authoritarian social system which prevails throughout the different regions of Pakistan and conditions the attitudes, behavior and institutional framework, the status of women as inferior and subordinate to that of men is accepted and promoted as the dominant ideology which has permeated to all levels of society. Combined with a traditional and culturally specific interpretation of Islam, separate spheres of activity and mobility are demarcated for women and men. This excludes women from most activities in the public domain unless they are performed in a segregated and secluded environment.

The co-existence of tribal, feudal and capitalist socio-economic formations in the different regions of Pakistan has also created class variations which exert their particular influence on the participation of women in politics. At one level this has allowed women of the ruling and elite classes a certain amount of freedom to enter politics which they have done as autonomous individuals and as family representatives. At the same time legitimacy of enforcing seclusion and denial of access to and control over opportunities is derived from tradition, custom and/or religion as is evidenced in the lack of cultural, social, economic and political autonomy of the majority of Pakistani women.

These contradictions are reflected and supported by a political system which exists to maintain the status quo instead of functioning as a democratizing process. Decision-making at all levels, from the household to the top rung of government, is considered to be a male prerogative, strengthened by an iniquitous distribution of resources and reinforced by law. With the exception of women who participate in elections on general seats, the majority of women on reserved seats are nominal representatives of the male members of their families.

Since independence in 1947 there have been about two dozen governments in Pakistan with the power base shifting between politicians, bureaucrats and the armed forces. This conglomerate of interests has not facilitated the evolution of a political system with the result that during the forty-six years of Pakistan's history as an independent, sovereign state, twenty-seven years or more than half the period has been under military rule while the remainder has been at times a cordial but often an antagonistic relationship between politicians (mostly feudals) and inherently patriarchal within which the religious orthodoxy can function with ease and continue to demand even stricter measures for the subordination and suppression of the weaker sections of society including women and minorities.

Instability coupled with the need to enforce legitimacy has entrenched authoritarian and male dominated structures which mitigate against the inclusion of women in the political process although Pakistan has the rare distinction of having had a woman Prime Minister. Few political parties have mobilised women to participate in political activity, the exception being the Pakistan People's Party. Thus, the participation of women in the political arena cannot be judged only from their participation in electoral politics, rather it encompasses a much broader spectrum of struggle extending from the personal to the formation of organisations and groups, and from demanding their rights and a place in society to actual representation in parliament.

Political Participation of Women

The participation of women in the area of politics can be traced during the different phases of the political life of the country. The first phase began with Independence in 1947 and continued till 1958; the second phase from 1958 to 1968 covers the period of Ayub Khan's martial law and often termed the 'Development Decade', the third phase extends from 1968 to 1977 and is dominated by the populist politics of Zulfiqar Ali Bhutto the first elected Prime Minister; the fourth phase from 1977 to 1985 is associated with Zia-ul Haq's dictatorial military rule and 'islamization' of laws and social norms. The present phase began in 1985 and can be described as the struggle to establish democracy. During this period the country has already seen a change of four governments and the present government is also relatively unstable.

From Independence to Martial Law

From the earliest days, the political involvement of women has been both at the level of formal political activity as well as through informal organizations and associations. Soon after independence, the most important development was the formation of a number of women's organisations especially the Democratic Women's Alliance, a left oriented political organisation and the All Pakistan Women's Association (APWA) with a focus on rehabilitating women uprooted by the division of the Indian Sub-continent by providing them education, training and employment opportunities. APOWA was formed by the wife of the prime minister, Begum Ra'ana Liaquat Ali who later started women's defence and military training but had to abandon these programmes because they were too controversial. The only organisation created by women political activists who felt that the political parties had failed to take up the issue of women's rights and concentrated on pushing for reforms in the legislative field was the United Front for Women's Rights. At the constituent level, there were two women members in Pakistan first Constituent Assembly who struggled for equal status, equality opportunity, equal pay for equal work and fundamental rights. (Mumtaz 1986).

The right of women to vote was recognised as early as 1928, but their election to the assemblies was not direct, instead there were reserved seats for women both at the National and Provincial level. However, women were given a two vote franchise and where allowed to elect their own representatives. Outside the political arena, women's agitated against polygamy which led to the formation of a Committee headed by a Chief Justice in 1956 to make recommendations to streamline marriage and other family laws.

Several other women's organisations were formed during these early years which reflected the growing the social consciousness of women working in business and different professions. These organisations have played a critical role in providing a training ground for women to enter into politics. It must be remembered though that the number of educated women was very few and the few professions open to women were education and health.

Ayub Khan's Martial Law (1958-68)

Ayub Khan's military dictatorship was progressive in the sense that he had a strong dislike for the obscurantist clergy. He revived the shelved 1956 Committee's Report which resulted in the promulgation of the Muslim Family Laws Ordinance of 1961. Among the most important statutes of this Ordinance were those that standardized the marriage contract, required the registration of all marriages and gave women the delegated right to divorce. What was even more significant was that the Ordinance was passed as a consequence of the agitation launched by women and despite opposition from the clergy. Till today, the Ordinance Symbolized a victory for women's rights and agitation. (Mumtaz and Shaheed 1987). It also continues to be a major bone of contention between women's organisations and the religious parties.

However, in the political field, under Ayub Khan's Constitution of 1962, the principle of female suffrage on the basis of women's constituencies, a right women had required under the 1956 Constitution was taken away. This paved the way for indirect elections for women to the National Assembly and their representation was further affected due to a reduction in the number of women's seats.

At a more popular level, the Democratic Women's Association which was the only left-wing women's organisation at this time, sought to organise women of the working class and articulate their demands for better economic conditions, employment opportunities and facilities for working women. These women also participated in the activities of other left-oriented political organisations and workers parties.

The Bhutto Period (1971-79)

In 1968 Ayub Khan was deposed. This was followed by a period of turmoil which ultimately resulted in the upsurge of the Pakistan People's Party (PPP) led by Ayub Khan's Foreign Minister,. Zulfiqar Ali Bhutto. The PP's politics mobilised the large mass of ordinary people including women who were drawn by its promise of equality and justice for all. A Women's Wing was formed in the PPP with branches at different administrative and local levels with the result that women from all social classes participated in the general elections. For the first time the entire polity of Pakistan was politicised and even subsequent martial law regimes have not been able to reverse this trend.

Under the 1973 Constitution the status of women was considerably improved. Article 25 of the Constitution stated that there was to be no discrimination on the basis of sex while Article 34 was to ensure the full participation of women in all spheres of national life. The Constitution also recognised women's right to the highest office in the land and women could contest for general seats in the assemblies. But, reserved seats for women were retained despite the struggle of APWA and other women's organisations to remove them.

Other measures which contributed to the emancipation of women included the Administrative Reforms (1972) which opened the administrative services to women including the foreign service and appointment to important posts. For the first time a woman was appointed as the Governor of a province and as Vice Chancellor of a university. The demand for the establishment of a Commission to determine the status of women resulted in the setting up of The Women's Rights Committee in 1976. Headed by one of the most active and vocal women members of the PPP the report of the Committee was extremely succinct and radical in the measures it proposed for improving the status and participation of women. It recommended the introduction of specific legislation to safeguard women's rights and emphasised the induction of women in all fields of life especially in politics. (Report of the Women's Rights Committee 1976). Although the report was never made public its recommendations have formed the basis for subsequent policy documents on women.

The intense political activity of this period had its impact on women's organisations in two ways; firstly existing organisations life APWA began to shift from being largely welfare organisations to becoming more development and issue oriented (this change was also partly the result of the 1975 International Women's Year); and secondly, new women's organisations were formed.

The leadership of these organisations was provided by professional and well educated women of the upper and middle class who had been motivated by the political programme of the PPP and other progressive ideas.

During the early seventies the organizations formed had decidedly political agendas in that they addressed themselves to working class women and defined their activities within the framework of revolutionary economic and social change. Women were organised in to unions and associations and literature was disseminated on women's rights and on the struggle of working women in other countries. Women students were particularly active in forming their own organisations as well as functioning as wings of other radical and left-wing students organisations. In the latter part of the same decade women's organisations focused on the need to conduct research on women, in providing legal and medical assistance, and in creating facilities for working women.

The politicization of women which occurred during this period has been critical in creating an awareness among women of their rights and capabilities. The participation of women in the celebrations of International Women's Year in 1975 and in international for a such the Mexico Conference where the Pakistan delegation was headed by the prime minister's wife, Begum Nusrat Bhutto increased the visibility of women. This impacted positively on women belonging to different strata of society. The educated women could for see a greater role for themselves in public life while middle class women recognised the need for education in creating upward mobility for themselves and their daughters as new avenues of employment were opened to women. Perhaps the greatest change occurred at the lowest levels of society where women (and men) of the working classes were for the first time in the history of Pakistan given a sense of importance and recognition as human beings.

Zia-ul-Haq's Period of Dictatorship (1977-1985)

The process of popular politicization was truncated by the imposition of martial law in July 1977 after the results of the 1977 elections were not accepted by the opposition who had formed a coalition, the Pakistan National Alliance (PNA) against the victorious PPP. The reactionary religious parties who had been the strongest and most vocal opponents to women's rights to work, equal opportunities and status, found it politically expedient to mobilise women and bring out *burqa* clad (shrouded) women on to the streets in the main cities. This compulsion to count women among their supporters was the direct outcome of the politics of the People's Party.

But, for the first time, the religious parties were on the side of the regime in power and not against it. This meant that the Jama'at-e'Islami, the most reactionary religious party, whose position on the status of women in society could only have a negative and regressive effect on women, could influence policy. (Mumtaz and Shaheed 1975). The Jama'at's propaganda was slow and insidious, it corroded the few gains women had made in the fields of education, employment and empowerment, and since it accompanied the most repressive martial law Pakistan has even known, women's reaction was also slow in crystallising. The right of women to certain specific types of employment was questioned, their personal liberties were circumscribed and their participation in sports and cultural activities was curbed; even the right of women to vote came under review. Since women belonging to the religious parties had also been mobilised, for every retrogressive step taken by the government two diametrically opposed points of view were expressed, those of the extreme right and those of the rest of the women. As the religious parties had been co-opted by the government they were in a position to force their standpoint, the progressive forces had yet to formulate their political agenda.

The several women's organisations individually were not in a position to take a militant stand against the policies of the government, also most of them were welfare and development oriented in their outlook. The need for a forum on which different women's organisations could come together so that a common protest could be initiated against the retrogressive policies of the government resulted in the formation of the Women's Action Forum (WAF) in 1981.[1] It became a platform for many of the existing women's organisations and although individuals from different social, economic and political backgrounds, whose common interest lay in safeguarding women's rights, became part of WAF, it was and continues to be dominated by upper and middle class women. The reason for this lay in the threat to personal liberties which these women experienced for the first time since the creation of Pakistan and thus felt the need to mobilise women belonging to those classes which had a greater voice in the affairs of the state.

WAF, created out of the need to challenge the government's attempts to segregate and limit women's activities as well to counter the legislative measures being taken in the name of religion which is Islam for the majority of people, was able to mobilise a representative number of urban women on the issue of women's rights. Between 1978 and 1981 a large number of ordinances and laws had been passed which had adversely affected women. WAF organised signature campaigns, meetings and press conferences against these and other attempts to seclude women. The concept of '*chador and chardewari*' (which literally meant the veil and the four walls of the house) promoted by the military regime and its co-opted religious parties as being the guidelines for female behaviour, was rejected by WAF. This was also a negation of the principles enunciated by the founder of the nation the Quaid-e-Azam, who had said in 1944: "It is a crime against humanity that our women are shut up in the four walls of the houses as prisoners."

The role of the Women's Action Forum has to be envisaged in the broader framework of a martial law regime which allowed no public expression of dissent. In this context the procession taken out by WAF in February 1983 against the proposed Law of Evidence[2] was the first by any organisation or group in direct violation of martial law regulations. The military crackdown on a peaceful procession followed by the subsequent imprisonment of many of the WAF members created in the minds of politicians, the government and women themselves the seriousness of the law and that it was possible to challenge it. This incident has been a turning point for the women of Pakistan and the fact that a women's movement existed in Pakistan was recognised nationally and by the international community. It was also the first step towards the revival of democracy in the country.

By not aligning itself to any political party WAF was able to mobilise a large number of women although its sphere of influence remained limited to a few large cities. Also, since the issues it raised affected all women its impact was much more than its numerical strength. After the lifting of martial law in 1985, WAF also began to lobby with the elected members of the government and other influential groups and individuals and since then it's role has expanded. WAF also generated a general politicisation of other women's organisations which had hitherto been welfare oriented, and together with women journalists it played a key role in articulating and bringing the question of women's rights on the national agenda.

The women's movement was not limited to the cities only, at the grassroots level in the rural areas of the Sindh Province the Sindhiani-Tehrik (Sindhi Women's Movement) developed into the largest and most militant women's organisations with a membership of over 1500 peasant women. Unlike the urban women's groups, the Sindhiani-Tehrik operated within the Sindhi nationalist movement and was against feudalism and for women's rights. It's programme was targeted against the specific problems of women in the rural areas which included women's right to education and medical care, and was against ingrained customs and traditions such as forced marriage, domestic violence and the exploitation of women.

If the political participation of women is to be judged from the activities of the above two women's organisation, it would appear that the women of Pakistan had made tremendous gains. But at the Nairobi Conference which marked the end of the 'Decade of Women' the Pakistan Commission on the Status of Women 1985 presented the true picture regarding the low status of women in Pakistan. In all fields including education, employment, health and public representation, women were the neglected section of society. Repressive feudal, tribal and religious customs and norms, in tandem, contributed to keeping women undeveloped and backward, and their participation in government and at decision making levels remained marginal.

At the same time, the 1985 elections were indicative of the generally low level of participation of women in the political life of the country. The unfavourable attitude to women's rights was reflected in the small number of female candidates. Similarly, the representation of women at other levels was minimal; neither the Senate nor the Federal Cabinet had any women members, and there was only one women Minister of State and two women in the cabinet of one province. One of the national newspapers commenting on this situation wrote: 'Two primary methods of political participation are voting and seeking an elective office. A third criterion for judging involvement is representation in the government. The record of Pakistani women on all three counts has been rather poor." (The Daily Dawn February 1985).

1985 to the Present : The Struggle for Democracy

Since the 1980's the visibility of women in political activity has increased to an appreciable extent and the question of women's rights, participation and role in society has come to be recognised at the national level. The challenge posed by a repressive martial law regime forced the women of Pakistan to come out into the public and protest against the draconian measures being taken to suppress them. What is even more significant is the fact that WAF was the first organisation to take positions on issues critical to the entire polity including specific legislation much before other organisations realised the implications of such measures.

With the return to democracy in 1985 the focus of the women's movement has been on trying to pressurize the elected governments to repeal all anti-women laws introduced by the last regime. This includes the Eighth Amendment to the 1973 Constitution by the non-representative *Majlis-e-Shoora* which indemnifies all actions taken by the martial law regime including all legislation in the name of religion, and the Ninth Constitutional Amendment passed by both the Senate and National Assembly which allows the Federal Shariat Court[3] to review all existing legislation to bring it in conformity with the *Qu'raan* and *Sunnah*[4] including the Family Laws Ordinance.

The election of Benazir Bhutto on the Prime Minister of Pakistan in 1988 had two implications which are unique to Pakistan; firstly, it symbolised the rejection of the majority of the policies of Zia-ul-Haq's regime which were aimed at undermining the status of women as in her party manifesto she resolved to remove all discriminatory laws against women; and secondly, her victory in an environment of entrenched religion was itself cause for optimism. Internally, the very presence of a woman Prime Minister had a visible affect on the psyche of women and men at all levels. As in the case of other South Asian countries where women have risen to the highest political office, women were able to identify themselves with a national leader and Benazir Bhutto was a very positive role model for the younger generation of women. For the men, it was a break in the established tradition of male domination and a negation of the commonly accepted inferior status of women. At the international level it helped to reduce the image of the country as a fundamentalist state.

There was both complacency and confusion on the part of the women's organisations following the appointment of Benazir Bhutto as they expected that all anti-women legislation introduced by the previous regime would be abolished. But not only did the government drag its feet in this area it appeared to be making overtures to the religious groups. The period of inactivity was shattered by the rape of two nurses in the ward of a hospital in the largest city, Karachi. This event brought out women's organisations from the whole political spectrum on the streets. For the first time women from the religious parties joined the women's movement even though they disagreed with the slogans and placards used during the demonstration which were clearly against legislation promulgated in the name of Islam and specifically the Hadood Ordinances of 1979.[5]

In appointments to government office, contrary to expectations, there were only two women Ministers of State and one woman Federal Minister in the new Cabinet. Almost no attempt was made to include more women at other levels of the government. Benazir Bhutto's government lasted only 18 months till it fell prey to the Eighth Constitutional Amendment under which the President had the powers to dismiss and elected assembly if he felt it was not performing its functions in accordance with the law and hold new elections within a period of three months.

Despite the increased visibility of women in meetings and demonstrations of all political parties including the religious parties, very few women were given tickets at the national and provincial levels. The PPP fielded three women candidates and the opposition one.

Following the defeat of Benazir Bhutto's party, there were large scale arrests of PPP women workers in the Sindh Province, the home province of the Bhutto family, by the new government of the Pakistan Muslim League. This was the beginning of a period of organised violence against women on political grounds and other human rights violations which resulted in public demonstrations by several organisations and the formation of a new organisation, Women Against Rape.[6] In order to present a liberal image to the West, the new government appointed Sydeda Abida Hussain a political women as ambassador to the United States of America. When the only women member of the Senate, Dr. Nurjehan Panezai, became its Deputy Chairman her appointment was opposed by both the Jama'at-e-Islami and the Jamiat-e-Ulema-e Islam, the two most reactionary religious parties. The PML government also lasted 22 Amendment.

Due to polarisation and distrust on the part of the political parties of the existing government and the opposition, a way out of the impasse had to be found. A Caretaker Government was formed with Mr. Moeen Qureishi a Pakistani working with the World Bank for several years and respected for his integrity and ability. His mandate was to hold elections within three months.

Within less than a decade the fourth general elections were held in October 1993 with the PPP led by Benazir Bhutto again emerging as the victor though with a lesser majority in Parliament than it had previously. In this election 13 women contested for general at the national level with more political parties fielding women candidates than in any previous election. At the national level only three women, Benazir Bhutto and Nusrat Bhutto of the PPP and Nasim Wali Khan of the Opposition were elected to office. More women have been given positions of political importance by the Government during its present tenure. The advisor to the Prime Minister on the social sectors Shahnaz Wazir Ali has been a PPP activist for many years and Dr. Maleeha Lodhi the ambassador to the US has also been associated with the PPP. After many years, there is a woman Secretary of the Ministry of Women Development and the recently constituted National Commission on Women is headed by veteran woman activist Tahira Mazhar Ali.

Women are being included at different levels of decision making and their views are elicited in matters which have social, economic and legal dimensions. Members of the Women's Action Forum (WAF), other women's groups and non-governmental organisations have been involved by the government in for example setting up of women police stations and establishing legal aid centers for women. An Inquiry Commission has also been set up by the government which has held a number of sessions and is open to the general public.

At the same time, laws such as the Blasphemy Law has targeted the minority religious groups and women have been in the forefront of agitations against the biased implementation of this law. In the recent case of Salamat Masih a young christian boy of 12 who was awarded the death penalty by the lower courts WAF's call for a demonstrations was participated in by men and women of several organisations. Later the sentence was overturned by the Lahore High Court amid violent threats and demonstrations by fundamentalist religious groups.

During the last decade the participation of women in political activity has increased with a number of political parties supporting active women's wings. However, most of the women's sections are motivated only at election time with the exception of the women's wing of the PPP which besides carrying on its own organisational work is articulate on many issues concerning women as well as participating in the programmes of other women's organisations. Issues which have drawn a large number of women from political parties and individuals include problems of violence against women especially rape, police brutality, maltreatment of women prisoners, more educational opportunities for women particularly for female medical students, rising prices of essential commodities, etc.

These actions have prompted the parties of the religious right especially the Jama'at-e-Islami to organise their women wings as a measure to counter the progressive and liberal politics of the women of the other political parties as well as concession of their own female supporters who are for the first completing higher education from universities and professional institutions, are entering employment and are having to cope in a environment for which they are not prepared.

More recently, women's organisations and human rights groups have been coming together on issue oriented platforms to raise a common voice and to pressurise the government in the area of Legal Reforms, Child Rights, ratification of the Convention on the Elimination of all Forms of Discrimination Against Women (CEDAW) and others. Political activism has become a part of the work of non-governmental organisations and is beginning to be recognised by the government as legitimate activity.

Women and the Electoral Process

Participation of women in the electoral process has been increasing since independence when only a handful of women were mobilised by the Women's Wing of the Pakistan Muslim League (PML). Two major problems have shadowed the inclusion of women in the political arena, firstly the question of how women are to be elected and secondly, whether women can contest for the highest political office, that is President and Prime Minister.

Women and Double Franchise

The first real elections on the basis of audit franchise were held in 1951 (for the Punjab Provincial Assembly), but these failed to draw women at a wider level. Women's elections were fought on five reserved seats on the basis of special constituencies. The two women representatives in Pakistan's first legislature Begum Jahanara Shah Nawaz and Begum Shaista Ikramullah belonged to known political families. They had been demanding a 10 per cent quota of reserved seats for women in the assemblies and other law making bodies, but although the draft bill for the Charter of Women's Rights was discussed in the Constituent Assembly, the quota remained at 3 per cent for both the Central and Provincial Assemblies. (Mumtaz and Shaheed 1987).

Under the 1956 Constitution the total number of reserved seats for women in the National Assembly was 10 and there were 10 seats for women in each of the 2 Provincial Assemblies. But in the 1962 Constitution their number was reduced to 6 at the national level and 5 each at the provincial levels. Women could contest for the general seats but since they continued to be indirectly elected as well their representation remained token especially as they were generally family members of the elected members of the National and Provincial Assemblies. This was, however, the first time that women of minority communities were given the opportunity to participate in the national elections and to serve in parliament. (Pakistan Commission on the Status of Women 1985).

Women as Head of State

The most significant event during the Ayub Khan period was the candidature of Mohtarma Fatima Jinnah, sister of the founder of the nation Mohammad Ali Jinnah, for the office of president in the 1965 elections. She was nominated as the candidate of the Combined Opposition Parties (COP) including the religious parties against Ayub Khan, since she was the most likely person to succeed and not because the COP was sensitive to giving representation to women. It indicated however that even the religious parties were willing to compromise on principles and accept a women as head of state when their interests were threatened. Ironically, it was Ayub Khan who used some of the *ulema* (clergy) to campaign against a woman becoming the head of state in a muslim country. It is also important to take cognizance of the fact that at the popular level, it did not matter to the common man whether a woman was head of state or not. (Mumtaz and Shaheed 1987). Although Mohtarma Fatima Jinnah lost the elections it is a commonly accepted fact that this was the result of the manipulation of the electoral process by Ayub Khan which was not a direct election but manoeuvered through an electoral college system known as Basic Democracies. There was, however, an overall increase in the participation of women in the electoral process during the 1965 elections and six women won National Assembly seats and served on various committees.

The anti-Ayub agitation which culminated in the general elections of 1970 had mobilised a large number of women both from the intellectual and working class to work voluntarily for the PPP. Women took it upon themselves to persuade others to vote, carry voters to the polling booths, supervise polling stations and ensure that the large women support of the PPP which was from the poorer sections of society would not be hindered from casting their votes. Consequently, the PPP won a landslide victory over its opponents. For the first time, women voted in very large numbers and often against feudal, familial and *baradiri* (caste/kinship) persuasions. But while no women contested on the general seats, reserved seats for women were raised to 13 under the legal Framework Order 1970 under which the elections were organised. Two women were elected as members of the National Assembly, Begum Nasim Jehan and Begum Ashraf Abbasi, both of the PPP and the later was elected Deputy Speaker of the National Assembly.

The 1973 Constitution and Women

The 1973 Constitution gave women equality, and was very strong on removing all forms of discrimination against them. But on the question of reserved seats it did not give women the double franchise; it did, however, recommend an increase in the number of women's seats to five per cent of the total strength of the house after a period of ten years. The two women members had presented a number of alternatives, which included women's elections to the reserved from urban constituencies, an electoral college of women's organisations, reservation of 20 constituencies of males and females to elect female representatives from there, and others, but all these were rejected. (Mumtaz 1988).

Despite the politicization of women, in the 1977 elections, the PPP did not put up a single woman candidate. However, the opposition coalition of centrist and extremist rightist parties the PNA, showed greater understanding of the situation and their candidate Begum Nasim Wali Khan became the first woman in Pakistan's electoral history to contest and win from a general seat. As has the case with other women politicians in Asia and some Third World countries, she belonged to a notable political family, and had entered politics after her husband's long incarceration. On the reserved seats 10 women were elected.

1973 Constitution in Abeyance

The democratic political process was subverted by the imposition of martial law by Zia-ul-Haq who tried two experiments of running the political affairs of the country through non-democratic institutions between 1977 and 1985. The first was the *Majilis-e-Shoora* an institution of hand-picked individuals in which the representation of women was minimal. The second was the non-party election of 1985 which eroded the political and economic and social base of the country as they were fought on the basis of *baradiri*, tribal and sectarian alternatives. However, the number of reserved seats for women was doubled to 20 at the national level and 23 at the provincial level. Only 64 women contested for the National Assembly seats, and 66 for the Provincial Assembly (compared with 3,853 male candidates for 483 provincial seats).

A smaller number of women (13) contested elections on general seats and the only woman who succeeded in winning a seat in the National Assembly was Syeda Abida Hussain who has consistently refused to be elected against a reserved seat. She was also the only female district council chairperson in the entire country to emerge successful in the Local Government elections of 1978. The other woman who contested on a general seat Gulzar Unar, faced one of the most powerful feudal lords of the area, and although she was defeated she was elected on a reserved seat. Gulzar Unar was described as "the new Pakistani woman-bold, articulate, daring—a symbol of revolt against the feudal-religious establishments." (The daily *Dawn* April 1985). It is also significant that both these women contested from rural constituencies which are generally thought to be more conservative and male preserves. In the by-elections another woman won a seat in the National Assembly.

At the provincial level only 2 women were successful. (Pakistan Commission on the Status of Women 1985). Another level at which women have participated in political activities has been Local Government. Women councillors constitute a cadre of leadership which is small in number but powerful in influence encompassing a wide scope of duties and responsibilities. With the sudden death of Zia-ul-Haq in 1988 a return to democratic politics became possible. A direct outcome of the women's movement was that most political parties participating in the 1988 elections included programmes for women in their manifestos and awarded more tickets to women; there were also more women contesting as independent candidates. The religious parties including the Jama'at-e'Islami had to concede to the right of women to vote and advocated education and employment for women albeit in a segregated situation. A change had also occurred among the women contestants who were more vocal on women's rights and issues.

For the second time in the history of Pakistan a woman, Benazir Bhutto as Co-chairperson of the Pakistan People's Party, was contesting for the highest political office, that of Prime Minister. She was the daughter of the country's first elected Prime Minister Zulfiqar Ali Bhutto who was hanged by Zia-ul-Haq. Benazir Bhutto was imprisoned for her activism and she remained in jail for several months. Her party won the most seats in the National Assembly and she became the first woman Prime Minister of a Muslim country in December 1988.

It was expected that more women would be fielded as candidates by political parties, but in the 1990 elections the PPP-led coalition, the Pakistan Democratic Alliance only gave tickets to three women for the national assembly. Of these Benazir and her mother Nusrat Bhutto won their seats. The opposition only fielded one woman candidate, Abida Hussain and she lost. Despite having a very large female constituency, the Mahajir Qaumi Mahaz (MQM) did not field any female candidates.

The number of women considerably increased in the 1993 elections with 13 women contesting general seats for the National Assembly. Several political parties including the PPP, Pakistan Muslim League (POML) and the MQM field women candidates. Some women also contested as independent candidates. Only the religious parties failed to put up any female candidates. Together with Benazir Bhutto four women were returned to the present National Assembly. Three women were also returned at the provincial level in Punjab, Sind and NWFP. Additionally a woman was also returned on a minority seat. (Shaheed et al May 1994).

Present Status of Women's Reserved Seats

With the 1988 elections the constitutional protection given to the issue of reserved seats for women ended. The 1973 Constitution had stipulated that reserved seats for women would only be maintained for a period of three elections following the promulgation of the constitution. A constitutional amendment would be required to restore these seats if it was felt that social conditions were still not conducive for women to contest on an equal footing with men which was the initial reason for having them.

Women's organisations have been divided on this issue as it is contrary to their demand for equality. However, it is also apparent that given the social milieu, women are unlikely to be elected to the general seats in sufficient numbers unless some conditions are laid down for the political parties to nominate women candidates. WAF in consultation with other women's organisations has developed a position on this issue which allows for the gradual phasing out of the reserved seats. It suggests that reserved seats should be restored and increased to 20 percent. Also that the women elected against these seats should have a record of having articulated gender issues and worked for the emancipation of women. At the same time women should be given a double franchise as they had prior to the abrogation of the 1956 Constitution. Also only those political parties should be allowed to contest elections who give 20 per cent seats to women. This is to be increased by 10 per cent during each following election, until parity is achieved. (Women's Action Forum 1992).

The position has however changed since the last election in 1993. The women's seats are yet to be resorted and as the government lacks the two-third majority in Parliament to push through its decisions, despite the passage of fifteen months it has not been able to bring women into the assemblies. Recently, WAF has initiated a dialogue with the government and opposition to arrive at acceptable modalities for restoring women's participation in mainstream politics. The National Women's Commission established by the present government has also opened a dialogue with the opposition and a formula based on proportional representation is currently under discussion.

Women in Local Government

Women's participation in Local Government has been steadily increasing although only a few women elected at that level have followed independent policies. In the 1992 Local Government elections a large number of women contested for urban seats. There were two to three times as many candidates as seats reserved for women who belonged to all social levels, including the wife of a minister and the wife of a tongawala (an animal cart driver) whose election programme was to fight for justice and oppressed women, and set up a vocational and embroidery training centre. Paradoxically, in another urban locality the two candidates, both male, unanimously agreed to the decision of the elders of the locality that women should not be "dragged to polling stations," (The Daily *Nation* December 1991) and did not allow the women of the area to cast their votes. These differences are indicative of the predominance of local, ethnic and customary social norms. At present elections at the local level are due to be held but the current political environment with the government and opposition at loggerheads has resulted in several postponements of the elections.

Women's participation in the electoral process has not only shown an increase but has elevated women to the highest political office. In few countries of the world has a woman been voted in as Prime Minister twice. This has important connotations in a country where the clergy has vociferously degraded and downgraded women in the name of religion.

Islamization and the Status of Women

The status of women can be defined in terms of their rights under law and their actual position in society. Submission to authority, whether it is the state, a superior, head of the family, elder, and in the case of women a male, is central to the social value system in Pakistan. (Zafar 1986). At the same time, in Pakistan, the social and belief systems are strongly bound together so that legal changes instead of modifying the prevailing ideology which is assumed to be Islamic have tended to be influenced by it. Thus despite constitutional provisions to the contrary, the legal and social status of women continues to remain very low. This situation has been aggravated by the suspension of Fundamental Rights during the long periods of martial law, the so-called 'islamization' policies of the Zia regime, while "discrimination in the laws and inadequacy of legal protections and safeguards, makes the already socially weak position of women even more insecure." (Zia 1991).

The dichotomy between the views of the founders of the country and politicians, and the orthodox *ulema*, which had its roots in the movement for creation of Pakistan, had begun to affect both political ethos and the formation of economic and social structures soon after independence and also impacted on the position of women in society. Any move to voice a concern for women's rights has been viewed as a threat by the religious forces which have almost without exception been reactionary. It was not surprising, therefore, that the Muslim Family Laws Ordinance was dubbed as 'un-Islamic' by the *ulema* and even today is considered to be violating among other things, the inherent right of a man under Islam-as interpreted by the *ulema*-to divorce his wife at will and practice polygamy.

Feminist scholars are of the view that "what is assumed

to represent Muslim culture and jurisprudence is actually the imposition of Islamic religious doctrines on pre-existing codes of behaviour." (Shaheed 1991). Differences are based on the sources of jurisprudence used, adherence to the several hundreds of a '*hadith*[7], and interpretations of the *Qura'an* and *Sunnah*, with the fundamentalists insisting on an interpretation which is mediavalistic and feudal while the more conservative adherents to Islam are willing to accept "modern" and "progressive" interpretations in some matters. (Zafar 1986). But almost without exception, all schools of thought in Islam tend to apply *Qura'anic* principles and injunctions selectively; and in the case of women specific strictures are given preference over broad principles.

Rise of Obscurantism

In the absence of a cohesive progressive Islamic movement cognizant of the social and economic changes taking place including the emergence of women as potentially independent beings, both economically and, therefore, politically, obscurantist forces have found it easy to establish themselves. The attitude of governments especially non-representative martial law regimes towards the orthodox clergy has been, at best, ambivalent. Although the founder of the nation Muhammad Ali Jinnah was vociferously against the formation of a theocratic state within a few years of his death, the *ulema* were successful in defining the objectives of the new state in religious terms in the Objectives Resolution of 1949, in getting Pakistan declared an Islamic Republic in the 1956 Constitution[8], and in acquiring for themselves an advisory role in the legislature. The founder of the *Jamaat-e-Islami*, Maulana Maududi who had earlier been against the creation of Pakistan, once it had come into existence, decided to turn it into a fundamentalist state, where all rights especially those of women were to be determined according to his interpretation of Islam. He advocated that only adult males and educated women should have voting rights, that women should not hold public office, and that there should be separate assemblies for women. (Mumtaz and Shaheed 1987). These attempts to exclude women altogether from the political process and to marginalize minorities were not accepted at this time.

The tendency to give concessions to the clergy especially on issues relating to women has steadily increased. The creation of a number of Islamic institutions by Ayub Khan which became increasingly powerful under Zia-ul-Haq including the Council of Islamic Ideology, Islamic Research Center and the Ministry of Religious Affairs have among other things concentrated on circumscribing a code of conduct for women. It is, however, since 1977 that a systematic policy of reducing the position of women in society through legal and extra-judical actions under a reactionary and retrogressive interpretation of the *Qura'an* and *Sunnah* has taken place.

Discriminatory Laws

In 1979 the Hadood Ordinances were introduced as a Martial Law Ordinance, which denies women the right to demand *hadd*, or maximum punishment for murder, theft or rape on their evidence. They also equate the punishment of rape and adultery, and since the onus of proving rape rests on the women, hundreds of women mostly from the disadvantaged sections of society have been jailed and subjected to degrading treatment. Since the law on registration of marriages and divorces has not been followed to the letter especially in the rural areas, there are several instances where a woman who thought she had been divorced remarried and was then implicated in a case of adultery by her former husband. With the enforcement of so called 'Islamic' punishments including flogging and stoning to death, the *Hadood* Ordinances are among the most discriminatory legislative measures enacted.

In 1984, the *Qanoon-e-Shahadat* (Law of Evidence) was passed, making the testimony of two women equal to that of one man in certain cases, thus reducing her status of that of a half person. Although the application of the law is restricted to specific areas it's implications are for all women and it is a negation of the rights given to women under the 1973 Constitution. Combined with changes in the existing Penal Code of Pakistan as in the case of the Law of *Qisas* and *Diyat* (9) and the *Qazf* Ordinance (10), both of which are emphatically discriminatory towards women as was all legislation passed by Zia-ul-Haq, a strict adherent of the *Jamaat-e-Islami's* philosophy that an Islamic society is based on the complete segregation of the sexes and that Islam subordinates women to men, the status of women suffered a decline from which the women are finding it hard to recover as all legislation has been given legal protection under the Eighth Amendment to Constitution. Furthermore, under the Ninth Amendment to the Constitution 1986, the Federal Shariat Court is empowered to question all existing and future legislation in the light of the *Qura'an* and *Sunnah*.

At the same time there has been an attempt to sanctify those prevailing cultural practices and values which negate the rights given to women in Islam and on which there is no ambiguity. These include for example, women's right to own, inherit and sell property including agricultural land, right to work and conduct business, control over their earnings, women's consent in marriage and right to divorce. On issues on which Islamic literature is ambivalent, the policy has been to follow a retrogressive approach rather than a progressive one.

Women and Government

Other attempts to legally reduce women's status included the appointment the Ansari Commission in 1983 to suggest an appropriate political system. In its report, with specific reference to women the commission recommended that women could not be appointed to the office of *Amir-e-Mumlakat* (head of state) and that the *amir* should Muslim and male. This was in direct contravention of Islamic principles and practice since Islamic history has several instances of women rulers as Muslim feminists have shown in their researches. (Mernissi 1986). Secondly, it suggested that while women could be members of the *Majlis-e-Shoora* they should not be below the age of 50 and should have the written consent of their husbands. This argument was also not based on any precedent from the

Muslim countries. That the recommendations pertaining to curtailing women's participation in elections was not adherent to by Zia-ul-Haq was indicative of the reality of the situation and political expediency of avoiding the alienation of almost half the electorate. (Mumtaz and Shaheed 1987). The Commission also advocated the setting up of a separate women's organisations not because they were opposed to a Women's University *per se* but because it was part of a programme to seclude women from the mainstream.

In the last three elections voting has been restricted to those male and female adults who are possession of a National Identity Card. (NIC). This policy has been discriminatory towards women who usually have to rely on the male members of their family to obtain this card. Also while men would automatically obtain this card the moment they are ready to seek employment, in the case of women, most of whom work in the informal sector, this is not considered a requirement. Similarly, in opening bank accounts and obtaining credit, women are handicapped when photographs are required on NIC's as in many areas it is not considered Islamic to publically display the photograph of a woman.

The Shariat Bill

The Islamic content of legislation has been growing with each succeeding constitution and government. The *Shariat* Bill presented in Parliament in 1986 was yet another move on the part of the Islamic fundamentalists to bring all laws in conformity with the *Qura'an* and *Sunnah* and the enforcement of the *Shariah* or Islamic code of life.[11] The women's Action Forum and its member organisations immediately rejected it on the grounds that it would take the country further along the road of theocracy and strengthen anti-democratic, obscurantist, and anti-women forces. (WAF 1986). It's vigorous campaign included a petition with hundreds of signatures which was sent to the Prime Minister and a demonstration outside the National Assembly at the time of its discussion. For the first time, the parties of the religious right organised a demonstration of its women supporters to counter of WAF propaganda.

The *Shariat* Bill finally pushed through, with unseemly haste, in 1991 was a modified version of the original. Nonetheless, it conceded to the clergy the right to question all existing laws and reiterated the theocratic nature of the state; It also overlooked women's rights and was again rejected by WAF, other women's organisations and this time by other progressive organisations including human rights groups.

Women and Work

In thc access to employment especially government which their largest employer, women are marginalised. The existing quota of 5 percent reserved for women in the public sector has not been enforced, and even where women work they are relegated to the lower echelons and to a few departments such as education and health. There is only a nominal representation of women at higher decision making levels and in politically influential Boards and Committees. The present government is making efforts to make women more visible at higher decision making levels but without affirmative action the pace of such change is likely to remain slow.

The gender-discriminatory policy of restricting areas of employment open to women derives legitimacy from cultural and religious norms. Obscurantist forces are more concerned with the enforcement of such restrictions on urban women especially those from the middle and upper classes. It is more difficult to subject women of the working class and rural women to such constraints because of their utility to the existing based on inequality. It is a well documented fact that upto a point upward mobility impacts negatively on women's access to the public sphere.

Violence and Women

When the state acts in collusion with patriarchal forces especially men to control women in the public and private realms with the support of a lethal combination of religion, the military and capital, the expression of control can become increasingly violent. (WAF 1993). Feudal and tribal social formations with their local baggage of norms and values combined with repeated impositions of martial law and anti-women Islamization process in Pakistan have created an environment in which the expression of male supremacy and *izzat* or honour is frequently directed against the weaker sections including women. Men, thus physically abuse, rape, murder and abduct women in the name of *izzat*, and seek sanctity from religion for their actions. Although this process is evident in all social classes, poorer women are more vulnerable as are working women and those who are constrained to move in the public sphere. This restricts the personal, social, economic and political autonomy of women and impacts negatively on their participation.

Crimes against women have shown a dramatic increase in recent years and particularly since women's organisations began focusing on the social, economic and political implications of violence. In a society where there is high premium on chastity, women are frequently the victims of violence for mere suspicion of infidelity or immorality. In rural areas, through the concept of women as male property epitomized by the common adage of *Zar* (wealth), *zamin* (land) and use of force, the patriarchal collective is able to subordinate and oppress women and justification is sought in the name of tradition and custom.

Women's access to development opportunities and employment is handicapped by the hostile social environment and sexual harassment. Together with the gender division of labour and high rate of domestic violence which effects their self image-although the latter is a cross-class problem-women are confined largely to informal and low paid employment. Women working in factories and active in trade unions have been threatened physically, and at the time when the *Shariat* Bill was under discussion, there were incidents of acid throwing on girl students at a University by the male students belonging to the Islamic *Jamiat-e-Tulaba*.

Incidents of rape have been increasing despite the *Hadood* Ordinances and the imposition of Islamic punishments including flogging and stoning. The *Zina* Ordinance which is one of the *Hadood* Ordinances, was enforced to put an end to adultery but has been used against women and to prosecute victims of rape since few women will report rape.[12] More recently, the use of violence against women as a political tool culminated in the rape of female political opponents. Yet another form of rape, custodial rape is increasingly occurring in police lock-ups, jails and other corrective institutions. Such incidents are on the rise ever since the religious right has targeted women as the perpetrators of obscenity and social evils. They are also indicative of the growing impact of the women's movement.

Over the last decade several women's organisations and resource centres have focused on crimes against women and there is a growing awareness of the different dimensions of the problem. Organisations with a specific focus have also been formed in recent years. Women Against Rape (WAR) is a comparatively new organisation which evolved from the Women's Action Forum to bring together women's groups and other organisations against the growing incidence of violence against women. It has taken up specific cases of violence especially rape, domestic violence, and death and injury caused to women through the explosion of oil stoves.

The insidious implications of violence has been exploited by the obscurantist forces against the mainstreaming of women's participation. Under the 'Islamization' policies of Zia-ul-Haq, the institution of public flogging and other barbaric punishments promoted a culture of violence which has impacted on all sections of society especially women. The public degradation of parading women naked and other such crimes have not been censured by the religious right, neither have any of the Islamic parties ever spoken out against rape for which they feel the onus is on the women.

Conclusion

In viewing the relationship of gender and politics in Pakistan the patriarchal nature of the state, socio-economic formations, culture and religion emerge as the strong components of a system determined to perpetuate the marginalisation of women and to deny them autonomy. The struggle of women to create space for themselves in the private and public spheres will thus in all circumstances meet with resistance. With the rise of obscurantism and religious fundamentalism the forms of resistance are becoming increasingly violent.

It is critical, therefore, for the women's organisations and groups to create an awareness and understanding of the bases of patriarchy to enable to larger number of women to participate in the struggle for emancipation. The limited access of most existing organisations and their concentration in a few large urban centres has to be systematically altered through the wider dissemination of information on issues which impact on women in their daily lives. Many of these are issues of fundamental human rights which have to be raised with governments and international organisations.

Notes

1. The case of Fehmida and Allah Bux versus the State (where a married couple were arrested under the *Hadood* Ordinances and the court awarded them the Islamic punishment of stoning to death) was the catalyst that activated women into forming a pressure group which became the Women's Action Forum.
2. The Law of Evidence or *Qanoon-e-Shahadat* stipulated that the evidence of one man was equal that of two women in all financial and future matters. What the latter meant was ambiguous.
3. The Federal *Shariat* Court was a nominated body by the President with the powers to examine any law that was brought to notice for being repugnant to the *Qura'an* and *Sunnah*.
4. The *Qura'an* is the holy book of the Muslims and is considered to be the word as revealed to the Prophet Muhammad.
5. The *Hadood* Ordinances (1979) cover the offenses of rape, adultery and theft. Under these the accused can get the maximum punishment of *Hadd* (or the *Qura'anic* punishment), but the testimony of women is not admissible and only the evidence of adult Muslim male witnesses is accepted. The *Zina* Ordinance was one of the Hadood Ordinances.
6. WAR was formed as a sub-committee within WAF in 1991, subsequently it became an independent organisation.
7. The *a'hadith* or "traditions" are a collection of incidents reputed to be the decisions, sayings and actions of the Prophet Muhammad.
8. The Objective Resolution was the first statement issued after the

creation of Pakistan in which it was stated that one of the objectives of the new state was to allow the Muslims of the Sub-continent to spend their lives in accordance with the *Qura'an* and *Sunnah*. This formed part of the 1956 Constitution.

9. The Law of *Qisas* and *Diyat* when proposed in 1980 stipulated that the life of women (and non-Muslims) was worth half that of a Muslim man. Because of criticism even from within the religious circles it was passed in 1990 without the gender-discriminatory clause.
10. The *Qazf* Ordinance was the Islamic law for punishing persons bearing false witness.
11. The *Shariah* means the injunctions of Islam in accordance with the *Qura'an* and *Sunnah*.
12. In one year between 1984 and 1985, 157 cases of rape were reported in the first six months at just one of Karachi's there government hospitals, and only 5 percent of these were reported in the press. (*The Herald*, September 1985)

References

1. Mernissi, Fatima (1986) *Women in Muslim History*, Simorgh Women's Resource and Publication Centre, Lahore.
2. Mumtaz, K. (1986) The Weekly *Viewpoint*. Lahore.
3. Mumtaz, K. (1988) "Women in Electoral Politics", (unpublished paper). Shirkatgah. Lahore.
4. Mumtaz, K. and Shaheed, F. (1987) *Women of Pakistan : Two Steps Forward, One Step Back?* Vanguard Books (Pvt) Ltd. Lahore.
5. Pakistan Commission on the Status of Women (1985) *Report of the Pakistan Commission on the Status of Women*, Women's Division, Islamabad.
6. Shaheed, F. (1991) "The Cultural Articulation of Patriarchy" in *Finding Our Way : Readings on Women in Pakistan*, (ed.) F. Zafar, ASR Publications, Lahore.
7. Shaheed et al. (May 1994) *Women in Politics : Participation and Representation in Pakistan*, Shirkatgah/WLUML Special Bulletin, Lahore.
8. The Daily Dawn, February 1985, Karachi.
9. Ibid., April 1985, Karachi.
10. The Daily Nation, December 1991, Lahore.
11. Women's Rights Committee (1976) *Report of the Women's Rights Committee*, Government of Pakistan, Islamabad.
12. Women's Action Forum (1992) Unpublished Documents, Lahore.
13. Ibid., (1993) Unpublished Documents, Lahore.
14. Zafar, F. (1986) "Islamization, Development and the Role of Women in Pakistan" in *Education for Learning and Living : Rights of the Third World*, Unesco Publication Pending.
15. Zia, Shehla (1991) "The Legal Status of Women in Pakistan" in *Finding Our Way Readings on Women in Pakistan* (ed.) F. Zafar, ASR Publications, Lahore.

Impact of United Nations Decade of Women on Sri Lanka

Vinitha Jayasinghe

Did the inauguration of the International Women's Year in 1975 and the Women's Decade (1976 to 1985) by the United Nations have any influence on feminism in Sri Lanka? These two major events were undertaken with the view to work out a strategy for the removal of any inequalities and disparities between the two sexes, it was thought they could lead to a new dimension in feminist consciousness. The theme of the Women's Decade was 'Equality, Development and Peace'. At the beginning of the decade, strategies were identified and the member states were requested to implement them, and at the end, the UN performed a monitoring exercise in order to examine the achievements, if any.

Sri Lanka participated in all major activities that were associated with the International Women's Year and the United Nations Decade for Women. It was represented at the conference held in Mexico City in International Women's Year, the UN Mid-decade World Conference held in Copenhagen in 1980, and finally, at the Post-decade Conference held in Nairobi. Sri Lanka was also represented at all the Regional Preparatory meetings and was signatory to the United Nations Convention on Elimination of All Forms of Discrimination Against Women in 1980, and presented its state party report to its Committee as well.[1] Government agencies, political parties, non-governmental organisations and trade unions in Sri Lanka celebrated International Women's Year by holding meetings and making speeches. For the first time, all these agencies talked about women's rights and issues that were included in their agenda. Several workshops and seminars were conducted, and the main theme was Rights of Women. Therefore, it can be said definitely that for the first time, there was concerted action on the subject of women in Sri Lanka.

These activities were well received by the media, the non-governmental women's organisations and particularly the government. The media played a major role in highlighting the event, and the newspapers carried several articles on the subject. Several funding agencies associated with the UN and other donor agencies gave financial support to the government and non-government organisations to implement action strategies and conduct studies and surveys related to women's issues. On the whole, all these activities gave a big boost to the women's movement. There was also more collaboration among the women's groups both at international and regional levels. An example is the networking that developed among the Asian women's groups.

It can be said that the International Women's Year brought a new dimension to the status of women in Sri Lanka. The women's organisations headed by the Sri Lanka Women's Conference acted as a pressure group in order to activate the government to set up a national machinery for women's affairs. The establishment of the Women's Bureau of Sri Lanka in 1978 as a Division in the Ministry of Plan Implementation whose Minister was the President of the country marks a milestone in the women's movement. When the Women's Bureau was established, it was considered as something unusual and therefore, not palatable to many, including the bureaucrats and political leaders. At this stage, I recall some of the remarks and quips made at me, the Founder Director of the Bureau from November 1978 to April 1983: 'Why a Women's Bureau and not a Men's?', 'What about the men – are they forgotten?', 'What wrong have men done to create a Bureau for women?', 'Are you intending to take our women away from us?', 'It is a very unusual thing to set up a similar organisation for women only; it has never happened before and looks a funny state of affairs!', 'Don't expect seats for women in buses or trains in the future if you women are going to ask for equal rights.' These are some of the remarks made that persisted.

When the Bureau first started, it had neither personnel nor equipment. No financial assistance was made available for its initial establishment by the government. A donor agency – Norwegian Agency for Aid and Development (NORAD) – provided the finance to set up the Bureau and run it until monies were allocated by the government in the second year. However, the UN bodies (Food and Agricultural Organisation, UNICEF, United Nations Fund for Population Activities and United Nations Development Program) rendered assistance to the Bureau for its programs. Other funding agencies such as the Swedish International Development Agency (which financed the first program to be implemented by the Bureau), the United States Aid Agency and the Asia Foundation also gave assistance to the Bureau for implementation of programs, including training.

It is worth mentioning at this stage that although the creation of the Bureau is considered as an off-shoot of the International Women's Year and initiated as a result of the active lobbying carried out by the Sri Lanka Women's Conference, it would not have survived if not for the external stimulus that it received. The existence of the Bureau in a Ministry under the President gave it a prestigious position, and facilitated the acquisition of any form of assistance, preferably local sources. Within the first year of its existence, staff were appointed and activities commenced. A whole series of training programs was carried out; the main object of the Bureau was to mobilise the participation of women in the national development process and improve the quality of their lives. This concept of Women in Development was a new area and required training. The staff of the Bureau at Assistant Director level was sent overseas to study women's issues. Thus, one can see that steadily and gradually, the Bureau expanded; simultaneously, there was a growing awareness of feminist perspectives.

In carrying out programs for integration of women in development, the Women's Bureau extended its activities to the rural sector. In addition, the Bureau had to coordinate all women's activities in the country. It was expected to ensure the granting of full equality for women in all sectors where such equality did not exist.[2] In an effort to accomplish this task, the Bureau also conducted research, collected data and disseminated information on women-related matters pertaining to women's issues and affirmative action. The Bureau also served as a central agency to channel foreign assistance from international agencies who were interested in promoting projects and programs related to the improvement of the status of women. It also serves a 'watch-dog' function to ensure that women's issues are dealt with sufficient care and attention and do not get bypassed.

In carrying out its functions, the Bureau established two panels: a Panel of non-governmental women's organisations and an Advisory Panel. Both contributed greatly to the formulation of action plans and programs for women. When acting as a pressure group, the Bureau worked together with non-governmental organisations; in this regard, by lobbying together, success was achieved in eliminating the quota system that existed in the intake of women into the Sri Lanka Administrative Service, Clerical, Accountants and Shroffs Services (1980).

The Sri Lanka Women's Conference (SLWC), inaugurated in 1934, is the only women's federation in the country with a membership of 39 women's organisations, and works closely with the Bureau. In planning, organising and conducting of seminars and workshops on women's issues, preparation of work content and presenting of relevant papers and other related matters, the women's NGOs always extended their cooperation. Thematic activities such as 'Women and Safety' and 'Women in Development' were associated with the International Women's Day and carried out by the Bureau annually. The main aim was to highlight areas that needed serious attention and due consideration by policy-makers. Areas of particular concern include the molestation of women on the streets, especially at night or on public transport; and incidents of rape. There was very close collaboration with the NGOs in these activities, including district-based programs that were carried out with the participation of women in the area.[3]

Together with assistance from US Aid and collaboration with SLWC, the Bureau sent 26 women to India in groups to study women's programs. They were selected from among the district-based training programs.

The Women's Bureau stretched out its programs to a wider representation and cross-section of women in various groups: in the rural, urban (low income-slum areas), plantations, fisheries and the manufacturing sectors. The activities concentrated on identification of needs of women and areas of oppression, shortcomings or hardships faced by them through studies and research, and training programs for income generation, leadership and family health improvement. As a result, several studies and consultancies had to be undertaken prior to the formulation of activity programs, which obviously encouraged and ensured the participation of women in the respective sectors. All these programs received financial support from funding agencies.

In addition, workshops, seminars and brain-storming sessions specifically designed for creating feminist consciousness were carried out by the Bureau. Discussion groups and the media as a vehicle for dissemination of relevant information were organised. A workshop was held with representatives from the media and they were questioned about using women in advertising. For the first time, a statistical bulletin pertaining to women was published by the Bureau.[4] These activities helped, to a great extent, to educate the political leadership and to gain a fuller picture of the status of women. The programs carried out for rural women for training in leadership and income generation helped them to form into groups. These women gained greater strength, became confident and felt recognised. New perspectives were realised through training programs (sometimes residential and of short duration), the initiation of projects for income generation, the marketing of products that entailed several visits out of home to the markets in the town areas, earning an income, obtaining credit and the opening of bank accounts, access to governmental and other extension services and above all, networking for sharing and exchanging of information and know-how.[5]

These activities helped women to build self-esteem and particularly provided possibilities for earning an income which had been hitherto primarily a male domain. The Bureau was successful in projecting the image of women as important partners in national development and raised the consciousness of women and improved their self-image through a series of workshops and media programs.[6]

In carrying out its advocacy role, the Bureau took several measures to improve the status of women with state intervention: extension of maternity leave, lobbying for equal pay for work of equal value, entry of women into the male-dominated preserves of training and employment, introduction of night work for women and the elimination of the quota system that prevailed in the entry to the administrative, accountants, Shroffs and clerical services.

The Maternity Benefits Ordinance was amended in 1978 providing nursing breaks for lactating mothers and for creches. The enforcement of these provisions, however, has not being brought to effect. A study carried out by the Women's Bureau highlighted the difficulties experienced by working women in combining their child care and economic roles.[7] The removal of the prohibition of night work for women in 1984 helped increase employment opportunities, particularly in the Free Trade Zone. This also tended to eliminate any form of discrimination against women in view of the three-shift based industries. The survey undertaken by the Women's Bureau on night work for women pointed out the reservations of advocates of women's rights, the objectives of trade unions and the lack of enthusiasm of women workers, referring to the conflict between economic pressures and welfare needs.[8]

The participation of women in modern sector manufacturing and service activities increased in the late 1970s, concentrating mainly around Colombo and the Gampaha districts. Nearly 90 percent of all private sector manufacturing establishments are located in the Greater Colombo Economic Commission area. From among females employed in the manufacturing sector, more than 90 percent are in assembly line type of jobs.[9]

The Free Trade Zone has led to migration of female

labour from the rural areas in large numbers, mostly between the ages of 18 and 25 years. More than 90 percent of the labour force in the Free Trade Zone factories which are predominantly large and medium-sized garment factories are women. Findings of a survey on women workers in the Free Trade Zone reveal: 'At the FTZ, 96%, 88%, 64%, and 100% of the workers at the large garment factories, medium garment factories, small garment factories and non-garment factories respectively, were of the opinion that overtime affected their health while at all categories of factories 100% of the workers felt that night shift adversely affects their health. All this seems to suggest that work was less strenuous at the factories outside the FTZ.' The exploitative nature of the work done by the women is thus evident.[10]

Within the public sector employment since 1975, the proportion of female professional and technical workers has increased. There is an increase in women working in administrative, managerial, clerical and sales services. However, the appointment of a woman as a magistrate and as a judge to the High Court took place only in 1979 and 1990 respectively.

Another phenomenon has been the exodus of female labour to the gulf region as house-maids or nannies, which began in the late 1970s. It has been estimated that almost half the migrant workers were women (47.7 per cent) and 82.8 per cent of them were employed in domestic service in the Middle East (1979).[11] In the early stages, they experienced difficulties and hardships particularly due to communication problems.[12] Subsequently, state intervention helped to improve matters; steps taken were the establishment of the Sri Lanka Bureau of Foreign Employment in the Ministry of Labour, expansion of the Foreign Service and the introduction of training programs for women before migration.

However, most of the female migrants leave their children behind with either the husband, grandparent, aunt or a friend while they work. Studies have shown that such substitution has failed in giving the children the necessary care, attention and affection and worse is when the husbands engage in extra-marital affairs leading to a family breakdown.[13] However, as a result of the wife migrating for economic gains, the husband is entrusted with the household responsibilities, and this has led to a reversal of roles in domestic affairs.

Large numbers of Sri Lankan Muslim women also migrated to the gulf region for employment. The impact on these women is therefore noteworthy, since culturally, male dominance decides that the woman should stay at home. Wimala de Silva explains that consequently, these women can make their own decisions on matters which were earlier outside their scope such as any improvements to the house or the education of their sons. Moreover, a sense of security was also developed.[14] The opportunities for estate women in social, cultural and educational advancement have been restricted, particularly due to the closed nature of the estate life and lack of time for other activities other than work in the estate and household chores. However, with governmental intervention programs, an improvement in the social sector has been witnessed during the eighties, with better childcare and health facilities.

New dimensions in the role of women have emerged. The first ever National Symposium on 'New Dimensions in the Role of Women' organised by the Women's Bureau in 1982 paved the way for a new awakening. Nearly 12,000 women from all parts of the country and all walks of life attended the symposium opening as did a number of political leaders.[15] The participants at the symposium were from the senior level officers from the public sector. Issues addressed included the law and the status of women; women at work; women in leadership and decision-making; single-parent families; aspirations of young women; and women and technology. This symposium drew the attention of the government towards fuller employment for women, just and adequate working conditions, support services to enable women's entry into employment, non-formal education and training, greater participation of women in leadership and decision making, and also helped to initiate action for the creation of a separate Ministry of Women's Affairs.[16] All these helped to create an awakening of feminist consciousness. In 1983 the Women's Bureau was transferred to the Ministry of Women's Affairs and Teaching Hospitals. Subsequently, in 1989, the Ministry of Health and Women's Affairs was established with the issues of Women's Affairs and the Women's Bureau held by a male State Minister. For the first time, a separate Ministry was set up exclusively for women's affairs and in the subsequent year, it was entrusted to a woman Minister, Chandra Karunaratne, who had been active in politics at grassroots level.

During this period, new feminist items entered the political agenda. Domestic violence, which had been previously accepted as part of the traditional superior male role in homes, was not criticised but was accepted as male superiority and as explained by Vijita Fernando as 'macho might of man who was the head of his home, the king of his castle'.[17] Such incidents are rarely reported, and are made known only if they are brought to court and then publicised in the media although this is very rare. Fernando states further, 'In Sri Lanka, there are no statistics or records on domestic violence. Cases are not reported and crime statistics are not gender specific. But there is a growing awareness of the need for such records and statistics and our study found that though no systematic study has been done by any group there are several organisations that have these records buried in general data' (27). Even in instances of rape, many of which go unreported and unknown, society will regard the woman as partly responsible. Police records show a total of 932 reported rapes from January 1989 to 1991.[18] Those counselling rape victims at Women in Need, an organisation which has been established to help women, believe that the figure barely shows one-fourth of the actual total. However, under Section 364 of the Penal Code, a rapist can be sentenced to a maximum period of twenty years.[19]

Violence against women takes many forms: harassment on the roads and on public transport, molestation, rape, incest and wife-beating. More and more the newspapers are regarding such acts as instances of violence. Such situations came up for discussion openly at seminars and workshops by feminists. The Women's Bureau conducted a seminar on the theme of 'Women and Safety' while highlighting a collection of newspaper reports of such events for over a period of six months. The main concern of the seminar was to highlight areas of violence against women.

Sexual exploitation and harassment and physical violence at the workplace became more visible during the early 1980s. Although an upward trend in its incidence is inevitable due to the increasing numbers of working women, they were not highlighted or reported. Most often the victims maintain secrecy about such incidents at the workplace, due to the fear of losing their jobs. It has been estimated that 56.5 per cent of women workers are actively employed in various fields today. In the employment profile, more than 60 per cent of women workers are concentrated in the low, semi or unskilled categories, where they are most vulnerable to harassment. A study has revealed that suggestive remarks and even verbal abuse are the commonest forms of harassment and rates 67 per cent of total reported cases in the state sector and 72 per cent in the private sector. Unnecessary physical contact accounted for 26 per cent in the state sector and 10 per cent in the private sector.[20]

Tourism is a major income earner in the Sri Lankan economy. However, this has increased prostitution – another means of exploitation of women for various sexual purposes. As a result of prostitution, the incidence of AIDS and sexually transmitted diseases has risen in Sri Lanka. This is evident from the fact that World Aids Day (1 December 1990) was used by a group of medical women (Public Health Network of Women, formed in 1990) in Sri Lanka to highlight the effects of AIDS on women and the safeguards.

So, after participating fully in the UN Decade activities; attending the regional preparatory meetings and other conferences associated with it; answering all the questionnaires; presenting papers and reports whenever required and conducting workshops and seminars locally as far as possible, how far has the decade been successful in creating feminist consciousness in the country? The Bureau's programs focused on the need for integration of women into the development process of the country. The planners began to include a chapter on women in the national plans of the country. Financial allocations were made for women's programs by the government.

In analysing the activities of the Bureau, Swarna Jayaweera, a feminist writer said:

> Reviewing its activities in the last six to seven years, it is apparent that the Bureau has been successful in increasing the visibility of women and in projecting an 'image' of women as important beneficiaries of development. It has sought to mobilise rural women through projects and its greatest achievement is its non-elitist orientation.[21]

Jayawardena has highlighted two new areas of feminist thinking and issues which surfaced in the 1980s. First, the right of the woman to control her own sexuality and the process of reproduction. This entailed the question of abortion which was taken up for debate. Secondly, Women's Studies became an important area of study and several students availed themselves of the opportunities that were made available and followed Women's Studies courses in foreign institutions (Institute of Development Studies, Sussex and Institute of Social Studies, The Hague).[22] The introduction of such courses in Sri Lanka is under consideration.

Non-governmental organisations also developed new dimensions by highlighting women's issues and rights although they were very restricted. An independent feminist group named Kantha Handa (Voice of Women), formed in 1978, included new issues in their agenda: equal pay, wife battering, sexual abuse, and so on. Several studies were conducted in order to highlight areas that need attention with regard to women's issues. Women's Action Committees, Citizen Committees, and a Mothers' Front were some of the new organisations that came into existence. The Seva Vanitha movement – based on the Dharma Wanita organisation in Indonesia – was established by the government in 1983. This organisation has as its members the wives of officials in various government departments and offices, with the wife of the President of Sri Lanka as the President of the organisation and the Minister's wife as the President of the body in each ministry. This movement helped mostly in supplementing government activities whilst the main area of concern is welfare-oriented. During the Women's Decade, a transition from the traditional ideology to an awakened feminist consciousness was evident. The women shifted their emphasis to economic gains either by means of self-employment or wage labour; this paved the way for sharing of domestic responsibilities by men and economic independence for women which in turn gave them a sense of self-confidence, security and a feeling of self-image and recognition.

It can be said that ideas about feminism are relative and vary from situation to situation. The main concerns among the rural women who form the largest number of women in the country are the uplift and the sustenance of the family: feeding the family, fetching of water and firewood and helping the family whenever needed are the main areas of concern. The word 'feminism', therefore, has no meaning for them. Their pre-occupation is in the interests of the family. Among women of all the three ethnic groups – Singhalese, Tamils and Muslims – this is a common characteristic. The family is their topmost priority and the husbands are responsible only for finding money for economic needs. The concept of the 'unpaid family worker' is not palatable to these women because family work is accepted as their prime duty.

Although prospects for career advancement and promotion are restricted and marginal among the working women in the formal sector, the experience has been that there is less agitation among them for betterment. Moreover, their participation in the trade unions is also low. As a result, their voice is not heard and their views are hardly represented. An awakening and an awareness has been created by several women writers for improvement of the status of women in the country. Some of the more prominent are Dr Kumari Jayawardena, Dr Swarna Jayaweera, and Dr Wimala de Silva. They are clear about the need for removal of any form of discrimination against women. An attitudinal change is the most critical need not only among men but also among women. The more educated women are increasingly beginning to understand the need for such changes. The writers who have highlighted these areas of discrimination have conducted studies. Workshops and seminars have been held and reports have been printed in large numbers with the recommendations and strategic action plans. But how far these ideas and thoughts have filtered to the target groups of women in the rural subsistence farming sector or the plantation sector or in the workforce, particularly among the semi-skilled and unskilled workers or in general, to all women, remains to be questioned. The day-to-day routine of the above categories of women continue, oblivious of the need for a change, neither do they realise that there could be an opportunity for them to perceive of a different perspective or dimension to their lives or for themselves. It is debatable whether they ever feel oppressed.

It is clear that women in Sri Lanka have continued to carry out their role not only in the upbringing of their families as their prime responsibilities but also in the economic uplift of the country. The dual functions have been carried out over the years oblivious of feminist concerns. Therefore, there is a need for feminism in Sri Lanka with the goal of eliminating all areas of oppression faced by women.

It is important to understand that the emergence of the women's movement was inspired by local situations in the country such as the struggle for independence. Within such a similar framework, Sri Lankan feminists are favourably placed, although outside influence has helped to a great extent to create an environment for feminism. Although similarities can be detected between western and Sri Lankan feminism, there is a disparity in the way it is accepted and practised. Creating an attitudinal change in the minds of both men and women in the home, workplace and society is an ongoing process. Stringent attempts and measures have to be made and prioritised by feminists. The awakening of feminist consciousness created together with the blossoming out with the Women's Decade has yet to be fully realised.

Notes

This paper was presented at Fourth Women in Asia Conference organised by The Women's Caucus of the Asian Studies Association of Australia at the University of Melbourne, 1993.

1. I attended all these meetings and led the Sri Lankan delegation to the Mid-Decade Conference in Copenhagen where I also signed the UN Convention on Elimination of All Forms of Discrimination Against Women on behalf of Sri Lanka.
2. Women's Bureau of Sri Lanka, Ministry of Plan Implementation, vol. 1, Nov 1979.
3. Sri Lanka is divided into 24 Administrative Districts.
4. Women of Sri Lanka in Statistics, Women's Bureau of Sri Lanka (1985).
5. When the Women's Bureau was established, several women and women's groups were consulted in order to formulate a program of action; the unanimous choice was for income generation programs.
6. K. Jayawardena & S. Jayawera, *A Profile of Sri Lanka: the Integration of Women in Development Planning* (Women's Education Centre, Colombo, 1986), p. 16.
7. Information derived from studies associated with the Women's Bureau Project for 'Women in the Plantation sector 1980'.
8. Fernando, V. 1982 'Maternity Benefits for Women in the Public and Private Sector', Women's Bureau of Sri Lanka.
9. V. Samarasinghe, *Women and Geographic Space: A Regional Analysis of Women's Well-Being and Productive Work in Sri Lanka* (Centre for Women's Research, Colombo 1989), p. 37.
10. Department of Census and Statistics, Sri Lanka (1979).
11. 'Women Workers in the Free Trade Zone of Sri Lanka', Voice of Women Publication, Series no.1 (1983).
12. 'Women and Night Work', Women's Bureau of Sri Lanka (1981).
13. S.T. Hettige, 'From Dependent Housewives to Breadwinners', in *Women, Poverty and Survival* (Centre for Women's Research, Colombo, 1991), p. 22.
14. W. De Silva, W. 'Political Participation and Decision Making', in *Status of Women in Sri Lanka* (University of Colombo, Colombo, 1985), p. 115.
15. V. Jayasinghe, *Report on Female Domestic Aides in United Arab Emirates* (Women's Bureau of Sri Lanka, 1982).
16. M. Endagama, 'Impact of UN Decade for Women in Sri Lanka' (Women's Bureau of Sri Lanka, 1985), p. 31–2.
17. V. Fernando, *Her Story* (Centre for Society and Religion, Colombo, 1991), p. 23.
18. 'Report of the National Symposium on Women', in *New Dimensions in the Role of Women*, Nov. 1982.
19. M. Wijesekera, 'Are Women an Easy Outlet for Violence', *Island*, 1982.
20. Penal Code Chapter 19, Sri Lanka.

21. K. Jayawardena, 'Some Aspects of Feminist Consciousness in the Decade 1975-1980,' in *UN Decade for Women Progress and Achievements of Women in Sri Lanka* (Centre for Women's Research, Colombo, 1985), p. 4.
22. S. Jayaweera, 'Integration of Women in Development Planning', in *UN Decade for Women Progress and Achievements of Women in Sri Lanka* (Centre for Women's Research, Colombo, 1985), p. 179.

(Ad)dressing Change: Working Women and the Resurgence of Purdah in Bangladesh

Gitiara Nasreen

Shamima is now a part of Dhaka's street landscape. Daily at dawn and dusk she walks swiftly, with a group of co-workers, lunch-box in her hand and a chaddor[1] worn over her dress. Like many other garment factory workers, Shamima has recently started wearing a chaddor. She believes that women should observe purdah while going in public. However, she does not like a burka[2] that her grandmother used to wear.

This paper focuses on the recent resurgence of *purdah*[3] observance among middle class and lower middle-class working women of Bangladesh. The compelling question for this enquiry is why women who have already broken the cultural notion of 'ideal Muslim woman', choose to revive *purdah* – a widely recognized symbol of women's subordination. This question touches upon two being currently debated: one on the new international division of labor among Third World women workers, and the other on the women's responses to the penetration of the market economy. Based on an analysis of contemporary social, economic and political changes in Bangladesh, I would like to suggest that working women are making use of *purdah* in order to deal with the complexities of their lives in a changing society.

Historically, a broad gender division of labour has existed in Bangladesh, in which field-based agricultural work is done by men while women are responsible for all activities carried out within the household. Because of the perceived public-domestic[4] distinction, any woman entering the public domain is perceived to be risking violation of her 'sotitto' (chastity), which is considered a loss of honour not only for herself, but also for the rest of her family.[5] The practice of *purdah* has effectively maintained the separation of public and private spheres. However, this gender division is no longer applicable in many households due to critical shifts at national and international levels. These shifts have impelled by the process of an uneven capitalist development, in which Bangladeshi female labour is being used in local and global capital accumulation. In this process, structures of family, kinship and production relationships are going through alterations and adjustments. Particularly, over the past several years, the accelerated reduction of landholding to non-viable units, the loss of land through indebtedness and forced sales, and growing impoverishment have transformed subsistence households into wage-based households.[6] Consequently, poorer women are gradually being forced into more public areas of employment, because women's income has become imperative for the family's survival.[7] Production for the market, which ensures cash returns, has taken precedence over production for household consumption, and women are becoming engaged in multiple production roles. The emergence of garment industry in the early 1980s made available a new form of urban employment for women.

The New International Division of Labor and the Rise of Garment Industry in Bangladesh

Since the 1960s, a massive restructuring has taken place in the global economy. Global restructuring refers to the:

> emergence of global assembly line in which research and management are controlled by the core or developed countries while assembly line work is relegated to the periphery nations that occupy less privileged positions in the global economy... Within developing countries,

restructuring is marked by the growth of the service sector and specialization in export industries such as electronics, garments and pharmaceutical as a development strategy.[8]

This 'new international division of labor' involves the transfer of the labour-intensive stages of production to countries that have an ample supply of cheap labor. Restructuring is particularly suitable for industries that are highly labour-intensive, which include but are not limited to textile, garment, toys, electric goods and electronics. Among these industries, the garment industry is especially susceptible to fluctuations in employment because of seasonal variations and fashion changes. This characteristic of the garment industry requires a highly flexible labour market, where labourers are easily available and can be easily disposed of when not wanted.

The new international division of labour is also based on gender division of labour, where the majority of the workers are young women. Several studies have shown that manufacturing industries prefer hiring women labourers because of:[9]

(i) low female wage rate, justified by the argument that women are only supplementing family income and the father/husband is the main earner in the family. Women's wages in world market factories are in general 20 to 60 per cent lower than wages paid for men in comparable jobs.

(ii) the belief that female workers are much more likely than men to be passive and non-organizing workers. They do not demand higher wages, benefits or better working conditions, can be easily laid off and fired.

(iii) women are considered best suited for assembly line work. Women's 'natural patience', 'nimble fingers' and 'manual dexterity' are needed to perform such monotonous work.

From the perspective of Third World governments, export-led manufacturing has become a primary strategy for national development. Throughout the past decade Bangladesh has encouraged export-processing as a way of alleviating the trade imbalance, of providing jobs for underemployed populations, of stimulating domestic industrialization and of promoting capital accumulation. The comparative advantage of a 'cheap labour reserve' helped Bangladesh to make a successful entry into the new international division of labor.

The first garment factory of Bangladesh began exporting in 1976. Since 1987 the garment industry has become the major export sector of Bangladesh surpassing jute, the traditional largest export sector. During 1990–91 Bangladesh derived 43 per cent of her export earnings from garments.[10] Garment factories of Bangladesh typically produce on subcontract to the order of particular overseas firms, such as, South Korea, Hong Kong and Taiwan. The customer arranges the marketing of the product. Factories in Bangladesh operate under different types of production arrangement. Most common arrangement is the cutting and making (C & M) arrangement, while the customer supplies the design and materials and the factories in Bangladesh do no more than cutting and sewing together the final product.[11] Most garment factories in Bangladesh are small-scale firms with low investment costs, producing less than 500,000 pieces annually. Bangladesh offers the cheapest wage among the garment manufacturer countries The abundance of cheap labour played a major role behind the success of the garment industry in the otherwise stagnant economic environment of Bangladesh. The garment industry now employs over 500,000 workers, of whom 85 per cent are women.[12]

Women's Involvement in Garment Industry and Gender Ideology

Social, cultural and religious traditions of Bangladesh emphasize the dependence of women on men. A woman's father or husband, or in their absence, her son or a distant male relative, assumes the responsibility of safeguarding her welfare. This argument has been translated into a notion of 'shame' and 'honour'. It is a matter of honour that a man should provide for his household, and failure to do so results in shame. Despite of a large number of female-headed households (nearly 15 per cent of all rural households and 25 per cent among the landless),[13] the culturally accepted structure of male headship is still intact. R. Jahan reported in 1975 that 70 per cent of rural and 80 per cent of urban men respectively considered women as inferior to men, and motherhood as the most desirable role for women.[14] This is stressed from the moment a child is born and elaborated in behaviour patterns prescribed for girls and women. Girls are taught the two virtues – patience and sacrifice – of ideal Bangalee womanhood. The folklore (stories of Gunai Bibi, Mahua, Malua etc.) idolize women who made immense sacrifices for their husbands. Religious stories insist women to follow the examples of Hazera, Aisha and Fatema – wives and daughter of the prophet Mohammed – who were obedient to their father and husband. Bengali synonyms for the word woman, for example, *greehinee, ghoroni, anntapurika, puranari, purabala* – are often related with words *pura, griha or ghor*, meaning 'home'. Manusmriti's[15] following dictum is still enforced in Bangladeshi society:

> She should do nothing independently, even in her own house.
>
> In childhood subject to her father,
>
> in youth to her husband,
>
> And when her husband is dead, to her sons,
>
> She should never enjoy independence.

Religion[16]

'Religion provides ideological basis for the accorded status and institutionalized roles of women in a society' while the roles women play and the restrictions on them 'are largely derived from the religious conceptions of a women's basic characteristics – such as her assumed virtues, vices, strengths, weaknesses and capacities' (Committee on the Status of Women in India, 1974, p. 38).

Bangladesh is predominantly a Muslim country. Bangladeshi women share many beliefs and forms of behaviour with other Muslim women of the world, yet they are also distinguished from their counterparts in other countries by the specific and unique history of Bangladesh. Islam came to Bengal in the thirteenth century through Muslim conquerors as well as preachers. Its egalitarian principles made for massive conversions among the low-caste Hindu population of Bengal who were despised of the prevailing caste oppression. A fusion of Hindu and Muslim traditions took place in Bengal, and within this synthetic system, it is impossible to disentangle the origins of various beliefs and customs that were shared by Muslim and Hindu commoners alike.

Regarding women's status in Bangali Muslim society it is worth mentioning Arnes and Beurden's remarks:

> Islam does not lie at the root of women's oppression since women were dominated by men even before the Mughal period when many were converted to Islam. Islam, however, has reinforced and consolidated women's inferior status. On the top of that it has provided men with an ideological instrument for dominating women.[17]

Therefore, the position of women cannot be read off solely from the religious texts. For example, a large section of women in Bangladesh has never used the veil, a widely held image of a Muslim woman's dress. Nevertheless, in Bangladesh, women's legitimate boundary is the household and they do not participate in the public domain. Typically, public gatherings and transaction points such as markets, mosques, public transportation or public meetings, are not considered 'women's places'. In other words, the Bangladeshi system of *purdah* symbolizes a division between masculine and feminine spheres.

I will return to a detail discussion of *purdah* in a later section. Before that I would like to focus on two very important factors: state and the foreign capital on the construction and reproduction of gender ideology in general and *purdah* in particular.

The Role of the State and the Influence of Foreign Capital in the Making of 'Productive Women'

This section attempts to understand the manner in which Bangladesh state policies have reinforced gender inequality in the export-oriented labor market and in turn influenced women's position in the labor force. The way the state contributes to gender ideology construction and reproduction is obvious in Bangladesh. To begin with, the economic development process is planned by the state, in conjunction with different class and global market interests.

Nearly two and a half centuries of British and Pakistani colonial rule hindered the rise of indigenous bourgeoisie in the then East Bengal and East Pakistan. Instead, colonial states helped to develop intermediate classes in order to serve the state apparatus. A severe lack of resources created by British and Pakistani colonial domination forced the postcolonial Bangladesh state to enter a dependency relationship with the core countries, specially through aid.

Women's work became of interest on the basis of a belief that women going out to work or having higher income may lead to a reduced birth rate. Therefore, explicit policies for women's greater involvement in the economic spheres have been articulated in all succeeding five-year plans of Bangladesh. These enabled both President Zia and President Ershad's regimes to claim more aid, to establish civilian legitimacy and thus to consolidate their power.

A policy decision in 1982 to privatize industries nationalized in 1972 has deregulated 558 industries in Bangladesh. The New Industrial Policy (NIP), introduced in 1982, and further liberalized in 1986 aimed to eliminate all restrictions of investment ceilings and other legal measures. The purpose of deregulation was to encourage the inflow of foreign capital. Besides tax benefits, tariff protection, income-tax exemption and employment of foreigners, another significant attraction that has been offered to foreign investors is the availability of a docile (female) labour force. According to a publicity brochure:

> The light-bodied Bangladeshis who are recognized as very intelligent people, can be turned into most productive and at the same time least demanding labor force.[18]

The Making of Working Mothers

Population control is the underlying theme of most of the development projects in Bangladesh. This theme is reflected in all five-year plans in priority basis. The population problem has been defined and formulated to a large extent at the assistance of donor countries and organisations. Resource allocation patterns by donors highlight women's reproductive roles and also the control of women's fertility and not reproductive health or reproductive rights. Women's health, education and productive roles receive lower priority. According to one estimate between 1980–86, only 19 per cent of projects allocations by donors have gone to the projects where women are sole targets or part of the target group; of these 55 per cent have gone to the population and family planning projects and only 2 per cent to health and 8 per cent to education. [19] The underlying motive of foreign aid and job creation for women is the assumption that economic opportunities can motivate women to accept contraceptives. The philosophy of the Mothers' Club sponsored by the World Bank, illustrates this motive: 'When a woman touches the first taka she has earned with her own labor, she feels liberated and her fertility behaviour changes to a great extent'.[20]

How are these measures affecting women? The exclusive targeting of women for population control, dumping and experimentation with birth control that are banned in the West clearly shows the relation between women's subordination, state control as well as international domination. By making women targets of the population programs the Bangladeshi state relegates women into a predominantly reproductive role. Population policies concerning women have been directed at controlling them, their sexuality and fertility, and endorsing their subordination.

Ideological Reproduction of Gender Relation

As Mandel has suggested, a capitalist state produces and reproduces capitalist social relations not only at the economic level but also through the manipulation of legal, religious, educational and other ideological apparatuses.[21] It is for us to see here to what extent the state is implementing processes to sustain and support discriminatory practices which help in the perpetuation of existing social structure which subordinates women.

Law is one area where the intentions of the state in relation to women may be more clearly demonstrated. On the surface, the legal status of women in Bangladesh appears to be almost at par with, yet not equal to, that of men. The constitution ensures equality of the sexes, but also acknowledges unequal status be reserving the right to make special provisions for women. Labour laws provide women with many benefits, but few women get to enjoy them. Laws relating to marriage, divorce, child custody, inheritance and maintenance are governed by community religious laws, and in certain cases, men have greater rights than women. Bangladesh accepted the United Nations' Declaration on the Elimination of All Forms of Discrimination against women with some reservation, because some articles conflict with the Shariah law.[22]

It is obvious that donors allocate aid in accordance of their political and commercial interests. On the question of women, the government's strategy is to balance between the conflicting gender ideologies implicit in different aid packages. The increasing significance of Islam in the state discourse is also a direct result of the oil-rich Middle Eastern countries aid. In 1977 Islam was introduced into the Bangladesh Constitution and thus ceased the ideal of secularism. In 1988 an amendment of the Constitution was made to declare Islam as the state religion of Bangladesh. This trend has special relevance for women. The Middle Eastern influence seeks to strengthen the traditional Islamic values through the resurgence of Islamic fundamentalist groups and the establishment of Islamic teaching and propagandist institutions. The resurgence and opposition of Islamic groups has created a tense political situation and made gender a contested arena. Some religious leaders of Islamic political groups who are concerned with perfecting society's adherence to Islam usually direct their attention to women's dress and women's proper Islamic behaviour. They strongly oppose co-education and women's involvement in the public arena.

Despite having a woman Prime Minister (Begum Khaleda Zia) and woman opposition party leader (Sheikh Hasina) in the Parliament (1991–present), women's relationship with the state remains substantially unchanged economically, socially and politically. It is important to note that both Khaleda Zia and Sheikh Hasina came to politics to inherit the power of their assassinated husband and father respectively, in order to sustain loyalty among their constituencies. Their public demeanour shows caution and compliance with the standard role of women as accepted by the society. Recently, the Bangladesh government gave instructions to women to clothe themselves properly to preserve their modesty and public morality.[23] The situation, following modernization policies dictated by Western donors, is an increase in the participation of women in public sectors. The 'traditional images' of 'Bangladeshi-Muslim' women in society are also being upheld at the same time. Although these two objectives of the state policy may seem contradictory, in reality, the state has been trying to create a docile labour force. On the one hand, making women targets of West-supported population control programs, the state is maintaining its control over women's body and biological reproduction. On the other hand, by strengthening Islamic values the state is reinforcing forms of social control and maintaining the reproduction of traditional gender ideals. The overall result is the perpetuation of gender inequalities in the household and factories and creation of a tractable workforce.

Understanding Purdah

Thinking of 'Muslim woman' conjures up the image of an all-concealing cloak-shrouded person in the Western mind. This image is unable to account for the important variations in women's situation both within and across Muslim societies. This image is not also able to portray the possible connections between purdah and other features of society such as economy, culture and the political system.

As I mentioned earlier, burka (which covers the wearer from top of head to wrist and ankle, allowing vision through netting over the eye-holes) is not a popular outfit among most women in Bangladesh. However, wearing burka is not the only form of observing purdah. Papanek identifies two instruments of seclusion – the physical segregation of the living space and the covering of the female face and body.[24]

> In the narrowest sense, purdah involves the seclusion of women within the four walls of their homes and the veiling of women when they move outside the homes. In a broader sense, purdah involves the exclusion of women from the public 'male' sphere of economic, social and political life.[25]

According to Mernissi (1975), purdah divides all social spaces into sex-related ones and keeps female sexuality firmly under male control. It is in this broader sense that we need to look at the purdah culture in Bangladesh.[26] Although very few women are strictly secluded from contact with unrelated men today, they are definitely expected to be modest in their presentation of self. Women must observe, as Sylvia Vatuk puts it, 'Shyness of demeanor, avoidance of eye-contact with males, avoidance of loud speech and laughter (particularly in the presence of and within the earshot of males), and the limitation of conversation with non-family males to necessary work-connected topic'.[27] Women should not go to other public places like tea-stalls where men congregate. When women venture beyond the home, a destination must be specified. In general, it is considered abnormal for a woman to go outside unless she has specific work to do. Constraints on the day-to-day physical mobility of women show not only the separation of male and female social arenas, but the dependency of women on men in the public context. The observance of purdah in its many variations is an expression of an underlying conception of domestic or inner realm protected from the larger world outside.

Studies of Papanek (1982), Jeffery (1979) and Sharma (1980) have shown that South Asian societies have two major cultural concerns with respect to women's place in the social order.[28] One of these is the concern with women's sexual vulnerability and the consequent need to protect her from possible violation or sexually motivated assault from non-family males. Related to this concern is also a set of notions about female sexuality and women's inability to control her own sexual impulses. The sheltering of a woman from the threat of sexual advances is felt to be necessary not only for her own sake, but also for the sake of maintenance of the social honour of the male centred group to which she belongs. Gender patterns, according to Ortner and Whitehead, are closely bound to prestige pattern of all societies. Much of the material that deals with this topic tries to explain the custom of purdah by reference to the twin notions of 'honour and shame'.[29] However, no society can seclude all women from all men under all circumstances, and all societies apply these rules selectively. There are wide variations in the physical and behavioural details of purdah observance. These relate to differences in class, income, place of residence, level of education, occupation, religious affiliation and individual life circumstances. The veil has always been a symbol of pride prestige and upward mobility. Veil's value as a symbol of high status derived from the fact that it interfered with a woman's work and therefore became the privilege of the well-off who could afford servants.

Bangladeshi women's recent participation in the industrial labor has broken the spatial norms of purdah. However, many working women have started to wear 'chaddor'. It should be noted that *chaddor* is different from the traditional form of veil, the burka. If we consider the veil as a symbol of tradition, and women's involvement in the industrial labor as a symbol of 'modernity', then the veil should be disappearing. Why then is it reappearing among the 'modern' women? It is to this question now we turn.

Purdah: resistance or compliance?

The situation of new veiling in Bangladesh can be read in different ways. Although factory workers are now earning wages, research show that women still adhere to the values of male supremacy and female modesty. As factory work is not socially prestigious, women encounter social disapproval in different forms. Working in public is associated with loose morals and loose character. Therefore, women try to impose greater discipline on themselves for fear of being charged as 'loose women', as they have left the symbolic protection of a home. Some men reinforce this social control on women in town streets by hooting, pinching and making sexually harassing remarks to passing women. The Islamic fundamentalist groups add insult to this injury by trying to build public opinion against women's 'un-Islamic' behaviour, such as, working in public and getting education in co-ed institutions. Factory women are frequently referred to as 'kharap mayalok' (bad women). Thus the different sections of people in Bangladesh have compelled factory women towards conformity. Therefore, chaddor can be described as a symbol of submission that women impose on themselves as a suitable substitute for the domestic realm. Purdah, a conforming behaviour of women workers can also be described as a direct result of the Bangladeshi state's crafting of a manageable, less reproductive and more productive labor force. Yet, a close reading of the situation makes it hard to reconcile a victim-centred picture. Chaddor is different from the traditional outfit in style, form, material and name. Chaddor conveys signs of upward mobility, honour and dignity.

In recent years, scholars have been focusing on the forms of opposition in which women and other marginalized groups have historically engaged. This resistance is particularly relevant to situations and relations embodying great disparities in power and access to resources.[30] It has been suggested that women engage in diverse acts of resistance everyday in their work and family lives. Following these arguments, we can perceive women's reconstruction of the veil as a resistance against gender segregation. Although I am sympathetic to the significance of above mentioned literature in recognizing women's agency, I find it somewhat problematic. It assumes that all humans are primarily engaged in the project of resistance. Resistance solely implies oppositional tactics, whereas women's re-veiling also expresses conformity to the social image of ideal women.

The contradictory ways of using purdah suggest against the dichotomy of resistance/helpless victims. Rather, the notion of *agency* provides a space for a subject focused analysis. Agency avoids the notion that women are either actively engaged in resistance or passively accepting any particular situation. Agency, as Joan Scott suggests, is 'action taken in specific context, but not entirely autonomously or without constraint'.[31] According to Wolf, agency is not synonymous with activity; agency can involve passivity, accommodation and withdrawal as much as it can involve defiance and resistance. The resurgence of purdah among the working women reflects women's tactic to cope with their conflicting and contradictory positions vis-a-vis the dominant discourses of the state, gender ideology, religious value and work. By wearing chaddor, women in Bangladesh have been able to move beyond the confinement of domestic and gain the right to work in the public spheres. At the same time, chaddor helps them to resolve their dilemma of traditional gender identity and new economic role. By wearing chaddor, a woman wants to convey that although in the masculine sphere, she does not cross the borders of ideal womanhood. She believes that chaddor can save her from sexual harassment and social stigmatization. Therefore, in her manipulation of an existing cultural symbol, a woman stretches her boundaries and creates new definitions of gender identity. The thoughts of some factory workers I have interviewed elucidate this point.

— If I maintain purdah, nobody can make bad remarks to me. (purdah as protection)

— You can go anywhere and do anything if you put on purdah. Bibi Aisha (wife of prophet Muhammad) fought against non-Muslims while maintained purdah. (purdah as prestigious and liberating)

— While I first started working, my husband was very suspicious of what I was doing. Now I wear chaddor and he does not bother any more.

The resurgence of purdah proves that working women in Bangladesh are questioning as well as complying with the existing notions of femininity. On one hand they are rejecting the spatial seclusion, on the other hand, they are reinforcing the bodily concealment. Women are accepting the definitions of the veil while redefining it. Additionally, we have to keep in mind that women's choice of veil is shaped by the Bangladeshi gender ideals, religion as well as state and the local and global market interests. It is from this perspective that this paper tries to understand Bangladeshi women's remaking of the purdah and its strategic position within complex field of power relations in Bangladeshi society.

Notes

1. A cotton shawl worn by women over their dress.
2. An overall which covers the wearer from head to wrist and ankle, allowing vision through netting over the eye-holes.
3. 'Purdah', the Persian word meaning veil or curtain, is the term most commonly used for the system of secluding women and enforcing standards of femininity. There are two broad forms of *purdash*: the physical segregation of the living space, and the covering of the female face and body.
4. I am not using public/private as binary oppositions. Private (feminine) and public (masculine) are not absolutely separate spheres and they often overlap. At the same time I also aware that there are symbolic boundaries of both feminine and masculine spheres (socially constructed and based on perceived differences between the sexes) in Bangladeshi society, and masculine sphere is historically marked by privilege.
5. See S. Adnan, "Birds in a Cage": Institutional Change and Women's Position in Bangladesh', *The Journal of Social Studies*, 46, 1989, pp. 1-34.
6. World Bank, *Bangladesh, Strategies for enhancing the Role of Women in Economic Development* (Washington D.C.: World Bank, 1990).
7. H. Hossain, R. Jahan, and S. Sobhan, *No Better Option? Industrial Women Workers in Bangladesh* (Dhaka: The University Press Limited, 1990).
8. K.B. Ward, Introduction and Overview, in K. Ward (ed.), *Women Workers and Global Restructuring* (Ithaca, N.Y. : ILR Press, Cornell University, 1990), pp. 1-2.

9. For further discussion, see, A. Fuentes, and B. Ehrenreich, *Women in the Global Factory* (New York : The Institute for New Communications 1983). M. Mies, *Patriarchy and Accumulation on a World Scale* (London: Zed Books Ltd., 1986); S. Mitter, *Common Fate Common Bond: Women in the Global Economy* (London: Pluto Press, 1986); J. Nash, and M.P. Fernandez-Kelly (eds), *Women Men and the International Division of Labour* (Albany: SUNY Press, 1983); K. Young, C. Wolkowitz, and R. McCullagh (eds), *Of Marriage and the Market* (London: CSE Books, 1981).
10. M. Mannan, *BAT Expo* (Dhaka: Export Promotion Bureau, Bangladesh and Bangladesh Garments Manufactures and Exporters Association, 1992).
11. R. Ahmed (ed.), Religion, Nationalism and Politics in Bangladesh (New Delhi: South Asian Publishers, 1990), p. 100.
12. H. Hussain, *BAT Expo '92* (Dhaka: Export Promotion Bureau and BMEA, 1992).
13. S.C. Rothschild and S. Mahmud, *Women's Roles in Agriculture: Present Trends and Potential for Growth* (Dhaka: UNDP and UNIFEM, 1989).
14. R. Jahan, 'Women in Bangladesh', in *Women for Women* (Dhaka: University Press Limited, 1975), pp. 1-32.
15. Manusmriti is one of the most authoritative lawbooks in ancient (approx. 200 BC) India.
16. For more information on religion, politics and women in Bangladesh, see Ahmed, p. 990; and Kabeer, 1991.
17. J. Arnes and J. Beuden, *Jhagrapur: Poor Peasants and Women in a Village of bangladesh* (Amesterdam: Authros, 1977), pp. 32-3.
18. Hossain et. al., p. 37.
19. T.C. Schaffer, *Survey of Development Projects and Activities for Women in Bangladesh* (Dhaka: The U.S. Agency for International Development, 1986).
20. Cited in N. Kabeer, 'Subordination and Struggle: *Women in Bangladesh*', *New Left Review*, 168, 1988, pp. 95-121.
21. E. Mandel, *Late Capitalism* (London: Verso, 1978).
22. Shariah law is based on the Koran and the Hadith (words, deeds and exemplary practices of the Prophet Muhammad, several authorized compilations available).
23. Proper length of the *saree* (6 yards) was specified by an official decree.
24. H. Papanek, 'Purdah: Separate World and Symbolic Shelter', in H. Papanek and G. Minault (eds), *Separate Worlds: Studies of Purdah in South Asia* (Delhi: Chanakya Publications, 1982), pp. 3-53.
25. M.C. Chen, *A Quiet Revolution: Women in Transition in Rural Bangladesh* (Cambridge, MA: Schenkman Publishing Company, 1983), pp. 58-9.
26. F. Mernissi, Beyond the *Veil: Male-Female Dynamics in a Modern Muslim Society* (Cambridge, MA: Schenkman Publishing Company, 1975).
27. S. Vatuk, 'Purdah Revisited: A Comparison of Hindu and Muslim Interpretations of the Cultural meaning of Purdah in South Asia', in Papanek and Minault, op. cit., p. 70.
28. See Papanek, op. cit.; P. Jeffery, *Frogs in a Well: Indian Women in Purdah* (London: Zed Press, 1979); U. Sharma, *Women, Work, and Property in North West India* (London: Tavistock Publications, 1980).

Bibliography

Abu-Lughod, L. 1985. "A Community of Secrets". *Signs*, 10, 637-657.

——— 1990a. "The Romance of Resistance: Tracing Transformations of Power through Bedouine Women". *American Ethnologist, 17*(1), 41-55.

——— 1990b. "Shifting politics in Bedouine love poetry." In Lutz. K. and L. Abu-Lughod (Eds.) *Language and the Politics of Emotion* (pp. 24-45). Cambridge : Cambridge University Press.

Adnan, S. (1989). "Birds in a Cage" : Institutional Change and Women's Position in Bangladesh. *The Journal of Social Studies, 46,* 1-34.

Ahmed, R. (Ed.). (1990). *Religion, Nationalism and Politics in Bangladesh.* New Delhi : South Asian Publishers.

Aptheker, B. (1989). *Tapestries of life : Women's Work, Women's Consciousness and the Meaning of Daily Experience.* Amherst : University of Massachusetts Press.

Arnes, J. & Beurden, J. (1977). *Jhagrapur : Poor Peasants and Women in a Village of Bangladesh.* Amesterdam : Authors.

Chen, M.C. (1983). *A Quite Revolution : Women in Transition in Rural Bangladesh.* Cambridge, MA l: Schenkman Publishing Company.

Gain, P. (1990). *Bangladesh Poshak Shiple Nari Sramik.* Dhaka : Bangladesh Manobadhikar Samannaya Parishad.

Guha, R. 1983a. Elementary Aspects of Peasant Insurgency in Colonial India. Delhi : Oxford University Press.

Guha, R. 1983b. "The Prose of Counter-Insurgency." In R. Guha (Ed.) *Subaltern Studies II : Writings on South Asian History and Society,* (pp. 1-42). Delhi : Oxford University Press.

Guhathakurta, M. (1985). Gender Violence in Bangladesh : *The Role of the State. The Journal of Social Studies,* 30, 77-90.

Hossain, H., Jahan, R., and Sobhan, S. (1990). *No Better Option? Industrial Women Workers in Bangladesh.* Dhaka : The University Press Limited.

Hussain, M. (1992). *BAT Expo '92.* Dhaka : Export Promotion Bureau and BMEA.

Jahan, R. (1975). "Women in Bangladesh". In *Women for Women,* (pp. 1-32). Dhaka: University Press Limited.

Jeffery, P. (1979). *Frogs in a Well: Indian Women in Purdah.* London: Zed Press.

Kabeer, N. (1991). The Quest for National Identity: Women, Islam and the State of Bangladesh. In D . Kandiyoti (Ed.) *Women, Islam and the State,* pp. 115-143. Philadelphia: Temple University Press.

Kabeer, N. (1988). "Subordination and Struggle: Women in Bangladesh." *New Left Review, 168*: 95-121.

Mannan, M. 1992. *BAT Expo.* Dhaka: Export Promotion Bureau, Bangladesh and Bangladesh Garments Manufactures and Exporters Association.

Mernissi, F. 1975. *Beyond the Veil: Male-Female Dynamics in a Modern Muslim Society.* Cambridge, MA: Schenkman Publishing Company.

Mandel, E. *Late Capitalism* London : Verso, 1978.

Mandelbaum, D.G. (1988). *Women's Seclusion and Men's Honor:* Sex Roles in North India, Bangladesh and Pakistan. Tucson: The University of Arizona Press.

Ortner, S.B., & Whitehead, H. 1981. Introduction: Accounting for Sexual

Meaning. In S. B. Ortner & H. Whitehead (EDs.), *Sexual Meanings* (pp. 1-28). Cambridge: Cambridge University Press.

Papanek, H. (1982). Purdah: Separate World and Symbolic Shelter. In H. Papanek and G. Minault (Eds.), *Separate Worlds: Studies of Purdah in South Asia* (pp. 3-53). Delhi: Chanakya Publications.

Rothschild, S.C., & Mahmud, S. (1989). *Women's Roles in Agriculture: Present Trends and Potential for Growth.* Dhaka: UNDP and UNIFEM.

Schaffer, T.C. (1986). *Survey of Development Projects and Activities for Women in Bangladesh.* Dhaka: The U.S. Agency for International Development.

Scott, J.C. 1990. *Domination and the Arts of Resistance: Hidden Transcripts.* New Heaven and London: Yale University Press.

Scott, J.W. 1988. *Gender and the Politics of History.* New York: Columbia University Press.

Sharma, U. (1980). *Women, Work, and Property in North-West India.* London: Tavistock Publications.

Sklair, L. (1989). *The Reformation of Capitalism : The Maquila Industry in Mexico and the USA.* Boston : Allen and Unwin.

Sobhan, R. (1990). *From Aid Dependence to Self-Reliance Development Options for Bangladesh.*

Vatuk, S. (1982). Purdah Revisited : A Comparison of Hindu and Muslim Interpretations of the Cultural Meaning of Purdah in South Asia. In H. Papanek and G. Minault (Eds.), *Separate Worlds : Studies of Purdah in South Asia* (pp. 54-78). Delhi : Chanakya Publications.

Ward, K.B. (1990). Introduction and Overview. In K. Ward (Ed.), *Women Workers and Global Restructuring* (pp. 1-22). Ithaca, N.Y. : ILR Press, Cornell University.

White, S.C. (1992). Arguing with the Crocodile : Gender and Class in Bangladesh. London, New Jersey and Dhaka : Zed Books Ltd. and University Press Limited.

Wiig. A. (1990). Non-tariff barriers to trade and development-the case of garment industry in Bangladesh. In O. Norbye (Ed.), *Bangladesh Faces the Future,* (pp. 139-166). Norway and Dhaka : Chr. Michelsen Institute and Bangladesh Institute of Development Studies.

Wolf D.L. (1992). *Factory Daughters : Gender, Household Dynamics, and Rural Industrialization in Java.* Berkeley : University of California Press.

World Bank. (1990). *Bangladesh : strategies for enhancing the role of women in economic development.* Washington D.C. : World Bank.

Section II
Thematic Issues with Relation to Religion, Law, Secularism and the Placement of Women in Trade Unions and in Organizations

The Changing Religious Role of Women in Pre-modern Southeast Asia

Barbara Watson Andaya

Claims that women in Southeast Asia enjoyed a relatively high status stretch back over hundreds of years. Observers as far removed in time and place as a tenth-century Chinese in Vietnam, an eighteenth-century Englishman in Sumatra, a New Zealander in eastern Indonesia around 1910, and a contemporary anthropologist have remarked on the respect with which females are regarded, and on their 'dominance' and 'freedom', even when imported traditions stress an ideal of female subservience.[1] Such comments have been echoed in a recent work by Anthony Reid, *Southeast Asia in the Age of Commerce*. In his view, the comparatively high position women held 'represented one aspect of the social system in which a distinctive Southeast Asian pattern was especially evident'.[2]

Despite the continuing affirmation of women's status, scholarly attention has been accorded to 'herstory' in Southeast Asia only in the last twenty years, undoubtedly as a result of the explosion of feminist-inspired work in other parts of the world. But while illuminating and welcome, it must be acknowledged that the consideration of gender issues in Southeast Asia has been dominated by anthropologists. Historical research has been limited, and concentrated heavily on the nineteenth and twentieth centuries. With some justification, it might be argued that our knowledge of the pre-modern period is as yet insufficiently detailed to attempt any sustained view of historical developments. Archaeologists have been particularly wary of engendering prehistory, although if the 'high status' of women is distinctively Southeast Asian, cultural patterns must surely have been laid down during a very early period. Indeed, the excavation of burial sites in Thailand has made one historian sufficiently confident to suggest that women skilled in pottery enjoyed considerable prestige in the community. Historical linguistics, while still in its infancy in Southeast Asia, may similarly throw up interesting theories: Robert Blust, for example, has argued that the emphasis on females in genealogical descent so frequently noted in the region can be detected in the very origins of Austronesian languages.[3]

Despite such limitations, it could also be argued that the available sources have not been fully exploited, and that in posing new questions the historical perspective can add much to existing understandings of how the position of women in Southeast Asia changed over time. However, if historians are to attempt a serious discussion of female experiences in the pre-modern period, they will need to pay due respect to the thoughtful discussions that have informed feminist historiography in recent times. They will also need to be aware of the increasing number of case studies from other parts of the world, since comments regarding the 'high status' of Southeast Asian females are usually made using an Indian or Chinese yardstick. Contrasts in economic roles and male–female relations might not be so marked if different comparisons were made. For instance, in much of Africa women were also active traders, and when the Arab traveller Ibn Battuta visited Mali in 1352 he observed with surprise that women there 'were treated with more respect than men' and that descent was calculated through the female line.[4] An assessment of how female experiences in Southeast Asia resembled or differed from societies in other parts of the world would undoubtedly go far in establishing the extent to which there were 'distinctive' Southeast Asian cultural attitudes towards gender relations. Before this can occur, however, much more basic research is necessary. In presenting some comments on the ways in which the arrival of the world religions in the region affected women's status, this paper presents a preliminary foray into an area as yet relatively unexplored.

Early Religious Roles

Isolated prehistoric remains such as rock paintings depicting human figures with exaggerated genitals combines with evidence from historic times to suggest that a veneration for fertility lay at the heart of Southeast Asian indigenous belief systems. In this the region is by no means unique, although a preoccupation with ensuring fertility may have been heightened because of the early development, prevalence and persistence of horticultural and agricultural societies.[5] With the life-principle infusing the natural world, the earth itself became a giant womb fertilized by the rain, from which fruits, edible plants, crops and ultimately animals and humans sprang. The cosmic intercourse of supernatural forces magnified, as it were, the sexual relationship between humans, which then became symbolic of an even more powerful creative force.

The world religions all tended to foster the notion that women played a passive role in reproduction, acting merely as the vessel into which Man placed life. Modern anthropologists have detected a similar pattern among some of those Southeast Asian societies that still follow indigenous religions.[6] Certainly it is not difficult to find early evidence of deep awe towards the creative energies manifested by men during the sexual act. The erect genital on a prehistoric sculpture found in Central Celebes is integral to the representation of the ancestral figure, and the image carved with a large penis to 'further female fertility' described by a Dutchman in seventeenth-century Ambon was obviously considered a potent counter to barrenness.[7] But it also seems that most of the small kinship communities that characterized early Southeast Asia conceived of parenthood as a union of complementary dualities, with the potency of males matched by the reproductive capacity of women as bearers of the next generation. Solicitations by women to supernatural agencies could be efficacious in both conception and a healthy birth, and the special bond between mother and child is repeatedly emphasized in the visual arts. Significantly, the most common image found among the famed Sawankhalok miniatures of Thailand, dating from between 1350 and 1500, is that of a woman holding a child, while ritual statues from various parts of Indonesia depict female figures with swollen bellies and women suckling their young.[8] The female element in fertility is suggested in the account of one district in Ambon, where Dutch preachers in the seventeenth century found that the people were worshipping a statue in the likeness of an old woman.[9] The interaction between male and female can also be seen in creation myths collected by Christian missionaries in the latter part of the sixteenth century. The accounts they recorded see the world and humankind arising from sexual union between equals; the male heaven couples with the female earth; the female egg from which a ruling house springs is no different from the male eggs; man and women emerge together from a single reed.[10]

Early European missionaries in the region also noted that certain men and women were believed to have particular skills in bridging the gap between the world of humans and that of spirits. As in numerous other societies, however, it seems that females were often considered to be particularly suited as spirit mediums, a role they have continued to play in some places to the present day.[11] Female mediation with the spirit world was fundamental to rituals of life and death such as birth, the planting of crops and funerals. With their knowledge of 'antidotal herbs' and their links with the spirits, women were also the society's principal healers. As one Spanish observer in the Philippines put it in 1582, 'The priestess chants her songs and invokes the demon, who appears to her all glistening in gold. Then he enters her body and hurls her to the ground, foaming at the mouth as one possessed. In this state she declares whether the sick person is to recover or not'.[12] In the mid-seventeenth century an ailing ruler of Palembang in southeast Sumatra thus asked the Dutch administration in Batavia to help him locate two female 'doctors' whom he believed would cure his illness.[13]

It may have been a popular belief in their magical powers that occasionally saw women emerge as leaders of rebellions against powerful outsiders. The legend of the Trung sisters of Vietnam, who led a revolt against Chinese overlords in 43 A.D., is well known; in seventeenth century Sulawesi, where Islam had only recently penetrated, female *bissui*, or indigenous religious leaders, led the army into battle against the Dutch swinging their spindles.[14] In the Philippines missionaries complained that Filipinos regarded the Virgin Mary as a more potent 'spirit' than Christ, and in some cases the rebels who fought against Spanish forces not only followed women 'priests' but carried images of the Virgin.[15] In Vietnam it was similarly reported that a male convert's adoration of the Virgin Mary enabled him to perform 'miracles'.[16]

This perceived access to magic secrets through association with a powerful female points up an inherent ambiguity in the attitude towards women which has been noted across many societies. Female sexuality, in its very non-maleness, was considered vital for the proper functioning of the world, but only if the correct balance were maintained. Too great an infusion of the female force would have disastrous results. In Southeast Asia a reconstruction of proto-Malay-Polynesian has used purely linguistic evidence to suggest that while women have always been associated with fecundity, they were also linked with calamity. When the forces of fertility were uncontrolled – that is., when sexual relations occurred with prohibited persons – the possibility of disaster loomed large. If sexuality was expressed in a manner unacceptable to the natural order, the world would be disrupted by volcanic eruptions, epidemic illness or famine. Early Austronesian society, for example, apparently believed that individuals guilty of incest and adultery would incur supernatural punishment, for they would be struck by lightning and turned to stone.[17] The sexual freedom that struck so many outsiders who visited Southeast Asia in later times was circumscribed by very strict limits.

Ambiguous attitudes towards sexuality, especially that of females, were manifested most in the beliefs and customs associated with menstruation. Here again Southeast Asia is by no means exceptional. There are various explanations advanced for why so many societies set menstruating women apart, among which is the notion that blood is closely associated with death, and the belief that during this period women can be of great danger to men.[18] In communities where blood was closely linked with sacrifice, menstrual blood was regarded as particularly powerful, and among numerous contemporary societies it is thought to be a key ingredient in potions designed to subordinate men to the whims of women. Significantly, a seventh-century Sumatran ruler placed his curse on those who charged members of their family to conspire against him 'making use of a bowl of blood'.[19] Early missionary reports from some areas in eastern Indonesia and the Philippines indicate that a girl's first menses, marking the advent of fertility, could be an occasion for solemnities and rejoicing. But it could also be a time of ritual seclusion, for of all the bodily fluids, menstrual blood had the potential to work the greatest magic. According to one Spanish account, a menstruating Tagalog girl was not allowed to talk to anybody except the spirit medium performing the ceremonies: 'It is their custom to enclose her with mantles and cover the windows, such that where she is becomes very dark.'[20]

Modern anthropologists have identified several societies in Southeast Asia where taboos attached to menstruation are minimal, but it is surely relevant that early reports consistently describe women who assumed a prominent place in indigenous ritual as 'old'.[21] Because they have ceased menstruating, they can no longer be regarded as dangerous. Political power occasionally fell into female hands, but the queens of early Southeast Asia were usually older women, widows who were beyond child-bearing years.[22]

The sexual neutralizing of old men and women can also be demonstrated linguistically. The notion of women's reproductive capacity as potentially disturbing comes through in one seventeenth-century account from the Philippines, where a missionary was told that although husband and wives were joined together in death the woman was no longer fertile.[23]

The need to retain a balance in male-female relations and contain the powerful forces of sexuality is suggested by the respect accorded bisexualism, evidence for which is particularly pronounced in Austronesian cultures. Among the Ngayu Dayak, for example, the complete godhead, like indigenous religious practitioners, embodies both male and female, 'the holy lance and the holy cloth'; in Java, the culture hero Panji is said to be bisexual, the inventor of the Javanese kris as well as the protector of the female occupation of weaving.[24] Tome Pires has mentioned numerous 'eunuchs' in Java who 'dressed in women's clothes', while in eastern Indonesia early missionaries described a particularly powerful group of people who, as spirit mediums and protectors of the regalia, took on the outward appearance of the opposite sex. Seventeenth-century Spaniards in the Philippines also remarked on 'sorcerers and priests of the demon' who were 'men in the garb of women'.[25] The female guards, armed with 'phallic' muskets that so struck Europeans in the courts of Java, are best considered not as an example of 'lady soldiers', but as an embodiment of deep-seated beliefs that considered sacral power to be most potent when male and female elements mingled.[26]

Because women could not control that most potent manifestation of femaleness, menstruation, it should not be surprising to find that individuals who combined the attributes of both sexes and most closely approximate priests in indigenous belief systems were commonly men, although in their role as spirit mediums, older females often dominated ceremonies at specific life crises.[27] Despite the prominent role of women in the indigenous ritual system, one should therefore be cautious in seeing historical Southeast Asia as an exception to what Valeri has described as a 'global inferiority of women relative to men in the sacrificial system, even when there may be equality in genealogy'.[28] Feminist prehistorians have commonly linked the beginnings of this process in western Europe with the Bronze Age, about four thousand years ago.[29] In Southeast Asia, however, it has been generally accepted that women maintained a comparatively 'high status' for a range of reasons, including their role in food production and trade, the looseness of pre-modern state structures, and the entrenched views of male–female dualities in kinship relations. Yet in religious practices the position of women was more ambiguous, and historical sources suggest that over time they were becoming increasingly subordinate to men. There can be little doubt that this tendency was fostered by the arrival and spread of the male-oriented, legalistic and hierarchical world religions.

Women and the World Religions

None of the world religions that came to Southeast Asia provides any textual basis for the participation of women at the highest levels of ritual.[30] It is certainly true that powerful indigenous female spirits survived; in their sexual coupling with great deities, they continued to personify the fertility notions embedded in Southeast Asian beliefs. In Java and Bali, for instance, the rice goddess Dewi Sri became Uma, Siva's wife, while in Champa the spouse of Siva was the ancient spirit Po Nagar, 'the Mistress of the Kingdom', depicted as Bhagavati. This linking of the new goddesses with the old is found across the region, albeit in different idioms. In eleventh-century Vietnam a female 'earth spirit' was thus accorded the name of a T'and Chinese goddess, while in the Philippines the success of Christianity was in many cases due to the metamorphoses of territorial spirits into 'patron saints' like Saint Rosa of Lima, charged with the protection of a parish.[31] Belief that the fertility of the land depended on a mystical union between the ruler and powerful female deity also survived, echoing Zhou Daguan's story of the nightly intercourse between the ruler and a snake serpent in Cambodia.[32]

But increasingly the male principle is assuming prominence, notably at the court level where images of male gods tower over their female counterparts and women are barred from certain rituals. While it is impossible to date myths, the written court traditions now appearing in the form of 'state chronicles' associated with one particular kingdom often depict male ancestors who produce progeny through their own power, by finding them in the forest, or by crafting statues, or through meditation. The fecundity of the earth-goddess is tamed, as in central Vietnam where, in the process of transformation into a Confucian tutelary deity, the Cham spirit Po Nagar loses her retinue of husbands and children.[33] Coupled with this trend is an emphasis on male possession and mastery of 'magical' women as a means of securing leadership. Burmese chronicles note that a queen was taken by an aspirant ruler 'because she was already part of the regalia'; in Java the female incarnate, the princess with the flaming womb, is nonetheless vulnerable to conquest. 'The poorest man who is able to make her his will become supreme ruler.'[34]

Although Hinduism stressed the power that came through the union of the gods and their female counterparts, it also brought to Southeast Asia a strengthening of the veneration accorded the male role in creation. In Hindu thought the world was formed from the body of Primal Man, and the personalization and worship of the *linga*, the phallic symbol of Siva, overshadowed the *yoni* (womb), the representation of female fertility, which, like the phallus, had been part of earlier Indian belief systems.[35] Indian-influenced sculpture in Southeast Asia retains the *yoni*, on which the *linga* rests; indeed, in some early Cham sculptures, which Paul Mus sees as closely related to prehistoric menhirs, the *linga* appears dwarfed by the *yoni*.[36] However, in most of Southeast Asia, as in India, the *yoni* is of far less visual and ritual importance than the *linga*. In Cambodia, where Hindu influence reached its height, the ruler identified himself with Siva, and the king's *linga* was the representation of the creative principle that he himself embodied. In the same manner, the worship of Siva and his reproductive force in Java elevated male practitioners far above females as guardians of the sacred rites and the secret mantras.[37]

These developments had little effect on the extensive economic activities of women.[38] Nonetheless, the beliefs associated with Hinduism foreshadowed trends that were continued as Buddhism, Confucianism, Islam and Christianity moved in to become the 'state' religions of the region. There is a much greater stress, for instance, on the duties of a wife to her husband, the most extreme example of which is the ritual burning of high-born widows on their husband's funeral pyre. In Bali the burning of women mingled with indigenous ideas of human sacrifice as demonstration of loyalty to any individual of royal birth, regardless of sex. By the nineteenth century the practice was associated only with males, but in 1633 twenty-two women were sacrificed at the cremation of a queen. Pires mentioned similar practices in his description of Java, although stressed that they did not occur among Muslim Javanese.[39] On the other hand, Muslim literature, like that of the other world faiths, constantly emphasized the need for a wife's obedience. As a Malay manuscript comments: 'We women believers should be devoted to our husbands, in the hope that we shall obtain the mercy of Allah the Exalted in the hereafter'.[40] Occasionally one catches a glimpse of notions that childbirth was inherently an unclean process, although for the most part such ideas, so widespread in India, were disregarded in Southeast Asia.[41] Such attitudes inevitably limited the role that females could play in ritual. Early Buddhism, for instance, originally allowed higher female ordination, but this tradition was lost early in the present millennium. In Cambodia there are indications that females were still involved in popular Buddhism in the pre-Angkorian period, but Zhou Daguan's account of 1296 categorically states that he saw no Buddhist nuns.[42] Inscriptions from Pagan certainly show that women in Burma continued to maintain a strong economic position, but the women of the time knew they were regarded as spiritually subordinate. The testimony they have left speaks for itself; one requested that she be born again as a man, since the 'status of wife is inferior'.[43] In another inscription of 1271 even a queen longs for the time when she will become 'a man and a spirit [*nat*]'.[44] In seventeenth-century Thailand de la Loubere noted Buddhist nuns, but commented that they were usually old women whose main function was serving the monks.[45]

One reason why women could not be spiritual leaders was their lack of access to the most prestigious forms of worship and to the religious books that contained the holy scriptures. Some high-ranking women could read and often produced texts of their own, but these were mostly concerned with entertainment, particularly stories of love and courtly life. Early European observers sometimes mentioned females 'reading and writing' love charms and poetic notes. However, theirs was almost certainly visual memorization of a very limited vocabulary, which was quite different from that found in religious and philosophical texts.[46] In any event, the latter were usually written in a foreign language such as Arabic, Pali or Chinese, and in an unfamiliar script that could be learned or memorized only through formal teaching. Although girls may have received basic religious instruction, at higher levels the students in religious schools were overwhelmingly male and thus the production and study of 'serious' religious literature was almost totally the preserve of men.[47]

A distancing from the sources of religious truths, the sacred texts, was reflected in a greater sexual differentiation in religious worship. Thus in sixteenth-century Brunei 'the common people go to the mosque and the women never go but it is the men'.[48] Nearly a century later in Makassar, where the women had their own mosque, the wife of one of the leading *ulama* had the effrontery to go to the public prayers on a fast day. Her husband deemed the mosque so profaned that he took her by the hand 'and publicly divorced her, as unworthy to be the wife of a priest of the Law'.[49] Indigenous rituals had emphasized the union of male and female; world religions stressed their separation. Something of this comes through in the style of Islamic gravestones from northern Sumatra. Up until the early sixteenth century they do not differentiate between the sexes in the style of design or in the inscription; however, from around 1520 there is a clear attempt to distinquish between male and female graves.[50]

Perhaps of all the religions that came to Southeast Asia, Catholic Christianity had the potential to offer the greatest appeal to women. Not only were both sexes encouraged to acquire knowledge of the scriptures and attend mass regularly, but they had before them the example of the veneration accorded the Virgin Mary. Indeed,

Portuguese observers in eastern Indonesia in the early seventeenth century commented on the zeal that females on the island of Siau showed for the faith, especially in terms of healing and baptism.[51] Spanish sources throw up repeatedly evidence that female participation made a significant contribution to the character and appeal of popular Christianity among Filipinos. In one parish in Nueva Segovia, for example, it became customary for women to carry the image of the Blessed Virgin on holy days. Priests disapproved, but found support for the custom so widespread that they finally specified that those involved should at least be clothed in a seemly fashion.[52]

Yet despite their undoubted dedication to the new teachings and ritual, Christian doctrine relegated Filipinas to a secondary role. Convents (*beaterios*) for pious native women were eventually established, modelled on those for Spanish females; for the most part, however, such *beaterios* stressed manual labour rather than spiritual growth, and there were few opportunities to develop independent authority structures and organizational skills. In view of the limited religious role provided for native women, it is significant that the greatest resistance from females to the penetration of a world religion occurred in the Philippines. Convinced that spirit worship was the work of the devil, Spanish missionaries mounted unrelenting attacks on what they saw as 'idolatry' and 'sorcery'. In so doing they struck at the bases of indigenous beliefs, and severely threatened the standing of those women who acted as spirit mediums, condemned by the friars as witches. It is not surprising, therefore, that priestesses were prominent in many of the rebellions against the Spanish, or that spirit practitioners incorporated Christian symbols and vocabulary into their ritual in an effort to maintain a hold over their following. A female *katalonan* (spirit medium) in an area near Manila said that the spirit (*anito*) who spoke through her also came from heaven and should be worshipped like the new deities brought by the Spanish.[53]

Spanish suspicions regarding the attachment of females to the 'devil and his ministers' were coupled with a belief in their spiritual weakness. As with the other world religions,

Christianity considered man's search after religious knowledge constantly vulnerable to female sexual wiles. The *Nitisastra*, an Old Javanese text, proclaims not only that women are the root cause of civil strife, but that they yearn for men to fight over them: 'All women long to be the cause of a dreadful war.'[54] Men must be constantly on their guard, for women have the capacity to cast spells over men that will make them set aside religious teaching. The immensely popular Malay tale, the *Hikayat Yusuf*, thus describes how the young Yusuf resolutely resists the advances of his master's wife; had he succumbed, he would have met the terrible punishments that await the adulterer in hell.[55] The Le Code of Vietnam specifically mentions the punishments that should be meted out to a wife who uses 'witchcraft or incantations to arouse love from her husband'.[56] The wiles of women and the sexual demands they make on their husbands are a distraction from the pursuit of true spirituality, that can only be properly undertaken by men. Fourteenth-century bas-reliefs from Candi Surawana in East Java graphically depict woman in her role as temptress. The message of the bas-reliefs is forthright: the truly religious man must be able to reject the companionship of women, and even men who are bound to this world through their relationship with females should ultimately be able to break free from their womenfolk.[57]

Linked with religious perceptions of female propensity to promiscuity was a greater stress on the notion that a woman should come to her husband untainted by previous sexual encounters. While frequently ignored, legal and social injunctions associated with the world religions restricted earlier sexual freedoms, being most enforced among women of high rank. With the idealization of a dutiful daughter and a virtuous wife personified by figures such as Sita, Fatimah, Mary, the greater stress on virginity before marriage meant that well-born women were living increasingly secluded lives. One early Chinese visitor had commented disapprovingly 'southern barbarian women . . . promisciously wander about', but a tenth-century Chinese scholar who lived among the Vietnamese for a decade claimed that females were being made to wear tinkling earrings to keep them from wandering. In Java in the seventeenth-century Dutch observers noted that ladies of high birth were very sheltered, and popular Islamic stories stressed that good Muslim women should be chaste, modest and above all obedient to their menfolk.[58] Even at the village level there is evidence that religious law attempted to limit the independence females had traditionally enjoyed in regard to marriage. In the Philippines, missionaries were particularly critical of the 'unchastity' of Filipino women and responded to what they regarded as moral profligacy by constantly stressing the sinfulness of premarital sex together with the sanctity and indissolubility of marriage.[59] A lessening of the old freedom of women to end a relationship with a man was also obvious in Muslim areas. In Ambon in eastern Indonesia, seventeenth-century Dutch observers remarked that discontented wives often ran away from their husbands. When Muslim men complained to Dutch authorities, orders were issued forbidding women to spend nights away from home without permission and imposing fines for 'carnal knowledge' before marriage.[60] In Confucian Vietnam, royal law codes gave women considerable protection from exploitation, and there can be no doubt that women here were more advantaged than in China, especially in terms of property inheritance. However, in legal terms they were almost always inferior to a man from the same social class.[61]

Scholars have made much of the fact that descent through the female line in Southeast Asia could be a significant determinant in royal authority. One scholar in Burma has gone so far as to contend that political power, though held by men, was transmitted through women'.[62] Nonetheless, the male-dominated religions so closely linked with developing state structures in Southeast Asia were still part of a conceptual package that saw men as the appropriate leaders of society. The new teachings even undermined the relatively privileged position of older women, who had occasionally assumed positions of political influence. One of the great thinkers of medieval Islam, Nizam al-Mulk, stressed that 'women cannot be allowed to assume power, for they are wearers of the veil and have not complete intelligence'.[63] God made the first woman Eve, from Adam's left side, says a Portuguese translation of an Islamic text, with the result that she was weak, not strong.[64] In Aceh four successive queens had ruled during the seventeenth century, but local chronicles allege that in 1699 a *fatwa* arrived from Mecca decreeing that no women should now be permitted to rule, since this was against the law of Allah.[65] One Javanese ruler explained his relationship to Dutch Batavia thus: 'Batavia is the man because of its *strijtbaaheid* (severity) and Mataram the woman because of her ignorance and laxity of discipline'.[66] The view of women as weak and unsuited to leadership is equally pronounced in Vietnam, where Confucianism constantly stressed the subservience of wives to husbands, and considered that village heads should unquestionably be male. Popular mythology itself suffered, for Confucianism downplayed the role of the Trung sisters, and a fifteenth-century account claimed their followers ran away because they saw that their leader 'was a woman [and] feared she could not stand up to the enemy'.[67]

This is not to argue, however, that existing attitudes and values were eclipsed or that women were being passively moulded by imported ideas. Even in the context of male-oriented religions, the old female-fertility motif resurfaces. One Islamic text, for instance, tells the story of how the daughter of the great teacher Abdul Kadir (1077/8–1166) successfully petitioned God to send rain.[68] Nor is the sexual aspect of worship lost. Muslim teachers of mystical Islam (which seemed to be more tolerant of female adepts) often compared the religious experience to marriage; an Acehnese text thus describes the bliss of oneness with God in terms of the sexual union between man and woman.[69] Certainly the 'official' view of appropriate female activities did not mean the end of pragmatism and humour. The seventeenth-century Malay text, the *Hikayat Bayan Budiman*, thus exhorts any woman who has lost her husband to act quickly and find another man, so that her youth and vigour shall not be wasted.[70]

Despite such continuities, it is clear that by the end of the eighteenth century the religious role of females in

Southeast Asia generally was considerably reduced from earlier times. Women certainly retained their old roles as midwives, as healers, and spirit mediums, and in southern Vietnam at the end of the eighteenth century an English traveller still commented on the number of 'priestesses' in the country.[71] Yet the prestige and influence of women in this area was diminishing. Islamic teachers and Christian missionaries alike railed against the continuing practice of spirit propitiation, where women had traditionally assumed such a prominent place. Such influence were also in places where world religions had not taken hold. In one Igorot settlement in the Philippines, for example, a chief and his son welcomed the Spanish priest, ignoring the warnings of a group of female shamans and even driving them away.[72] Through the Malay–Indonesian world men learned in Islam also filled many roles once taken by shamans in state ceremonies. The phenomenon known as *latah*, associated with spirit possession, came to be regarded as a female malady that provided evidence of women's 'weaker spiritual strength'.[73] In the same mode, seventeenth-century Vietnam Confucian edicts attempted to reform popular customs by reiterating that it was not appropriate for a woman to preside over offerings to the spirits of deceased male forebears.[74] The amalgamation of female with male, so integral to indigenous religions, also aroused doctrinal ire; the famous Islamic scholar Abd al-Samad al-Palembani, in translating a well-known Arabic treatise, may even have altered the original slightly to strengthen the Malay version's condemnation of men who wore women's clothes and did women's work.[75]

In the Theravada Buddhist countries, often regarded as more tolerant of indigenous practices, there was a continuing effort to limit spirit propitiation. A king of Laos even issued an order in 1527 banning spirit worship and ordering the destruction of all sanctuaries associated with them. Rama I of Siam (1782–1809) listed the various types of spirits and deities who could be legitimately honoured, but reminded his subjects that good fortune came from *kamma*, not from the intervention of spirits and gods.[76] Such edicts must have contributed to a lessening of the status of spirit mediums. An English sea captain in the early eighteenth century described how women and 'hermaphrodites' at a Burmese feast 'danced a dance to the gods of the earth', but there is a significant absence of any *nat kadaw* (nat wives) in spirit appeasement at the court levels, where brahmins and monks were in charge of ritual. Because women were the principal practitioners of 'village' as opposed to 'court' magic, they were far more likely to be accused of unacceptable practices such as witchcraft, and a Burmese law of 1785 provides detailed instructions for immersion of a woman in water 'to find out if she is a witch'.[77]

Conclusion

The relationship between men and women lies at the heart of Southeast Asian societies and should therefore be an important focus for historical research. The implications of sexuality underlay all indigenous religious ritual, yet studies devoted specifically to this topic have only recently begun to appear.[78] In the religious context, as elsewhere, it should be possible to bring a comparative perspective to a discussion of women's 'high status' in Southeast Asia, and to place greater emphasis on changes in 'traditional' society, all too often regarded as essentially static. It has been suggested here that despite the undoubted prominence of women in indigenous religious beliefs and practice, there was always an ambiguous attitude to the sexual potency they represented. Ritual prestige may have been ultimately vested not so much in women but in males who incorporated female attributes. In a number of ways the introduction of the world religions strengthened underlying fears of the 'danger' inherent in female sexuality, and to this was added a political and legal system that affirmed women's lesser position.

Current research is demonstrating that the male-female interaction in religious beliefs is characterized by an ongoing process of adjustment to changing circumstances. For example, a recent study sees the dominance of male mediums among the Temiar of the Malay Peninsula as a modern,

Malay-influenced phenomenon, while showing that women still play an important role as 'spirit guides'. The fragility of the male–female ritual linkage, however, is suggested in other research from northern Thailand; here the introduction of new crops and consequent economic change has led to increasing gender disparity. A series of studies in Borneo and eastern Indonesian societies reminds us of the range in male–female relationships, and of the fact that every generalization needs to be constantly tested.[79]

Anthropologists have been at the forefront of gender studies in Southeast Asia. The research produced has been exciting and has undoubtedly fundamentally and permanently influenced the way in which we approach the region. However, the concentration on contemporary developments has fostered an implicit assumption that change, adjustment, and the socialization process are only characteristic of recent times. Historians of pre-modern Southeast Asia have a particular responsibility to return to their material to search for possible answers to new questions. Lying at the cultural core of Southeast Asia, religion and ritual provide a specific environment in which the interaction between men and women can be explored. A strong historical base is vital if the diverse ways in which this relationship has evolved are to be satisfactorily explained.

Notes

Earlier drafts of this paper were presented to the 10th International Asian Studies Conference, Victoria University of Wellington, July 1993; to the Fourth Women in Asia Conference, University of Melbourne, October 1993; and to the Centre of South East Asian Studies, SOAS, October 1993. I am grateful to Judy Ledgerwood for her comments.

1. Edward H. Schafer, *The Vermilion Bird and Images of the South* (Berkeley and Los Angeles, University of California Press, 1967), p. 80; J. Macmillan Brown, *The Dutch East: Sketches and Pictures* (London, Kegan Paul, 1914), p. 125; William Marsden, *The History of Sumatra* (Kuala Lumpur, Oxford University Press, 1975), pp. 265–66; Robbins

Burling, *Hill Farms and Paddy Fields Life in Mainland Southeast Asia* (Englewood Cliffs, New Jersey, Prentice Hall, 1965), p. 2.

2. Anthony Reid, *Southeast Asia in the Age of Commerce 1450-1680.* vol. 1; *The Lands Below the Winds* (New Haven and London, Yale University Press, 1988), pp. 146; 162; see also his 'Female Roles in Pre-colonial Southeast Asia', *Modern Asian Studies*, 22, 3 (1988), pp. 629-45.
3. Charles Higham, *The Archaeology of Mainland Southeast Asia. From 10 000 BC to the Fall of Angkor* (Cambridge University Press, 1989), p. 77; Robert Blust, 'Linguistic Evidence for some Early Austronesian Taboos', *American Anthropologist*, 83. 2 (1981), p. 292 and 'Early Austronesian Social Organization: the Evidence of Language', *Current Anthropology*, 21. 2 (April1980), p. 215.
4. Ibn Battuta, *Travels in Asia and Africa 1325-1354*, trans. and ed. by H. A. R. Gibb (New York, Augustus M. Kelley, 1969; Reprint of 1929 edition), p. 321; George Brooks, 'The Signares of Saint-Louis and Goree: Women Entrepreneurs in Eighteenth-Century Senegal', in Nancy J. Hafkin and Edna G. Bay, *Women in Africa: Studies in Social and Economic Changes* (Stanford University Press, 1976), p. 20.
5. Peter Bellwood has argued for the agricultural ancestry of Austronesian-speaking hunting and gathering groups in contemporary Southeast Asia. Peter Bellwood, *Prehistory of the Indo-Malaysian Archipelago* (Sydney, Academic Press, 1985), p. 132.
6. See Jane Monnig Atkinson, 'Gender in Wana Society', in Jane Monnig Atkinson and Shelly Errington, *Power and Difference; Gender in Island Southeast Asia* (Stanford University Press, 1990), p.76.
7. Claire Holt, *Art in Indonesia* (Ithaca and London, Cornell University Press, 1967), pp. 12, 25; Gerrit Knaap, 'Kruidnagelen en Christenen. De Verenigde Oost-Indische Compagnie en de Bevolking van Ambon 1656-1696', Ph.D. Dissertation, Utrecht University, 1988, p. 108.
8. Roxanna M. Brown, *The Ceramics of South-East Asia. Their Dating and Identification* (Kuala Lumpur, Oxford University Press, 1977), pp. 53, 260-61; Holt, pp. 26-7.
8. Knaap, p. 108.
10. Leonard Y. Andaya, *The World of Maluku. Eastern Indonesia in the Early Modern Period* (Honolulu, University of Hawaii Press, 1993), p. 53; *Readings in Philippine Prehistory* (Manila, Filipina Book Guild, 1979), p. 199; Holt, pp. 26, 173; Knaap suggests early stories resembled those collected in later times (pp. 88–9). See also the figures with exaggerated genitalia depicted in a traditional design on a cloth from Lampung, South Sumatra in Robyn Maxwell, *Textiles of Southeast Asia: Tradition, Trade and Transformation* (Melbourne, Australian National Gallery and Oxford University Press, 1990), p. 133. A detailed account of the pairing of male and female in contemporary Kodi Society is in Janet Hoskins, 'Doubling Deities, Descent and Personhood: An Exploration of Kodi Gender Categories', in Atkinson and Errington, pp. 273–306.
11. Teresita R. Infante, *The Woman in Early Philippines and among the Cultural Minorities* (Manila, University of Santo Tomas, 1975), pp. 167-94; Walter Irvine, 'Decline of Village Spirit Cults and Growth of Urban Spirit Mediumship: the Persistence of Spirit Beliefs, the Position of Women and Modernization', *Mankind*, 14.4 (August 1984), p. 315. One

notes, however, the preference for men in some societies, e.g. Atkinson, 'Gender in Wana Society', in Atkinson and Errington, p. 89; Albert E. Jenks, *The Bontoc Igorot* (Manila, Bureau of Public Printing, 1905) p. 205.

12. *Readings in Philippine Prehistory*, pp. 202, 212.
13. *Dagh Register Gehouden int Casteel te Batavia* (Batavia and The Hague, Bataviaasch Genootschap; Nijhoff; Kolff, 1887-1931), 1646, p. 64.
14. See Reid, *Southeast Asia in the Age of Commerce*, I, p. 167; Keith Taylor, *The Birth of Vietnam* (Berkeley and Los Angeles, University of California Press, 1983) pp. 334-39; Leonard Y. Andaya, *The Heritage of Arung Palakka. Southwest Sulawesi (Celebes) in the Seventeenth Century* (The Hague: Nijhoff, 1981), p. 86.
15. Eric Anderson, 'Traditions in Conflict: Filipino Responses to Spanish Colonialism, 1565-1665,' Ph.D. Dissertation, University of Sydney, 1977, pp. 97, 100.
16. Solange Hertz (trans.), *Rhodes of Vietnam* (Westminster, Maryland, The Newman Press, 1966), pp. 117-18.
17. Blust, 'Linguistic Evidence', p. 300; see Barbara Watson Andaya, *To Live as Brothers: Southeast Sumatra in the Seventeenth and Eighteenth Centuries* (Honolulu: University of Hawaii Press, 1993), pp. 27-8.
18. The most thoughtful discussion of this topic in Southeast Asia is Valerio Valeri, 'Both Nature and Culture: Reflections on Menstrual and Partuitional Taboos in Huaulu (Seram)', in Atkinson and Errington, *Power and Difference*, pp. 235–72. Eastern Indonesian societies may be more similar to those of Australia and Melanesia in the degree of polluting qualities attached to menstruation and childbirth.
19. J. G. Casparis, *Prasasti Indonesia* (Bundung, Masa Baru, 1956), pp. 4; 30; 39; 40-1.
20. Chou Ta-Kuan, *Notes on the Customs of Cambodia*, describes ritual deflowering, although such practices may have occurred only among the elite; Knaap, p. 92; *Readings in Philippine Prehistory*, p. 355.
21. See Laura W. R. Appell, 'Menstruation among the Rungus of Borneo: an Unmarked Category', in Thomas Buckley and Alma Gottlieb, *Blood Magic. The Anthropology of Menstruation* (Berkeley, University of California Press, 1988), pp. 94–112; Anna Lowenhaupt Tsing, 'Gender and Performance in Meratus Dispute Settlement', in Atkinson and Errington, p. 100.
22. Taylor, p. 28; for further references, see Barbara Watson Andaya, 'Statecraft in the Reign of Lu Tai of Sukhodaya (ca. 1347-1374)', in Bardwell L. Smith, *Religion and Legitimation of Power in Thailand, Laos, and Burma* (Chambersburg PA.: Anima Books, 1978), pp. 7 and 17 n.37. The position of Puteri Jamilan in Minangkabau provides a telling Indonesian example. See Leonard Y. Andaya, *The Kingdom of Johor 1641-1728. Economic and Political Developments* (Kuala Lumpur, Oxford University Press, 1975), pp. 250–51; 260–62; 331.
23. James J. Fox, 'The Ordering of Generation: Change and Continuity in Old Javanese Kinship', in David Marr and A. C. Milner, *Southeast Asia in the 9th to 14th Centuries* (Canberra, Research School of Pacific Studies, Australian National University, 1986), p. 324; Francisco Demetrio, *Myths and Symbols* (Manila, Metro Manila, 1978), pp. 103–4.

I am grateful to Dr Jim Collins for reminding me that sexual differention in Malay kinship terms may be relatively recent.

24. J. M. van der Kroef, *Indonesia in the Modern World* (Bandung, Masa Baru, 1956), II. p. 152.
25. Tome Pires, *Suma Oriental: An Account of the East from the Red Sea to Japan*, trans. A Cortesao (London, Hakluyt Society, 1944), II. p. 179; B. F. Matthes, 'Over de Bissoe's of heidensche priesters en priesteressen der Boeginezen' (originally published in 1872), in H. van den Brink, *Dr. Benjamin Frederik Matthes. Zijn leven en arbeid in dienst van het Nederlandsch Bijbelgenootschap* (Amsterdam, Nederlands Bijbelgenootschap, 1943); Gilbert Harmonic, *Le Langage des Dieux. Cultes et Powoirs Pre-Islamiques en pays Bugis Celebes-Sud, Indonesie* (Paris, National Centre for Scientific Research, 1987); Anderson, 'Traditions in Conflict', pp. 97, 146.
26. For examples of women as soldiers, see Reid, pp. 637-38.
27. Infante, *The Women in Early Philippines*, p 194.
28. Valerio Valeri, *Kingship and Sacrifice. Ritual and Society in Ancient Hawaii* (Chicago, University of Chicago Press, 1985), p. 113.
29. Margaret Ehrenberg, *Women in Prehistory* (London, British Museum Publications, 1989), p. 77.
30. For a fuller discussion, see Arvind Sharma (ed.), *Women in World Religions* (New York, State University of New York, 1987).
31. Urs Ramseyer, *The Art and Culture of Bali* (New York, Oxford University Press, 1977), p. 107; Schafer, *The Vermilion Bird*, p. 74; Keith Taylor, 'Authority and Legitamacy in 11th century Vietnam', in Marr and Milner, p. 161; Bruce Cruikshank, *Samar 1768-1898* (Manila, Historical Conservation Society, 1986), p. 86.
32. An eleventh-century Vietnamese hero, for example, is portrayed as a man so virtuous he wakens a powerful female spirit who promises to bring prosperity to the realm (Taylor, p. 161). Senapati, the legendary founder of the dynasty of Mataram, was according to legend taken below the water and taught how to make all the spirits serve him. See H. J. de Graaf, *De Regeering van Panembahan Senapati Ingalaga* (The Hague, Nijhoff, 1954), pp. 75–7; see also Andaya, *To Live as Brothers*, p. 113.
33. For further discussion, see Nguyen The Anh, 'Texts related to the Vietnamization of the Cham Deity Po Nagar', presented to the SEASSI Symposium of Vietnamese History, Cornell University, July 1991.
34. G. E. Harvey, *History of Burma* (London, Frank Cass, 1967. Reprint of 1925 edition), p. 104; B. Schrieke, *Indonesion Sociological Studies*, II (The Hague and Bandung, W. van Hoeve, 1957), pp. 72-3.
35. R. C. Zaehner, *Hinduism* (New York, Oxford University Press, 1966), pp. 16; 44.
36. Paul Mus, *India Seen from the East: Indian and Indigenous Cults in Champa*, translated and edited by David Chandler and Ian Mabbett (Melbourne, Centre for Southeast Asian Studies, 1975), pp. 14-15; 39. See the plates reproduced in Nora Taylor, 'La sculpture tardive du Campa et son complement malais', in *Le Campa et Le Monde Malais* (Centre d'historie Civilisations de la Peninsule Indochinoise: Paris, 1991), Fig. 3.

37. Th. G. Th. Pigeaud, *Java in the 14th Century*, IV (The Hague, Nijhoff, 1963), p. 105; N. J. Smith-Hefner, 'Pembaron: An East Javanese Rite of Priestly Rebirth', *Journal of Southeast Asian Studies*, 23. 2 (September 1992) pp. 237–75; Holt, p. 26.
38. For evidence of female economic roles, see Reid, I, pp. 164–65. Tenth-century inscriptions from Java show that village women entered into contracts, incurred debts, owned property, and took an active part in ceremonies connected with the granting of land for freehold domains. Women could either inherit or acquire titles in their own right, and there is evidence that they took a prominent part in village decision-making. N. C. van Setten van der Meer, *Sawah Cultivation in Ancient Java*, Oriental Monograph Series no. 22 (Canberra, Australian National University Press, 1979), pp. 94–6; Antoinette M. Barrett Jones, *Early Tenth Century Java from the Inscriptions. A Study of Economic, Social and Administrative Conditions in the First Quarter of the century* (The Hague, Nijhoff, 1979), pp. 96-8.
39. Alphons van der Kraan, 'Human Sacrifice in Bali: Sources, Note and Commentary', *Indonesia*, 40 (October 1985), p. 119; Pires, II, p. 176.
40. Russell Jones (ed and trans.), *Hikayat Sultan Ibrahim bin Adham* (Berkeley, Center for South and Southeast Asian Studies, University of California, 1985), pp. 173-5.
41. See Valeri, pp. 243-61; Anke Niehof, 'Mediating Roles of the Traditional Birth Attendànt in Indonesia', in Sita van Bemmelen et al., *Women and Mediation in Indonesia* (Leiden, KILTV Press, 1992), pp. 17-15. In J. Ras, *Hikajat Banjar: A Study in Malay Historiography* (The Hague, Nijhoff, 1968), p. 345, a court lady is cut open on her left side, dying so that her daughter, destined to marry the king, will not be born through an unclean passage. But according to an eighteenth-century text on Malay customs, kings were present at the birth of their children. Panuti H. M. Sudjiman (ed.), *Adat Raja-Raja Melayu* (Jakarta, University of Indonesia Press, 1983), pp. 60; 220.
42. Laurence Palmer Briggs, *The Ancient Khmer Empire* (Philadelphia, Transactions of the American Philosophical Society, 1951), p. 50; Chou Ta Kuan, *Notes on the Customs of Cambodia*, p. 24. Women in Khmer Buddhism are discussed by Judy Ledgerwood, 'Changing Khmer Conceptions of Gender: Women, Stories and the Social Order', Ph.D. Dissertation, Cornell University, 1990, pp. 33–64.
43. G. H. Luce and Pe Maung Tin, *Selections from the Inscriptions of Pagan* (Rangoon, British Burma Press, 1928), no. 53, p. 149, cited in Michael Aung Thwin, *Pagan. The Origins of Modern Burma* (Honolulu, University of Hawaii Press, 1985), p. 34.
44. Aung Thwin, p. 36.
45. Simon de la Loubere, *The Kingdom of Siam*, ed. David K. Wyatt (Kuala Lumpur, Oxford University Press, 1969), p. 113.
46. My view of indigenous female literacy here differs somewhat from that of Reid, p. 639.
47. In Malacca in the late eighteenth century the grandmother of Munshi Abdullah, the daughter of an Islamic official, was a well-known teacher of the Koran. See A. H. Hill, *The Hikayat Abdullah* (Kuala Lumpur, Oxford University Press, 1970), p. 38.

48. John S. Caroll, 'Beranai in the Boxer Codex', *Journal of the Malaysian Branch of the Royal Asiatic Society*, (hence JMBRAS), 55. 2 (1982), p. 9.
49. Nicholas Gervaise, *An Historical Description of Macassar in the East Indies* (London, Leigh and Midwinter, 1701), pp. 158–59.
50. Othman bin Mohd. Yatim, 'Ancient Gravestones in Peninsular Malaysia. A Brief Survey', *Federation Museum Journal*, vol. 21, New Series, 1976, cited in Wayne A. Bougas, 'Some Early Islamic Tombstones in Patani', *JMBRAS* , 54. 1 (1986), pp. 97; 99.
51. Hubert Jacobs, *Documenta Malucensia* (Rome, Jesuit Historical Institution, 1980), III, p. 539.
52. Pablo Fernandez, *History of the Church in the Phiippines (1521-1898)* (Manila, Metro Manila, 1979), pp. 72; 164; 173–74.
53. Elizabeth Uy Eviota, *The Political Economy of Gender: Women and the Sexual Division of Labour in the Philippines* (London, Zed Books, 1992), pp. 41-2; de la Costa, *The Jesuits in the Philippines 1581-1768* (Havard, Harvard University Press, 1961), p. 156.
54. Schrieke, II, p. 78.
55. Ismail Hamid, *The Malay Islamic Hikayat* (Kuala Lumpur, University Kebangsaan Malaysia, 1983), pp. 64; 86; 90; 119; 177; the Koran, 24: 2-4 says an adulterer should be stoned to death if married, or given a hundred lashes if not.
56. Tan Van Tai, 'The Status of Women in Traditional Vietnam: A Comparison of the Code of the Le Dynasty (1428-1788) with the Chinese Codes', *Journal of Asian History*, 15 (1981), p. 102.
57. Peter Worsley, 'Narrative Bas-Reliefs at Candi Surawana', in Marr and Milner, pp. 335-68.
58. Chou Ta-Kuan, *Notes on the Customs of Cambodia*, p. 25; Taylor, *The Birth of Vietnam*, p. 77; Pires, *Suma Oriental*, II p. 178; Izaak Commelin, *Begin en Voortgangh van de Vereenighde Nederlantsche Geoctroyeerde Oost-Indische Compagnie* (Amsterdam, Theatrum Orbis Terrarum, 1970. Reprint of 1646 edition), I, p. 69; Hamid, *The Malay Islamic Hikayat*, p. 57.
59. See Miguel de Loarco's remarks of 1582 in *Readings in Philippine Prehistory*, p. 198; Eviota, *The Political Economy of Gender*, p. 41.
60. Knaap, pp. 103; 109. One recent study has pointed out that 17 of the 44 chapters in the Malacca Code mention women, but all except three are concerned with sexual offences, usually illicit intercourse. See further Brenda M. Fane, 'Against the Grain: A Post Structuralist Analysis of the Representation of Women in Traditional Malay Literature'. B.A. Honours Thesis, Australian National University, 1993.
61. Tan Van Tai, 'The Status of Women in Traditional Vietnam', pp. 97–145.
62. A. Thomas .Kirsch, 'Kinship, Genealogical Claims, and Societal Integration in Ancient Khmer Society: An Interpretation', in C. D. Cowan and O. W. Wolters, *Southeast Asian History and Historiography: Essays Presented to D. G. E. Hall* (Ithaca, Cornell University Press, 1976), pp. 190–202; J. S. Furnivall, 'Matriarchal Vestiges in Burma', *Journal of the Burma Research Society*, 1. 1 (1911), p. 21.
63. Cited in John A. Williams, *Themes of Islamic Civilization* (Berkeley and London, University of California Press, 1975), p. 105.

64. Commelin, *Begin en Voortgangh*, I, p. 38.
65. 'Translation of the Annals of Acheen', *Journal of the Indian Archipelago and Eastern Asia*, 4, 1850, p. 599.
66. H. J. de Graaf, *De Vijf Gezantschapreizen van Ryklof van Goens naar het Hof van Mataram 1648-1654* (The Hague, Nijhoff, 1956), p. 145.
67. Taylor, *The Birth of Vietnam*, p. 41.
68. G. W. J. Drewes and R. Ng Dr Poerbatjaraka, *De Mirakelen van Abdoelkadir Djaelani* (Bandung, Nix & Co., 1938), p. 50.
69. P. Voorhoeve, 'Three Old Achehnese Manuscripts, *Bulletin of the School of Oriental and African Studies*, 14 (1951-2), p. 340.
70. Cited in R. O. Winstedt, *A History of Malay Literature* (Kuala Lumpur, Oxford University Press, 1969), p. 118.
71. John Barrow, *A Voyage to Cochinchina* (Kuala Lumpur, Oxford University Press, 1975, Reprint of 1800 edition), p. 329.
72. William Henry Scott, *The Discovery of the Igorots. Spanish Contacts with the Pagans of Northern Luzon* (Quezon City, New Day Publishers, 1974), p. 97.
73. Aihwa Ong, 'Japanese Factories, Malay Workers: Class and Sexual Metaphors in West Malaysia', in Atkinson and Errington, *Power and Difference*, p. 389 Robert L. Winzeler, 'The Study of Malayan Latah', *Indonesia*, 37 (April 1984), pp. 77-104.
74. Insun Yu, 'Law and Family in Seventeenth and Eighteenth Century Vietnam', Ph.D. Dissertation, University of Michigan, Ann Arbor, 1978, p. 137.
75. G. W. J. Drewes, 'Further Data Concerning Abd al-Samad al-Palembani', *Bijdragen tot de Taal-, Land-, en Volkenkunde*, 132, 2-3 (1976), pp. 279-81.
76. George Condominas, 'Phiban Cults in Rural Laos', in G. W. Skinner and A. Thomas Kirsch (eds), *Change and Persistence in Thai Society. Essays in Honor of Lauriston Sharp* (Ithaca, Cornell University Press, 1975), p. 253; A. Thomas Kirsch, 'Complexity in the Thai Religious Systems: an Interpretation', *Journal of Asian Studies*, 36. 2 (Feb. 1977), p. 241.
77. Alexander Hamilton, *A New Account of the East Indies*, William Foster (ed.), (London, Argonaut Press, 1930, reprint of 1727 edition), II, p. 31; Than Tun, *Royal Orders of Burma, A.D. 1598-1885. IV A.D. 1782-1787* (Kyoto, Center for Southeast Asian Studies, University of Kyoto, 1886), p. 102.
78. A few years ago one Indonesian even complained that 'the position of women in religion has received relatively scant interest, even by anthropologists working in eastern Indonesia, a region in which women and the feminine principle are of especial religious importance'. David Hicks, *A Maternal Religion: The Role of Women in Tetum Myth and Ritual* (DeKalb, Northern Illinois University, Center for Southeast Asian Studies. Special Report No. 22, 1984), pp. 3-4.
79. Marina Roseman, *Healing Sounds from the Malaysian Rainforest: Temiar Music and Medicine* (Berkeley, Los Angeles, University of California Press, 1991), pp. 123; 127-8; Otome Klein Hutheesing, *Emerging Sexual Inequality among the Lisu of Northern Thailand* (Leiden, Brill, 1990). See also Nancy Everhardt (ed.), *Gender, Power and the*

Construction of the Moral Order: Studies from the Thai Periphery (Madison, University of Wisconsin-Madison, Center for Southeast Asian Studies, Monograph 4, 1988); Vinson H. Sutlive, Jr. *Female and Male in Borneo: Contributions and Challenges to Gender Studies* (Williamsburg, VA: The Borneo Research Council, n.d. [1992?]); Atkinson and Errington, *Power and Difference.*

From Theory to Practice: Reflections on Legal Literacy Work with Women in India

Ratna Kapur

Feminism and the Liberal Discourse of Rights

The Women's Movement is not a universal movement in India. It is a diversity of movements, ranging from party affiliated women's organizations to regional autonomous women's groups that differ in terms of class, ethnicity, language and region. To speak of a homogenous group would obscure the diversity of the movement, which has in many respects been its strength. While there is no common experience of the women's movement, the law has, nevertheless, been a common site of struggle for many, although by no means all, women.

Rights and law have played an integral part in the women's movement for social change in India over the past decade. In a country where there is no uniform family law, it is governed by the laws of the different communities. Therefore, Hindus are governed by Hindu law, Muslims by Muslim law, Christians, Parsis and Jews by their respective personal laws. Feminists have struggled for, and to some extent achieved, legal reform of the rape and dowry laws and are still demanding reform in different personal laws, and in laws relating to *sati* and amniocentesis.[1]

In the area of rape, women have secured significant reforms in the laws governing rape by persons in authority, including police officers, in which case a presumption in favour of the rape survivor and a mandatory minimum sentence of ten years for the offender have been established.[2] The dowry issue was addressed through several amendments in the Dowry Prohibition Act and its succeeding acts. The amendments aimed at preventing the giving or taking of dowry at the time of, or in connection with, a marriage.

With respect to personal law, there has been considerable debate over the question of lobbying for a uniform civil code that would be applicable to all persons regardless of their religious conviction or affiliation.[3] Several petitions are currently pending in the Supreme Court of India challenging the *sati* law and seeking the closure of temples glorifying or worshiping *sati*.[4] Women's organizations are also lobbying for legislation to ban the practice of amniocentesis. The main strategy pursued by the women's movement has involved lobbying for law reform, and raising constitutional challenges by using the discourse of rights in the courts. This strategy can be seen to be informed by a liberal understanding of law that focuses on the individual and on the need to protect individual rights from the state. Although the approach taken by the women's movement has secured formal rights for women, this liberal approach precludes an understanding or inquiry into the deeper relationships of oppression underlying and sustained by the law, particularly of the economic relationships that make people unequal, notwithstanding formal equal treatment.[5] For example, although the women's movement has put a considerable amount of energy into securing reform of the dowry law, the demands for dowry and dowry murders persist, and are on the increase. The Act remains unworkable, primarily because of the liberal discourse adopted by the Act and used by much of the women's movement in lobbying for change. The strategy of liberal discourse precludes an analysis of the underlying factors responsible for dowry, the unequal economic relationships between men and women and the patriarchal relationships on which the family is based. The issue can be addressed only in terms of individual rights and remedies, rather than the relationships within the family and the broader socioeconomic context that deny women access to property and wealth.[6] Similarly, despite the challenges and amendments to the rape law, rapes continue to happen, women do not report them, and the acquittal rates remain disturbingly high in those cases that are reported and tried. The failure of the rape law reflects the movement's failure to sufficiently inform women of how such laws can be useful in their struggles for some semblance of equality.

An interactive approach to education about law must also be adopted in which the women actively participate in the learning process. Recognizing the limitations of a mere information-giving approach, it is important to work with methods that do not treat participants as passive listeners, but as active participants in producing knowledge for their benefit. As Paul and Dias see it, the role of the educator or facilitator is to actively engage the participants, contextualize the learning process within their own lives, and provide the legal and technical tools for the participants to decide if and how law can be useful in their struggles for social transformation [7]

A feminist approach to legal literacy involves education to empower women for action and change rather than simply conveying information about law. The objective of a feminist approach to legal literacy is to develop consciousness that enables participants to think critically about the power relationships sustained by the law that affect women's lives, and ultimately, to take action to challenge and transform these relations. It begins from and includes this understanding of both the limits and possibilities of law.

In terms of pedagogy, we must place ourselves within the framework of the learning process, and attempt to break down the hierarchy and distance from the women with whom we are working, recognizing that there is no such thing as the universal 'we'.[8] We are not all situated similarly in terms of power and privilege. Yet we must also move beyond the 'us and them' approach to education. Such an approach treats the other as unknowledgeable and inexperienced, and the educator as possessing all relevant experience and knowledge. It sets up a hierarchy between the participant and the educator that treats the former as passive and ignorant. Ideally, the pedagogical process must involve a sharing of our experiences, placing our differences before the group, and most importantly, acknowledging our positions of power and privilege. We need to be conscious of our power and acknowledge it. We must work with it so it does not cultivate dependence, but works to politicize women struggling for self-empowerment. We need to continuously think about our use of power and the equations we set up with one another.

It is also essential that legal literacy be integrated into broader educational programs for women who similarly seek to provide other women with opportunities to participate in learning, acquiring information, and understanding their social context. In isolation, legal literacy programs will only reinforce a non-contextualized conception of law and its role in our struggles for social change. Isolated legal literacy could lead to a further reliance on law and lawyers, and hurt the women it is intended to benefit by encouraging them to see law and rights as the solution to their problems. Only by integrating legal literacy strategies with these broader programs will women learn about the law in the context of the broader social movement they are creating, and strategies for using law will be developed that are responsive and accountable to this social movement.

A feminist approach to legal literacy, therefore, provides knowledge about law that will be empowering to women and bring them to understand what the law means in the context of their lives. Women must be allowed to reflect upon their lives, to work towards an understanding of the violations that have occurred in their lives, link these violations with broader structural causes such as class, caste or gender, and understand how these structures are supported and sustained in the law. The process develops critical consciousness about women's subordinate position in society, the role of the law in reinforcing that subordination, and hopefully leads to the development of strategies for social change.

Legal Literacy: In Action

The most difficult challenge lies in translating this preferred approach to legal literacy into action. Beginning from the premise that legal literacy for women should be situated in broader-based educational programs involving issues such as health, public administration and labour, I have done legal literacy with different community-based groups and programs involved in such processes. Through these experiences, I have become aware of the extent of differences among their approaches, their process of interaction with the communities, and their understanding of empowerment.

In the following sections, I will describe and evaluate the extent to which these different approaches facilitate and/or limit legal literacy. My remarks are based on my experiences and observations in attempting to conduct legal literacy with various groups. They are tentative and mediated through the partiality of my experience and perspective. I am attempting to build on my previous work where I have tried to explore how legal literacy can contribute to the transformation of women's lives. I will relate the stories of three different experiences with three very different approaches to community-based development and education. The first story concerns a development organization working with women in some urban slums in a northern industrial city in India. The second story is about rural women from a southern state participating in a government education program for women's equality. The third story relates to a workshop conducted by a feminist organization with rural women from a northern state.

The First Story: The Development Organization

The first group involved a development organization working with women in some urban slums in a major industrial city in northern India. I visited the organization to explore the possibility of doing legal literacy workshops with the women.[9] The organization, like many other development organizations working with women, focused its activities on saving schemes and income generation. Little or no attention had been given to consciousness raising and participatory education for women from a feminist perspective.

I visited the slums and in my conversations with women, became aware of the horrors of dowry and its effect on poor women's lives. When I inquired into the nature of these demands I learned that dowry demands over the past two years had risen to extortionate proportions. Yet women did not question the giving and taking of dowry and accepted it as a part of being born a daughter. There had been little focus on the question of dowry by the development organization ,whose major concern was the economic empowerment of women. The issue of dowry had been discussed and some space created, perhaps for women to speak about their pain or the violence in their lives. However, the discussions were limited to sharing some experiences of dowry without addressing the underlying conditions that are responsible for the harms caused by dowry. Without making these connections, women will not begin to understand that dowry is not a natural condition, but socially determined. Naming the personal pain is not adequate for changing consciousness. Naming women's pain in relation to structures of domination is also an essential part of the process for coming to political consciousness.[10] This understanding must then be linked to the overall struggle for developing collective political resistance.

The development organization had not emphasized developing critical consciousness in their interactions with the women. Their focus on economic empowerment reflected their analysis of women's condition primarily within the structures of international class inequalities. Like many development organizations, they operated from the assumption that women's position will improve if and when international structures become more equitable.[11] In the meantime, the organization focused on developing intervention strategies designed to address women's under-representation in economic, political and social structures. Savings schemes and income generating activities were encouraged. The common assumption is that access to income will be a sufficiently powerful stimulant to encourage women to rearrange their time so that they can take part in yet another activity. However, these schemes often exhibit a lack of awareness of the experience of women's lives, particularly the extent to which women are already overburdened with tasks and responsibilities.[12] Yet when participating in a savings scheme, women will most often save on themselves, by eating less or spending less money on their health care. The internalized notions of good wife and mother keep women from spending less on their husbands and children. Such schemes do not challenge the traditional system or structures of power within the home, nor do they analyze women's situation in terms of the relationship between patriarchal attitudes, differing modes of production, and women's subordination.[13] It did not, and does not work toward a fundamental shift in the social relations of gender.

This approach to development affects the approach to legal literacy. Focusing on income generation or savings schemes for women does not create awareness of the connections between such developmental activities and women's position in society, a necessary condition for empowering education and for situating legal literacy. Further, if the organization is involved in income generation or savings schemes, it would be primarily interested in learning about those aspects of law related to these schemes. Other aspects of women's lives such as violence in the home, contraception, and child bearing and rearing would not necessarily be addressed and thus remain invisible because of a focus on income activities.

There is a direct link between the model of development being pursued and the issues that will be addressed in a legal literacy scheme set up by the organization. Unless such groups question their development approach and its lack of gender focus, any effort to do legal literacy for women that is empowering will be limited. Instead of focusing exclusively on service-oriented activities, there needs to be a greater emphasis on critical consciousness. This involves developing a process that encourages a critical understanding or approach to development and its impact on women. Legal literacy should be incorporated into this broader educational process. Otherwise, legal literacy would give rise to all the standard problems associated with the traditional model; that is, information-giving and looking to the law for solutions. There is a need for groundwork, in the form of critical consciousness, to be done before legal literacy programs are introduced.

The Second Story: The Government Program's Equality Fair

A second experience with conducting legal literacy involved a large number of women. An information or knowledge fair was organized for village women participating in a government program of education for women's equality in Karnataka. More than 1300 village women participated in the three-day fair.

A law workshop was organized for the fair, to be conducted with the participation of three to four hundred different women per session.[14] Each session was four hours, and one session was conducted on each of the three days. Conducting the workshop had both strengths and limitations. Ideally, the process should be conducted with small numbers of women in spaces that are specifically for women, over a long period of time. At the fair, it was not possible to adopt such a process to produce a feminist consciousness about the law.

Given the limitations, as facilitators we still had to work out methods that did not reduce the workshop to merely giving information to women about the law. We focused on our objective of enabling women to challenge the understanding of the law as a solution to the problems and violations they had experienced in their lives. The first concern was to identify the issues to be addressed with the participants. As gender consciousness had been a focus of the program over the two years, some specific issues concerning women emerged from each area.[15] Women had become aware of oppression within their lives as they were given space in the program to articulate and understand these experiences. Different communities of rural women attended the workshop, including *devadasi* women,[16] *adivasi* women,[17] and scheduled caste women.[18] They experienced a range of problems including the dedication of women to temples, the expulsion of tribal women from their forest dwellings, sexual assault, domestic violence, cruelty, bigamy, and desertion. Accordingly, we decided to address the specific concerns of a different community of women each day.

On the first day we addressed the problems of *adivasi* women and the forest laws. On the subsequent day, the issues of *devadasi* and prostitution were addressed, and on the final day, we dealt with the concerns of other rural women, specifically in the context of the family. We found that the fear or experience of sexual assault was common to all women, regardless of their diverse cultural and economic background. We decided to address the issue of sexual assault with each group, on each of the three days.

Within this framework, we then decided to use only one hour to convey some information on the issue of particular concern or relevance to the group being addressed. In the second hour, we divided into smaller groups to explore the issue in greater detail and to allow women to listen to one another's experiences. We formulated stories for the women to consider and decide the extent to which the law could assist or limit their efforts to address the violations. In the final half hour, the groups reported back to the group as a whole.

The first day mainly *adivasi* women attended the session on forest laws. We shared with them basic information on forest laws and sexual assault. During the discussion period, the *adivasi* women spoke about the changes that occurred in their lives as a result of their forced removal from the forests, their original habitats. Both as tribals and as women, the shift to a settled way of life had resulted in economic and cultural deterioration.[19] The effects of these changes included an increase in violence both inside and outside the home, erosion of *adivasi* culture, and the lowering of women's status in their community. We then talked of the role of the forest laws in bringing about changes in the lives of the forest dwellers more generally, and the women of those communities specifically. We looked at the interests served by the laws, particularly the state's interests in securing revenue by reserving forests for its purposes. We discussed the role of the law in forcing *adivasis* out of the forests into settled agricultural lifestyles and the waged economy. All of the groups came back together and a participant from each shared the discussions with the entire group of women.

On the issue of sexual assault, the participants were given information on the rape law and domestic violence. In the smaller group sessions, women were asked about the definition of rape and how it was distinct from sexual assault. Was this distinction valid? What was the difference and should there be a difference? In most groups women felt that sexual assault that did not involve penetration did not make the offence less harmful to women. Most forms of sexual assault were violent and humiliating for women. The women were asked to discuss different problem situations, such as what they might do if their daughter was raped by a neighbour or if her son raped a village girl. No consensus resulted in either discussion group as to how to resolve these situations; the women were torn between the rights of the family and those of the woman. These discussions forced the women to think about the institutions that challenged and frequently took priority over women's rights. It further forced them to think about how to meet this challenge through consciousness raising and using rights as a strategy for mobilizing women.

We followed a similar format on both the second and third days. We began by providing basic information about the subject areas, and then broke into smaller groups. Despite the format, the second day began rather spontaneously, with the participants singing songs. One group of married women sang a song about the duty of all women: if they were good women, to serve their husbands regardless of his nature, appearance or treatment of her. The *devadasi* women then sang a song of how they were born from a diseased womb and destined to serve one 'master'. The images of the good and bad women provided the basis of discussion on the law governing *devadasi* and prostitute women.

In the discussion on *devadasi* practice, prostitution and child marriages, some *devadasi* women shared their experiences with the group. They were all rural *harijan* women who had little economic security and frequently had to resort to prostitution, unable to find employment or participate in society because of social stigma and rejection from other women.[20] We looked at the different legal provisions governing the dedication of women as *devadasis* and prostitution, and the extent to which such laws helped protect or further hurt these women. We attempted to illustrate how the law continued to reinforce the stigma attached to *devadasi* and prostitutes as it penalized them for the kind of work they did. The law is based on assumptions of morality, that is, the moral conduct and behaviour of women (not men), and is concerned with protecting public rights as opposed to women's rights. Women who are engaged in offering sex for money or under the guise of religion, are immoral and threaten public moral values, in particular the values on which the family is based. It does not protect the rights of these women or attempt to address the economic conditions, compulsions or the class interests responsible for their situations.

In the small groups, the participants were presented with different situations and asked to respond to each in light of the knowledge they had acquired about the law.

Situation 1

There is woman in your village who is a *devadasi* with two children? How do you treat her?

Situation 2

You see a dedication taking place. A 12 year-old girl in the village is being dedicated. What do you do? A pimp will take her to Bombay. What can you do?

The group consisting of *devadasi* women were asked: what is your self-perception? Do you see yourselves as workers? Are you different from prostitute women? Should the law treat *devadasi* women as immoral? Should the law treat prostitute women as immoral? Do you see either of these women as immoral?

The purpose of this discussion was to force the women to question the assumptions on which the law is based and whether the distinction between prostitute/*devadasi* women and all other women is a legitimate distinction. Should women be denied access to their rights because of the nature of the work they do? Furthermore, it challenged the distinctions that women themselves practised, and the need to break down these distinctions between women if there was to be any possibility of developing solidarity among women.

On the third day, virtually the same format was followed with regard to domestic violence, cruelty, bigamy and desertion. In general, both the large and small discussion groups were used to provide an opportunity for women to think about the law differently and think about its role in changing their lives/conditions or in reinforcing their situation. The purpose was to internalize an understanding of the possibilities and limits of the law. It was possible for women to share their experiences on specific issues, then talk about and convey a sense of the limits of the law with respect to each issue. Yet the process was limited primarily by the large numbers present, the lack of familiarity between the participants and the facilitators, and the limited amount of time allotted for conducting the legal literacy workshop. It is essential for such a process, where the main achievement has been in getting women to think about the law differently, to be followed up in the different districts or villages of the participants. The follow-up will enable educators or facilitators to work with smaller numbers, build on familiarity and truth, and enable further exploration of the issues of specific concern to them, and the role of law in addressing those issues.

The Third Story: The Feminist Organization's Ten-day Workshop

The third group consisted of approximately fifty women who attended a ten-day workshop on women and health, and women and law. The workshop had been preceded by a continuous feminist educational process that had been going on for almost two years. Out of this process emerged a need expressed by the participants for a workshop on health and law. The law sessions were conducted primarily by activists from a feminist group with the assistance of two lawyers, including myself. The focus of the workshop was on the right of equality and non-discrimination. We took up different issues affecting women's lives, gave information about laws governing those issues, and the extent to which such laws facilitated or undermined a women's right to equality. Some of the issues raised during the workshop concerned wages, rape, marriage, divorce and alcoholism. These issues were explored primarily through the medium of plays and songs. We used facts from different cases and asked the participants to enact the cases, bringing out the questions raised by the particular issue.

Women enacted plays on decided cases about abortion and the restitution of conjugal rights. They divided into small groups to discuss the cases and then put together a play to be enacted before the entire group. One case concerned the story of a woman who had an abortion without her husband's consent.[21] Her choice was held to constitute an act of cruelty and grounds for divorce under the Hindu Marriage Act, even though a woman had a right to terminate her pregnancy under the Medical Termination of Pregnancy Act without seeking any other party's consent, including that of her husband.

On the issue of restitution of conjugal rights, the facts of two cases were presented. The right was primarily used by men, and could result in forcing a woman to return to the matrimonial home and his conjugal 'company'.[22] In their play, the participants raised important questions about a Supreme Court decision that held that the man's right did not violate a woman's right to equality and that, in any case, constitutional rights to equality and liberty had no place in the family.[23] The play raised important questions for discussion, such as whether a man has the right to order his wife return home when she is unwilling? How is this different from rape? Why didn't women enforce their right of restitution of conjugal rights when their husbands left the home without good reason? One response was that the women were essentially homeless, that if they have no real home, how can they ask their husband to return?

Through the discussion of the plays, the participants concluded that the law was primarily functioning as a mechanism for protecting man's right to have an heir, a son to light his funeral pyre, to have unhindered sexual access to his wife, and to protect a husband's rights over his wife's body. The method enabled women to understand the limits of the law and to develop critical consciousness about the laws, the primary objective of a legal literacy workshop.

The question arose that if the values of decision makers/ judges are so biased, what is the solution? Should more women be in places of power from where they can shape the law? ('No, because even in that place she is surrounded by men, she doesn't have the space to develop herself.') Can the law ever benefit us if this is the situation? Some bold answers included the responsibility of women to claim their rights and change the law. In a subsequent group discussion consisting only of single women, we heard some women argue for property rights in their natal family, something that is not acknowledged in the law. They also felt entitled to rights to education, to control their bodies, to speak, to wear the clothes they wanted, and to move about freely.

Voicing needs or rights that women consider relevant to their lives did not merely raise expectations. In fact, the group proceeded to talk about how to secure rights that are not recognized by the law. Honest, genuine, empowering stories of resistance, struggle and opposition emerged. We listened to the story of Asha, a village woman, who told us how she was sexually assaulted. Her assailant made several attempts to rape her, but she was able to struggle free. She brought the issue before the *panchayat*, a local body of village elders, all male, who determines disputes arising from the village. She refrained from making a complaint and going to court, where she had already experienced a bitter lesson. Asha had gone through a divorce and was presently fighting for the return of her dowry. Her initial enthusiasm diminished as the court process turned out to be lengthy, the lawyers appearing to be the only ones to benefit materially. She decided not to use the courts to fight the case of sexual assault. Her experience taught her that her struggle in the courts would be a lonely one, where she would have to fight as an individual against her aggressor and would also, at best, secure a decision long after the assault occurred and no one would hear about it. The assailant attended the meeting accompanied by local thugs hoping to intimidate Asha. Yet she arrived at the meeting accompanied by a large number of women from nearby villages to whom she had related her story. This display of solidarity was sufficient to intimidate her assailant, who was forced to apologize and was publicly humiliated by his family, who beat him with a sandal. Asha did not resort to traditional legal processes that could not have delivered justice to her in the same manner or speed, if at all.

By working with a feminist group we were able to conduct the legal literacy workshop using feminist approaches. The process was intensive, involved working with small numbers of women, and used consciousness raising as a specific method of empowerment. Such an approach provides a space in which women can talk about or share their experiences, work through those experiences to achieve a greater understanding of their material context, and with that awareness, ultimately work together to transform that context. It is the ideal place to situate legal literacy that enables women to critically consider when and how law may be a useful tool in their lives.

There were some important limitations of the workshop that need to be understood and further explored. The discussions raised many contradictions, frictions and inconsistencies. The main obstacle to the process was that women attended from different areas and raised different issues that were relevant to their particular context. It may be more useful to explore these issues in much smaller groups, and in relation to laws that are of particular relevance to each district.

What conclusions can we draw from these different experiences of doing legal literacy? What are the implications for our understanding of rights and the role of law in women's struggle for social transformation?

Legal literacy will only be effective to the extent that it

is compatible with broader approaches to education and development. It must be premised on an adequate understanding of class and gender. This means probing beyond the grassroots experience or nature of an organization or program with which we are working. We need to understand the nature of the relationship they are attempting to establish with the communities in which they are situated. This understanding involves looking at the relationship with the community being established, the assumptions of gender and development that are being pursued, and the understanding of empowerment informing the organization's approach.

Further, the experiences related also indicate the need to develop a flexible approach to legal literacy. That is, the structure of a workshop will be determined by the nature of the group attending in terms of its class, caste and religious identities, the number of women participating, as well as the level of gender consciousness in a group. Where there is little or no gender awareness, then a consciousness-raising process must precede a legal literacy program. Consciousness raising enables women to reflect on their lives, critically analyze and evaluate their experiences, and understand the possibilities of transforming their lives. A legal literacy program must enable women to apply that critical awareness to the law and legal process, discovering both the limits and possibilities of law in the struggle for social transformation.

In a legal literacy workshop, we need to talk more about the use of rights both inside and outside the courts. It is important to come together and relate struggles of women, both successful and unsuccessful in court, and try to understand the reasons for success or failure. We also need to continue to share the struggles that have taken place outside the courts. This sharing is important for expanding the use of the law for social change in women's lives. Our purpose is not to exclude the traditional approaches to law, but to expand the scope and dimension of rights strategies, to explore the full potential of rights, and use them in ways that can be more effective and practical for rural women in particular. Information giving is essential, for an informed woman might at least have a change to challenge persons in positions of power who are prone to abuse their power. Yet legal information must be placed in context if we are to understand its full potential and its limits. To tell a women that bonded labour is illegal is to provide her with information that will make no difference to her life. To work towards formulating strategies for social and economic empowerment with the knowledge that bonded labour is illegal must be the goal of an effective legal literacy strategy.

Notes

1. The amendments were brought about as a result of protests by academics and agitation by the women's movement against the decision of the Supreme Court, acquitting two police officers of the rape of a young girl named Mathura. See Tuku Ram, *State of Maharashtra*, AIR 1979, p. 185; *Report of the National Meeting of Women's Organizations Against Rape*, 1990; A. Rao, M. Juneja & S. Vaid, *Rape, Society and State*, PUCL, 1980; Indian Penal Code (1860), amendments to sections 375 and 376 by the Criminal Law (Amendment) Act 1983 and insertions of sections 376A, 376B, 376C and 376D.
2. The women's movement has used a variety of methods for women's empowerment, primarily in the form of consciousness raising, using plays, songs and workshops for generating critical awareness about women's oppression and the factors responsible for that oppression.
3. 'Towards a Uniform, Secular and Non-Sexist Civil Code', 27–30 December 1989, Bombay, N. M. Tripathi Private Limited; M. N. Menon, *Uniform Civil (Family) Code for the Citizens*, New Delhi, 1986; C. Singh, 'Rehabilitation and the Right to Property', in W. Fernandes & E. G. Thukral (eds), *Development, Displacement and Rehabilitation*, (New Delhi, Indian Social Institute, 1989).
4. *All India Democratic Women's Association and Janwadi Samiti* v. *Union of India and Others*, AIR 1989, p. 1280
5. P. Williams, 'Alchemical Notes: Reconstructing Ideals from Deconstructed Rights', *Harvard Civil Rights-Civil Liberties Law Review*, 22 (1987); E. M. Schneider, 'The Dialectics of Rights and Politics: Perspectives from the Women's Movement', *New York University Law Review*, 61 (1986); C. Smart, 'The Problem of Rights', in *Feminism and the Power of the Law New York* (London, Routledge, 1989); J. Fudge, 'The Effect of Entrenching a Bill of Rights Upon Political Discourse: Feminist Demands and Sexual Violence in Canada', *International Journal of the Sociology of Law*, 17.6 (1989).
6. M. Kishwar, 'Rethinking Dowry Boycott', *Manushi*, 48 (1988); M. Kishwar, 'Continuing the Dowry Debate', *Economic and Political Weekly*,

9 December 1989; Kusum, 'Concept and Function of Dowry and Bride Price', *Indian Bar Review*, 14. 3 (1987); C. Lakshmi, 'On Kidneys and Dowry', *Economic and Political Weekly*, 28 January 1989.

7. J. Paul and C. Dias, *Developing Law and Legal Resources for Alternative, People-Centered Development: A Human Rights Approach* (New York, ICLD, 1985).
8. In referring to we, I am talking about those of us working in and through the law using feminist processes; those of us working to use law to empower women. The use of we is intended to critically engage the reader in the struggles and challenges that face us.
9. I was assisted by Geetenjali Gangoli, a Masters in Philosophical History student at Delhi University.
10. b. hooks, 'On Self-Recovery', in *Talking Back, Thinking Feminist-Thinking Back* (Sheba Feminist Publishers, 1989).
11. E. M. Rathgebar, *Trends in Research and Practice* (Ottawa, International Development Research Centre, 1989).
12. A. Gupta (ed.), *Women and Society: The Developmental Perspective* (New Delhi, Critierion Publications, 1986).
13. S. Stichter & J. L. Parpart (eds), *Women, Employment and the Family in the International Division of Labour* (London, Macmillan Press, 1990); L. Dube & R. Patriwala (eds), *Structures and Strategies: Women Work and Family* (New Delhi, Sage, 1990).
14. The workshop was conducted with the assistance of three law students and a faculty member of the National Law School of India. University.
15. Mahila Samakya Karnataka, *A Progress Report* (January–June 1990).
16. *Devadasi* refers to the class of women, who through various ceremonies of 'marriage', dedicated themselves to deities of temples and other ritual objects. The practice is subtly sustained by feudal landlords, normally of a higher caste, who use religion as a guise for keeping a mistress. Further, pimps and touts frequently recruit these women for prostitution in urban centres.
17. *Adivasis* are people who have traditionally resided in the forests and have developed a culture and heritage that is directly linked to their relationship with the forests.
18. Scheduled castes are those castes, races or tribes, or part of groups within such castes, races or tribes that have been historically disadvantaged or deprived as a result of discriminatory practices. They consist primarily of the economically weaker sections of society. See further definition under Article 341 read with 366 (24) of the Constitution of India.
19. W. Fernandes & G. Menon, *Tribal Women and the Forest Economy: Exploitation and Status Change* (New Delhi, Indian Social Institute. 1987); V. Shiva, *Staying Alive: Women Ecology and Survival in India* (New Delhi, Kali, 1985); C. Singh, 'Development, Displacement and Rehabilitation', in *Dams and Other Major Projects: Impact on and Response of Indigenous People* (New Delhi, Indian Social Institute, 1988).
20. J. D'Cunha, 'The Suppression of Immoral Traffic in Women and Girls, 1956: A Critical Review' (Bombay: SNDT, 1986); Fight for Prostitutes' Rights as Citizens [Proceedings from Maithri Forum for Women] *Manushi*,

58 (1990); Demand for Legalisation of Prostitution, *Manushi*, 3.4 (1983).
21. *Sushil Kumar Verma* v. *Usha*, AIR, Delhi, 86, 1987.
22. *Sareetha* v. *T. Venkata Subbaih*, AIR, Andhra Pradesh 3561983, 1984.
23. *Smt. Saroj Rani* v. *Sudarshan Kumar Chadha*, AIR, 1562, 1984.

Redefining the Agenda of the Women's Movement Within a Secular Framework

Flavia Agnes

A New Challenge to Existing Social Movements

Bombay has a reputation of being the home of many progressive social movements during the pre-independence and post-independence period. Although the first communal riots recorded in the history of Bombay took place in 1893,[1] during the period when the city grew into an industrial capital it acquired a cosmopolitan image, with the migrants providing the necessary vibrancy for the growth and expansion of the city. In fact this migrant character was conducive to many refugees taking shelter here after the partition. The riots during the later period did not affect Bombay in any significant way.

Hence the scale and intensity of the riots which broke down in the wake of the demolition of the Babri Masjid at Ayodhya took the Bombayites by surprise and dealt a serious blow to the cosmopolitan and progressive image of the city. The city, which had welcomed with open arms refugees of all natural and man-made calamities and provided them with at least the basic minimum means of sustenance, witnessed a large-scale exodus. Many of its age-old trades as well as its endeared traditions went up in flames with the tacit approval of thousands of spectators.

The riots in their wake posed a new challenge to the social movements in the city. Every stone, every pebble thrown by the frenzied mob became the touchstone upon which their work had to be tested. And sadly, faced with this new challenge, they failed miserably. It was evident that building a counter secular force had not been in their agenda (or at least not been addressed effectively) and hence they could not counter the rising wave of communal passions. So when the riots broke down the feeble voice raised by a few groups was drowned in the sea of venom and hatred into which the city had plunged. At another level, the trade unions and community organizations became the fertile collective on which this venom was nurtured and nourished.

As the city 'went back to normal' the organizations tried to pick up the threads again but found that the basis of their work had collapsed. The beneficiaries of a program or the members of a union had been divided into two sectors: the majority and the minority. The question foremost in the minds of the secular-minded was an obvious one: 'Why did this happen, and when? And where did we go wrong?' Did the venom of communalism spread overnight? If not, did the movements themselves consciously or unconsciously participate in this process? The riots affected different social movements in different ways. Since our work has primarily been within the context of women's movement, I am posing the questions within its confines.

The Women's Movement in India

Around late 1970s and early 1980s the autonomous women's movement began to take shape mainly around the issue of rape and bride burning.[2] Women marched the streets of several major cities in protest, shouting slogans and demanding for legal reform. The groups that mushroomed in various cities consisted of women from left and liberal backgrounds, many of whom were professionals from the middle and upper strata of society. The initial spontaneous protest marches led to more sustained activities of counselling centres that offered aid and advice to victims of rape and domestic violence.[3] Women from both lower and middle sections approached the centres for help in a crisis situation. Their ideology was pro-women, and can be categorized as broadly feminist (although several groups refrained from using this term). They helped to challenge the traditional and conservative role of the women as subordinate partners within domestic and social relationships.

Although the groups remained small in number, the movement was highly visible as it received wide media publicity. In the face of such pressure tactics, the state was forced to respond. Women's issues were placed on the agenda of state-sponsored developmental schemes and social work programs. The government set up anti-dowry police cells to deal with victims of dowry harassment and bride burning. There were also several cosmetic efforts at legislative reforms although the faulty and badly formulated laws did not have the desired effect.[4]

While the counselling centres remained at the crisis intervention level, women were also mobilized through community programs and income-generating activities by several non-governmental agencies. Some of these were managed by women who subscribed broadly to the feminist ideology and hence were able to transgress the narrow boundaries of 'women's welfare' and incorporate the new ideology of 'women's empowerment'.[5] Although they did not directly challenge the subordinate role of women within marriage nor address 'personal' issues like domestic violence, they indirectly helped in the empowerment of women through economic activities.

Secular Culture as an Agenda

The autonomous women's movement focused on issues that challenged the patriarchal power structures and at times even issues concerning caste and class within a broad liberal framework. The broad premise on which this ideology rested was that all women were equal and issues such rape and domestic violence affected them equally across class, culture and religious constraints. The leaders of this autonomous movement remained predominantly urban and upper class Hindu. Their work centred mainly in areas away and outside their own immediate neighbourhood and community context. In order to reach out to women from a different class and culture and to propagate the new ideology of the strong and assertive woman, the movement adopted a populist approach and relied upon mythical symbols of *Shakti* and *Kali* to convey the newly constructed feminist ideology. The movement relied more upon myths and fictions rather than on the history of a pluralistic society encompassing within its framework symbols drawn from minority cultures.

The intention of using the symbols from mainstream culture was not to propagate the Hindu ideology. But since the movement did not have 'secularism' as one of its prime objectives, no conscious efforts were made to evolve alternate symbols. Hence the cultural symbols with which the women who were in the forefront of the women's movement were familiar with, had surreptitiously crept into the women's movement.

One of the reasons for adopting symbols from Hindu mythology was to counter the allegation that the 'feminist' ideology is Western. To establish the 'Indianness' of the movement it relied on Hindu symbols and Sanskrit idioms denoting woman – power thus inadvertently strengthening the communal ideology that Indian, Hindu and Sanskrit are synonymous.

Women and Communal Forces

With women's concerns gaining prominence in both governmental and non-governmental organizations during the 1980s, women's issues became an important agenda for all political parties. Initially the political parties refrained from raising issues of domestic strife and male dominance within party organizations. The women who needed support against violent husbands or a male colleague would still approach a women's organization to deal with this issue. This conservative approach was maintained not for traditional reasons of preserving the family but more in order to preserve the existing status quo within party cadre.

In Bombay the communal party Shiv Sena, which was gaining popularity within the lower middle class was able to mobilise a large number of women around support such activities as income generation, creches, and midday meals for children. The movement also appropriated cultural forums of public celebrations of Hindu festivals like *Ganesh Utsav* and *Satya Narayan Pooja* which was popularized by Tilak during the nationalist struggle in the pre-independence era. Another forum through which both men and women could be mobilized was trade union activities. Many trade unions have been taken over by the Shiv Sena in recent years.

These organizations were headed by local leaders with a more coherent Hindu ideology that the women found more acceptable than the alien culture of the Western-influenced 'feminism'. But these groups also used the forms of protest popularized by the women's movement and the left movement of road blocks and street plays that are contrary to the conservative domestic role of the traditional Hindu woman.

The communal groups and in particular the Shiv Sena, through a systematic hate campaign was able to whip up communal tensions among their woman cadre. The image of the modern Hindu woman constructed while advocating the communal Hindu ideology was not the traditional subservient and docile domestic being but a new modern *Durga*, a woman of the world and by and large a working woman. This construction of the modern Hindu woman resembled very closely the Indian construction of the new 'feminist' woman.

This new woman could come out on the street with equal ease just as the men from the community to avenge the wrongs. And in this action she had the blessings of the political party and community leaders. Women found this role not only exciting but also more comfortable in comparison to the protests against a violent husband or a rapist from within the community because then they would not have the protective mantle of the party nor the blessings of the community elders.

The irony lay in the fact that the communal forces were able to mobilize women far more easily adopting the ideology of the modern *Durga* and adapting the external forms of protest than the women's movement itself which had popularized these forms of protest. But to its dismay the women's movement found that the new found *Shakti*, the modern *Durga*, was not used to combat violence within the home and community but was directed externally towards the Muslim — both men and women. Hence slogans such as 'Sisterhood is Powerful' or '*Hum Sub Ek Hai*' (We are all United) lost their relevance. But what was even more shocking was that the women from the communal organizations used slogans such as '*Hum Bharat Ki Nari Hai; Phhol Nahi Chingari Hai*' (We are the Women of India, not delicate flowers but fire flames) while leading the demonstrations during the riots.

Charter of Demands of Opposing Sections

The merging of lines did not stop just at an abstract level of symbols and images but also found expression through some of the more concrete demands raised by women's movement although at times the reasons were contradictory.

Obscenity was one such issue. The women's groups had taken up a campaign against obscenity in the media. The focus was to protest against using women as sex symbols and violent, derogatory and subservient images of women in the media. This campaign attracted people from all sections and the women's movement could not clarify its position away from more prudish and conservative, and at times even anti-women, supporters of the campaign. The issue became very popular with communal parties. The BJP and the Shiv Sena organized protest marches of women against the late-night screening of classic films on the television including films which portrayed an assertive woman.

The women's movement had a sustained campaign for reforms within the segregated and religious-based marriage laws and pressurized the state to evolve a non-sexist secular code. This demand found an echo in a similar demand by the communal forces.

The family laws in India are termed 'personal laws',

and divided along religious lines, the laws of the minorities remaining archaic and anti-women. Even after independence no effort had been made to evolve a uniform civil code in spite of the constitutional mandate. The ruling party continued with the 'divide and rule' policy of the British era for political gains, sacrificing the rights of minority women in its wake. A glaring instance of this tendency was the passing of the Muslim Women's Act 1986. A judgment passed in 1985, popularly known as the Shah Bano judgment,[6] which gave Muslim women the right to maintenance, aroused the wrath of the leaders of the Muslim community because of certain adverse comments made by the judiciary against Islam. The adverse campaign led to passing of laws that deprived divorced Muslim women of their hard-won right to maintenance.[7]

It was not surprising that the demand of uniform civil code raised by the women's movement aroused contradictory responses from fundamental elements, depending on whether they hailed from the majority or minority section. While very popular among the Hindu fundamentalists, the code was strongly opposed by Muslim and Christian religious leaders who perceived it as a threat to their cultural identity and a violation of fundamental rights guaranteed by the constitution. By raising the demand for a uniform civil code, the communal forces were not only to gain popularity amidst the Hindu male who envied his counterparts within the Islamic code which permitted polygamy, but could also pose as the champions of women's cause.

There was a very clear difference between the demand made by the women's movement which was based on a pro-woman, secular and non-sexist ideology and the anti-Muslim demand of the communal forces. But this did not clearly manifest through active campaigns or court litigation. This is because quite a few minority women initiated court proceedings to challenge the sexist biases within their personal laws. But unfortunately, not sufficient numbers of Hindu women challenged the Hindu Code. This resulted in the women's movement focusing primarily on lacunae within laws concerning the minority family laws. For instance, the Muslim Women's Bill which deprived the Muslim women their right to maintenance was strongly criticised. But an earlier amendment of 1976 to a secular code — The Special Marriage Act, 1954 – through which two Hindus marrying under this code were taken out of the purview of the secular code in matters of property rights went unnoticed by the women's movement.[8]

The ambiguities of the procedures which solemnize the Hindu marriage that enables the Hindu male to contract second marriage with relative impunity in spite of a progressive legislation, the lacunae within the laws concerning the property rights which denies the Hindu woman equal property rights and the sexist laws of guardianship and child custody, denial of right to matrimonial and ancestral home etc. were seldom challenged nor did they receive much publicity. So by default, the women's movement contributed to the fiction popularized by the fundamentalist that the Hindu Code is the perfect family code which ought to be extended to other religious denominations in order to liberate women.

This was broadly the situation when the riots broke in Bombay and the rest of the country. The riots broke some of the earlier presumptions of the women's movement in their wake and brought minority concerns centre stage. No longer could women's issues be addressed only as a woman's issue but had to be placed within the context of majority and minority politics.

Changing Equations during the Post-Riot Situation

Around October 1992 the Add. Commissioner of Police had issued directions to the subordinate police stations that cases of domestic violence should not be registered against women who do not have marks of physical injury. This direction undid the hard-won gains of the women's movement which had succeeded in getting the state to recognize the issue of domestic violence by passing a law to deal with violence within the matrimonial home. The Add. CP later retracted his statement, and to clarify the issues raised by his statement, a seminar was planned for January 1994 with police and legal authorities.

The riots ,which broke in December, however, changed drastically the original context of the seminar. In the wake of the large-scale police brutality on 7, 8 and 9 December, where groups of young boys picketing on the roads were shot down by the police, the faith of the minority community in the law-enforcing machinery had totally broken down. Men with bullet injuries were hiding in their homes haunted by the fear that they will be locked up if they came into the vicinity of the police stations.

In such a situation where one whole community was being held at ransom, the issue of domestic violence lost its earlier context. By holding a seminar on domestic violence we would be helping the police to defuse the more pressing issue of police excesses during the riots. By interacting with them in a forum on women's issues would amount to condoning of their acts during the riots.

The police were too eager to arrest Muslim men under any pretext. They would have entertained Muslim women's complaint with undue eagerness and responded to it promptly. Viewed from within the context of the women's movement, it would have been an ideal situation, but the response would in fact be anti-Muslim rather than pro-women. By applauding this move on the part of the police the movement would be segregating the issues affecting the Muslim women along gender and religious lines into isolated compartments. Suddenly the number of women approaching the agencies for help had decreased. The number of Muslim women following up their court cases reduced even more drastically. Additionally, the Family Court was situated in midst of one of the worst affected areas. The violence and instability had corroded the social fibre, an essential pre-condition for raising the question of internal domestic strife and instability.

Rape was another issue that raised newer dimensions. Although rape had been an important issue, the context in which it was addressed had remained within the parameters of a patriarchal ideology with emphasis on penetration. The women's movement had grappled with the question of shifting the onus of proof in rape cases that had brought about a sharp cleavage within the women's movement in the early 1980s. Ultimately the burden of proof was shifted only in custodial rape cases.

Rape is a weapon used during any riot. In Surat mass rapes of poor Muslim women took place under floodlights. Fact-finding teams of civil liberty groups and women's movement visited these areas and talked to the women, and came across allegations of rape from the majority of women in the dominant community. But upon further probing they realised that these were cases fabricated to malign the men from the minority community. In the charged atmosphere of communal violence, the stigma attached to rape in peace times is diminished as both sections view the women as the property of the menfolk. Traditionally the rape of women by the opposing camp was used as a weapon to punish the men. But now it had gone a step further and the community was ready to tarnish the image of women's chastity to malign the men from the opposing camp. Women's sexuality had always been at the disposal of the men within the community, but now its use had been charged with a strange mixture of feminist and communal ideologies. If the community wanted its women to use their sexuality to advance the cause of the community, women would be too willing and happy to be the sacrificial lambs. The women themselves were ready to risk not only their life, but even their 'honour' for the cause of the community. They were willing to invoke a 'state worse than death for the Indian woman' – an expression often used in rape judgments – to further the communal cause.

Women from both communities were being used or became willing martyrs in aid of the community, defying traditional norms and roles. For the Muslim community, women became the buffer between police and the community youth and hence suffered casualties. Ironically the freedom that was denied to them in peace times was now being offered to them on a platter in the face of grave adversity. The elderly neighbours of 50-year-old Neelam Bano, who was shot dead on 8 December 1992 in a slum in Bandra East say, 'As the police opened fire, a group of us elderly women came out. We were under the impression that the police never fired at women'. While men went into hiding, the women braved the bullets to fend for the children with a great sense of pride and honour.

On the other side, the Shiv Sena was able to mobilize a large section of women to hold traffic blocks and demonstrations outside police stations to protest against detention. Women slept on the road to prevent army trucks from entering the area to rescue Muslim hostages or put off the blazing fires. The same slogans which the left and women's movement used to strengthen collective actions were now used to whip up communal frenzy among violence mobs such as '*Hum se jo takarayega, Mitti me woh mil jayega*' (Those who confront us will be destroyed or in other words might is right). Suddenly with a sinking feeling we felt that there is a thin line between collective action and mob frenzy and one can easily lead into another. But sanctions to oppose traditional norms did not imply that they would not be victims of sexual jealousy and domestic violence within the homes. So the women who threw stones at the Muslim men who were set on fire in the middle of the road, would yet have to approach a women's organization for help in personal problems.

With the Muslim community the situation was the reverse. Those who were opposing the women movement's demand for a uniform civil code and had opposed the Shah Bano judgment were our allies in the anti-communal force, fighting for a legitimacy and a right to dignified existence in a riot-torn situation. And even while we were being welcomed with open arms during peace rallies we are apprehensive that riot-time allies might become peace-time adversaries. The same men may deny us access to their women once normalcy is returned if we work on the issue of maintenance to the divorced Muslim woman.

The riots dealt a severe blow to the premise that the women have a separate existence away from their communal identity where we can discuss problems of rape, divorce and maintenance on a common platform. The same issues affect different women in different ways at different times. We also realised that our allies and adversaries would change depending on the external realities. If social action means reacting to external social reality, then as the external reality changes the internal positions have to be redefined or else the movement itself would be redundant in the wake of newer challenges.

A Moment for Reflection

In conclusion it is necessary to emphasize that the critique of the movement is made from within, having participated in all the different stages of the development of the movement. The contradictions and confusions are as much a part of the movement as its strength and gains and are signs of a movement that is alive and growing while reformulating its earlier premises and positions in response to external shifts in the configuration of powers.

The women's movement does not stand in isolation and is an integral part of other social movements. Hence the contradictions and ideological shifts expressed here within the context of the women's movement hold true for other social movements as well. During the last decade the trade union movement in Bombay has become communalized, with the Shiv Sena dominating many important trade unions in the city. During the riots they not only led riots but also campaigned for the reduction of the Muslim workforce. There were many stabbing and burning instances within factory premises and Muslim labourers were terrorized, which resulted in large-scale absenteeism. Finally establishments like Tatas had to issue a public statement inviting the Muslim workers back to work and promising them adequate protection. This is an indication of the level to which the trade union movement was divided.

A similar situation also arose within the Dallit and other caste-based movements. The Mandal issue that had divided the Hindu community along caste lines stood united as a Hindu force against the Muslims. The progressive groups which had stood by the Mandal campaign found that this alliance could not withstand the stress of communal pulls. Within the government bureaucracy those who were occupying reserved seats expressed deep-seated communal biases even while implementing relief programs declared by the government. Shanta Dharia, a Republic Party woman corroborator (political organization of the Dallits), was shot down by the police while leading a rioting mob. A similar re-scrutiny of carlier presumptions and premises of other social movements might help in building up a consolidated secular force that can stand the onslaught of rising communalism and counter its challenges effectively.

Notes

1. E. Padgaonkcr, When *Bombay Burned* (Bombay, UBSPD 1993), pp. 152–53.
2. *Manushi: A Journal About Women & Society*, nos. 1–10, contain several articles on campaigns around the issue of rape and dowry death during the initial phase.
3. Women's Centre, Bombay; Saheli, Delhi, Vimochana, Bangalore etc.
4. F. Agnes, 'Protecting Women Against Violence?', *Economic & Political Weekly*, 25 April 1992.
5. Self-employed Women's Association (SEWA), Ahmedabad; Working Women's Forum, Madras; Annapurna, Bombay.
6. *Mohd. Ahmed Khan v. Shah Bano*, AIR, SC 945, 1985.
7. The Muslim Women's (Protection of Rights on Divorce) Act, 1986.
8. Amendment of 1976 — Section 21-A of the Special Marriage Act, 1954.

The SEWA (Self Employed Women's Association) Trade Union Model

Helen Lay

It is hardly likely that an Australian organization sporting the title 'Self Employed Women's Association' would instantly be thought of as a trade union. On the contrary, the image of a group of business women – probably of small-scale entrepreneurs – is more likely to come to mind. Some might even conjure the epithet 'petit bourgeois'. That the members of such an organization could qualify for, and indeed desperately require, the sort of anti-exploitative support normally associated with trade unions might indeed be thought laughable. Why? The clue lies in the label 'self employed'. We have become accommodated here in Australia to the idea of a trade union being '*at least* an association with a membership confined to employees'.[1] Ergo, trade unions exist to protect *employees*. Thus in thinking about who trade unions represent, and who they argue against, we tend to rely on a notional line that divides employees from employers. There is a reality to this: whether one is an employee or not can be of great significance in determining what protection is available under labour law. Generally speaking, non-employees or those seen as 'atypical' workers have not been protected by labour law nor represented by trade unions (even allowing for modifications to the law such as the 1992 amendment to the Federal Industrial Relations Act, which extended union membership eligibility to independent contractors).[2] As for the 'self employed', axiomatically, they need no protection against exploitation.

Representation of employee interests is one facet of trade unionism in Australia. The question of women or gender is another. For many years Australian trade unions have been dominated by men – in part because of the persistence of the male breadwinner ideal.[3] We may note the occasional and ephemeral existence of women-only trade unions, like the Victorian Lady Teachers Association and various colonial tailoresses unions in nineteenth and earlier twentieth century Australia, but it has taken the more recent increase of women both in the workforce and union movement for so-called women's issucs to be advanced in the industrial sphere. In this we may see a femocrat style operating; meaning, as Anne Summers has noted, that successes have come via Australian women working within and through established bureaucracies and institutions.[4] Groups like the WEL (Women's Electoral Lobby) are not about setting up alternative women's organizations but rather about putting women into existing organizations and having an impact upon their agendas. For example, in the Australian union movement there are some notable women holding significant executive positions: Anna Booth, National Secretary of the Textile, Clothing and Footwear union and an ACTU (Australian Council of Trade Unions) vice-president, is one. Yet she was reported on the front page of *The Weekend Australian* on 4–5 December 1993 as enduring whispered comments from male colleagues about continuing to hold her vice-president's position while on twelve months maternity leave. Working from the inside is one way of forcing change, but change is not thereby guaranteed.

We may use these two aspects – of employee representation and gender – as a comparative starting point to consider the Self Employed Women's Association (SEWA), which draws on the women's, trade union and cooperative movements for its modus operandi.

Beginnings

SEWA was legally registered as an Indian trade union covering informal sector workers in April 1972. In itself this was an important achievement since Indian labour law (inherited from the industrial West) restricted registration of trade unions to situations where an employer-employee relationship existed, in other words, to employment in the formal sector.[5] The restriction is probably a contributory factor in the poor unionization of the Indian workforce. Only some 10 per cent of Indian workers operate in the so-called formal sector, where regulation and labour law apply, and only about 30 to 40 per cent of these are unionized. The rest of the workforce in the informal – or, as it is often referred to – the unorganized sector, is largely untouched by labour law or trade union activity.[6] The workers SEWA embraced would not normally be eligible for trade union membership.

SEWA's beginnings sprang from the needs of women who worked in a variety of casual and 'self-employed' jobs in the textile mill city of Ahmedabad. In 1917 Ahmedabad had been the birthplace of the powerful Textile Labour Association (TLA), a union which had grown to be influential in the Indian trade union scene under Mahatma Gandhi's patronage and promotion. In fact it was a belief in the TLA's reputation that caused a number of poor, unprotected and financially insecure women – working as headloaders and cartpullers – to approach the TLA for help.[7] Having spoken to the head of the TLA Women's Wing, they were advised that they needed to become organized.

Their adviser, Ela Bhatt, knew what she was talking about. Long experience with the TLA and labour issues had alerted her to the vast numbers of informal sector workers outside the bounds of trade union and labour law protection. She had also spent some time in Israel at the Afro-Asian Institute of Labour and Cooperatives and had been impressed by the joint success of the trade union and cooperative movement.[8] By the time of her return to India she was convinced that 'unless those who are in the unorganized sector are brought into the mainstream of the labour movement, there is no labour movement worth its name in [India] – or in other countries like [India]'. She was also supportive of a women's movement, believing that those making up the majority of the female population, 'the eighty per cent rural, poor, illiterate and economically active', should be the ones taking a leading role. SEWA was a way of putting these beliefs into action and its name, chosen by Bhatt, was not just a recognition of the fact that SEWA members were women workers in the informal sector and thus more readily described as 'self employed' but, as importantly, because she found other alternative descriptors to 'informal' (such as 'unorganized', 'unprotected', 'marginal', 'peripheral', 'unregistered', 'undocumented') to be negatives.[9]

Hence the beginnings of SEWA: a union for informal sector women workers but operating under the patronage of the TLA, which meant, among other things, that while Ela Bhatt became General Secretary, there were also TLA male office holders able to exert their own gender influence on the SEWA executive.[10] This was not destined to last, however. In 1981 the TLA expelled SEWA and Ela Bhatt from its ranks after differences of approach emerged between SEWA and the TLA to communal disturbances in Ahmedabad. Following the expulsion SEWA members took the opportunity to change their rules of membership so as to exclude men.[11] From that time on SEWA has been an all-women organization, now operating in a number of other Indian states under an umbrella federation called SEWA Bharat.

Policies and programs

How have Ela Bhatt's twin convictions of the importance of including informal sector workers within the mainstream labour movement and of encouraging rural women (the 80 per cent rural, poor, illiterate and economically active) to take the lead in a women's movement been addressed? Largely, it is in the way SEWA has tried to realize its stated goals of bringing visibility to women as *workers* and of improving their economic position via access to resources and control over an income.[12]

1 Economic control and access to resources

Early research by SEWA women found that one of the major problems encountered by the workers they were trying to help was a lack of access to credit. Although an initial strategy was to try and link the women to established banks, ingrained bank policy and attitudes to poor slum-dwelling women meant continuing problems. SEWA's answer was to set up its own cooperative bank. It required a large amount of share capital to start such an enterprise but the women contributed what small amounts they could spare and raised what was needed in six months. The man responsible for registering such cooperative ventures objected to the idea but eventually agreed, provided that fifteen promoters could be found – all of whom had to be able to sign their name. SEWA had fifteen suitable women but only one could sign her name. Undaunted, they overcame that problem with an all-night name-signing lesson and the next day were able to demonstrate the mandatory skill and proof of intent.

Such an innovative way of addressing problems is what characterizes SEWA operations. For instance, having a bank to provide credit to SEWA members was not the end of the problem. Bank practices had to be devised to overcome the fact that borrowers would be unlikely to be able to read or write. Also their earnings, such as they are, can be erratic and easily siphoned away from the practice of saving or repaying loans to addressing innumerable demands created by ill-health, family emergencies or even husbands who find the temptation of drink a buffer against the harshness of life. Consequently the bank has adopted strategies like providing a mobile service collecting deposit monies from women who might find it difficult to be away from work or household, or by encouraging women to use their borrowings for goods and services that will enhance their economic prospects. And rather than seeing the women as careless defaulters when loans are not repaid (although repayment rates are high at some 93 per cent) the bank makes every effort to assist and advise.

In a similar vein SEWA has assisted women to form cooperatives so that they may become more economically independent. These range across a variety of producer and service activities including land and animal cooperatives, artisan cooperatives, vendor cooperatives and the provision of such services as childcare and waste-paper collection. Our view of trade unions as organizations bargaining on behalf of their member might seem inconsistent with such ventures, but not if one also sees trade unions having a legitimate role in supporting their members to earn a livelihood. To this end, SEWA provides training for those engaged in cooperatives so that the necessary skills of marketing, accounting, purchasing of materials and so forth can be acquired. Training however is not just restricted to cooperative activities for there are SEWA members who in effect are employees, albeit employed on a casual or contract basis. The driving idea is to help women overcome their problems by responding to their priorities. In the words of Ela Bhatt, 'If they [the women] have to participate in the women's movement, then we have to look into their priorities and take up such problems which are relevant to them. Otherwise they are not going to be interested in a women's movement. And their priorities are, as I understand, more work, more income [and] a better life for their children.'

Responding to the women's priorities also means representing them before the relevant bodies or authorities. In this sense SEWA *is* a bargaining agent on behalf of its members. In fact this was part of the argument Ela Bhatt put to the Labour Commissioner, who registers trade unions, when he said to her, 'Where is the employer? Against whom are you going to agitate?'. Her response was that, although there wasn't one employer against whom SEWA could argue, nevertheless there were a number of government and social policies against which the union would have to agitate. Besides, she said, 'the objective of a trade union is not only to agitate against the employer but . . . also to build up solidarity amongst the workers for social change and to be equal partners in the development of the country'. This is a step removed from traditional industrial relations theory which, according to Cohen, is a restricted model based on a contained system of collective bargaining within an employer-employee milieu or relationship, meaning that 'The world of work [is] not only separated from politics, it [is] separated from society'.[13] By agitating for SEWA members in a number of forums and against a number of policies

SEWA has furthered its aim of bringing visibility to its members *as workers*. This is the other dimension to SEWA's goals, and fits with Ela Bhatt's desire to bring informal sector workers into the mainstream of the labour movement.

2 Bringing visibility

Informal sector women workers are invisible in many ways. For instance, they are often not fully accounted for in national employment statistics. In addition, they have been invisible insofar as having their needs understood by governments, agencies and policy makers.[14] For example, on what would seem to be the simple matter of supporting pregnant and antenatal women so as to ensure against deleterious health and/or income-earning effects, SEWA found that even the services of the Gujarati Government's own Life Insurance Corporation were closed off to the sorts of women workers they were representing. SEWA was forced to implement its own maternal protection scheme and finally has been successful in its lobbying of the State, with a scheme now being administered through the Labour Ministry.[15]

Wrestling with this problem of invisibility, Ela Bhatt asked herself how industrial workers in India had their rights recognized. She found that much Indian labour law and policy had developed from a 1929 commission – the Whitley Commission – which looked into the situation of workers. It became the desire of SEWA women to have a similar commission investigating the needs of the self-employed. After years of lobbying, the then Prime Minister, Rajiv Gandhi, granted their wish and the National Commission on Self Employed Women and Women in the Informal Sector was instituted in 1987 with Ela Bhatt, recently appointed to an upper house (Rajyah Sabha) seat in central Parliament, as its chairperson. A report, *Shramshakti* (meaning, women's labour power) was produced in 1988.[16] While it is still difficult to claim the same significance for *Shramshakti* on the lives of the self-employed as the Whitley Commission came to mean for industrial workers, nevertheless the report's many recommendations, based on a wide-ranging investigation, are at least documented. Time will tell whether they are to have an impact.

In representing its members needs, in trying to make them visible as workers, SEWA has not limited itself to the stage of nation-state. It has also tackled the international labour movement through the International Confederation of Free Trade Unions (ICFTU) and the International Labour Organisation (ILO). In 1983 Bhatt addressed the ICFTU Congress being held in Oslo, Norway where she argued for the inclusion of 'the self-employed' within the trade union movement, otherwise 'the labour movement will remain incomplete . . . decisions on employment, poverty and peace will remain unfruitful and [the] ICFTU Congress will remain unrepresented.'[17] She addressed the ICFTU Congress again in 1988, this time to argue for the needs of homeworkers (those doing paid work at home), which also SEWA numbers amongst its membership.[18] The successful passage of her resolution to Congress meant at least in principle support for the issue among the workers of 91 countries. Finally, SEWA and Ela Bhatt have been instrumental in bringing the issue of protection for homeworkers to the attention of the ILO through research and lobbying. Following the failure of a Home-based Workers Employment Rights Bill to gain passage through the Indian Parliament it became clear that another solution might come through an ILO Convention. In fact the topic of homework and the 'social protection' of homeworkers has now been scheduled for discussion at the 1995 and 1996 International Labour Conferences, where the decision will be made whether or not to adopt an ILO Convention. Homework is a global phenomenon but homeworkers (mostly women) are largely unprotected by the labour laws of the countries in which they operate.[19] SEWA's efforts on this front have had important implications for women both inside and outside of India.

Conclusion

Union movements in so-called developing countries like India have, as I have shown, often inherited their traditions from the industrialized West. This has meant that trade unions have tended to be restricted to a field of operations created by the employer-employee relationship or milieu. Those not clearly defined as employees can easily fall outside this field of operation. Thus it is with informal sector workers. One has to acknowledge the view, as conveyed by the ILO Director General that informal sector workers are only to be found in developing countries, but not all hold to this. There are also those, like Castells and Portes, who would want to argue that it is possible to observe a (growing) informal sector even in highly institutionalized economies.[20] Arguments like these often turn on definition and selected indicators. Regardless, the growth of unemployment in advanced economies, accompanied (as it has been in Australia) by a growth in part-time/casual employment as well as in 'self-employment' means, by virtue of the restrictive ambit of labour law, that much of the workforce is moving outside the protection of both the law and trade union coverage. How is this situation to be addressed? Does it mean that trade unions have to change their ways of operating? What does it mean for women workers who have been the ones taking up part-time and casual work, and no doubt, by virtue of their 'home duties', taking in paid work at home, generally under a banner of 'self employment'? Anna Booth's address to an Evatt Foundation after-dinner conference on strategies for the twenty-first century in the labour movement acknowledged the need for the Australian labour movement's need to adapt to change.[21] While she did not talk about informal sector workers, she did talk about the sex composition of the Australian labour force and the imperative for Australian trade unions to restructure their organizations and operations – including the idea of unions being more responsive to their members. It is particularly in this sense that SEWA represents a model worthy of consideration.

Notes

1. R.M. Martin, *Trade Unionism: Purposes and Forms*, Oxford, Clarendon Press, 1989, p. 9.
2. See J. Burgess, 'Non-Employee Status in Australia: Trends and Issues', *Australian Bulletin of Labour*, vol. 16, no. 4 (1990), pp. 233–53 regarding

the problems inherent in the definition and classification of "non-employees" and A. Stewart, '"Atypical" Employment and the Failure of Labour Law', *Australian Bulletin of Labour*, vol. 18, no. 3 (1992), pp. 217-35 for a discussion of labour law in connection with 'atypical' employment.

3. K. Hargreaves, *Women at Work*, Ringwood, Penguin Books, 1982, pp. 284-89.
4. A. Summers, 'Feminism of Two Continents: Comparing the Women's Movement in Australia and the United States', *Inkwell*, no. 5 (September 1992), pp. 9-10.
5. K. Rose, *Where Women Are Leaders: The SEWA Movement in India*, New Delhi, Vistaar Publications, 1992, p. 45.
6. L. Rudolph, and S. Rudolph, *In Pursuit of Lakshmi: The Political Economy of the Indian State*, Chicago: The University of Chicago Press, 1987, p. 22; J. Pathy, 'The Structure of the Indian Working Class and Conventional Unionism', in *Labour and Unions in Asia and Africa*, ed. R. Southall, Basingstoke: Macmillan Press Ltd., 1988, p. 127.
7. See Rose, p. 41.
8. M. H. Esterline, *They Changed Their Worlds: Nine Women of Asia*, Lanham, University Press of America, 1987, pp. 75-6.
9. Interview with E. Bhatt conducted by Helen Lay in New Delhi, India, on 9 April 1990.
10. Ela Bhatt, 'SEWA Women Break Free from Parent Body', *Manushi*, no. 8 (1981), pp. 13-15.
11. Rose, p. 80.
12. Rose, p. 45.
13. R. Cohen, 'Theorising International Labour', in *International Labour and the Third World. The Making of a New Working Class*, eds. R. E. Boyd, R. Cohen and P. C. W. Gutkind, Aldershot, Avebury, 1987, p. 5.
14. National Commission on Self Employed Women and Women in the Informal Sector, *Shramshakti: Report of the National Commission on Self Employed Women and Women in the Informal Sector*, New Delhi, The Commission, 1988, pp. 7-8.
15. Rose, pp. 26-7.
16. See Bhatt interview and Rose, p. 99.
17. E .Bhatt, 'Address to 13th ICFTU Congress', in *Report of the Thirteenth World Congress*, Brussels, International Confederation of Free Trade Unions, 1983, p. 551.
18. E. Bhatt, 'Address to 14th ICFTU Congress', in *Report of the Fourteenth World Congress*, Brussels: International Confederation of Free Trade Unions, 1988, pp. 446–47.
19. G. Schneider de Villages, 'Home work: A case for social protection', *International Labour Review*, 129.4 (1990), pp. 423-39.
20. M. Castells, and A. Portes, 'World Underneath: The Origins, Dynamics, and Effects of the Informal Economy', in *The Informal Economy: Studies in Advanced and Less Developed Countries*, eds. A. Portes, M. Castells, and L. Benton, Baltimore, The Johns Hopkins University Press, 1989.
21. A. Booth, 'Evatt's Internationalism', in *Labour Movement. Strategies for the 21st century*, Sydney, Evatt Foundation, 1991.

Changing Patterns of Women's Identity and Social Change in Modern India

Indira J. Parikh & Nayana Shah

This century has provided nations, societies and individuals opportunities to crystallise new identities for themselves. An individual's identity and role-taking are shaped by the society, culture and the family each one is part of. In the 5000 years of man's existence, there have been four major historical discontinuities. Each has given rise to a model of society, man, collectivity and man's relationship with collectivity. These have affected the roles and identities of men and women. From the era of hunting, man has moved to nomadic way of life, to the agrarian era, and finally to the current industrial and technological era.

The shift from an agrarian to technological era has also coincided with mass exodus from rural to urban areas. This transition generated experiences, encounters, demands and impact of urban industrial living that began to erode the agrarian social fabric. This in turn brought changes in the process of socialization from the culture, society and family and as such, the role and identity of both women and men.

The agrarian era had a continuity of over 2500 years. It gradually crystallised role differentiation; organizations and institutions were established with specific functional definitions. Bio-physiological differentiation that set men and women apart as counter yet complementary points for continuing life of the species seemed to have been capitalized by the agrarian culture to design differential roles and linking of these roles to distinct patterns of role activities.

Agrarian society then set about to reinforce these differences. Over a period of time the classification and patterning of role activities acquired an absolutism for conduct as well as visualizing of the role by individuals. The agrarian model identified women as anchored in stability, continuity, consistency and permanence. In this design women managed the internal interface of home and family and the extended network of roles and relationships. They also became the holders of values and virtues on behalf of the society. The social history of Indian agrarian society had slowly, but over a period of time evolved a traditional ideal role for women that emphasized and glorified sacrifice, surrender of the self to the role, victimhood and martyrdom. The women's only salvation lay in their spiritual freedom of worship.

The women too internalized the agrarian model crystalized by Manu: 'Women are to be the property owned and protected by a successive set of males'. They never recognized their own potential, aspirations or inner urges. Their role was to adjust, adapt and accommodate; they were expected to sacrifice and suffer for the wellbeing of their families. The agrarian social design further encountered the moguls and then the British. Both influenced women's identity and role-taking processes. As such, the transition from agrarian to industrial, from rural to urban and the universalization of education where women had opportunities to educate themselves drastically changed women's roles in the society.

The shift of Indian society from agrarian to industrial and from rural to urban is characterized by two distinct features:

— in the agrarian society men managed the external interface while the women managed the internal, social and relational interface of the environment. In the industrial society of today's times men and women have to manage both the external and internal interfaces of the environment.

— in the agrarian society men worked alone and in isolation while women lived in groups. In the formal work structures of organizations men worked in groups while women lived alone during a large part of the day.

As such, all the processes of cultural, social and familial socialization anchored in the agrarian model of living and relationship come into direct confrontation with the experiences, expectations and aspirations of today's requirements of women. This century and specifically in the last five decades have seen women make significant shifts in their location in the social structure, in their role in family settings and the external environment. One such significant shift has been their transition from homes to the formal work organization, and their role from social affiliative relations to managerial roles.

The post-independence era, which is moving at a high rate towards industrialization, complex technologies, professionalization and institutionalization presents a very confused but a challenging arena to women. Industrialization has created new opportunities and new role spaces for both the women and men of India. This new space is that of formal work organizations and managerial roles that is a unique dimension of today's time and age.

Changing Patterns of Women's Identity Concept of Identity

Before we take a look at the changing patterns of women's identity, let us first explore the concept of identity. The social science literature has many definitions of identity. For example, in the context of this paper, and after Pulin Garg, identity is postulated four dimensions: meaning making; role taking; action choices and replenishment.

The socialization and acculturation of a child generates experiences of people and systems. These experiences generate emotive and cognitive maps in an individual of significant people and systems. Before language develops the human child has absorbed the experience of people and introjected some of the people and systemic qualities . It is with the development of language that meaning giving appears, and a cognitive map develops of people and systems. Some meanings are embedded in the experience with people and systems while other meanings are postulated by the self. These meaning giving processes then determine the nature of transactions the individuals will have with others and the systems. The meanings can focus on the social, psychological or symbolic, and thus influence role and identity formulation.

Role taking is the process by which the individuals transact with the world. No individual can transact with the world as a pure self; the self is mediated through a series of social and psychological roles. The social roles reflect being a son or a daughter, a husband or a wife and a father or a mother. The psychological role is the core around which feelings and meanings converge; they influence the quality of social role taking. For example, underlying the social role of a daughter or a son, a wife or a husband and a mother or a father may be a psychological role of a martyr, a victim, an orphan, an Atlas and a Hercules.[1] These psychological roles are anchored in role models from culture, society, epics and myths.[2] Both the social and psychological roles are anchored in identity.

Action choices are determined by the meanings given by the self, others and situation, and the quality of role taking in the system. The action choices may be governed by societal and familial expectations, the given norms and what is acceptable or unacceptable, or what is considered socially desirable or undesirable. An individual may conform with the socially desirable and perpetuate the existing norms and beliefs, or may act given the context, situation, era and time. The action choice of an individual is largely determined by the quality of the social and psychological role, the meaning giving processes and identity. For example, Indian women are largely focused on affiliative and relational aspects and the expectations of them from the culture, society and family. Women more often conform to the norms of the sociocultural context, systemic expectations and the family's affirmation. They surrender their beings to ideal role models, and find it difficult to own up their existence in their own right independent of relational and affiliative linkages.

Replenishment processes are squarely anchored in the proactive identity of the individual. The individual can replenish the system when s/he acts with values and convictions. Replenishment processes add to the wholesomeness of systems and the wellbeing of individuals. It is only these processes that bring about the reshaping and refashioning of existing cultures, social structures and role-taking processes.

Indian women give of themselves to people and systems through sacrifice, denials and deprivations. They will fight for the maintenance of relationships and the perpetuation of norms and beliefs based on traditions, something society seems to idealize and glorify. However, Indian women find it difficult to assert, define and take charge of their destiny in their own hands. As such, they often end up making compromises or pseudo choices rather than replenish and redefine themselves, their roles or systems.

All these four processes put together contribute to the emergence of an identity of the individual. When the four processes are dominantly influenced by socio-cultural structures and processes and normative expectations, identity gets masked and only social roles emerge. When only social roles emerge action choices get limited and no replenishment occurs. Only in the unfolding of identity can new responses emerge and as such the redefinition of roles, the redesign of systems and the replenishment necessary to refashion responses.

Socio-cultural Influences on Women's Identity

Socialization processes through culture, society and family have influenced women's roles. These patterns reflect the era and history of various ages and the existing models of society. However, there have been some common threads running through these patterns in varying degrees. The agrarian design of society considered women to be the weaker sex, and accordingly designed a marginal role in decision-making concerning external environment. She was a victim of biological differentiation and predispositions, psychological and social oppressions and a denial of processes of being and of becoming her own self. There was overemphasis on conformity to the social roles as per the social design. Like its culture and country Indian women carry a rich heritage of role models, however, their location seem frozen in the social structure of the agrarian era.

In the Indian context, women have been worshipped and identified as goddesses or mothers since time immemorial. She is considered to be a source of strength, devotion, understanding, purity; her symbolic existence as 'Ardha Nareeshwar' or 'Ardhangini' itself goes to prove her status as a co-partner or an individual and not a gender. This ideology has percolated since the Vedic age and to that extent Indian culture is largely responsible in maintaining a dignified status of women in society. Her role is complementary to a man's. Though she was supposed to be vulnerable, in her all powerful form she can be the ultimate saviour or destructor of the universe. These processes of identity, however, only unfold in crisis and for a macro cause or relationship. Indian women rarely use these aspects of their identity.

Though the Scriptures have provided her legitimate space and due respect the sociocultural structures have postulated her idealism by glorifying the roles of Seeta, Savitri, and Kannagi as portrayed in the great epics. Women are supposed to follow without stating what they feel or believe is right for her, others or the system. She is bound by role performance with devotion. In today's times the continuity of the roles that women play in society have also generated images and stereotypes not only from the exigencies of biological differentiation and social situations but are deeply rooted in myths and legends and the religion of that particular culture.[3]

Influence of Family on Women's Identity

Given the baggage of society anchored in the agrarian model today's women have entered another era and another space of formal work organizations. Their entry has raised many issues as it directly confronts all those roles and expectations which were once held sacrosanct.[4] In this creation of new space families and role holders in families and society continue to bemoan the loss and erosion of traditional roles.

Families with male and female role models shape the child's role taking. The Indian family has a deeply embedded social design of conformity, surrender and becoming to a duty-bound role of a daughter, wife, daughter-in-law and mother for its daughters. Organizationally, there was a carry-over of the familial structures and role models to formal work settings.

Although the Indian family setting provides eventual support to women working in organizations, it also creates tremendous guilt and stress. Each new step the woman takes, she is shown the prescriptive social ideal role model of an ever-sacrificing woman who is both a victim and a martyr. Her own ambition, achievement, involvement in work generates threats and anxieties in the significant role-holders of the family, viz. the husband, the in-laws and the children. The husband puts her in the middle of two systems and questions her loyalty to the family. The in-laws demand the traditional ideal of a daughter-in-law; and the children demand her presence at all times. Indian women executives who hold the responsibility of a dual career as mother and worker find themselves belonging in two competing systems, getting pulled and pushed between the multiple roles and expectations.[5]

At the family level, marriage as an institution and social living gets loaded with expectations of traditional roles. In spite of genuine efforts by both, men and women keep regressing back to older models. Men regress to the role of a provider and controller of resources and matters outside the home. He does not sustain the new role of sharing the turmoils of the outside world. The woman tends to regress back into a homemaker and mother. She expects the husband to bestow all love and care and also to sustain the initiative to keep the marriage as a partnership.

A cultural lag is created as western models and behaviour patterns are adopted in the eastern environment. At the cognitive level the Indian woman wants to gain total freedom from social and familial role expectations. However, at the emotive level they remain anchored in the traditional culture of the agrarian era in affiliative and relational dimension. An approach avoidance conflict is created, resulting in the woman vacillating between her aspirations and emotions.

Caught between rising aspirations for a new world view and role definitions, and the persistence of centuries' old beliefs of a traditional agrarian society, India created the metaphor of women as martyrs and the persecuted. Their life space became overloaded with the struggle to create a sense of psychological equality, respect and autonomy. The universe of identities of the cultural lore also gets replayed by the Indian female child. Perhaps the role models of the cultural lore are internalized as deeply as the universe of identities are introjected. The three significant and persistent models through mythology to history are that of a virtuous woman who suffers (Sita); the virtuous and assertive woman who fights (Rani of Jhansi); and the one who escapes into religion (Meera). In terms of the three role models from history, women attempt to either conform, react or sidestep the system without directly confronting it or modifying it. All models chose either physical or psychological death. These women become martyrs who, despite all good intentions and personal struggle, perpetuate further the processes of dehumanization of women in the system.[6]

The Current Stance of Indian Women

Out of the deep-rooted social order, there emerged three types of women in today's times. They are the adjuster, the asserted and the drifter. The *adjuster* accepts the traditional roles and lives by them. They are content in their prescribed roles and experience no internal nor external conflict. Family is their focus of being and becoming, and they are greatly satisfied in their stance of conformity.

The *asserters* are the women who are constantly pushed and pulled by both systems. They are aware of their potential and react aggressively to their restrictive lives and the inevitable nature of their life space. They constantly create conflicting situations to assert themselves.

The *drifters* are those who have chosen to create a new location and define a new meaning for themselves. In doing so, they attempt to redefine their roles, the system and the nature of relationships. They wish to bring something more to themselves and the system they live in. These capable, intelligent, persistent and hard-working women act with courage and conviction. With every step they take, they create a space. The road they travel is unknown and lonely and each step is a discovery towards freedom.

Within these frames of identity and role models Indian women of today attempt to transcend the social milieu but fail to create real space for themselves in the social system. They attempt to define new roles but fail to trigger new processes within the system. They are captives of social traditions and role prescriptions.

Women's Movement in India

Indian women have attempted to borrow new role models from the west. These borrowed models are very often acceptable in both the family as well as work settings. The borrowed models do not acquire emotive roots or responses. Rational logical responses anchored in alien models create barriers and inhibitions. Women's movements have emerged from time to time. From the pre-independence period, the women's movement was very much a part of the nationalist movement. The radicalism and militancy that was characteristic of the women's movement during that period has substantially come down. The powerful women's movement of the pre-independence period based on social and political work among women has lost both its vigour and sense of purpose afterwards. The first two decades after independence were marked by stereotypical activities by women's organizations and apathy towards crucial issues concerning women.

During the 1960s women tried to get mobilized in large numbers and they joined the general struggles of the rural poor, tribals, industrial working class and other mass movements. The participation of women in Naxalbari movement, anti-price rise demonstrations, Navnirman Youth Movement, rural revolt in Maharashtra and the Chipko Movement provided a backdrop for the ensuing struggles on women's issues. However, the fact that women participated in other larger struggles but had not evolved their own platform for focusing and pressing for their own issues till the mid-1970s has been observed by various scholars and activists.

The International Women's Decade (1975-1985) has brought to the limelight a number of crucial issues relating to women, and it was felt that the 'Women's movement is the organized effort to achieve a common goal of equality and liberation of women and it presupposes sensitiveness to crucial issues affecting the life of women.' Although women's movements have taken considerable strides since the mid-1970s they have not been able to sufficiently obtain involvement of the rural women or urban poor. Individual groups have been working with all these women, yet a semi-permanent network has not been evolved, though many a time the need has been felt.

Women's movements gave rise to special interest groups such as cultural groups, professional women, working women, and centres where women could go for emotional, legal and medical support. In various states organizations like the 'Shramik Stree Mukti Sangathana', 'Mahila Mukti Morcha', 'Self-Employed Women's Association' have established themselves.

Research on women is not new but studies regarding them offer a variety of concerns with shifting emphases and perspectives, depending on one's theoretical orientation, ideological alignments, changes in the contemporary situation and in priorities in development. Women's question is no more a woman's concern but an important issue in the development debate and policy. Today's women attempt to deal with the inhibiting forces of societal barriers, and some have actually come up with new responses that are meaningful and relevant for the times. These new responses are anchored in today's times and have had no earlier role models or affirmation from societal structures.

Apart from women taking the initiative to help themselves and recreate an identity for their lot, society and government agencies too can work towards this end. Laws have been formed in favour of women. 'Abolition of Sati', 'Anti Dowry Bill', raising the age of marriage and 'equal pay for equal work' are positive advances by the government and concerned groups. The United Nations had declared 1975 as the 'Year of Women' and the period 1975-1985 as the 'decade of women'. There is an all-round recognition of the issues facing women and various groups, committees and forums, are discussing and formulating policies to raise the status of women. Instead of reinforcing existing realities like discrimination and deprivation, actual sources of problems that can provide new directions are to be discovered.

However, all the external barriers to growth are the result of Indian culture, societal design and history. The government policies are also reactive in the sense that they are designed on lacunas, deprivations and discriminations. As such, in the absence of monitoring and concomitant deterrents they do not change the tide. What the government can do is to design policies that facilitate new choices and directions. Education, infrastructure for women to feel respected and dignified and support systems so that they find freedom to leave oppressive people and situations have been ongoing concerns. Similarly, the social stigma attached to divorce, separation and or widowhood need to be eroded so that men and women can live a life and redesign life and relationships if it becomes necessary. Policies are for living issues and not only for emergent problems. As such, policies need to be designed for people and today's relational, structural and systemic scenario of society.

Though the rate of development in India is high, women have gained marginally because the pattern of development has been superimposed on a pre-existing system with social structures severely in disfavour of women. The main thrust should be to uplift the consciousness of women's issues. Without a change in the consciousness no social transformation will be able to set women free. Mass media which usually glorifies the subordination of women can help in a big way by influencing and reorienting the philosophy and attitudes of people. Values have to be internalized which no external force can help. What is required is a re-examination of existing systems, structures, relationships and the culture of the environment. Only if prevailing practices are analysed can one move towards a change for the better.

New Patterns of Identity for Indian Women

What should be the strategy of women to experience life, work, family and their own selves to the fullest? How can they make more meaningful action choices in the complex and ever-changing environment where they have to deal with the unknown and the unfamiliar? It seems that Indian men and women in modern society have failed to delink the absolutism of role activities associated with that of being male and female. Women often get caught in their primary biological role of nurture and sustenance. While some remain job-oriented and anchored in economic criteria, many deny themselves the unfolding of their potential. They accept routine, lower paid and lower status organizational positions. They give exclusive priority to the family demands and surrender their potential at the altar of familial roles. However, the younger and more educated generation create greater rationality between family and work responsibilities than do their older peers. The last decade has undergone some dramatic change. Women have experienced that role processes anchored in the agrarian model were inadequate and insufficient for the industrialized and urbanized living of today. Nevertheless, with all the clarity and understanding, the strengths of sociocultural structures and familial socialization tend to influence women's growth, status and career conditions. Can we provide any alternatives for women to define new roles and crystallise new identity patterns for themselves? Can we provide a role model for them to follow?

Professional women who have attempted to work with their potential, capabilities and resources and who have entered the world of occupation and career get caught up with the pathos of the traditional past and the ethos of modern times. They accept the responsibilities and expectations of both the past and the present, thus getting overburdened. This leaves them very little scope to disengage themselves from the pulls and pushes of dependence, surrender and control, and generate for themselves processes of autonomy and commitment.

As a result such women are continuously struggling in the system to find freedom from dependent and controlling relationships, to redefine their status from being passive performers and being acted upon by the system, to being actors and acting upon the system for their own wellbeing. Economic independence is only a mask to avoid confrontation with the basic issues of becoming a person in social interaction. Many women in their struggle become victims of the fear of social stigma, isolation and loneliness. To break the barriers to self-actualization, growth and independence, women have used economic independence as a medium to rise above their usual subdued level. But in the process they do not realize that economic independence is not the only factor to release them of their bond. It may just be the beginning of self-realization and assertion.

Women are at a crossroad. What choices do they make for themselves, their aspirations, urges and ultimate release? In today's times one charismatic woman cannot generate an ideal model for other women to follow. This kind of follower model would only repeat the historical process of turning others into echoes and shadows of a giant model; women will only turn out to be pale replicas of others. The only alternative seems to be that women become 'heroines' unto themselves to initiate a search to discover their own identity without condemning men, society or the system. Some women have opted to create a landmark for themselves. They have had the courage and conviction to choose the dimensions of their existence and grapple to discover an integrated identity that includes the multiple facets of social and work roles. They have claimed their existential and psychological identity beyond the social roles. Only then fulfilment and wider horizons have been experienced, acted upon and actualized.

The most enduring and difficult internal barriers are women's own social stereotypes, their psychological feeling of martyrdom and victimhood, their recipient status and doubts about the legitimacy of their formal roles in work organizations. These have been deeply embedded through the cultural lore and processes of socialization. Evidence of achievement aspirations and success does not free the woman to accept her action choices, courage of conviction and ownership of her own life; instead she ends up mortgaging her life to significant relationships and disown her potential and creativity. Her identity is influenced by the internal cultural, social, familial, psychological and personal barriers. The future scenario for women in India is an uphill journey to transcend existing monolithic social structures, to create new processes in the culture, the organizations and other families. The professional women will influence the social structures and culture by presenting a new role of being a professional, a new kind of a daughter, wife and mother.

Exploring beyond the Horizon

Most women experience terror at crossing the threshold to a space beyond the horizon. This space demands that women take charge of their destinies and their own life-spaces. It demands that she refashion her response, and confront the values that they hold and especially, to search for ways to encounter human existence with resilience.

One of the anchors of the space beyond the horizon lies in the freedom to make a choice and to experience the present. In order to do that, women have to free themselves from the associative universe and the overwhelming symbols of past experiences. The other anchor of the present lies in the space beyond the horizon where, instead of hope there is engagement with the world, instead of dreams there is commitment, instead of aspirations there are choices, instead of ideals there are convictions, instead of bestowal and affirmation there is courage.[7]

There are many complexities that envelop an Indian woman. There are pulls and pushes from her being to create an awareness/awakening o break away from conventional stereotypes. There is a pull to look beyond being a helper or a procreator of children. All these issues are merely the tip of the iceberg. Awareness is just a stepping stone towards bringing about change. Today's women need to pro-act rather than react to bring about a change in the existing system.

Patterns of identity that have changed at the macro-cultural level is the mother Goddess and the power Shakti. One fosters and the other destroys. At the micro-family level identities are role bound into either idealization or subjugation. At the societal level either they are marginal and exploited or glorified.

None of these are relevant for today. Alternatives for today's times are that women accept their multiple roles in multiple contexts and create space for themselves so that they can meet the challenges of tomorrow. Many women have lived the identity patterns of being treated as a Goddess, Mother, Shakti, power and essence of goodness and virtue. Many have lived their lives as idealized daughters, wives and mothers. Many have reactively or proactively made choices and been stigmatized, called names, labelled as whores and prostitutes. Many have burnt themselves in the name of social decadence and perpetuated the syndrome of a female child being a burden. Many have lived a lifetime in misery, burdened by the drudgery and surrender of themselves. Far too many have clung as dependents and derived their meaning of existence in relationships that have been abusive, exploitative and violating in the sugar-coated names of romance and love. Many women have led invisible lives being echoes and shadows of significant role holders and articulators of their norms. And millions of others have been lost in the jungles of giant figures and their voices lost in the wilderness, lives laid waste by non-choices. Women have turned their beings into non-beings and disowned their options of discovering new meanings and new definitions of roles in the emergent industrial context of today's times. Women refashion their responses to the new challenges in their role in the urban complex settings of today, and their action choices with multiple roles in multiple membership.

Indian women would have to cross a major threshold and enter an unknown land. They will have to design a path where none existed with a sense of discovery. They will have to encounter and live with threat, fear, anxiety and terror.

In the creation of a new path the women will discover new dimensions of their being and create their own landmarks. Women in their emerging new identity will have to open their eyes and look at people anchored in themselves and respond. They will determine and make choices as to who and in what manner their world will be postulated and with what quality of relatedness. Women will discover what offerings they will make and what they will receive. They will also create a space where others will feel included as well as excluded. Women in their identities will discover the infinite quality of relatedness as well as the finiteness of boundaries.

With structures and systems women will locate themselves with courage and conviction. Their own locations will provide them with stability and security rather than anchor them in structures and systems. The women will stand steadfast in their convictions to fight oppression and to generate autonomy and shared human values to live by. All in all the new patterns of women's identity will give shape to their own destiny in an ever-changing environment.

Notes

1. See Pulin Garg, and Indira J. Parikh, *Managers and Corporate Cultures*, Case of Indian Organization, International Management Review, vol. 3, 36, (1986).
2. Pulin Garg, 'International Conference on Transience and Transitions in Organizations', in *Corporate Culture of India*, ed. Parikh et al., Ahmedabad, ISISD Publications, 1989; Pulin Garg, *Designing for People*, Presentation in the IIMA Alumni Seminar, Bombay, 1987.
3. Rehana Ghadially (ed.), *Women in Indian Society*, New Delhi, Sage Publications, 1988.
4. Indira Parikh, *Models of Role and Identity: Barriers to Growth*, Indian Express, 3 January 1982; Indira Parikh and Nayana Shah, *Women Managers in Transition: From Homes to Corporate Offices*, Working Paper 941, Ahmedabad, Indian Institute of Management, 1991; P. Kapur, *The Changing Status of the Working Women in India*, New Delhi, Vikas, 1974.
5. P. Sinha, *Role Conflict among the Working Women*, New Delhi, Anmol Publications, 1987.
6. Indira Parikh, *Women in Management*, Ahmedabad, Indian Institute of Management, 1981; see Parikh, *Models of Role and Identity: Barriers to Growth*, op. cit.
7. Parikh and Garg, op. cit.

Section III
Regional Representations

Boundary as Predicament : The Case of the *Dai* in Rural Bangladesh

Santi Rozario

In my earlier work I have explored the ways in which women, their bodies and sexuality are used to maintain the boundaries of various Bengali social groups, e.g. lineages, classes and religious communities. I have shown how class and communal domination in turn reinforce gender domination. In this paper I look at women who through economic necessity are forced to engage in a profession which places them on the margin of the Bengali moral community. I examine the way these women understand and make sense of their anomalous position.

Related issues have been raised by a few recent studies of South Asian society which explore the self-understandings of marginalized and devalued groups. One study which has several points of contact with my material is Margaret Egnor (Margaret Trawick)'s article on *sakti* and Tamil women (1980). Others include works which deal with the predicament of untouchables, notably R. R. Khare's *Untouchable as Himself* (1984; see also Appadurai's comments, Appadurai 1986). In a wider sense, Ashis Nandy's work on the psychology of colonialism, notably *The Intimate Enemy* (1983) concerns how colonial India as a whole dealt with its relationship of inferiority to the colonial powers.

All these studies run some risk of dismissal by varieties of postmodernist discourse for their involvement with the essentially humanist project of understanding and listening to the experiences and the voices of the marginalized, the minorities and the oppressed. Their approach is, however, too important to be dismissed so easily. Kalpana Ram has argued recently for the need to rescue the concept of 'experience', and humanist values in general, as potentially useful for the counter-mobilization of minority groups against class, race and sexual oppression. She comments that some such concept is necessary 'in order to develop a satisfactory account of the way in which particular subjectivities are constructed' (1993: 24). My paper is intended as a contribution to this rescue. In seeking to understand and locate the experience of the Bangladeshi *dai* and to make sense of what they have to say, I have no intention of romanticizing the negative features of childbirth in rural Bangladesh (see Rozario 1992A), but I do hope to make some contribution towards the validation of the lives that are lived within this despised and negatively valued space.

My research on the *dai* was carried out in the context of fieldwork on women's reproductive health in late 1991 and early 1992 in the Rupganj subdistrict, which is located in Dhaka district, three hours by road from the city of Dhaka. The area is well known to me from my previous doctoral fieldwork (Rozario 1992B), and my family originates from a nearby community, so that despite the brevity of the fieldwork period I was able to carry out useful research. My initial aim was to examine the impact of modern medicine and contraception, and the significance of local concepts of purity, on women's reproductive health. My data consists mostly of interviews with *dai*, family planning workers, folk healers (*kabiraj*), biomedical (allopathic) and homeopathic doctors, pregnant women, and mothers with small children.

The Pollution of Childbirth and the Marginal Status of the *Dai*

To understand the marginal status of the *dai*, we need to begin with the most central and most problematic aspect of her role: the *dai's* involvement with the pollution of childbirth. In the North Indian context, Jeffery et al (1988) argue that the *dai's* function is centrally concerned with the removal of pollution: pollution associated with their task of delivering babies, and to give meaning to and legitimize their role. For the sake of convenience, I will classify the strategies used by the *dai* to counter their devalued status under four categories:

(a) seeing their work as chartacterized by the possession of significant professional skills, particularly in comparison with doctors and other medical personnel;
(b) taking pride in their individual skills in comparison with other *dai* ;
(c) seeing themselves as engaged in the performance of charitable work;
(d) claiming spiritual or religious sanction for their work.

I shall discuss these one by one, although there is often significant overlap between them.

(a) The *dai* as possessor of significant professional skills.

In my interviews, the *dai* often made it clear that they were proud of their skills and went on to elaborate on the various method they employ in different problem situations. The *dai* take pride in the special knowledge they gained from more experienced *dai* on how to deal with difficult labour. Thus Gaynoda, a Hindu *dai* , said that the way she decides whether or not the baby is due is by pulling out a certain plant. 'If the plant comes up with the root then the baby is ready to be delivered, if the plant breaks somewhere in-between then the baby is not due.' By following this method Gaynoda apparently successfully predicted in a case that the pain felt by the birthing mother was not labour pain. She said ' I delivered that baby after eight days.' Gaynoda uses various other techniques in dealing with difficult labour. She said to bring on labour pain a root of a special tree is tied to the left thigh and taken off as soon as the mother delivers, 'otherwise the whole of the mother's inside will come out with the baby' since the root is thought to be so potent. Alternatively, the woman in labour is sometimes given basil leaves to sniff or the root of a young tamarind tree is placed in her mouth in order to bring on her labour pains. Another *dai* told me that she uses the root of a plant to correct the position of the baby inside the mother's womb. If the delivery looks like a really difficult one, the *dai* looks for a rare plant the root of which has to be collected when she is absolutely naked. These practices are common among most of the *dai* in Rupganj as well as in other parts of Bangladesh as reported by Blanchet (1984).

The *dai* also compared their skills and integrity of their work with the village doctors or city hospitals. Even though the families give higher status and higher value to doctors it is interesting to see the way *dai* compare their work to that of the doctors.

Although it is a common custom that a family give a sari to a *dai* after she delivered a baby, the *dai* claim that they do not necessarily attend a birth for this reason. They cite examples of performing difficult deliveries and yet not receiving any form of remuneration. On the other hand, they refer to the enormous amount of money that the family have to pay to a village doctor if he is called, not to mention the costs involved in sending a birthing woman to a city hospital. Thus when I asked the *dai* why they thought that the families called them, instead of a doctor, the reply usually was because doctors are very expensive. 'A *dai* is merely given a sari, if anything, and maybe a meal of chicken curry.'

There is a clear distinction between the way a family treats a doctor on the one hand and a *dai* on the other. This is so despite the fact that the *dai* , who are accorded low status, are recognized as experienced women, whose presence is desirable at a birth. Within the limited options available to rural families, it is not surprising that a *dai* is often perceived as the only person who can help. After all, unless there are complications, delivering babies is a relatively simple task for *dai* who have sufficient knowledge of female anatomy.

However, when complications arise, a *dai* will usually advise the family to call a doctor or to take the birthing woman to a hospital. She does this (i) because she feels unable to tackle the situation, and perhaps more importantly (ii) because she does not want to be responsible for any mishap or to ruin her reputation by being involved in a problem delivery which may lead to the death of the birthing mother and/or the baby. In such a situation, if a family can afford it, a doctor (usually uncertified) will generally be called. Usually he simple watches the *dai* deliver the baby without making any physical contact with the birthing mother or the baby. At other times, the baby may be killed as a result of the doctor's attempts to deliver it by force. Whatever the case, and even if the mother or the baby dies, the doctor, who is almost always male, has to be paid a very substantial amount.

While in the above accounts we see the *dai* being concerned about the validity of their profession vis-a-vis other medical professionals, and the community of the *dai* is presented as a united front, in this section we see that the *dai* are also at the same time anxious to preserve their individual professional reputation vis-a-vis other *dai*. Thus when I asked an elderly Christian *dai*, trained by the dispensary nun some 30 odd years ago, what she does in difficult deliveries, she said 'It has never happened that I could not deliver the baby — yes, once I had to call the sister (midwife-nun from the Catholic dispensary) who gave a saline to the birthing mother'. She said 'in my hands nothing happens to babies, there is no trouble'. She added 'people do not call the *dai* in whose hands babies have died, or the birthing mother had hemorrhage. With God's blessing no baby died in my hands, or no woman experienced haemorrhage in my hands. This is why people call me all the time. People do not call other *dai* because they do not know about haemorrhage, when it happens, how or why it happens they do not understand'. Then she continued to explain why a woman may haemorrhage. Note the emphasis placed on my hands signifying the importance of her expertise, not necessarily characteristic of other *dai*.[2]

The stories from another middle-aged *dai* and her elderly mother bring out a similar emphasis on individual professional skills. Teri was called to attend a delivery case which was already being attended to by a nurse. By the time Teri arrived on the scene the nurse had apparently administered a douche to the birthing mother and made her lie down. Teri told the nurse (with whom she enjoyed a joking relationship): '*kiyer Baler nurse tumi!* (What sort of a nurse are you!) It is more than time for the delivery. You had better get out of here.' Then Teri locked herself inside the room with the birthing mother. 'I helped her get up, and, holding her by her waist, shook her up. At that moment the birthing mother said 'I can feel the baby coming forward'.' Then Teri delivered the baby. She reported to me with apparent pride that after the delivery the nurse said 'Oh, Teri is the one with the degree, I am really embarrassed.' Teri's personal reputation is then said to have increased. The father of the newborn baby said 'if we did not bring Teri today but sent the baby's mother to a hospital we would be in for Tk4000.00 (A$100.00) bill.'

Obviously enjoying telling me the stories of her high reputation, Teri went on to tell me yet another story: Malati was taken to the hospital by her husband to deliver. Malati watched the way in which women's legs were tied up to poles. She got frightened and ran away from the hospital, leaving her husband behind. Teri said 'this baby was then delivered in my hands'. According to Teri, the dispensary-trained midwives are amazed at her courage. One dispensary nun told her '*Hai Hai*, how do you handle such big cases, the doctors get scared but how do you do this?' Teri added 'the kind of cases I do, the Medical Hospital staff often do not know what to do'.

Teri's elderly mother, also a *dai*, chimed in: 'you need courage, the one delivering needs the courage as does the birthing woman'. She then told me the story of a case in which the husband of a birthing woman came to call her: 'He touched by feet and said 'you are my Godsister, save me'. Another birthing woman she attended was apparently in labour for 14 days but Teri's mother did not have any trouble delivering the baby.

These stories clearly reveal the individual *dai's* concern about their reputation. The popular *dai* are the ones who enjoy a good reputation when compared with other *dai*. The competitive attitude of the *dai* is understandable given that most *dai* engage in this task for material gain.

(c) The *dai* as engaged in public service or charitable work

In Rupganj, the *dai* often said things like 'I cannot say 'no' when people call, so I go', or 'what can I do, I know the job, they call me', etc. None of the *dai* interviewed explicitly described their role in helping the birthing woman as being primarily a source of income. It is true that almost all the *dai* are from poor families, but they do not focus on the material gain from their involvement in childbirth. Instead they will relate their involvement in childbirth in terms of 'so and so came to call me middle of the night, he was desperate, his wife had been in labour for three days'. This way of relating their task of delivering babies immediately removes any question of payment. It is often an emergency, people are desperate, there are no alternatives, especially for the poor families — so the impression one forms is that a *dai's* prime motive is to save the situation, save the mother from terrible pain by relieving her by delivering the baby.

Pishima is a well known *kabiraj* . She said that she is confident she can cure any illness or problems villagers come to see her for. On questioning she said that she received her power almost 25 years ago from a *pari* (female benevolent spirit) whom she can call upon whenever there is a danger. Beside her usual clients with *sutika* (post-natal diarrhoea), stillbirth and abortion problems, a vast number of her clients come to see her for other reasons. For example, a cook/bearer working in an expatriate's household might have been facing problems with the employer, or someone else looking for a job might have been unsuccessful, or someone might want to know whether her husband has arrived safely in Kuwait or Bahrain. Pishima said she even has overseas clients — their relatives in the village take the medicine from her and send it by post or through personal couriers. However, interestingly she emphasises that for all of these she uses roots and plants to offer help and never uses *jharfuk* (exorcism of evil spirits). It seems she is anxious to dissociate herself from *bhut* and align herself with her *pari* , a benevolent spirit. She said she is possessed by this *pari* every now and then, and when she is possessed she prays, sings religious songs and goes to the Church. In other words, her religious activities takes a priority.

In these examples we have seen a variety of ways in which *dai* claim that their work has some kind of spiritual or religious sanction, thus again countering their low status and polluting occupation.

Discussion and Conclusion

As we have seen, the *dai* (midwife) occupies a precarious position in rural Bangladesh. She is vital to the system because birth cannot take place without a *dai* . However, she is at the point of maximum conflict and contradiction. For example, fertility is of utmost importance, and a Bengali woman is anomalous until she is married and bears children. Yet at the same time childbirth is associated with the worst pollution. As one main function of the *dai* is to remove birth-pollution, it is not surprising that she is accorded low status in Bengali society. This is true both for Hindus and Muslims (Blanchet, 1984; Rozario 1992A).

In Margaret Egnor (Margaret Trawick)'s paper on the concept of *sakti* among Tamil women (Egnor 1980), *sakti* is a kind of power separate from the formal status of the caste hierarchy and in some ways countervailing to it. *Sakti* is explicitly associated with women, who are by definition subordinate in Tamil (as in Bangladeshi) society. It is also associated with suffering, servitude and self-sacrifice. I see these values as very much part of the Bangladeshi context as well, if perhaps less explicit than in the Hindu society of Tamil Nadu. Several of Egnor's case-studies have points of similarity to my own material (in particular those of Valliammae and Sarasvati).

R. S. Khare's emphasis on the importance of the ideology of asceticism and of the values of world-renunciation among untouchables (specifically Lucknow Chamars, Khare 1984) also has points of contact with my material, in that, in both his material and mine, poverty and low status is to some degree given positive value by linking it with ideas of renunciation of conventional society.

The discussion could be taken further into the area of the South Asian reaction to the colonial predicament. Ashis Nandy's work (Nandy 1983) emphasizes how deeply this has marked the self-understanding of modern South Asians. It is interesting to think about, for example, Mahatma Gandhi's self-presentation as a poor ascetic, and the enormous resonance which this had among the Indian population, in relation to the *dai's* attempts to construct their role as one of spiritually-sanctioned public service.

All this material suggests that, particularly in articulating a construction of their role as one of public service and as having religious sanction the *dai* are developing a mcans of representation that extends–slowly–beyond their traditional roles.

The Girl Child in Bengali Women's Literature of the Nineteenth and Early Twentieth Centuries

Shivani Banerjee Chakravorty

This paper is an attempt to explore the representation of the 'girl child' in Bengali literature by Hindu upper-caste and class women in the nineteenth and early twentieth century. Taking into consideration the fact that the 'girl child' was at the core of the reform movements in Colonial Bengal — the abolition of *satidaha*, child marriage, Kulin polygyny, female infanticide; the sanctioning of widow-remarriage; raising of the age of consent; the introduction of women's education, it was natural that she was one of the most important features of the reformist discourse and became the object of all the ideological debates which took place first in Bengal and then spread all over Colonial India.

In these debates, the Reformers made of Hindu upper-caste girls symbols of their cause of improving the condition of all Indian women who they felt were oppressed by retrogressive values and barbaric customs. According to them, the emancipation of women would eventually pave the way for the modernization of the entire nation. On the other hand, the upholders of cultural nationalism saw women (again considered normative for all Indian women) as repositories of Indian tradition and culture and authentic Hindu values, guardians of chastity and honour of the country. The Colonial state wooed both groups according to their own convenience; supporting the former was in tune with their 'civilizing goals'; at the same time they did not want to alienate the latter too much by interfering in 'native rituals;'. By the turn of the century, the social reform movements had receded into the Nationalist movement, and once again the icon of women as spiritual and moral strength was constructed. Now, the imagery of traditional religion was combined with progressive ideals of the reformers and the puritanical restrictions derived from the now idigenized Victorian moral code. The new symbol was that of a deified being, who could bring a sense of wholeness to community by energizing her men in their struggle to free the captive 'Motherland', and who would create an ideal family by producing worthwhile citizens of the nation. The boundaries of the family was extended to that of the nation, so that women's participation in the Nationalist movement was part of their domestic duty of servitude, sacrifice, self-denial and endurance.

All these ideological battles were carried on by man and the organizing principle remained patriarchal. Each perspective reduced women to cultural constructs — ploys used to idealize emotions in order to serve the patriarchal family structure. History and culture tended to ignore what they themselves thought of the social and political changes taking place, or of the repercussions of these on their own lives.

Despite all the debates and controversies, some of the social changes did permeate to the inner courtyards. Hindu girls from the middle and upper classes gained an access to some education which facilitated the growth of inquiry and self-expression. Eventually they could appropriate the patriarchal hand-outs to create a space for themselves and articulate their own anxieties, struggles and resolutions. One of the chief vehicles they used in order to articulate their ideas was writing. Interestingly, in their writing too, the girl child assumed significance. Not as the icon she was in the national debates, not as a passive object of discourse, but as the main protagonist. In text after text, the world and society, family and relationships are seen through her eyes. The authors seemed to be reconstructing their past in an attempt to catharsize the pains of their deprivations and unfulfilled yearnings, as well as to discover the sources of their strengths.

It is interesting to note that in these texts, even when the point of view is that of a child, she is not considered a child, nor does she think of herself as one. She is a 'woman' from birth and has to be socialized to become an efficient server of the prescribed code. The joys of childhood — games, laughter, toys, playing with friends, — are all forbidden to her. Any tendencies towards 'unwomanly behaviour' incites social disapproval. She has to be forcibly weaned away from deviant behaviour and channeled towards her rightful task — the upholding of the stability and the honour of the family and thereby of nation. It is only from a contemporary perspective that she is seen as the child she really is. In recent years, a special focus on the girl child has become a felt need, as there is an increasing realization of the fact that most problems related to women's status and rights evolve from childhood.

We can see documented in women's literature (which essentially emerges from the Hindu middle and upper classes; the voices of subaltern women were still not audible) in the nineteenth and early twentieth centuries how gender discrimination begins at birth or even before, through conscious and subconscious neglect of the girl child's nurture and education, through social taboos, prejudiced double-standards and gender-specific behavioural expectations. There are clearly two levels of narrative. From the social perspective the girl child is not a human being with individual needs but a convenient receptacle for the changing ideologies. For the author, she is a living, feeling and suffering entity, a projection into her own childhood experiences. On the one hand, we see the process of the construction of gender, on the other we see the individual woman's attempts to negotiate with and subvert this official construction of femininity.

Moving to the texts, we discover the unwantedness of the girl child and the high value placed on the male child as a recurrent theme. Such discrimination can be traced back to centuries of historical processes which have legitimized this as a social system. In the Hindu patrilineal family structure, the son is responsible for carrying on the family lineage; he is responsible for looking after his parents in their old age; he is the natural heir to ancestral property; and only he can perform the funeral rites of the parents without which they cannot reach salvation. Religious, economic and social factors combine to make the birth of a son the most desirable event in a person's life. This leads to a strong preference for the son, who is an asset, a good investment, an insurance for the future. The daughter, on the other hand, is nothing but a liability. She has to be given away in marriage to another family, and a dowry has to be paid for her marriage. Any money spent on her is a waste, as her loyalties must change on marriage, and her parents can have no further claims on her. She cannot perform the funeral rites, cannot carry on the family name, and hence can have no right to ancestral property. Religious customs and economic factors collude to perpetrate and perpetuate patriarchy. Hence, gender discrimination, which begins even before birth, is considered to be a natural phenomenon. All kinds of strategies are contrived to ensure the birth of a male child — medical treatments, herbal concoctions, talismans, visits to the atrologers, special prayers and religious rituals, even witchcraft is sought. If a son is born, the event is celebrated with great pomp and ceremony, the gods are propitiated, relatives, friends and neighbours are fed, in accordance to the social status of the family. If the child turns out to be a girl, it is an occasion to mourn. All the necessary rituals are limited to what is absolutely essential. A novella *Annakali* by Jyotirmoyee Devi (1894-1989) depicts this unwantedness of the girl child most poignantly. Jyotirmoyee Devi has written a number of stories on this theme. In a short story, '*Beti ka Baap*', she shows how the grandmother poisons the sixth female child, a normal, beautiful baby, who everyone loves from the moment of birth, and the atrocity is accepted as a natural act by everyone in the family. There are no dissenting voices, except the mother's silent grief. Ironically, the principal agents of gender oppression are women who have been made to internalize centuries of myth-making about women's inferior status.

One of the major reasons for this unwantedness of the girl child is the fear of dowry, which renders a child bride an inanimate toy in the barter that is Hindu marriage. In Saralabala Sarkar's (1875-1960) short story '*Kanyadaya*', the young girl Toru is taunted because her wedding cannot be fixed due to a lack of resources. Her elder brother, little more than a child himself, can only sympathize:

> 'She was rebuked at every step. And for what crime? That she wasn't getting married! I thought, what can the poor girl do? She had never said that she didn't want to get married. Even if she had said that, that wouldn't prevent her marriage.
>
> The only obstacle to her marriage was money. Where did her fault lie? *Ma* was really unjust. If Toru asked for food, *Ma* said, 'You old maid! You are not getting married, yet you want to eat all the time and grow big like an elephant!' Wasn't that strange? Should she starve just because her wedding wasn't taking place? And if by chance she refused to eat, she was taunted, 'Oho! So you are worrying about your marriage and are unable to eat!' She wasn't allowed to go out of the house and play with her friends, 'It doesn't look good for such a big unmarried girl to roam around outside the house!' How much more the little girl had to suffer, I wonder! I used to think "Why ever are girls born?'

But it is his duty, in the absence of a father, to marry her off, and the only way he can do it is through subterfuge, fully realising the painful consequences of his deception the young girl would have to face at her in-law's home.

The narrative of *Annakali*, begins with the birth of the fourth female child in an upper-middle class Hindu family in rural Bengal at the turn of the century. The event brings to the desolate grandmother's mind an 'image of an inevitable future — the responsibilities and obligations, the humiliation of being burdened with unmarried daughters'. Neighbours taunt, ridicule and pity, and the infant is named '*Annakali*' — a plea to the deity to bring an end to the procession of girls. The conch-shell is not blown, no naming ceremony is held, and all rituals are performed perfunctorily. Anna grows up a neglected child — whose first smile, first word, first step are of no significance to anyone. She is fed and clothed and left to fend for herself. At every step, she is reminded of her worthlessness. When she cries over a broken doll, she is laughed at. 'Why are you crying for such an unimportant thing? — Imagine anyone grieving for a daughter — you have had a lucky escape from the ordeal of getting her married!'

In due course of time, the unwanted Anna grows up, gets married and gives birth to three girls. But she becomes a mother in the real sense of the term, in fact, is publicly proclaimed to have 'attained the glory of motherhood' only at the birth of a son. This is perfectly in tune with the official construction of motherhood — the creator of community, — 'the divine mother of the godly son'. The female child is not in the same position. Although she has to become a mother herself, her upbringing has to be geared around and outside her brothers' growth. So, when Anna's son is born, she feels that doors to a golden future have been opened before her. Earlier she had vowed to herself that she would never differentiate between a daughter and a son. Now she reasons with herself that a son is more precious as he will remain her own, whereas the daughters will have to go away to other homes. Consequently, the three girls fade into the background, much as their mother had in her own childhood, while lavish signs of affection, expensive clothes, toys, food, are bestowed on their brother. When the five year old Atasi wants to play with his toys, she is rebuked by her mother. The little girls realize that their brother is far more important than they are, and retreat silently. Annakali suppresses her own memories of a deprived childhood, and continues to favour her son. When her husband suggests leaving the girls a small share of his property, she strongly opposes it, 'it would cut into Dipu's (the son's) inheritance'. And she believes that if need be, Dipu would look after his sisters. Her faith in her son is rooted in centuries of conditioning of 'patrilineal heritage, that there should be no disruption in the flow, the son's happiness or comforts should not be impaired. As for the daughters, if they have to suffer, it is their destiny'. Even when it becomes obvious that Dipu, when he assumes a position of power, considers his widowed mother and sisters unwanted burdens, Annakali quells her doubts and maintains her faith in him.

The daughters (one a young widow with two children, the other poor and sickly, and the third still unmarried) are pushed to the peripheries of family life, aliens in their parents' home, and realize the significance of their mother's name, 'it meant not only for her mother, but for all of them. They are collectively saying to all the girls, no more. We don't need you. You have no future. There is no place here for you. We don't need you. No more. No more'.

Who is this 'they'? The entire social structure that considers only males as worthy of being called 'humans'. Sarat Kumari Chowdhurani (1861-1920) attacked the popular notion of 'What use can girls ever be?' in her analysis of the neglect and deprivation of the girl child in the short story, '*Adorer Na Anadorer* '. Her spokesperson, a young woman, addresses a representative of the older generation of women, criticizes gender discrimination bitterly:

> What use can't they be now... a woman is an asset to the family... You people jump up as soon as you hear a girl has been born and say, 'Now we'll have to marry her off'. Well, don't you have to spend a lot of money on a boy too? We've all seen the way the girls are given the leftovers to eat from plates the boys have already used. The boys wear shoes and shiny spotless garments and girls go around in cheap grimy wraps...The boys sleep on soft beds with mattresses and girls sleep on rush mats and a tattered quilt spread out on the floor... The other day, the second aunt's daughter... asked for rice in the morning and Grandmother turned round and said, 'Whoever heard of a girl eating rice with the first lot — to come and ask for rice when nobody has eaten yet! Let your father and your uncles eat first: You can sit and eat off their plates after that'... She's just a little girl of six or seven — how could she know?

This is one of the first voices of protest by a woman. And it is in this voice that the roots of social change lie, not in the ideological battles being fought outside. But change is still a long way off.

Despite all the arguments against child marriage, high caste Hindu girls continued to be married before the age of ten. In colonial India, the optimum age of marriage for girls was eight. *Gouridaan*, the gift of the virgin daughter before she is eight years old could guarantee salvation for the father. Women were property, and their virginity was necessarily bound to family honour. The objective of early marriage, was, like the earlier practice of *satidah*, the prevalent custom of *kuli* polygyny, and the oppression of widows, to ensure the maintenance of family honour and purity of lineage through the controlling of female sexuality within the family fold.

Since early marriage was the norm, little girls had to be conditioned to accept their fate, and to be trained to perform their future duties effectively. This training program began very early, and older women took on the role of teachers of duties and transmitters of values. Satyabati, the protagonist in Ashapurna Devi's *Prothom Protisruti* (1962) is a child of eight in an upper-middle class Hindu joint family of nineteenth century rural Bengal. She is surrounded by a huge network of women whose function is to train her to fulfil the predestined mission in her life — to be a 'good daughter-in-law, wife and mother'.

For this, she has to first chant hymns to God, and perform a number of rites to propitiate the deities so that they would bless her with a good husband and kind in-laws. These rites — *bratas* — are socio-religious observances which are an integral part of the Hindu girls' upbringing. They are used to socialize young girls to traditional feminine roles by teaching them a sense of self-discipline, self-sacrifice, and patience — qualities necessary to cope with the inevitable travails of a woman's life. Next, she has to remain indoors and perfect the crafts of domesticity, which included cooking, knowledge of religious rituals, taking care of children, sick and aged, domestic crafts like stitching, drawing *alpana*, etc. And finally, she must inculcate the values of submissiveness, servitude, and dependence. Only by perfecting all these can she be worthy of her onerous future role.

In *Prothom Protisruti*, the women in Satya's family collaborate to caste her into this mould. However, Satya refuses to be tamed. A brilliant personification of protest, she becomes the source of horror, anger, and admiration in an age women were not supposed to be seen, let alone heard. She is repeatedly warned that by defying norms she was jeopardizing her future happiness, and threatened with the catastrophe of being thrown out by her future in-laws. She pays no heed to these threats, and from the age of eight embarks on a life-long quest for gender justice. She romps around with the village boys, laughs aloud, speaks out, and constantly criticizes double-standards in society. In her parental home, she can get away with this defiance, mainly because of the class structure. The only daughter of an affluent patriarch, no one can really control her outspokenness, as she has her father's support. She appeals to him every time she sees injustice, even in his own actions, and arouses his admiration for her courage. Yet he has internalized traditional values enough to feel a little regret that she is female and all her potential would get restricted to housework and childbearing. He cannot conceive of an alternative option for her, performs *gouridaan* and sends her away to her in-laws' home at the age of ten to meet her inevitable fate.

This experience of being sent away, being 'given away', is extremely traumatic for little girls. Social reformers argued against child marriage on the grounds that young girls did not have the capacity to be fitting partners to the new enlightened Bengali youth, and more importantly, were not physically or mentally prepared to assume the responsibilities of motherhood. The agony of these children in having to leave their home and family to live among strangers forever was never taken into account. Even when it was noted, it was not an important factor to necessitate social change. The anguish is most poignantly described by Rasasundari Devi (1809-1900) in her autobiography *Amar Jiban* (1897). Here she describes how she is married at the age of twelve, considered very late in those days, but is as naive as a child of five at the time. Exceptionally shy and timid, she has no idea what marriage means. All she knows is that everyone has to get married. Initially, the new clothes, jewelry, crowds, music, everything delights her. But she soon realizes that she has to leave her mother and family, that she is being 'given away', she becomes desolate with grief and terror. She compares her anguish to that of a sacrificial goat which has realized that its end is near. In her new home she feels imprisoned. Although she receives love and affection from her in-laws, she can never forget the grief of leaving her parental home. She is so tied up with household duties that she has to gradually sever all her links with her parental family, and is not even able to visit her dying mother. Her bitterness over this is severe, and she writes, at the age of 88, that if she had been a son, no one could have prevented her from flying to her mother's death-bed. As a daughter, she has to remain trapped in her cage. It is not the back-breaking domestic drudgery to which she is bound all her life that pains her so much as the complete loss of freedom.

The custom of child-marriage ensures not only the control of a woman's freedom and sexuality, but also control of her development as a human being. In the story '*Akritagya* ' by Anurupa Devi (1861-1920), Leela the child-bride, enters her in-laws' home to face taunts and rebukes at every step. Her mother-in-law firmly believes that 'a daughter-in-law is like a dog and requires strict disciplining, or else she will get above herself'. So she dictates what the child must wear, eat, speak, how she has to spend her leisure, and even how she must feel. Her devotion for her father is misinterpreted by her husband and mother-in-law as a craving for the comforts and affluence in her parental home. To 'break her arrogance', all kinds of vicious methods are used, as their possession of her mind and body has to be complete. What Leela finds most painful to endure is their refusal to permit her to visit her father. And what hurts her even more is his advice that 'that is your home, this home you have known since birth is not yours'. In order to spare him the extent of her misery, Leela informs him that she is happy and well and she doesn't want to visit him. She has internalized the code of self-denial well. A child herself, she continues to play the role of mother which she had assumed on her own mother's death, and protects the father/child at the cost of her own silent suffering. He accepts her 'ingratitude' with mortification, and concludes that 'A daughter is born for another, but a son remains one's own forever'. Despite his deep love for her, he is incapable of understanding the extent of her sacrifice.

In *Raibari* (1962), Giribala Devi (1890-1983) focuses her entire narrative on a child-bride. The novel traces the growth of a child-bride, starting with her being uprooted from her familiar surroundings and placed in a traditional *zamindari andarmahal*—the inner courtyards of an affluent rural land-owner. Twelve year old Binu is at home only amidst nature, plucking berries, climbing trees, swimming in the family pond, and playing with her companions, cushioned by the affection of her mother and grandmother. It is extremely traumatic for her to adjust to the rules and regulations of the elaborately ritualistic household she is married into. She is bitterly criticized for not having the qualities befitting the daughter-in-law of *Raibari*, and has to endure taunts for her ignorance of the traditional customs, religious rituals, domestic duties. At every step she makes mistakes and is rebuked severely. Once she forgets the code of dolcility and swims in the family pond instead of confining herself to the expected dip, she is told by her mother-in-law and sister-in-law that:

> Even if people don't have shame, at least they have fear. You have neither. Your parents taught you to swim, didn't they teach you any shame or manners? You are a disgrace to the Rai family, I am unable to show my face in the neighbourhood because of your lack of manners. Such a beast had to be written in my destiny. The cheat and swindler father from Calcutta found a rustic simpleton and forced this lunatic on him...Such a daughter-in-law deserves a broomstick on her face, fire on her forehead. A person who does not have fear or respect, shame or shyness, is worse

> than a dog or a cat. A girl from the banks of a river has completed her dalliances at the *Jamuna* and has come here to play her lascivious games in *Mathura.* Glory to her guts, glory to her audacity! A new bride, swimming in the pond in the middle of the afternoon! *Maago,* where can we hide? How repulsive, how shameful, fie! Fie! (*Raibari,* p. 51).

Binu's only allies in the household are the old grandmother, who is as unwanted and unloved in *Raibari* as Binu is, and the housemaid, who offers to help her adjust to the rules and regulations of the household. The maid talls Binu:

> Listen, let me first train you. They [the mother-in-law and sisters-in-law] will return soon after their bath. After you have bathed, you will also go straight to the room where they are working, you will help your mother-in-law and sisters-in-law with the work. You will not leave the room till they do. After everyone has finished eating, you will serve them *paan.* When it is time to bathe, you will put oil on their hair. Nabne makes everyone's beds, when it is time to do to bed, you will dust the beds once again with your *aanchal.* You will stay close to them, press their arms and legs when necessary. Tell Taru that the *thakur* should not serve your food before everyone else's, say. 'I'll eat with *Ma* '. You will go to bed when everyone else does, not earlier. Why will people love you if you don't do all these? To fit the bark of one tree into another tree requires care, requires perseverance. Tell me, didn't your mother and grandmother teach you anything?

Binu tries her best to conform, yet at the same time secretly yearns for freedom from the monotony of the endless chores which bind the women's lives firmly to the kitchen and inner courtyards. She longs for the carefree days in her parents' home and for her mother's love and affection. Her only form of escape from this real world which represses her highly creative mind is to live in a secret imaginary world where she can roam around freely.

Jnanadanandini Devi's (1850-1941) trauma at leaving her family and entering the *Thakurbari* as a seven-year-old bride is feelingly expressed in her autobiography, *Smriti-katha* (1895). Hardly more than an infant, she can barely understand what is happening to her and sits like a bejewelled doll weeping for her mother. It takes her a long time to learn to live among strangers, merge with them, comply with their norms, suppressing the interests of the child she is. Annakali, in Jyotirmoyee Devi's story, is also married at ten. Her husband is about twenty years older than her. The wrangling of this match, for a dark-complexioned fourth daughter, without having to pay a large dowry, has been a feat achieved by her father. The bride herself is quite happy with her wedding finery, which is all that the marriage means to her. She assumes the responsibilities of her new household as uncomplainingly as she had accepted her neglect in her parents' home. Her conformity to the demands of traditional femininity is spontaneous. She is quite happy to live under the wings of her affectionate husband., So much so, that his death renders her completely helpless and dependent for her very existence on her uncaring son.

However, not all little girls agree to be cast into a preconceived mould as easily as Annakali. Satyabati, in *Prothom Protisruti*, realizes when she enters her new home as a child-bride, that she is bound to a narrowness for life. Her early training has been thorough, and she assumes her role of daughter-in-law without complaints, performing all her domestic chores dutifully. But she doesn't hesitate to speak out, defying all norms of 'correct' behaviour for brides, and actively fights for gender justice. She is only a child, but her strength of character and determination to achieve her goals make her an object of fear and awe among her contemporaries and even older women. In fact, Satya reveals a maturity far beyond her age. In an interview, her creator Ashapurna Devi, said that as a child, growing up in a conservative home, she used to observe the restrictions and double-standards which bound women. She herself could not articulate her protest at that time. When she eventually found a voice in her pen, she went back in time in an attempt to retrace her personal history. She created Satyabati as a symbol of her critique of patriarchal double-standards. But Satyabati does not remain merely symbolic. She is a very real intelligent and outspoken little girl who must have existed outside the realm of fiction.

At the age of eight, Satya sees the roots of women's deprivation in the denial of education. For her, education is the basic civilizing factor, the lack of which reduces women to the level of beasts. Around the 1840s schooling for girls was gaining some acceptability among a few urban-based, westernized families. The public debates on women's education was getting vociferous. The cultural nationalists feared the disruption of traditional family and declared women's education sacrilegious. The reformers insisted that this was the only way to prove to the Western world that India was as civilized as they were. However, upper-middle class Hindu families, especially in rural Bengal, remained untouched by these controversies. Here, it was still considered a sin for females to touch books, a rule, if defied could lead to dire consequences. Satyabayti not only struggles to learn to read and write by observing her male cousins, she soon masters it, and even tries to compose verse. Her family, specially her mother, reacts with deep shock and dismay. She is told that God has ordained that education is one of the 'higher pursuits' reserved for the naturally superior sex, while the 'baser activities of cooking, childbearing and child-rearing' are meant for women. Satya refuses to accept this. 'God cannot be so prejudiced, this has got to be a creation of man's distorted interpretation of the holy texts', she says. And in any case, 'the deity of learning, Saraswati, is female' (*Prothom Protisruti*, pp. 157-61). Even at this young age, Satyabati has a clear perception that 'gender' is not a natural phenomenon. All her life, she attacks this social construction, defies the code, and eventually makes it her mission to sensitize women to the fact that women's helplessness is a myth created by men, and to educate women as a means of self-respect and self-awareness, so that they can create a space for themselves and actively fight for their rights.

The real life counterpart of Satyabati is Rasasundari Devi. She too displays a similar single-minded determination to transcend the inferiority imposed on her and achieve self-worth. Her source of strength in this quest is a sense of faith, a deep trust in God, instilled in her by her mother in her early childhood, which sustains her even in the most adverse of circumstances. Like Satyabati, she too resents her enforced illiteracy. At eight, she has been allowed to attend the local *pathshala* (school), the only girl among boys, where she had tried to secretly memorize all the lessons taught to the boys. Even this education ended before her marriage. At fourteen she is filled with a desire to read religious texts. The institutionalizing of schools at that time was being opposed by the threat that education for girls meant ill luck — it would induce widowhood. Rasasundari, whose faith is her greatest strength, is terrified lest she be punished for her secret yearnings, yet continues to plead with her God to teach her to read and write. Her yearning has nothing to do with the reformist concepts of women's education as a precursor to the nation's modernization. It is aimed at increasing her own self-esteem, her desire for knowledge, her wish to read religious texts. Rasasundari remained within the realms of domesticity all her life, and continued to struggle and persevere to achieve her childhood dream. She wrote her autobiography at the age of 88 (one of the first Bengali autobiographies by a woman)

By mid-century, the movement for women's education began to make headway, and *zenana* education (education at home) became the norm in the upper-class liberal urban households. By now, a reconstruction of femininity with some redefined parameters took place as a result of a growing need for a new kind of woman who would adjust well to the new type of urban family. It was now reiterated that education for girls would not threaten the basic principles of femininity. On the contrary, it would teach them to serve their families far more efficiently. To achieve this result, it was necessary to create separate curricula for girls and boys. While it was necessary for boys to be trained to face the external competitive world with assertiveness and ability, to earn money, their education had to be all-rounded. But for a girl, it was enough to have some basic information so that she could run her future household more efficiently. So, *zenan* education was a perfect system, as she could remain at home and learn what was necessary. A primary education would suffice for reading religious texts, writing letters, keeping household accounts, and at the most teaching children the basics. The rest would be geared around the acts of cooking, serving, nursing the elderly and sick, looking after children, stitching, domestic crafts, etc. With these qualities, she would earn praise as a good wife and mother.

Ironically, a number of women who had the benefit of *zenana* education and were tutored by Western educated husbands, internalized this redefined patriarchal code, and became active agents in the construction of this new femininity. These were women like Kailasbasini Devi (1807-1861), who wrote extensively on the virtues of the educated woman as the fitting partner for enlightened men, a better mother and a more efficient housewife. A number of semi-fictionalized manuals teaching proper behaviour and appropriate education for girls like *Stri Shiksha* (Ramtanu Gupta, Calcutta, 1861), *Bala Bodhika* (Kaminisundari Devi, Calcutta 1868), or the later *Balika Jiban* (Uma Devi, Calcutta, 1927) became extremely popular, as they perpetuated the new construction of gender, in an amalgam of traditional values, progressive ideas and Victorian concepts of femininity.

This amalgam is best exemplified in *Raibari*. In this semi-autobiographical novel, there are two versions of femininity offered to Binu, which are in a way complementary. The traditional one of the dutiful daughter-in-law, submissive, docile, devoted to maintaining and carrying on the domestic rituals is apparently a deliberate attempt to preserve indigenous Hindu culture from the onslaught of westernization. On the other hand, Prasad, Binu's idealistic young husband wants to train his young bride to be a fit member of the changing social order. He wants to infuse into her a sense of duty to the nation. She has to transcend the endless rituals engulfing her and prepare herself for her future role of wife and mother and work beside him in the service of the country. This is in keeping with the Nationalist image of the ideal India woman at the turn of the century, whose basic role was to have an energizing effect on her husband and thus act as the ideal helpmate in his pursuit of independence for the nation. However, to do this, Binu has to fulfil all traditional domestic duties and then enter the world of knowledge, enlightenment and social responsibility. The two forces become complementary as the conflicts between the traditional and the modern dissolve in Binu, as she matures, and within a year of her arrival in *Raibari*, she moves from childhood to the threshold of womanhood.

Like Prasad in *Raibari*, Jnanadanandini's husband, Satyendranath Tagore is the emancipated young son of the renowned social reformer Maharishi Debendranath. In this progressive Brahmo household, Jnanadanandini has the benefits of *zenana* education, conducted by younger brother-in-law, Hemendranath. She has had some exposure to education in her early childhood, when, like Rasasundari, she was allowed to attend the *pathshala* — a timid four-year-old girl among much 'bigger boys'. Here she learnt to read and write. This early education helped her a great deal in later life, as she writes in *Smritikatha*. This shy girl from a remote village in Bengal, grew up to be the first Bengali woman to take on the role of the official hostess to her husband's social get-togethers, and to actively aid and complement his career. She was also one of the first women in India to travel abroad on her own. In fact, Jnanadanandini's development as a public figure, within the realms of domesticity, is one of the best examples of the new definition of femininity. She is the personification of the 'ideal Indian woman' of reformist discourse. Like Jnanadanandini Devi, her niece Madhurilata Devi, the daughter of the Nobel Laureate poet Rabindranath Tagore underwent a similar upbinging of education at home, an environment which encompassed both Western and traditional Indian culture. As Madhurilata reveals in her letters to her father, she was brought up reading Byakarankoumudi and Brahmodharma on the one hand,

Pickwick Papers on the other. She was taught Sanskrit, Bengali and English, she read all the major works of Indian literature as well as Moliere and Mark Twain. She was encouraged to read, write, socialize in mixed groups, to actively pursue women's education and social reform. Yet she writes to her progressive father that 'I will try to follow all your advice with all my heart. I will always remember that my husband is superior to me in all respects and I am not his equal. I will try my best to see that his household prospers in every way. He expects a lot of good qualities in me as a girl from this family, I will see that he is not disappointed in any way'. (*Madhurilatar Chithhi*)

However, this kind of upbringing is accessible only to the urban upper-class, upper-caste Hindu or Brahmo families. For the average Bengali woman, the achievements of Jnanadanandini Devi or Madhurilata Devi have no bearing on the actuality of her day-to-day life. The lives of lower caste, working women, tribal women, peasant women, women from Muslim, Christian, or any other religious backgrounds are outside the scope of this paper, but even the average middle-class, traditional Hindu families remained entrenched in patriarchal double-standards and women's education continued to be strongly opposed. Marriage, motherhood and domesticity remained the destiny women were born to fulfil. Child marriages were very much the norm, and young girls were married off early, often to men much older than themselves.

A common consequence of such marriages was early widowhood. The hardships imposed on the widow, irrespective of her age, were many. In fact, the rigid maintenance of rules and regulations regarding food, clothes, behaviour, often rendered the personal tragedy of bereavement insignificant. Sometimes young girls were widowed even before they had left their parental homes. An upper-caste Hindu widow, even a child of seven, was made to follow strict restrictions on what she wore, what she ate, how she behaved, what she said, etc. Her life had virtually ended with her husband's death, even if she wasn't made to commit *sati*, like her predecessors. She had to spend most of her time fasting, or performing religious rituals, or working as the unpaid servant in the home of whichever of her relations gave her food and shelter. Her presence was considered unlucky at auspicious occasions. She was conditioned to feel that her existence was unnecessary and could be justified only if she served her benefactors faithfully and lived a chaste and austere life as long as she lived. The objective of the oppression of widows, as was the earlier custom of *satidaha*, was to control her sexuality, to prevent sullying of the family honour, to prevent insurgency, and to prevent ward off claims on property. In-laws often abandoned her as an ill-omen or an unwanted burden. Even in her parental family, she was usually considered a burden, and had to live the rest of her life as a liability. Oppression of widows and the issue of widow remarriage became the focal point of intense debate and legislation by the reformers, cultural nationalists and the colonial state, but there is little evidence of these debates making a marked difference in the actuality of widows' lives.

How women widowed in childhood cope with their lifelong deprivation is depicted in various ways in women's literature. Saraswati, Binu's sister-in-law, steeps herself in an obsessive maintenance of sanctity and rituals, making herself and everyone in the household absolutely miserable (*Raibari*). Some young widows like Saraswati take on an assertive role to overcome their deprivations and grow up to be like Mokhkhada, Satyabati's great-aunt who bullies everyone in the household, in an attempt to forget the barrenness of her austere life. Mokhkhada eventually turns insane, spending her last days searching among the kitchen garbage for fish and meat, which have been forbidden to her from early childhood when she had been widowed (*Prothom Protisruti*). Sometimes, widows are little girls like the ten-year-old Shanu who dies of thirst having been forced to observe the fortnightly *Ekadashi* fast, [when even a single drop of water is not permitted] in an intensely hot summer ('*Ekadashi*,' Jyotirmoyee Devi). Or they fall prey to their sexuality, like the sixteen-year-old Khanaprabha, who is seduced and abandoned and when she seeks refuge with her family, her own parents reject her and she is driven to suicide as the only alternative ('*Amar*,' Jyotirmoyee Devi).

Or they are girls like Annakali's eldest daughter Uma, who suffers her misery in silence, enduring humiliations and destitution, apologetic to the world for her very existence. She is ever fearful of being abandoned by her parents, her brother, at the same time yearning for a life of respect for herself land her three children. Encouraged by her younger sister's going to school, Uma wants to study in order to be able to support herself in some way, but is refused permission by her in-laws. Though these people have abandoned her, they have the right, by virtue of 'family honour' to dictate all her actions. Repudiated by in-laws, with no rights to parents' home or property, unwanted by brothers, with no source of economic support, no skills or social acceptance of working for an income, what can girls like Uma do? ('*Annakali*'). By 1872, widow remarriage had legal and state sanction. But in actuality, remarriage for the majority of child-widows from conservative Hindu families remained an unthinkable blasphemy. Just like child marriages continued to be the norm, widows continued to be oppressed lifelong.

Another reformist measure was rendered meaningless by actual events. While the 'Age of Consent' was being debated heatedly in public and, in 1860, was officially fixed at ten years, a young girl was brutally beaten to death by her husband and mother-in-law as a punishment for the 'crime' of refusing the husband's sexual advances. The event is included in *Prothom Protisruti*. What makes the event even more painful is the girl's family's acceptance of the tragedy with complete equanimity. Only Satyabati is infuriated by this apathetic grief and demands justice for this child and for the thousands of such girls in the country suffering in similar ways. She makes of her daughter Subarnalata a symbol of the girl child who must be saved; a symbol of the girl child's potentialities which must be nurtured; and a symbol of the new woman who will get opportunities she and other women never had. But Satya's husband and mother-in-law conspire to marry off eight-year-old Subarna in Saty's absence. Satya cannot condone this betrayal, and leaves her home and family forever. She aims to spend the rest of her life seeking answers to questions on the systematic oppression of women and challenging the practice of child marriage, which to her denotes the end of a woman's life even before it begins. It is a system which gives unscrupulous people the power and right to brutalize young girls for no reason other than their powerlessness. Another such victim is little Tulu in the story '*Anadrita* ', by Madhurilata Devi's (1886-1913), who is abandoned by her father after her mother dies, unwanted by her relatives who are forced to give her shelter, and eventually tortured by her in-laws, for whom she is no more than a beast of burden.

In *Prothom Protisruti*, Satyabati asks her recalcitrant husband if he could restore Subarna to her unharmed by the flames of the holy matrimonial fire. Even the thought is a blasphemy. Subarna cannot be saved. Can any girl child be saved? In fact, is seems doubtful whether there ever was girl child. To the custodians of social order, she did not exist beyond representing an icon — the site for gender construction; the repositories of tradition and culture, the future mother who would create the ideal family/nation. Her duty lay in the regeneration of society, and she can do her duty best only if she fits into the mould imposed upon her. If she is deprived or oppressed in the process, it is only a minor side-effect of the larger social need. She has to sacrifice unimportant and selfish yearnings for personal fulfillment. In any case society has clearly defined for her what brings her fulfillment, and she has only to conform to the demands of the social code to achieve it.

The personal tensions, anxieties, fears and anguishes of young girls come to life in these women's writings. We have seen how these texts deal with their helplessness as they assume adult responsibilities while they are still children. They yearn for the carefree joys of childhood, for freedom from the prison of domesticity, and for the untrammeled life they have always been denied because of their gender. Most of the reform movements geared around their upliftment have not had a widespread impact, as female children in India, not only in the past, but even in contemporary India, continue to be deprived, discriminated against, and subject to gender-based behavioural expectations. They have very few of the rights and privileges male children are natural heirs to. In fact, seen in the context of the nineteenth century, a lot of apparently progressive ideas of reform were actually reactionary preconditions placed on the girl with the objective of reconstructing femininity to fit the new demands of a changing society.

However, what transcends the victimization of the young girls by the family and the socialization process, are the glimpses of questions and critiques of the official construction of female roles these texts display. The very fact that these women have been able to create a space for themselves and have left behind a legacy to us in their writing is indicative of the success of their struggles to find a voice. And they have discovered in the girl child the most appropriate vehicle to articulate their anguish and anger, their weakness and strengths.

References

Anurupa Devi, *'Akritagya'*, *Ranga Sankha* (Calcutta, Ray M. C. Sarkar Bahadur and Sons, 1916).

—— *Sahitye Nari.* (Calcutta, Calcutta University, 1949).

Ashapurna Devi, *Prothom Protisruti.* (Calcutta, Mitra & Ghosh, 1965).

Bagchi, Jasodhara, *'Amader Nibedan' Raibari.*, Giribala Devi 1962 (Calcutta, De's Publishing Co. 1991).

—— *Naribadi Protibhangite Adhunik Bangla Kathasahitye Du-Charti Katha, Bharat Itihase Nari.*, Ratnabali Chattopadhyay and Goutom Niyogi, eds (Calcutta, K. P. Bagchi & Co., 1989), pp 119-28.

—— *Narimuktibadi Jyotirmoyee Devi. Paschimbanga Bangla Akademi Patrika,* 3, 1990.

—— 'Representing Nationalism, The Idealogy of Motherhood in Colonial Bengal', *Review of Women's Studies Economic and Political Weekly,* October 1990.

Banerjee, Himani, 'Fashioning a Self: Educational Proposals for and by Women in Popular Magazines in Colonial Bengal', *Economic and Political Weekly: Review of Women's Studies,* vol. 26, No. 431, 26 October 1991, pp. WS 50-62.

Bhattacharya, Malini. *'Meyeder Itihas o Sahitya Sakhhya'', Bharat Itihase Nari,* pp. 110-18.

Borthwick, Meredith, *The Changing Role of Women in Bengal 1849-1905* (Princeton, Princeton University Press, 1984).

Chakravorty, Usha, *Conditions of Bengali Women around the Second Half of the Nineteenth Century* (Calcutta, Bardhan Press, 1963).

Chatterjee, Partha, 'The Nationalist Resolution of the Women's Question', *Recasting Women: Essays in Colonial History,* Kumkum Sangari and Sudesh Vaid, eds (New Delhi, Kali for Women, 1989), pp. 233-68.

Choudhurani, Sarat Kumari, *'Adorer na Anadorer'. Women Writing in India Volume I: 600 B.C. to the Early Twentieth Century.* (New York, The Feminist Press, 1991).

Desai, Neera and Maithreyi Krishnaraj, eds *Women and Society in India.* 1987 (Delhi, Ajanta Publications, 1990).

Dutt, Romesh Chunder, *Cultural Heritage of Bengal.* (Calcutta, Punthi Pustak, 1962).

Fruzetti, Lina M., The Gift of a Virgin: Women, Marriage and Ritual in a Bengali Society (Delhi, Oxford University Press, 1990).

Giribala Devi, *Raibari* (Calcutta, Dey's Publishing Co., 1990).

Guha, Shibani Pal, *Bangla Upanyashe Nari Charitrer Bibartan* (Calcutta, Delight Books, 1969).

Gupta, Ramtanu, *Stri-siksa Pratham Bhag.* (Calcutta 1861).

Jayawardene, Kumari, *Feminism and Nationalism in the Third World.* (New Delhi, Kali for Women, 1986).

Jnanadanandini Devi, *'Smritikatha'. Ekshan,* 1990, pp. 1-35.

Jyotirmoyee Devi. *'Amar', Jyotirmoyee Devir Rachana Samkalan,* (Dey's Publishing Co., 1991.

—— *'Annakali'. Anakalir Jhaanpi.* (Calcutta 1965).

—— *'Beti ka Baap'. Sona Rupa Naya.* Ed. Ashoka Gupta (Calcutta, Mitra and Ghosh Publishers, 1974).

—— *Chirantan Nari Jigyasa: Sekaler Smriti.* (Calcutta, Ananya Prakashan, 1988).

—— *'Ekadashi', Sona Rupa Naya.* Ed. Ashoka Gupta. (Calcutta, Mitra and Ghosh Publishers, 1974).

Kaminisundari Devi, *Balabodhika Prothom Bhag.* (Calcutta 1868).

Karlekar, Malvika, *Voices from Within: Early Personal Narratives of Bengali Women* (Delhi, Oxford University Press, 1991).

Liddle, Joanna and Rama Joshi, *Daughters of Independence: Gender, Caste and Class in India.* (New Delhi, Kali for Women, 1986).

Madhurilata Devi, *'Anadrita', Sabujpatra,* 1898.

——, *Madhurilatar Chithhi,* edited by Purnananda Chattopadhyay (Calcutta 1977).

Mahindra, Indira, *The Rebellious Home-makers* (Bombay, SNDT Women's University, 1980).

Mani, Lata, 'Whatever happened to the *Vedic Dasi*? Orientalism, Nationalism and a Script for the Past', *Recasting Women,* pp. 28-67.

Mehta, Sushila, *Revolution and the Status of Women in India.* (New Delhi, Metropolitan, 1982).

Mukherjee, Meenakshi, *Realism and Reality: The Novel and Society in India.* (Delhi, Oxford University Press, 1985).

Mukherjee, S. N., 'Raja Rammohan Roy and the Debate on the State of Women in Bengal', *Women in India and Nepal,* eds Michael Allen and S. N. Mukherjee (New Delhi, Sterling Publishers, 1990), pp. 155-70.

Murshid, Ghulam, *Reluctant Debutant: Response of Bengali Women to Modernization, 1849-1905.* (Rajshahi, Sahitya Samsad Rajshahi University, 1983).

Rasasundari Devi, *Amar Jiban.* 1876 (Calcutta, Mohesh Press, 1987).

Ray, Bharati, 'Beyond the Domestic/Public Dichotomy: Women's History in Bengal, 1905-1947', *Modern Bengal: A Socio-economic Survey,* eds S. P. Sen and N. R. Ray (Calcutta 1985).

Roy, Monisha, *Bengali Women* (Chicago, University of Chicago Press, 1972).
Sangari, Kumkum and Sudesh Vaid, *Recasting Women: Essays in Colonial History* (New Delhi, Kali for Women, 1989).
—— (eds) Women and Culture (Bombay, SNDT Women's University, 1990).
Sarkar, Saralabala, 'Kanyaday', *Saralabala Śarkar Rachana Sangraha*, Volume I, edited by Chitra Deb. (Calcutta, Ananda Publishers Ltd, 1989), pp. 450-6.
Sarkar, Sudhangshubala, *'Smritir Malika.' Ekshan*, pp. 36-62.
Sakar, Sumeet, 'The Women's Question in Nineteenth Century Bengal', *Women and Culture.* Kumkum Sangari and Sydesh Vaid, eds (Bombay, RCWS, SNDT Women's University 1985), pp. 157-72.
Sarkar, Tanika, 'Bengali Women in Politics — the 1920s and 1930s', *Women and Culture.*
—— 'Hindu Conjugality and Nationalism in Late Nineteenth Century Bengal', *Toward Equality: Status Committee Report on Women in India*, eds Vina Mazumdar et al.
Tharu, Susie, 'Women's Writings in India', *Journal of Art and Ideas* Nos 20-1, March 1991, pp. 49-66
—— and K. Lalitha, eds, *Women Writing in India Volume I: 600 B.C. to the Early Twentieth Century* (New York, The Feminist Press, 1991)
Uma Devi, *Balika Jiban*, (Calcutta 1927).

The Hindu Wife and the Hindu Nation : Domesticity and Nationalism in Nineteenth-Century Bengal

Tanika Sarkar

The intelligentsia in nineteenth century Bengal was engaged in a convoluted critical exercise that simultaneously interrogated problems of power within indigenous custom and tradition (especially their gender norms, albeit within definite patriarchal limits), as well as within the colonial connection. The problems so interanimated and complicated one another that far from reaching a resolution, it was unable to set itself an agenda with any absolute certainty. Emergent nationalist consciousness, which straddled a complex range of forms and possibilities, posed more questions and doubts to its own convictions than resolutions.

It is, perhaps, time to remind ourselves that colonisation did not necessarily simplify the range of questions and problems for the colonised, since tendencies within recent historiographical and cultural studies reduce the whole complex enterprise to the manageable yet impoverished proportions of a crude binary framework: whether it assented to or refused the structures of colonialism. A further surgery displaces these structures from the realm of colonial political economy into a conveniently attenuated rump of the epistemological-ontological aspects of colonial mastery — now to be regarded as the *real* structures. The historiographical shift further simplifies its own task by locating these structures in a single form of western power-knowledge with monolithic and fixed signs. A flat, uninflected, deductive, structural determinism then reads the consciousness of the colonized mechanically off these signs. Moreover, since these signs are vested with totalitarian powers, the consciousness of the colonized may be divested of all claims to an autonomous life of its own and be made parasitic upon the master discourse of colonialism that constitutes the iron cage of language and meaning within which the colonized mind may only perform mimetic gestures.[1]

There is no denying that colonialism had spawned the nineteenth century intelligentsia. It is equally true that history of the new middle classes was marked by many absences and voids — the absence of economic and political leadership being the dominant constitutive principle. The aftermath of 1857 had left little doubt about the coercive, violent aspects of colonial rule. The sense of racial discrimination was heightened steadily through Lyttonian repression in the 1870s: the muzzling of the vernacular press and the theatre as well as the forced disarming of the Indian population. The rabidly racist rhetoric during the Ilbert Bill agitation of the 1880s and a relatively moderate Government's capitulation to it constituted crowning proof. Given the new political conditions which largely demystified the colonial myths of non-discrimination and rule of law, earlier reformism, soon passed its hopeful youth. The Brahmas were split right down the middle and Vidyasagar spent his last few days in bitter disillusionment about his own agenda.[2] Earlier creative innovations within the new education lost its initiative as a standardized and officialized uniform education policy proceeded to unfold itself from the 1880s.[3] The initiative would not be recovered till the Swadeshi days.

The formation of a nineteenth century political sphere is usually located within the religious and political associations that began to acquire pan-Indian aspirations from the 1870s. An alternative and often opposed area is seen to be constituted by mass protest movements — tribal revolts, the Indigo mutiny, the Pabna riots, the post-seventies agrarian unrest where sections of the bhadralok could participate as critical/sympathetic observers, active sympathisers and sometimes even as leaders. In the late nineteenth century middle class context, however, the politics of associations, of self-government bodies and of lower class protest acquired immediacy and substance largely through the mediation of vernacular printed journals which described these developments in close and vivid detail, and opened up their activity to widespread debate and comment.[4] The debate did not stop there. The public sphere, at this stage, remained integrally linked to domestic issues. A substantial number of journals and newspapers came into existence to debate issues of sati, Kulin marriage, widow re-marriage[5] — domestic issues which generated a wide range of authors and readers from Bankimchandra to Battala farces.

Bengali prose, contrary to established belief, was not the creation of the Serampore Baptist Mission or the Fort William College, but had a longer and authentically home-grown lineage. Certainly from the sixteenth century onwards, and particularly in the eighteenth century, it developed a number of crucial features and reasonable fluency through the exercise of an epistolary tradition, through Vaishnavite theological expositions and descriptions of pilgrimage.[6] Missionary and colonial efforts contributed a significant but by no means formative moment in a much larger process. Print culture, far from displacing earlier traditions and freezing writing habits into cultural translations of foreign norms, actually continued and expanded much of the earlier conventions. Vaishnavite literature, for instance, continued to form a substantial part of the new printed material. Nor was the new print a displacement and marginalisation of earlier popular oral-performative traditions, substituting for them a single line of new, largely derivative and sanitized, educated middle class values. Much of the recent work on nineteenth century new Bengali culture, which is eager to brand it as alienated and elitist, chooses to wander only within the elitist productions, counterposing to it a rather utopian, healthy, sensual, earthy, popular pre-colonial cultural past.[7] Not only were there very substantial popular writing traditions even before the entry of print but print itself stimulated new expressions of urban popular culture — the theatre, the woodcut prints, Battala literature. Battala groups of minuscule yet numerous and highly solvent publishers-printers produced a large corpus of cheap booklets, tracts and pamphlets — mostly pulp, but also a significant volume of serious religious work.[8] They were written by and for a literate but little educated, sprawling readership and authorship who would rarely read or write anything else. Up to the 1940s these presses had a rapid turnover, enormously brisk sales and continuous production.[9] Cheap woodcut prints and later oleographs, similarly, carried pictures of religious matters, of current scandal, and of the new city elite, into a much larger number of lower middle class and even rural homes.[10] The new Calcutta theatre, again, boomed largely through lower middle class patronage, and, in its turn, stimulated the growth of print, through the continuous turnout of play scripts. In the Battala areas of North Calcutta even today, small printing presses and tiny theatre groups (called 'operas') jostle each other, creating an unbroken circuit of script publishers and playhouses and of even actors and actresses: the red light area of Chitpur Road borders on it and this, in the nineteenth century, was the main source for the supply of actresses. The success of the theatre depended significantly upon lower middle class themes and preferences. While the classical themes and the chaste language of Madhusudan Dutt's early plays were displayed to depressingly empty halls, the fortunes of the just established Bengal Theatre picked up and flourished in the early 1870s with the performance of a popular farce — *Mohanter Ei Ki Kaj* — a play enacting a scandal that had then rocked popular imagination ;when the Mohunt of the Tarakeswar pilgrimage seduced a young girl who was later murdered by her husband, an employee, interestingly, at a printing press.[11]

Print revolutionized reading habits and possibilities. It penetrated into all sorts of times and spaces within everyday life by its sheer portability. Earlier, manuscripts were not only extremely rare commodities with a slow and thinly spread-out circulation, but the reading time and space devoted to them had to be carefully selected and limited: they were inscribed on heavy yet fragile paper pressed together between flat wooden covers and not sewn together since that would strain the delicate material. Each page had to be carefully extracted from between the wooden *pattas* , read and restored to its proper place. The whole complicated, delicate and time-consuming exercise could be carried out only in special times and places involving fixed postures. The new, plentiful, cheap, portable and replicable printed books, on the contrary, inserted themselves everywhere and into any kind of time effortlessly. This unprecedentedly easy availability was augmented by the introduction of primers and textbooks in school and *pathshalas* . Earlier *pathshala* training was largely oral arithmetic and the acquiring of writing skill, usually to the near complete exclusion of reading matter of any sort (students usually read only what they wrote themselves following set pieces dictated from memory by the teacher).[12] New educational institutions reversed the process and the proportion between reading and writing. Within the confines of a limited class, reading became a non-specialized, fluid, pervasive, everyday activity. This is why vernacular presses developed and mushroomed with an avidity that all observers of contemporary society commented on.

The growth of vernacular prose and press made possible the incorporation of a new range of themes within literate culture which neither English works nor classical Sanskrit/ Persian education, nor theological or imaginative literature could have included within their scope: themes concerning every day life. In the Bengali language catalogues of the Imperial Library holdings for the three decades between 1870s and the 1890s, roughly two-thirds of prose works deal with problems in the organization of everyday living. Simultaneously with the entry of new themes, an extended range of new authors was created. A cross-section of thinking men, and even a few exceptionally fortunate women could, without formal learning, develop and express ideas within a public debate over the shape of their own daily lives. A vast range of non-authors could at least follow the debates, on themes involving themselves. Within this shared yet contested enterprise, the middle class could recuperate something of what it lacked in terms of an articulated position within the production process and the power structure. By marking out an autonomous discursive field of force which drew within its orbit men as well as a few women, highly educated professionals as well as petty clerks, artists, artisans, hack writers and theatre persons, the Bengali middle class was certainly present at its own making.

The autonomy was expressed primarily through a paradox. A deep, pervasive awareness of political subjection did not elicit from it a direct or explicit demand for independence for a long time. What it did was make the middle class dourly deny its own energies, to refuse any description of itself except deeply negative, bleak ones. Early reformist expectations of radical social improvement or Moderate nationalistic assertions about the 'providential nature of the British connection' might indicate an optimism about colonial prospects; yet the hopes were usually brittle and small. They stemmed from sporadic, rather tentative expectations of strictly specific gains rather than from grand visions of emancipatory possibilities. The general run of popular observations as well as more erudite literary production would equally characterize the present times as one of degeneration, recasting the old trope of '*kaliyug*' to express new kinds of anxiety about a modernity ushered in under alien direction.[13] For a long time unease about foreign rule would be obliquely expressed through a critique of modern times. Spectacular signs of technological growth and breakthrough that were revolutionizing their own life experiences — railways, electricity, telegraph, urban growth, city crowds, street scenes — were steadfastly refused recognition into their symbolic order except in a tangential and negative sense. It is disconcerting, to find how scantily Calcutta was being represented as a city, whether in Bankim's novels or in bazaar paintings or in woodcut pictures which dwelt on domestic situations and interior scenes. The only comments on the city centered on the series of bans that restricted public civic activities.[14] In

1829 the newspaper *Bangadoot* had pioneered one of the first definitions of the new middle class. It was then described in terms of a marked increase in the size and circulation of wealth.[15] In the last few decades of the century, all vernacular journals were unanimous in their description of a diseased unproductive, morally decaying, *bhadrlok* .

Middle class Bengalis chose to read certain features of their physical and economic environment obsessively as symptomatic elements, as metaphors of their larger condition. I would point out a few such physical and economic changes which particularly engaged their attention and the ways in which these were used as narrative devices to describe their lives and times. Concrete physical reasons shaped much of the bleak mental landscape which the nineteenth century middle class inhabited. Hindu nationalists of these times belonged largely to Calcutta or to the western, southern and central parts of the province which had been, for the past few centuries, the key cultural zones of the region. This region was the home of Vaishnavite Bhakti as well as of Shakta music and poetry, of the Bengal school of Navyanyaya philosophy, of Tantric practices and of Smarta orthodoxy, of esoteric and syncretic popular religious sects. It saw the rise of the Bengal school of temple architecture. Seats of large zamindari estates provided patronage to art and manufacture while the growth of foreign trade from the seventeenth century stimulated local artisanal, commercial and peasant economies.[16] The rise of the port of Hooghly bore testimony to the growth of new commerce, Political turbulence and economic disasters of the eighteenth century, however, had combined to destabilise the entire region to a fearful extent. Eighteenth century Shakta devotional poetry expressed these experiences in terms of existential uncertainties: coming back again and again to the unknowable countenance and the inscrutable intentions of the Divine Mother.[18]

From the late seventeenth century onwards, and especially throughout the eighteenth century, the very land itself was going through a major crisis.[19] The western arm of the Ganga, which used to bear most of the river's flow of water, was silting up gradually, leading to the formation of a moribund delta in this region.[20] Productivity was markedly lowered due to the infrequency of inundation: by the 1830s, some of the land which used to yield two crops a year was producing a harvest only every three or four years.[21] Low food supply weakened the Bengali constitution and made it vulnerable to the fevers and epidemics that the stagnant waters produced: the Burdwan or the Hooghly fever which was a great killer, cholera epidemics from 1817, and smallpox that raged once every seven years.[22] The silted up waters, which became more stagnant with the construction of railway embankments from the mid-century by the colonial state, produced the malaria-bearing annopheles mosquito, causing 'remittent' and 'intermittent' fevers which went undiagnosed till 1897.[23] Little children, women of childbearing age and poor agricultural labourers were most prone to all of them[24] but there was a marked and general decline of health over entire areas. The dread of either prolonged and fatally weakening fevers or of sudden and unexpected epidemics structured the self-awareness of Bengalis. Enough ecological information had come in by the first three decades of the century[25] to build up a pessimistic picture of the land, the air and the people. Contrasts between an earlier era and the present times were most often made in terms of impaired health.[26] The woman in much of nineteenth century literature presides over the sickbed.[27] It is interesting that even though it would be children, young women or agricultural labourers who were the worst victims of fevers and epidemics, it was the vulnerability and degeneration of the body of the Hindu male babu which became the most significant sign of the times. One might even say that this is how the Bengali middle class sought to express its hegemonic aspirations; not by attributing to itself political or economic leadership roles, not through claims to power, but through ascribing itself all the ills and deprivations that marked nineteenth century Bengali society as a whole.

As the volume of water flowing down the Hooghly branch of the Ganga shrank and as early colonial depredations shattered established economic and political patterns, a number of flourishing commercial, manufacturing and administrative centres went into decline. The decay of the great port of Hooghly was dramatic. The ruin of Dacca (though this did not lie on the moribund delta) caused extensive comment. Malda, Murshidabad, Krishnanagore, Vishnupur — all were broken cities.[28] In course of his boat rides in the early years of the century, Diwan Kartikeya Chandra Ray passed along a whole string of ruined towns, decaying with disease and destitution and teeming with ghost stories: how travellers would return home to find their once-flourishing habitations entirely taken over by the spirits of the dead.[29] Mid-century famines and ravages caused by forced indigo cultivation by white planters led to havoc and panic in rural areas. Bengali journalists agitated extensively over these issues.[30] The sense of depression produced by such sights and news came to make a larger sense when they were fitted into a framework of systematic, critical knowledge shaped by theories of drain, deindustrialization and poverty.

The growth of the colonial urban sector could provide little comfort or hope. Higher reaches of the new liberal professions were racially structured and congested. The massive tertiary sector could provide scope for very small-scale investment. The larger part of the middle class found employment as petty clerks in foreign administrative or commercial establishments. In the discourse of the master race, manhood was defined not just through financial solvency but by the nature of relationship to property. A passive and subordinate working life produced therefore a deep sense of emasculation.

Yet, in the early decades, the bhadralok had seemed poised on the brink of a major entrepreneurial breakthrough when several wealthy Calcutta houses began to make substantial fortunes from shipping, insurance, mining and some amount of foreign trade.[31] The boom was over by the 1840s and after the 1860s hardly any new fortunes were made that way. Hopes of business success had already formed a new economic vocabulary. Debendranath Tagore, in his autobiography, talks about the failure of their business enterprise as the time 'when we lost all our property'[32] even though the Jorasanko Tagores still retained substantial rural estates and a solid Calcutta establishment. Property, for some time at least, meant a specific kind of activity, i.e. business. Significantly, an elegy to the lost golden era of Bengali entrepreneurship was composed in the early 1870s when a biography of a Bengali business magnate described Ramdulal Dey's financial success as a condition of self-respect and even political equality.[33] Perhaps, even more significantly, the book was reprinted in 1978 when a further round of flight of capital had taken place from West Bengal.[34]

Bengali capital was to be tied up largely in urban real estate and rural landholding which did not require much acumen or entrepreneurship and in local trade which had little growth potential.[35] By the late nineteenth century the second rung in business activities had been monopolised by Marwaris whereas the top rung had long been an European preserve. By the mid-nineteenth century Bengalis had only a marginal presence in Burrabazar — the heart of indigenous business in Calcutta.[36]

Colesworthy Grant has left a vivid description of Burrabazar in 1850. It reveals that the bulk of goods circulating from here were foreign imports.[37] What made matters worse was that imports were most often luxury articles or modern, household utensils that replaced indigenous products. Lal Behari Dey's novel on Bengali peasant life in the 1870s noted their penetration into even tiny village fairs.[38] A late nineteenth century autobiography describes the disappearance of flint with the influx of foreign matchboxes. This was taken to denote the disappearance of honest labour and self-sufficiency, driven away by laziness which led to enslavement.[39] *Sambad Prabhakar* complained in 1892: 'The Lakshmi of sound commerce had abandoned Bengal. Mother Bengal now produces coolies and clerks alone'. The tragedy was caused, said the paper, by the self-destructive inclination towards easier or more luxurious foreign alternatives.[40]

Women were primarily responsible for deciding on household purchases. They, therefore, served as the target of both nationalist appeal and blame. A large body of tracts and folk art depicted the modern woman as a self-indulgent spoilt and lazy creature who cares nothing for family or national fortunes. The charge encompasses the triadic relationship between women, gold and servitude — *kamini, kanchan, dasatva* — that the nineteenth century saint Ramakrishna was to engrave so deeply upon the Bengali moral order.[41] The archetypal evil woman of these times was not the immoral or the economically independent one, but one who, inspired by modern education, has exchanged sacred ritual objects (the conchshell bangle, the ritually pure fabric, sindur) for foreign luxury ones.[42] There was thus an interchange between economic compulsions and pleas for feminine commitment to ritual.

The rent-revenue gap that the Permanent Settlement had generated and guaranteed had constituted the major security area for the middle class bhadralok. It had ensured a whole spectrum of fairly comfortable rentier incomes at many levels. Certainties of absolute manipulative power over rent began to be breached — though in a very limited sense — from the mid-nineteenth century by the Rent Acts of 1859 and 1885. They intended to give a measure of security to upper tenants and curb some of the arbitrary coercive powers exercised by the landlord's *kutcheries* or unofficial courts-cum-dungeons. The Rent Act of 1859 had come about partly as a result of missionary pleas on behalf of the tenant.[43] Missionary-inspired colonial interference into the hitherto closed world of largely upper caste Hindu zamindar and the lower caste or Muslim peasant was curiously coextensive with very similar intrusions into the closed world of Hindu domestic practices. Both aroused a keen sense of the fragility of economic and domestic arrangements that had cushioned some of the traumas of the Hindu bhadralok. After the 1859 Act, landlords had been complaining that the loss of disciplinary power had eroded their moral authority and had affected rent collection. The grievance closely parallels the dirges that were composed over each colonial or reformist suggestion for new conjugal laws. Clearly, the moral order of Hindu patriarchy was in peril.

If an alien, imposed modernity was represented as a series of deprivations, then nationalism could situate its emancipatory project only by enclosing a space that was still taken to be inviolate, autonomous. Much of nineteenth century nationalism identified this space as the Hindu way of life. The fundamental distinction between reformers and Hindu nationalists of nineteenth century did not lie in the fact that the former were less patriotic or that the latter was more rooted in indigenous tradition. It stemmed from two different readings of Hindu domestic practices and custom. While liberal reformers described them as a distortion of earlier purity and a major symptom of present decay, Hindu nationalists celebrated them as an excess reserved over and above colonization, any change in which would signify the surrender of the last bastion of freedom. 'That household is our motherland, that family is our India', affirmed a tract on marriage, referring to the network of intimate human relationships into which lost independence had been folded back.[44] Colonization had made it imperative to introduce an absolute distinction between the Self and the Other while emergent nationalism made it equally imperative to stake out claims to sole representational authority over the self. It would be wrong to imagine that the middle class did not write about things beyond itself. Energetic enquiries were made into obscure religious cults and festivals, folk tales and poetic tradition were compiled; there were antiquarian and ethnographic surveys galore. Prizes were offered on writings on peasant plays and reports were written on peasant risings, about Assam tea plantation labourers. Yet at every point, a troubled intelligentsia, keenly aware of the absence of organic links with any stable social formations in the past and the present, of the fragility of its social moorings, felt unable to distinguish confidently the nature of its enterprise: was it anthropology or was it autobiography? What was being probed? The self or the Other? It was in the representation of their own women that the tension was most acute and productive, the ambiguity at its richest. The object of investigation was enclosed within the Self, was immediately outside it and possibly opposed to it. Enquiries were therefore endless.

The concern with domestic practice initiated much discussions and debate. The consequent transparency of concrete practices demystified the self-legitimising arguments around custom and eventually put far too many strains on the commitment to it. The Hindu nationalist agenda, consequently, moved out of the area of human relationships into the more public and reified domain of social service and patriotism towards the turn of the century. I would, then, relocate some of the vital beginnings of Bengali nationalism away from the recognized kinds of issues in the political sphere into the politics of relationships within the family.

The Hindu home would be the one sphere where improvement could be made through our own initiative, changes could be wrought where ed7ucation would bring forth concrete, manipulable, desired results.[45] The home, then, had to substitute for the world outside and for all the work and relations there that lay beyond one's comprehension and control. 'Just as the King reigns over his dominion, so the head of the household (karta) rules over his household'[46] — began a mid-nineteenth century tract on domestic management. 'The karta sometimes rules like a King, sometimes needs to legislate like the lawgiver and sometimes he adjudicates like the Chief Justice',[47] said another. 'Whoever can run a Hindu family can administer a whole realm',[48] was an assertion that was frequently made within this body of writing. Yet another tract advised the karta on how to marshall his forces to face a rebellious woman within the family.[49] The karta, therefore, becomes within the home, what he can never aspire to be outside it— a ruler, an administrator, a legislator or a Chief Justice, a general marshalling his troops. Apart from compensatory ones, the strategic placement of the home assumes other functions as well. Management of household relations becomes a political and administrative capability, providing training in governance that one no longer attains in the political sphere. The intention is to establish a claim to a share of power in the world, a political role that the Hindu is entitled to, through successful governance of the household. A possibly unintended consequence, however, is that, in the process it also renders household relations into political ones.

This was an unintended consequence because the Hindu nationalist strategy centered its critique of colonialism primarily on the loveless, purely deprivational, unrequited nature of its political arrangement which endowed the dominant group with absolute power and profits and the subject people with helpless surrender without any possibility of self-fulfilment. If the home was not merely an escape from this world but its critique and an alternative order in itself, then love and affection had to be the organizing principle of this inner, hidden nation and the exercise of power needed to be replaced with the notion of self-surrender and general self-fulfilment. Household relations had to be shown as supra-political ones, relations of power must be represented as purely emotional states.

Out of the entire gamut of household relations, it was conjugality that was found to be ideally relevant for this project. It was based on the apparent absolutism of one partner and the total subordination of the other. As such, it was the one relationship that seemed to replicate colonial arrangements most precisely. Hence, this would be the ground for challenge and contestation of colonial arrangements: by showing the supposedly real and radical difference between the two sets of relationships despite their apparently similar basis and by establishing where the moral superiority of the one lay over the other. Success in this endeavour would then lend political strength to the contestation of reformist-cum-colonial-cum-missionary intervention into conjugality that had begun with renewed vigour from the 1870s — the Brahmo Marriage Act of 1873, proposals to introduce divorce in the 1880s, and the Age of Consent Act of 1891.[50]

Conjugality provided a variety of possible registers which could test, confirm or contest the Hindu's political condition. Conceived as an embryonic nation, this relationship could also define ingrained Hindu dispositions that might mirror or correct or criticise and overturn the values structuring colonialism. Virtues accumulated through a proper expertise in conjugality could equip the man to a share to power in the world. Equally, proof of the absence of moral leadership here would disqualify him and explain his subjection. The terms for describing Hindu marriage, then, also formed a language for rethinking relations in the political world and allowed Hindus to articulate both worlds simultaneously as they appeared to speak of only one or the other. A satirical poem conveyed this double message:

> The Bengali male goes out
> And gets thrashed everywhere he goes
> The Bengali male appears terrible only within his home.[51]

While its chief intention is to portray the husband's tyranny at home, the poem simultaneously refers to the colonial order which has deprived him of everything else except the right to domestic tyranny.[52]

As we have already seen, Hindu nationalists needed to naturalize love as the basis for Hindu marriage, a higher form of love that excelled over allegedly utilitarian, materialist and narrowly contractual western arrangements. They argued that non-consensual Hindu marriages could, indeed, be more loving than the western pattern of courtship which was based on class and property qualification more than on love. In the Hindu case, a lifetime of togetherness since infancy guaranteed a superior and more certain compatibility. They disclaimed that the production of sons was the sole aim of Hindu marriage: it was a complete spiritual union through perfect love. It was kinder to women since it ensured not just a hold on the husband's affection but an integration with the family which gave her greater security. While the entire system of non-consensual, indissoluble, infant marriage system was to be preserved intact and inviolate, each aspect of the Hindu marriage needed to be written as a love story with a happy ending.[53]

Let us take up a very typical description of a child bride. 'People in this country take great pleasure in infant marriage. The little bit of a woman, the infant bride, clad in red silk ... Drums are beating and men, women and children are running in order to have a glimpse of that lovely face. From time to time she breaks forth into little ravishing smiles. She looks like a little lovely doll.' The key words are little, lovely, ravishing, pleasure, infant, doll — inserted at carefully chosen selected intervals.[54] The community of 'men, women, and children' formed round this figure is bonded together by great visual pleasure, by happiness. Loveability bathes the trauma of patrilocality in warm sensuousness and grounds non-consensual indissoluble infant marriage on mutual desire alone.

Given this sensual starting point, the absolute and unconditional chastity of the Hindu wife, extending beyond the death of the husband was equally strongly grounded in her own desire. This purity, since it is supposedly a conscious moral choice, becomes at once a sign of difference and of superiority, a Hindu claim to power. The politics of the women's monogamy then is the condition of the possible Hindu nation. The one is often explicitly made to stand in for the other., 'We are but a half civilized, poor, sorrowful, subjected, despised nation. We have but one jewel and for us that is the treasure of seven realms, a priceless gem.'[55] Or, 'this so called subjection of our woman produces this sacred jewel of chastity which still glows radiantly throughout the civilized world despite centuries of political subjection'.[56] Woman's chastity, then, has a real and stated, and not merely symbolic political value.

Willed chastity enables the widow to desire the austerities and sacrifices that her condition imposes on her. Since spiritually she still belongs to her husband in an extra mundane world, worldly comforts have actually ceased to matter and her body and soul draw pleasure, not pain, out of the rigours of her material existence. Her life is not marked by loss or absence but by surfeit since her voluntary abdication of an earthly life is a form of *sanyas* within the household.[57] It not only gives her a moral and spiritual energy but also ensures a reservoir of spirituality in each home and for the Hindu order as a whole. Also, the strict ritual observances roots the widow's body in ancient India, thus miraculously escaping foreign domination. The cloth she wears is necessarily indigenous, the water she drinks is to be carried from the sacred river and not through foreign water pipes and the salt that goes into her food is special rock salt, untouched by machines. The nation therefore needs ascetic widowhood.[58]

The final and highest test of the supremacy of Hindu

conjugality was the proved past capacity for self-immolation by widows.[59]

The satu was an adored nationalist symbol, her figure representing the moment of climax in expositions of Hindu nationalism. Bankimchandra saw in it the last hope of a doomed nation.[60] Jyotirindranath Tagore's patriotic plays reached dramatic finale with the song:

> Flames burn higher, burn higher
> The widow has come to immolate herself.[61]

Rabindranath's writings of the early Swadeshi period recall her glory.[62] An immense body of patriotic tracts routinely invoked the act as an unfailing source of nationalist inspiration and pride.

Yet another register for comparing and discussing and thereby masking power relations developed somewhat sketchily within Hindu nationalist discourses on the family. As *adhinata* was the crucial term on gender as well as political relations, so *dasatya* (slavery or servitude) became a key concept to explicate, or rather, to deny a third dimension of power — that of class and caste. Within this household-bound discourse a lower class, lower caste person could only assume the figure of the domestic servant whose servitude was constructed as willed surrender to enlightened paternalism and thus provided yet another justification of Hindu patriarchy.[63]

It was the nature of the woman's commitment to the conjugal order that bound the system together. Moral initiative, therefore, passes on to the woman, uniquely privileging her activism. If the household was the embryonic nation, then the woman was the true patriotic subject. The male body, having passed through the grind of western education, office, routine, and forced urbanization, having been marked with the loss of traditional sports and martial activities, was supposedly remade in an attenuated, emasculated form by colonialism.[64] The female body, on the other hand, was still pure and unmarked, loyal to the rule of the *shastras* alone.

The construction of the Hindu wife could also bind together wide ranging social segments around her practices and norms to formulate a middle class which, in colonial Bengal, lacked a clearly articulated economic base.[65] Since the new economic man did not appear in Bengal; it would be the new domestic woman who had to carry the image of a class.

The image of the loving heart of Hindu conjugality was, understandably, more an act of heroic imagination and conviction, than of lived experience. Paradoxically, the stronger the expression of conviction in the vision, the more strongly critical attention would focus on concrete aspects of the reality and render the project enormously complicated. Four developments problematized the Hindu nationalist discourse on conjugality in the last two decades of the nineteenth century. There was already an old and deeply influential counter tradition of folklore and verse that described marriage and domesticity as a source of profound unhappiness for the woman.[66] Nineteenth century discursive prose would extend these desperate sobs into critical argument, interrogation and frontal challenge, into a movement for change. From the 1860s women's own writings began to appear, further confirming this tradition.[67] And, finally, there were reformist campaigns for change that, from the mid-eighties under Malabari, assiduously picked up and wove together all material evidence on force and coercion within Hindu marriage. Two sensational events — Rukmabai's demand to be released from a marriage contracted at her infancy and a little girl Phulmani being raped to death by her husband seemed to abundantly vindicate the reformist critique and added strength and urgency to their campaign.[68]

Women's voices had frequently been borrowed by male authors to express a profound sense of bleakness about her existence. Jaydev's Radha had remained implacably angry about sexual double standards.[69] A particular stream within eighteenth century Shakta devotional poetry — the Agamani songs — would use the mother's voice to mourn Durga's imminent parting at the end of her annual visit to her parent's home: 'Do not pass away the night of Nawami, leave her with me just a little longer'.[70] These songs, enormously popular throughout the nineteenth century, would find a double resonance from within a very wide ranging age group among Bengali women. Thanks to the widespread custom of infant marriage, women, by their early twenties, might be daughters longing for their mothers, and, simultaneously, young mothers pining for their married daughters. In lullabies and folk verses, probably composed largely by women themselves, married sisters threatened to drown themselves unless their brothers came and took them away from 'this place of torture'. A little girl would plead with her playmate to have a last game with her, 'for the son of a stranger is coming to take me away and I shall never play again'. A young mother, hungry for the sight of her baby from whom the endless duties of a joint family routine separate her, plans: 'I'll run away to the forest with my baby, and there, in solitude, I'll gaze upon the face of my treasure'.71 A complicated variety of female rites — *vrats* — were evolved to eliminate the threat of the co-wife.[72]

Experience of their own subjection gave to colonized men a fresh and acute sensibility about bondage. *Adhinata* became a peculiarly loaded word, fraught with a double guilt: the sin of submitting to foreign domination which would necessarily conjure up the associated guilt of submitting the woman to a state of subjection. The two senses of the word would continuously flow into each other, interanimate each other. They would sometimes be posed as cause and effect. 'When our white masters kick us, we return home and soothe ourselves by kicking our wives.'[73] Or, 'Our women lost their freedom when we lost ours'.[74]

Sometimes the order of cause and effects was reversed. A women's magazine published this poem in 1894:

> Men, you have inflicted a terrible wrong
> On the defenceless women of this land
> And because of that
> You will forever remain exiles in your own
> land of birth.[75]

Reversal also introduces the theme of expiation.

Occasionally one kind of subjection was so closely linked to the other that they interchanged as metaphors.

There is a poem on the caged bird whose title refers to the incarceration of women within the home:

> Free bird, how do you hope to be happy within the cage?
> Imprisoned, you have forgotten your own speech.
> And you repeat words of others mindlessly.[76]

Loss of one's own language was also the most familiar trope for describing political subjection.

A whole alternative, contestary description developed from the extended guilt over subjection, representing the Hindu home as the very antithesis of pleasure. 'Our home knows no joy, no pleasure. Our home is filled with a spirit more nightmarish than that which reigns over the cremation ground.[77] It was the grave of pleasure, not its home. The interrogation was not restricted to reformers alone. Hindu nationalists themselves, by relentlessly focusing on conjugality, problematized the entire arena. Even the most status quoist tracts, which conclude with very orthodox prescriptions, do so not with confidence and certainty, but after compulsive and obsessive probing of all the tension spots.[78] The endless preoccupation reveals continuous doubts rather than a final resolution since excessive speech points at anxiety just as surely as silence does.

The alternative, challenging description gained in authenticity once Hindu women began to write about themselves from the 1860s. They wrote about the trauma and not the beauty of infant marriage, the deprivations of the widow, the absence of love in the lives of wives. 'Conjugal love has disappeared from our country,' wrote a Hindu woman in 1863. She also claimed that Hindu women suffered more than anyone else in the world.[79] The Hindu household was described as 'a most terrible mountain range, infested with wild beasts'.[80] Another woman stated that nothing in her life — not conjugal love, nor children — could compensate for the deprivation of knowledge. 'Ignorant and cruel men have segregated us from this priceless and endlessly pleasurable jewel that is knowledge, and yet foolish women serve them and care for them like servants.'[81] All varieties of women's writings unanimously identified and condemned two problem spots within the Hindu woman's existence — the pain of patrilocality and the longing for knowledge. Whatever the format and whatever the basic political stance towards patriarchy, women's writings at this time agreed on these points of criticism. The longing for systematic learning was not a desire implanted by male reformers, missionaries and colonialists. A pious Hindu housewife, spending her life in a non-reformed domestic environment where no woman ever learnt to read, was so driven by this sharp desire that she taught herself the letters in great secrecy and difficulty. When she finally started reading, a measure of her triumph was conveyed by her coining of a magnificent new word to describe her own achievement — *mastery over the world' — jitakshara* [82] Instead of reducing the pain and the triumph of the whole process to yet another form of male patriarchal manipulation we need to explore what historical conjuncture gave focus and direction to certain kinds of established and diffused experience of deprivation among women themselves — and why at this time and why in this form?

In 1884 Rukmabai, a low caste, educated, Maharashtrian girl sought to repudiate an unconsummated marriage contracted at her infancy with an illiterate, dissolute, sick husband.[83] Over this sensational challenge, Malabari mobilised reformers and renewed his campaign for the introduction of divorce and for a higher age of consent — demands that seriously eroded the principles of indissolubility and of infant marriage. A higher age of consent for the girl would also jeopardise the fundamental Hindu tenet of *garbhadhan* that is, the obligatory ritual cohabitation as soon as the wife attains her puberty for otherwise her womb is tainted and her sons lose the right to serve up ancestral offerings.[84] Since in the hot climate of Bengal puberty may occur quite early, a higher age of consent, it was feared, would interfere with this injunction.

For some time in Hindu nationalist circles, Rukmabai became a name more dreaded than Malabari's or colonial legislators.[85] They would still valiantly argue that a true Hindu wife must find the husband desirable, irrespective of all external circumstances — a problem that Rabindranath would continue to ponder on as late as the novel *Joga Jog*.[86] Already, however, the basis of conjugality had shifted from love to prescription as soon as the imperative 'must' was introduced in the statement. A structured duality thus complicated the representation of conjugality. The two compulsions and possibilities of construction — preservation of conjugal discipline and accent on love — would inevitably prove mutually non-accommodating.

Reformers had an easier time of it since they were willing to surrender the principle of sacrament to the principle of willed and regularly consummated conjugal love. Widows could remarry since for them the physical relationship was over and hence the marriage was over as well. Similarly, wives of endlessly polygamous Kulin Brahmins were really not married since in their case, consummation was rare, if not impossible. Infant wives, thrown into a relationship not chosen by them, could similarly repudiate their marriage tie. Hindu nationalists, on the other hand, fused love into sacrament which, once performed, must reign supreme, irrespective of absence of consummation or of consent. There were no gradations within marriage — a child widow who had not seen her husband was as meaningfully married to him as the wife of a monogamous, loving and living husband. Once love and willed surrender were separated out from the sacrament, however, Hindu nationalists had to take their stand on the latter alone in order to preserve the totality of the conjugal system.

They continued to sensualize the discipline of the sacrament — up to 1889 at least, when a more severe jolt occurred. Phulmani, a girl of ten, was raped to death by her twenty-nine-year-old husband Hari Maiti. Since she was beyond the statutory minimum age of ten, Hari Maiti could not be punished under existing Penal Code provisions. The event seemed to fully justify Malabari's allegations and a very hesitant Government was at last inclined to give in to proposals for a higher age of consent.[87]

The narrative of Hindu marriage could no longer use the language of love; it had to be rewritten in terms of force and pain. If the element of difference from other systems was so obviously be seen to lie in discipline, then Hinduism had to be celebrated as a superior coercive power. "'The Hindu is truly very severe, even cruel,' exulted Chandranath Basu in 1892 in his rejoiner to Rabindranath on the question of *Hinduvivaha* .[88] Self-fulfilment and pleasure were now demoted to a rather lower order of values. If infant marriage led to violence, to even bloody death, then it was the unique privilege and strength of the Hindu woman to accept the risk. Its practice could lead to weakened progeny and racial degeneration. But 'the Hindu prizes his religion above his life and short lived children.'[89] Hindu scriptures did impose harsh injunctions on the wife as well as the widow. Yet 'this discipline is the prize and glory of chaste women and it prevails only in Hindu society.'[90]

A typical argument on age of consent would run thus;

> The performance of the *garghadhan* must be after the first menstruation. It means the first cohabitation enjoined by the Shastras. It is the injunction of the Hindu Shastras that married girls must cohabit with their husbands at the first onset of their menses and all Hindus must implicitly obey the injunction. And he is not a true Hindu who does not obey it. If one girl in a lakh or even a crore menstruates before 12 it must be admitted that by raising the age of consent the ruler will be interfering with the religion of the Hindus. But everyone knows that hundreds of girls menstruate before 12. And the *garbhas* of hundreds of girls will be tainted and impure. And the thousands of children who will be born of those impure *garbhas* will become impure.[91]

Even in translation the power of the voice comes through. Repetitive short phrases, joined by many 'ands', the frequency of the word 'must', the deployment of increasing numbers — all add up to an incantatory, apocalyptic mode of speech that is very typical of fundamentalist millenarianism. All external arguments have been chipped away, and the bare mandate is repeated on rising notes of urgency. Hindu nationalism has learnt to speak the authoritative word in the appropriately authoritarian voice.

Yet the grounding of an imagined notion on sheer pain could not proceed beyond this point. Hinduism has come far too close to its own description of the prescriptive, loveless, disciplinary regime that is colonializm. The discourse reaches its breaking point and begins to collapse into self-travesty, the beginnings of self-disgust. When Joygobinda Shome said in 1891 that what if infant wives died in childbirth since female scorpions always do so in any case, the limits of this discourse had been reached.[92] Ragendralal Mitra had earlier raised a laugh at a Shobhabazar Raj palace meeting when he described the Hindu wife as 'an article of gift ... she is given away even as a cow or any other chattel'.[93] I suspect that the laugh was an uneasy one. Hegemonic desires of Hindu nationalism clashed too violently with the starkness of its discipline. Love had to re-enter the nationalist narrative.

Over the last decade of the century a new organizational principle, a new center of gravity was sought beyond conjugality. The axis was eventually located in the loving relationship between the mother and the son. This time, however, this was no flesh and blood woman, all too easily visible within an all-too accountable household, but the new and supreme deity within the Hindu pantheon — the Motherland, the reified woman.[94] With the reoriented figure of the woman came a crucial shift in the very placing of the patriotic project. It was taken out of the problematic home space, into the wider and more public arena of the Hindu community which is an abstraction. Defence of Hindu domesticity, the preservation of the Hindu home, fell away from the nationalist agenda. Vivekananda, who had found the whole age of consent agitation profoundly uncomfortable, proposed to add muscles and sinews to the decadant Hindu through work-oriented asceticism and social service. Bankimchandra in his last political novels, envisioned salvation through an apocalyptic war with the Muslim.[95] The experience of something approaching a mass upsurge over the Age of Consent issue generated enabling rhetoric and techniques for political mobilization and agitation that were, for the moment, found to be more efficacious than the politics of petitions or the annual Congress forums. The very success of the struggle over domestic issues, paradoxically, carved out a political sphere that could now be delinked from the domestic arena.

Questions of internal power arrangements were not to be completely resolved. They constituted — as I suspect or hope they still do now — implacable pitfalls, the internal limits within the discourse. Bankim in the last pages of his last novel had mocked the grandeur of his own apocalyptic vision through the casual gossip of common people who dismissed the Hindu-Muslim war as supremely irrelevant for themselves. Vivekananda was asked by an American woman missionary in 1898 if he foresaw any hope of eliminating child marriage and cruelty to widows. Sadly, he said no. The missionary went on with her account: 'Even at the height of his popularity, with the Hindu world at his feet, the Swami shows a strange foreboding of ultimate failure. I cannot give you an adequate impression of the effect, but sitting there at twilight, in the large, half-lighted hall, it seemed like listening to a cry'.[96]

Notes

1. Edward Said's *Orientalism* (London 1978) has acquired enormous canonical value for recent perspectives on the colonial period. For an equally influential application of Saidian dicta, see Partha Chatterjee, *Nationalist Thought and the Colonial World:: A Derivative Discourse* (Delhi 1986).
2. See Asok Sen, *Iswar Chandra Vidyasagar & His Elusive Milestones* (Calcutta 1977). In fact, the presumed naive faith and hope of the early reformers can be looked at very differently. For a more pessimistic reading of that phase, see Sumit Sarkar, 'The complexities of young Bengal', *A Critique of Colonial India* (Calcutta 1985).
3. All experimentation with courses and pedagogic methods gradually dried up after the Despatch of 1854 which introduced a drab uniformity through a systematic examination system. See Romesh Chandra Mitra, 'Education: 1833-1905' in N. K. Sinha, ed., *The History of Bengal, 1757-1905* (Calcutta 1967). See also Kissory Chand Mitra, *On the Progress of Education in Bengal*, July 1887, reprinted in *Nineteenth Century Studies*, January 1975.

4. See Swarajit Chakraborti, *The Bengali Press, 1818-1868 — A Study in the Growth of Public Opinion* (Calcutta 1976). According to Rev. Long's evidence before the Indigo Commission, in 1860, the controversy on widow remarriage alone gave birth to 25 new publications in the vernacular press and the issues of early marriage and female education were similarly widely discussed. Benoy Ghose, 'The Press in Bengal' in N. K. Sinha, ed., *The History of Bengal, 1757-1905* (Calcutta 1967), p. 227.
5. *ibid.*
6. Asit Kumar Bandyopadhyay, *Bangla Sahityer Itibritta*, vol. IV (Calcutta 1985). See also vol. V (Calcutta 1985).
7. This seems to constitute the consensus about the new printed prose in several articles in Svati Joshi, ed., *Rethinking English: Essays in Literature, Language History* (New Delhi 1992). See also Sumanta Banerjea, 'Marginalization of women's popular culture in nineteenth century Bengal', in Kumkum Sangari and Sudesh Vaid, ed., *Recasting Women: Essays in Colonial History* , Kali for Women (Delhi 1989).
8. Asit Kumar Bandyopadhyay, *Bangla Sahityer Ittibritta* , vol. V.
9. See Bireswar Bandyopadhya, *Heto Bai, Heto Chhara* (Calcutta 1984).
10. William G. Archer, *Bazar Paintings of Calcutta* (London 1953).
11. See Brajendranath Bandyopadhyay. *Bangiya Natyashalar Itihas, 1795-1876* (Calcutta 1943), p. 151.
12. See Kazi Shahidullah, *Pathshalas into Schools: The Development of Indigenous Elementary Education in Bengal, 1854-1905* (Calcutta 1987).
13. For the reorientation of this traditional myth under colonial conditions, see Sumit Sarkar, 'The Kalki avatar of Bikrampur: A village scandal in early twentieth century Bengal' in Ranajit Guha, ed., *Subaltern Studies VI, Writings on South Asian History & Society* (Delhi 1989).
14. A Survey of excerpts from a collection of mid-nineteenth century newspapers — among other things — indicates that while most technological breakthroughs went largely ignored, Calcutta registered itself as a city which forced the indigenous urban population into recasting their ingrained bodily disposition and public activities according to strange, non-customary norms imposed by the city's rulers. A ban on religious processions with music was seen with apprehension: 'now our officials are publicly opposing Hindu religion'. The streets were to be withdrawn from the sphere of religious activity. (*Sambul Prabhakar* , editorial, 12 December 1858.) A similar reaction followed the ban on Indians urinating in public places. The ban was read as a forced westernization of bodily gestures as well as a sign of racial discrimination. 'We are poor Bengalis, much oppressed by officials ... Whenever Sahibs feel like urinating, they stand like plam trees, choose the wall of a (native) gentleman's house and then let go of a stream of piss ... The pissing law should be the same for everyone.' (*ibid* ., 2 August 1858). A complexly inflicted text uses the device of newly departed Bengali souls reporting on major changes in the city to the long dead ones. While the obvious format is that of deadpan, factual reportage, the balance sheet carefully and unobtrusively stacks up very minor, unimportant gains on the credit side while the debit sheet reveals the loss of fundamental values. They start with the

replanting of public parks with colourful but non-perfumed western flowers replacing the white, fragrant varieties. At the end they build up to larger and more direct comments: 'The Legislative Assembly is displacing Dharmashastras. Now one freely retains ancestral property even while changing religion and adulterous widows inherit their husband's property without difficulty'. This refers to a new ruling that the widow's moral standing would not prevent her from inheriting the husband's property. It raised a storm of protest from the city's prominent gentlemen. Haranath Bhanja, *Suraloke Banger Parichay* (Calcutta 1875), ed., Aloke Ray (Calcutta 1976).

15. *Bangadoot*, 1829., cited in R., C. Majumdar, *History of Modern Bengal, Part I, 1765-1905*, (Calcutta 1975), p. 253.
16. Hiteshranjan Sanyal, *Social Mobility in Bengal* (Calcutta 1981), pp. 36-64.
17. See P. J. Marshall, *Bengal: The British Period in Eastern India 1740-1828* , CUP, 1987, pp. 25-9, 139.
18. See a discussion on Shakta poetry in Shashibhushan Dasgupta, *Bharater Shakti Sadhana O Shakta Sahitya* (Calcutta 1960).
19. Frank Perlin, 'Proto Industrialization and Pre-Colonial South Asia', *Past & Present*, 1983, p. 56. Although he ascribes the major structural changes to a period well before the establishment of colonial rule, there is no doubt that colonial innovations and interferences sharpened the processes in the nineteenth century.
20. Marshall, *Bengal* , p. 4. It is interesting that findings about the formation of the moribund delta became widely known by 1833.
21. *ibid.*
22. Chowdhury, 'Agrarian Economy & Agrarian Relations in Bengal 1859-1885', in N. K. Sinha, ed., *The History of Bengal* , pp. 241-3. Also Marshall, *Bengal*, pp. 5, 18-19.
23. *ibid.*
24. Chowdhury, 'Agrarian Economy', pp. 243-44. Also Marshall, *Bengal*, p. 20.
25. Marshall, *Bengal*, p. 4.
26. See, for instance, Rajnarayan Basu, *Sekal O Ekal*, reprinted, (Calcutta 1988), pp. 31-6.
27. *Garhasthya* (monthly journal) (Calcutta 1884).
28. Marshall, *Bengal*, pp. 160-1.
29. *Diwan Kartikeyachandra Rayer Atmajiban Charit* (Calcutta, reprint 1956), pp. 36-39.
30. Ghose, 'The Press in Bengal'. See also Chakraborti, *The Bengali Press.*
31. See Nilmoni Mukherji, 'Foreign and inland trade', in Sinha, ed., *op. cit*, pp. 339-62. See Sabyasachi Bhattacharya, 'Traders & trade in old Calcutta', in Sukanto Chaudhuri, ed., *Calcutta: The Living City*, vol. I (Calcutta 1990), pp. 204-8. Also Marshall, *Bengal*, pp. 166-7.
32. Debendranath Tagore, *Atmacharit* (Calcutta 1898), reprinted in *Atmakatha* (Calcutta 1981).
33. Girish Ghosh, *Ramdoolal Dey: The Bengali Millionaire* (Calcutta, reprint, 1978). The book, though undated, seems to have been published in 1878. Around the same time Kissori Chand Mitra delivered a lecture on the life of Motilal Sil, in a very similar vein, calling him the 'Rothschild of Calcutta'. See Pradip Sinha's 'Foreword' to *Rumdulal Dey.*

34. See Sinha's 'Foreword' written in 1978.
35. Marshall, *Bengal*, p. 13.
36. Bhattacharya, 'Traders and Trade in Old Calcutta'.
37. *ibid.*
38. Rev. Lal Behari Dey, *Bengal Peasant Life*, 1878 (reprinted, Calcutta 1970).
39. Dinendra Kumar Ray, *Pallichitra* (Calcutta 1904, reprinted Calcutta1981), p. 30.
40. *Sambad Prabhakar*, 11.8.1892 in Ghosh, ed., *Samayik Patre Banglar Samajchitra* (Calcutta 1978), p. 127.
41. Sumit Sarkar, 'Kaliyug, Chakri & Bhakti: Ramakrishna and His Times', *Economic & Political Weekly*, 18 July 1992.
42. See Tankia Sarkar, 'Nationalist Iconography: Image of Women in 19th Century Bengali Literature', in *Economic and Political Weekly*, 21 November 1987.
43. Chowdhury, *Agrarian Economy*, pp. 295-9.
44. Chandra Kumar Bhattacharya, *Banga Vivaha* (Calcutta 1881), p. 51.
45. A mechanical application of a simple divide between the home and the world is derived from an untenable extension of a mid-nineteenth century Victorian situation into a very different socio-political context. Partha Chatterji argues along the lines of a series of binaries since he sees the nineteenth century 'nationalist' agenda as being a mimetic gesture. See Partha Chatterji, 'The Nationalist Resolution of the Women Question' in Sangari & Vaid, eds, *Recasting Women*. The concept of the Victorian home and its separation from the public sphere, again, is an undifferentiated social construct, taking an active entrepreneurial segment as presentative of the middle class. For a very different positioning of the domestic sphere within a less activist, non-entrepreneurial world of the clergy, see Howard M. Wach, 'A 'Still, small voice' from the pulpit: Religion and the creation of social morality in Manchester, 1820-1850', *The Journal of Modern History*, September 1991.
46. Narayan Ray, *Bangamahila* (Calcutta, n.d.), p. 51.
47. *Garhasthya* (monthly journal) (Calcutta 1884), p. 1.
48. Monomohan Basu, *Hindur Achar Vyavahar* (Calcutta 1279), p. 99.
49. Chandrakanta Basu, *Sangyam Shiksha* (Calcutta 1311), p. 81.
50. See Tanika Sarkar, 'Hindu Conjugality in 19th Century Bengal — A Study of the Age of Consent Controversy', forthcoming.
51. Surendranath Majumdar, *Mahila* (Calcutta 1287), p. 4.
52. The narrowly political intention is enriched by the admission of socio-political deprivations and emasculation of the Bengali male. Love within conjugality is evoked as a restorative, the wife confirming the male desirability of the husband:

    Our horrible labour is spiced with the discipline of clock time
    And with words like 'Swine', 'Nigger'
    Let that red face & grey eyes recede for a few days
    Let my lotus-eyed darling take his place
    And with her loving hands, clasp me to her bosom.

    See Srinibas Basu, *Khokababu Prasange* (Calcutta 1304).
53. See Tanika Sarkar, 'Hindu Conjugality'.

54. *ibid.*
55. Basu, *Hindur Achar Vyavahar* , p. 31.
56. *Ibid.* , p. 60.
57. Pratapchandra Majumdar, *Stri Charitra* (Calcutta, n.d.) Interestingly, the model for the chaste Hindu widow is Queen Victoria. Also Kamakhyacharan Bandyopadhyay, *Stri Shiksha* (Dacca 1308). Interestingly, even Rev. Lal Behari Dey, who had converted to Christianity, became rather lyrical in his praise of chaste Hindu widows. The most unqualified admiration was evoked in Sister Nivedita. See *The Web of Indian Life* (first published Calcutta 1904, reprinted Calcutta 1955).
58. *Ibid.*, p. 57.
59. Sati was routinely evoked as the climax, the highest proof and the essence of the Hindu wife's chastity. 'The woman's chastity is the bright jewel of an Aryan family. The chaste wife is sitting at the heart of flames, with the feet of her husband clasped to her breasts. She is chanting the name of Hari with a face radiant with love and joy. Whenever we think of that, we are filled with pride.' See Girijaprasanna Raychaudhury, *Grihalakshmi* (Calcutta 1294), p. 67.
60. Bankimchandra Chattopadhyay, Kamalakanter Daptar, *Bankim Rachanabali* , vol. II (Calcutta 1954).
61. Jyotirindranth Tagore, 'Sarojini Natak' 1875, *Jyotirindranather Natyasangraha* , first published 1891.
62. Rabindranath Tagore, 'Jagajog', *Rabindra Rachanabali* , vol. 9 (Calcutta 1961).
63. Basu, *Hindur Achar Vyavahar* , p. 51.
64. See Tanika Sarkar, 'Hindu Conjugality'.
65. This was enabled by the fact that since the late seventeenth century, commercial and agrarian prosperity had generalized upper caste conjugal practices among a wide spectrum of low peasant and trading castes as the inescapable mode of social respectability. See Sanyal, *Social Mobility in Bengal* . Conjugal norms, at the same time, were becoming more strict and inflexible. Raghunandan had made pre-pubertal marriage obligatory in the sixteenth century and from the eighteenth century, the royal court of the Krishnanagore Raj enforced a Smarta orthodoxy, tightening the practices of austere widowhood. See Sibnath Shastri, *Ramtanu Lahiri O Tatkalin Bangasamaj* (Calcutta 1903). From early nineteenth century, foreign accounts reported on the ubiquity of the ban on widow remarriage and the custom of child marriage which were to be found even among the low castes. See Abbe Dubois' account of 1792-1823, Abbe Dubois, *Hindu Manners, Customs and Ceremonies* , Translated by H. L. Beauchamp, (Clarendon Press, 3rd edition, 1906). Sati, similarly, was practised very widely by Sudra castes of Bengal. Risely found infant marriage and ban on widow remarriage the two uniform practices even among untouchable castes. H. H. Risley, *Tribes and Castes of Bengal.*
66. Bhabataran Datta, *Bangladesher Chhara* (Calcutta, n.d.)
67. On this see Ghulam Murshid, *Reluctant Debutante: Responses of Bengali Women to Modernisation,* (Rajshahi 1983).
68. See Tanika Sarkar, 'Hindu Conjugality'.

69. On the importance of this twelfth century text, see S. K. De, *Early History of the Vaisnava Faith & Movement in Bengal* (Calcutta 1961), pp. 9-11.
70. Rasikchandra Ray, 'Nabamir Gan', Prabhat Goswami, ed., *Hajar Bachharer Bangla Gan* (Calcutta 1969).
71. Datta, *Bangladesher Chhara*.
72. Nandalal Sil, *Vratakatha* (Calcutta 1930).
73. Prasad Das Goswami, *Amader Samaj* (Serampore 1896), p. 14.
74. Bhattacharya, *Banga Vivaha* (Calcutta 1288), p. 76.
75. *Narishiksha*, Part II (Calcutta 1884), p. 210.
76. *ibid*., p. 194.
77. Bhattacharya, *Banga Vivaha*, p. 60.
78. See for instance, Saudamini Gupta, *Kanyar Prati Upadesh* (Dacca, third edition, 1325). Even though it teaches the daughter how best and most graciously she can submit to patriarchal discipline and demands in her married life, the text simultaneously undermines the patriarchal hegemonistic claim by asserting, again and again, that this was going to be a life of sorrow and problems, 'All women must live out their lives without their relatives or close ones near them (p. 3)... My child, I cannot advise you on when or how much to eat, for whatever you do, you must know that, you will most probably be criticised.' (p.41).
79. Kailashbashini Debi, *Hindu Mahilaganer Heenabastha* (Calcutta 1863), p. 62.
80. *ibid*., p. 45. Also *Narishiksha*, Part I (Calcutta 1884, first edition 1275), p. 6.
81. *Narishiksha*, Part I, p. 134. See also Kailashbashini Debi, *Hindu Mahilaganer Heenabastha*, p. 67.
82. Rashsundari Debi, *Amar Jiban*, 1876, reprinted in *Atmakatha*, Calcutta, 1981. See also Sarada Debi, *Atmakatha* (Calcutta 1979), for a similar longing for the written word. In her case, however, it remained unfulfilled.
83. Charles Heimsath, *Indian Nationalism and Hindu Social Reform*, (Princeton University Press, 1964), pp. 91-4.
84. Tanika Sarkar, 'Hindu Conjugality'
85. On folk poems about the Rukmabai episode sung on Calcutta streets, see Asit Kumar Bandyopadhyay, *Bangal Sahityer Itihas*, vol. V.
86. It explores whether the marriage sacrament can or should generate love within a chaste Hindu girl or, if it must do so. Interestingly, the novel was composed at a time when yet another round of controversy about a higher age of consent was going on over the Sarda Bill proposals. *Rabindra Rachanabali.*
87. See Tanika Sarkar, 'Hindu Conjugality'
88. Chandranath Basu, *Hindutva (Hindur Prakrita Itihas)* (Calcutta 1892).
89. *Bangabashi*, 25 December 1890, RNP (Bengal 1890).
90. *Dainik O Samachar Chandrika*, 14 January 1891, RNP (Bengal 1891).
91. *Bangabashi*, 25 December 1890.
92. Cited by Nagendranath Bandyopadhyay, *Balyavivaha* (Calcutta 1888), p. 31.
93. Cited in *Hindoo Patriot*, 19 September 1887.
94. On the composition and control of a dominant cultural symbol and its relationship to a real physical support in society, see Luisa Accati, *The*

Larceny of Desire: The Madonna in Seventeenth-Century Catholic Europe, in Obelkevich, Roper and Samuel, eds, *Disciplines of Faith: Studies in Religion, Politics and Patriarchy* (London 1987).

95. Tanika Sarkar, 'Bankimchandra and the Impossibility of a Nationalist Agenda', forthcoming.

96. Lucy E. Guiness, *Across India at the Dawn of the Twentieth Century* (London 1898), p. 147.

Women and Education in Kerala

Lashvinder Kaur

Feminist theory is gaining a lot of popularity in this present day and age. A lot of people have misconceptions about women's struggle against the rigid norms of a patriarchal society. Feminism is not just about burning bras or walking about with under-arm hair. Feminism is politics of women, that is aimed towards changing the existing power relations between women and men in society (Weedon, 1987, 1). It is all about male domination and female subjugation in any society. The struggle is all about the things women do and are expected to do, with the tight reins of patriarchy and it covers every aspect of a woman's life. It is mainly concerned about the oppressions of patriarchy that compound many women by class and race; in the case of India, by caste (Weedon, 1987, 1). Analyzing the position of women also brings in the social differences between men and women that are underwritten by the biological inequalities between the sexes (Hamilton, 1978, 50). There is a greater need to examine these differences in some countries than others.

Countries in the Middle-East and many other Asian countries have the most sexual discrimination. The very fact that a Moslem woman is expected to go around in a purdah is discrimination. The existence of suttee and dowry system in India is discrimination as well. Gender inequality has existed for many centuries. Some women more than others are breaking out of the chains of patriarchy that bind them. Women have a great influence in any country's achievements, and India is no different. Indian women have for decades been portrayed as docile and submissive. This is not entirely true. Women in India have played a major role in the independence of the country, although they have not received the accolade they so richly deserve. For instance, how many people are aware of the fact that women were very active in Gandhi's passive resistance campaign? In fact, when Gandhi was in prison, a woman called Sarojini Naidu took over temporary leadership of the party (French, 1985, 226).

One state that stands out in this area is Kerala. Kerala has shown a lot of interest in the nature of a woman's role in society. Kerala has achieved what no other Indian state has achieved. It has the highest female literacy rate in India as well as the highest age at marriage for Indian women. They are more successful than their Indian counter-parts and are quite independent. The interest in women's issues in Kerala led to their hosting of the All India Women's Conference on the 27th to the 29th December, 1975 (Omvedt, 1978, 397).

Kerala as a whole is far more advanced than any other Indian state or low income country. In many aspects, Kerala has far surpassed all the Indian states and stands too far ahead for any of them to catch up. In fact, Kerala can be compared to the United States in many areas. For instance, Kerala is the most literate Indian state; the adult literacy rate is 78 percent while India's is 43 percent. In comparison, the United States literacy rate is 96 percent (Monthly Review, 1991, 20). The high infant mortality rate which is a major problem in India, has almost been overcome in Kerala, which only has 27 per 1000 infant mortality while India has 86 per 1000. The infant mortality rate of ten per 1000 in the U.S. is much closer to that of Kerala's (Monthly Review, 1991, 20). With Kerala being so advanced, it also means that its women have opportunities that are not available to the women in the rest of India. The status of women in Kerala is very high and can be mainly attributed to the matrilineal system that existed as well as the high literacy rate of Keralan women, which is incidentally the highest in India. 66 percent of Keralan women are literate while only 25 percent of Indian women generally are (Jeffrey, 1989, 14). With the high literacy standard, the women in Kerala are given the opportunity to develop and be socially independent. They have opportunities to improve their living standards as well as fight against oppression which exists in every patriarchal society. The better living conditions also mean that Keralan women generally live longer than their female counter-parts in India. They live up to an average of 66 years while the women only live up to an average of 50 years (Jeffrey, 1989, 14). These women are lucky because they have been treated better than other Indian women, mainly because of their matrilineal system and their high literacy rate. Keralan women have many privileges and rights that other Indian women cannot even dream of. There is a deep cleavage in the status of women especially if we compare Kerala to a more backward state like Rajastan, which only has a 11.3 percent literacy rate (Ratcliffe, 19, 68). The whole picture becomes much clearer once the reasons for these vast differences are analyzed.

The differences in the status of women between Kerala and the rest of India are very clear. As mentioned before, Keralan women are the most literate and they also have a longer life span. The reasons for these differences are many and far-reaching. This can mainly be attributed to the fact that Kerala has for many generations had a matrilineal caste system (Jeffrey, 1989, 15). This basicallly means that descent is through the female family line (Oxford, 1976, 673). This gave the woman greater sexual freedom and autonomy as she could choose her own partners. Women were treated almost as equally as men and this meant that female children were given equal opportunity as male children in getting an education as well as other privileges that other female children in India could not have. In traditional Hindu society, women had to be docile and follow their men submissively. This meant that women had less rights than men and thus were not as valued as men. Kerala's matrilineal caste system changed this as women had almost equal opportunity as men to attend schools. Because of Kerala's matrilineal caste system, more importance was given to women as men are marginal in matriliny. This led to the decline in female infanticide in Kerala. In fact, Kerala has had an increase in the ratio of females to males (Franke & Chasin, 1991, 15). Although matriliny meant that descent was through the female line, women still did not inherit property as in matriarchy. Their oldest brother or 'karanavar' would control their property as well as being the guardian to their children (Duvvury, 1989, 103). He was basically the man of the house. Matriliny dissolved after some time, as there was a shift toward patriliny. There also emerged European Christian practices which had an effect on the women's position (Jeffrey, 1987, 17). The Christian women had in reality, less freedom than their matrilineal Indian counterparts.

Christianity has affected the status of women in Kerala in many ways. It does not have as much influence as the matrilineal system in promoting the status of women but it has its advantages as well. Christianity only had importance once matriliny was on the decline. It became important upon the emergence of the 'New Kerala' which led to the contradiction of the 'Old Kerala'. The most famous example would be Mary Poonen Luise, who became Kerala's first woman doctor in 1915 (Jeffrey, 1989, 23). In the old Kerala, Christians were quite against sending their daughters to school as they did not want them to appear as brazen as the matrilineal caste Hindus (Jeffrey, 1989, 23). Christianity also had an effect on education in a different way. Education was used as bait to lure low-caste Hindus especially the untouchables to convert to Christianity (Jeffrey, 1984, 79). This saw to the spread of education to all sections of Keralan society, including the low-caste women.

What both matriliny and Christianity have in common is education. Although matriliny meant that women had more autonomy than men, it resulted in women being allowed to attend school and have an education. This was also the case with Christianity as women were allowed to go to school especially after the missionary influence came in. All this meant that women in Kerala have been exposed to education for a long time. Almost every woman born since 1960 is literate and this is the state with the highest standard of literacy in India and other low-income countries in the Third World (Jeffrey, 1989, 18). Education is a far ranging factor and affects many aspects of the lives of Keralan women.

Through education, women were able to be more independent of their spouses as well as have more say in their family life. What is especially important about education in Kerala is that it does not discriminate. Education is available to everyone, even the poorest people (Franke & Chasin, 1991, 12). 56 percent of Keralans are literate while only 21 percent in India are. There is also a vast difference in the rural sector in Kerala where 69 percent are literate while only 30 percent are in India (Franke & Chasin, 1991, 21). This only proves that education in Kerala is not only confined to the rich. Free education was actually introduced in Kerala at the turn of the century (Ratcliffe, 19, 67). Several other programs have been implemented to ensure that every Keralan has an education and this includes the school lunch program which enables the poor children to attend school (Franke & Chasin, 1991, 13).

The Keralan women who enjoy the status of being the most literate, use their education wisely. It is not merely a statistic for them. They use their knowledge wisely and apply it to their daily lives.

Kerala excels in its health standards and level of health awareness among its people, especially the women. As a result, Kerala has a very low infant mortality rate. In comparison to Kerala, the states of Orissa and Uttar Pradesh have a very high infant mortality rate of 126 per 1000. Because health care is abundant and readily accessible, Keralan women use these services readily. Their literacy also encourages them to apply what they learn to their daily living conditions. Not only has infant mortality declined in Kerala, the fertility rate too has dropped.

Through education, women would have greater independence and have a chance at decision-making at home. She would be in a better position to practise birth-control methods as she would be aware of all the contraceptives available. She would also be wise enough to know that having more children is not going to secure her comfort and protection in her old age. Because infant mortality is high in most Indian states, many couples have larger families as the chance of all their children surviving is very slim. This situation does not arise in Kerala because of the low infant mortality rate. The birth rate in Kerala is low as a result, it is only 22 per 1000 while it is 32 per 1000 in India. As Ratcliffe (19, 72) concludes '. . . education interacted with preventive health measures in a strong, positive fashion to facilitate reductions in mortality'. There is an inverse relationship between education and fertility (Ratcliffe, 19, 76).

Kerala is also a highly co-operative state where government 'ration-shops' are available and accessible to everyone. Almost every household has ration cards that enables them to purchase food and other basic necessities at highly subsidized prices (Franke & Chasin, 1991, 8). This ensures that every Keralan has adequate nutrition. This has an effect on the childrens nutrition level which in turn lessens the chances of infant mortality caused by malnutrition. Because food is easily available, parents do not only feed their sons, their daughters receive the same level of nutrition. The school lunch programs also ensures that children can be sent to school as well receive a healthy and nutritionous meal in the process. Keralan women have been found to place an importance on the nutrition of their families. A survey of housewives showed that education level has a positive correlation with the nutritional level of their families. Although Kerala has the lowest average, per capita caloric intake in India the nutritional intake of pre-school children is high (Ratcliffe, 19, 74). This is crucial as children are most vulnerable at this stage and need to be well nourished in order to achieve maximum growth. The chances of catching contagious diseases is also minimised if the children are well nourished as their bodies would have more resistance. This clearly states that Keralan women use their education wisely to ensure that their children are well nourished, even if they are in the low income level.

Keralan women themselves are healthier than their female counter-parts. As I mentioned earlier, they live longer than other Indian women; their average life-span is 66 years. Because health care is readily available, Keralan women have no problems getting health care and treatment. They are also more aware of need for personal hygiene as well as immunisation. Keralan women and their children are also given the chance of a free meal everyday at the government funded village nurseries (Franke & Chasin, 1991, 9). Horowitz and Kishwar found that Indian women consume less calories than men and female children are more likely to suffer from malnourishment. They found a discrepancy in the weight related to height in all classes of Indian society (Duvvury, 1989, 104). This problem is overcome to a certain degree in Kerala as the women are educated about nutrition as well as given the opportunity to have free food. Self-awareness gives rise to better living conditions, and this is what Kerala has achieved. The fact that pre-school children have an adequate caloric consumption only serves to support this. In Indian society, as it is elsewhere, women are responsible for the domestic part of their household. The correlation between the high literacy level of women and the high nutrition level is rather obvious. Their understanding of hygiene is applied well as most women have been found to boil their drinking water if it is found to be contaminated (Jeffrey, 1989, 18). This is very important as water is the main carrier of many diseases. Hepatatis B and cholera are examples of diseases that can be controlled by boiling drinking water.

Education means that Keralan women are more independent and socially mobile. More and more women are joining the workforce and are a major contributor in their household. As mentioned earlier, fertility rates have declined substantially in Kerala. This is mainly due to the other alternatives that are available to an educated woman. More Keralan women are putting off marriage to pursue their careers and as such, Kerala has the highest female age at marriage in India (Ratcliffe, 19, 77). The data from studies reveal that many Keralan women do not marry at all; around 22 percent remain single (Ratcliffe, 19, 77). The dowry system is also widely fought against in Kerala by women's associations. They organize mass protests and rallies to fight it as well as force investigation whenever there is a suspicious bride death (Franke & Chasin, 1991, 16). This itself is a major step forward for Keralan women as the dowry system has existed for many generations in India, and fighting this gives the women great independence and autonomy from men. A survey in Kerala found that wives decided independently about contraceptive methods in 35 percent of the families surveyed (Jeffrey, 1989, 18). The very fact that Keralan women are independent enough to refuse marriage as well as have a say in the number of children they have, sets them poles apart from other Indian women. In places like Rajastan, not only child-marriages are practised, bride burning or suttee also exists. Kerala certainly stands far ahead where women's position is concerned. Fighting against suttee and dowry expectations, is actually fighting the rigid expectations of a patriarchal society. Kerala more than any other Indian state has succeeded to a certain degree in its fight against patriarchy. It is male supremacy that makes women suffer, especially in countries where women are considered inferior to men. This is the case in Hinduism as women are considered impure due to their menstrual cycle. Hinduism teaches close supervision of females and promulgates a special ideal for womanhood (French, 1985, 254). By breaking out of the chains of patriarchy that bind them, women are in the position to demand greater autonomy and status.

Although the status of women in Kerala has a great effect on the overall success of Kerala, there are many other underlying factors that need to be discussed. It is not merely the women who have gained much from the high literacy level in Kerala. The whole state has advanced greatly due to the literacy level. All Keralans are aware of the need for an education to succeed. This level of mass education has created a political consciousness which has resulted in more political participation (Ratcliffe, 19, 79). Through their political consciousness, they have been able to demand better facilities and amenities. Education is the root of all development in Kerala as it has also broken down traditional social barriers and created a more equitable society (Franke & Chasin, 1991, 18).

Breaking down Kerala's structure to its very roots is the best way to find the reasons for its amazing success. Kerala is geographically well located, as there are many rivers and backwaters as well as rich deltas (Jeffrey, 1984, 77). These provide not only irrigation but transportation as well. Kerala's position also meant that trade was carried out in the early days as there was a port there. Trade is the best way to widen one's horizons, and Kerala did just that. If one looks back in history, all the major ports or coastal regions were very advanced as the people were exposed to diverse cultures. Traders normally brought news of the happenings in other places and this would bring great knowledge. Trading regions also were the first to have their own form of currency as well as a method of keeping their records. A certain degree of education would be necessary to enable such record keeping. This meant that there was always a need for education in Kerala.

Kerala has a unique crop as it is the single largest producer of rubber, cardamom, coconut, banana, tapioca and lemon grass oil (Jeffrey, 1984, 77). The dependable rainfall meant that agriculture was less demanding and that other areas could be explored (Jeffrey, 1984, 79). This led to the interest in education among the Keralan people, as they did not need as much time to tend their farms.

One of Kerala's greatest successes is its agrarian reform, especially land reform. The fact that Kerala did not depend on industrialization to succeed is rather amazing as most developing states and countries have resorted to it for development. This is clearly not the case for Kerala. Kerala's land reform carried out in 1969 is the most successful among any Third World state or country (Franke & Chasin, 1991, 5). Agrarian reform is the most effective way to ensure an equitable income level in developing countries. Land reform in Kerala is mainly aimed towards redistributing income among all its people, not just the rich peasants and land-owners (Ratcliffe, 19, 66). The main aim of the newly elected communist government in 1957 was to implement tenancy reform, where it would be illegal to evict tenants (Franke & Chasin, 1991, 6). Land reform has improved the living standards in Kerala greatly. Larger scope for wage employment is made available through land reform which aims at reducing income disparities (Ratcliffe, 19, 67). With better chances at joining the workforce, unemployment would be reduced to a certain degree. Kerala has gone one step further. Wage rates in Kerala are the second highest in

India after Punjab (Ratcliffe, 19, 67). This would lead a labour intensive workforce to contribute to their own share of an equitable income distribution.

Land reform was only implemented after pressure was put on the government by the defeated communist party. They had in actual fact lost their power when they introduced their land reform in 1957 as it was considered too radical. The communist part, CPM is independent of any other country and provides healthy competition and criticism to the government (Franke & Chasin, 1991, 19). They demanded many reforms in Kerala. This is not all. Communists were the first to include women's liberation on their agenda and managed to mobilize women especially in Kerala, West Bengal and Andhra Pradesh (Duvvury, 1989, 107). The CPI (M) leadership in recent years has also led to the success of labour organization as well the achievement of high wage rates (Omvedt, 1978, 393). The fact that there were times that Kerala has had a communist government has helped push several long standing issues forward.

It does not mean that a communist government would ensure the success that Kerala has achieved. The government of any state or country has to be there for the people. The people of Kerala have been very vocal and active in their political consciousness and participation. Because of the widespread public participation, all the government based services run smoothly and effectively. If it does not, one could expect major protests and demonstrations until everything runs smoothly again. To sum it up briefly, Kerala's success has been a result of a class struggle which was led by the communist party (Amin, 1991, 28).

A unique characteristic of Kerala is the apparent absence of caste discrimination in government bureaucracy and society. Although castes still do exist, the people seem to have put aside their differences to pool their resources for the success of their state. Through the means of education, rational and scientific thought was promoted to fight the caste system (Franke & Chasin, 1991, 13). The CPI party in Kerala has also had a hand in organizing the lower class and castes that it seems that the poor would never be suppressed again (Ratcliffe, 19, 69). No matter where, united people would lead to the success of the country. Where racial tension or bias exists, there would be unrest and no progress can take place. By ensuring that no one is discriminated against due to colour or caste, equality can be achieved. The hegemony in Kerala has been attained due to this.

There are constant references to the 'Kerala Model', obviously through which Kerala managed to attain so much success. If examined closely enough, there does not appear to be such a model. Kerala is different to all other Indian states in India. What really does exist though is the co-operation of the people no matter what caste or colour and the great autonomy of women. The strong position of women in Kerala has had a tremendous effect on the social development of this state. No other state in India can even be close enough to Kerala for a comparison to be made in terms of female literacy. The lesson to be learnt of-course, is that gender inequality is lessened to a certain degree by education. Education gives women a chance to stand on their own two feet as well as provide competition in the work place. By bringing in an income, women would also have a greater say in their homes, which brings in issues of nutrition and fertility.

Matriliny was the foundation on what the women have achieved today. This system ensured sexual independence as well as a greater chance of social mobility. Although several advantages were lost in the process when there was a shift towards patriliny, what remained was the right to an education. It appears as though it was more tradition than anything else, but whatever the reason, it served the purpose well. Women became independent enough to make decisions about their lives and their futures. Women were in a position to decide when they wanted to marry as well as have a major say in the number of children they had. The women have as much capability as men to earn a living and this makes parents value their daughters as well as they would their sons. This overcomes the sense of inferiority which prevails in India.

Education is another major factor which I feel can be attributed to Kerala's success. Every aspect discussed so far is linked either directly or indirectly to education. Matriliny, mortality, fertility, health . . . the list is endless. Education is important in Kerala because it does not discriminate, it reaches all corners of Kerala, right from women to the tribal people. Mass education has achieved Kerala's state today. Although it has been reported that the standard of education is deplorably poor, I feel this is not very important when one considers what Kerala has achieved. Keralan people use their education wisely, whether it is for knowledge or leisure. The daily newspaper circulation in 1983 was 60 per 1000. This is far ahead of Punjab which comes in next at only 36.6 per 1000 (Statistical outline, 1989/90, 10). Through education, a greater awareness of health and hygiene arises. The medical facilities are the best in India. The population per hospital bed is the lowest with only 391, while Bihar which is the highest, is 2876 people per bed (Statistical outline, 1989/90, 10).

All this only serves to show that Kerala has succeeded due to the sheer ingenuity of its people. Mass education has achieved what no other state in India has achieved. Women have greater autonomy due to this as well. This only serves to show all the other Indian states that there is a lot to be learnt from Kerala.

References

Amin, S. (1991), *Comments on Kerala* , Monthly Review, 42 (8), January 1991.

Duvvury, N. (1989), *Women in Agriculture: A Review of the Indian Literature* , Economic and Political Weekly, 28 October 1989.

Franke, R, W, & Chasin, B. H. (1991), *Kerala State, India: Radical Reform Development* , Monthly Review, 42 (8), January 1991.

French, M. (1985), *Beyond Power* (New York, Belles-Lettres Inc.).

Hamilton, R, (1978), *The Liberation of Women* (Great Britain, George Allen & Unwin Ltd.).

Jeffrey, R. (1984), *Learning Is Sold Like Snakeoil in India's Most Literate State* , Far Eastern Economic Review, 19 July 1984.

Jeffrey, R. (1989), *Women and the 'Kerala Model': Four Lives, 1870s to 1980s* , South Asia, XII (2), 1989.

Omvedt, G. (1978), *Women and Rural Revolt in India* , Journal of Peasant Studies, 1 (3), April 1978.

Ratcliffe, J. (19), *Social Justice and the Demographic Transition: Lessons from India's Kerala State* , Practising Health For All.

Weedon, C. (1987), *Feminist Practice & Poststructralist Theory* (New York, Basil Blackwell Inc.).

The Coor System in Goan Clubs in Bombay and its Effect on Female Members

Olga Valladares

I undertook this study despite the constraints imposed by the volatile Goan political situation at the time, as the uniqueness of the system interested me. In 1961, Goa was liberated from Portugal by the Indian Army and became part of the Indian Union. In the light of the political, economic and developmental changes that followed in Goa, I decided to investigate the repercussions of these changes on the lives of members of Goan *coors* (also known as *cudds*) in Bombay and in 1968, undertook a small sample survey. I found that changes were few and far between. At the time of writing this article, in 1994 the premises of several coors have been sold some odds have sold or developed their premises into multi story structure.

The word *cudda* or *coor* literally rendered, means "room". A Konkani word, it is probably derived from the Portuguese *cuadd* of similar connotation. The use of the word *cudd* may have some relation to the ancient dormitory system of living prevalent on the West coast of India, and was certainly not a new word coined or adapted by Goan emigrants to explain their mode of habitation. Houses in coastal villages of the Konkan, usually had provision for a guest-room (known as *cudd*) to accommodate the casual traveller. This term *cudd* or *çoor* was brought to Bombay, and the place where the village people lived together was also known as a *cudd* or *coor*. So, what was originally used to denote only a place, later on came to be identified as a system of living.

The *coor* system is an associated form of living that evolved from a way of life adopted by a section of migrant Goans in Bombay and other parts of India. It emerged naturally and spontaneously from the social consciousness of migrant people, in contrast to the scientifically formulated, deliberately planned and organized associations like the community centres in the USA, which served the same purpose-the rehabilitation of the immigrant and the prevention of social and psychological disintegration that such displacement sometimes brings in its wake.

For the early emigrants who were the originators of this system, the cudd was only a temporary home for the duration of their working life, after which they would return to retire in Goa. Coming from the agricultural classes, being untrained for an occupation and having little or no education, they were in the majority, employed in the "lower-income" groups semen, cooks, domestic workers and clerks being the most popular occupation avenues open to them. Their primary need was accommodation that would be cheap, yet provide as far as possible "Home comforts" and the "atmosphere of home", yet for them it would be only temporary, to last for their sojourn in Bombay. The *coor* and *cudd* or club, answered their needs. It was cheap and provided the companionship of fellow villagers, since membership was restricted to people hailing from a particular village or group of villages in Goa. Gradually, from this simple act of "clubbing together", there evolved a system of living governed by rules and regulations and providing certain benefits.

Within the Goan community itself, the clubs cropped up occasionally as the subject of journalistic comment and talks, but had otherwise been neglected and not infrequently eschewed as being an organization for "the lower classes". This led some literate, progressive *coor* members to refer to their *coors* as "clubs". The use of this word "club" has often led those unaware of the *coor* system to confuse Goan clubs with the club of Western origin.

At the time this study was undertaken, Goan *coors*

served a population of about 40,000 Goans in Bombay, i.e. about 50 per cent of the total Goan population.

Early Emigrants and the First Cudds

Emigration from Goa has been evident from the advent of the Portuguese in that part of India. The earliest exodus has been attributed to fear of proselytization. Over the seventeenth and eighteenth centuries, the religious policy of the Christian conqueror, sporadic no doubt, led to mass migration of the Hindu inhabitants towards the Konkan and the south.[1] In early 1835, the first Christian emigrants from Goa, too, field the home-country for Bombay, with the deposed governor, Bernard Peres da Silva (a Goan), actuated by the same fear of persecution from the subsequent rulers.[2] Bombay at the time, was seeing the beginnings of commercialization. European commercial houses, just beginning to open up, found themselves in need of white collar workers and minor officials who were familiar with the Roman script. The demand for copy clerks and scriveners was far in excess than could be filled by the local population and the arrival of Portuguese-educated Goans solved the problem. But, it was not these political emigres who represented the educated classes more or less, nor the 'boys' (cook/bearer/sacristan) who accompanied the *Padroado* (goan) clergy to Bombay, who were the Pilgrim Fathers to the *coor* members. The former were comparatively well-off, able to afford their own private residences and as they came as families, established their own homes. The later, though, came singly and ensconced themselves in quarters attached to parochial houses. Those who returned home on visits, may have spread the word about opportunities in the rising metropolis of Bombay.

Perhaps it was these echoes of easily-gotten wealth linked with other causes that aroused the uneducated middle and labouring classes to venture in hand-hewn *patmaris* (country craft) across the seas. These men who came only as temporary migrants, were pioneers of the immigration movement of founders of the Goan *cudd* system. The migration to Bombay began in the 1840s and most of the migrants were men who left their families at home.[3]

The occupation of Goa by British forces, for 16 years, towards the end of the eighteenth century and the beginning of the nineteenth century, opened yet another avenue to the emigrants-the local people served as domestic staff to British officers, who when they were transferred to Bombay and other stations in British India, took their servants with them.[4] One of the *coors* studied in Bombay, was established by 'cooks in military messes'.

With the growth of Bombay as a seaport, foreign passenger ships, steamers and tramps began to employ Goans as seamen.[5]

The last to arrive were the 'women and children.' The former were, in all probability, not the wives of the immigrants, who more often than not left the women-folk behind to keep the home fires burning, but were relatives or co-villagers of the uneducated, middle and labouring class immigrants, of the kind who needed employment badly, 'mostly widows'.[6] The majority found employment in European and Parsi houses while a few were adventurous enough to open *pousadas*[7] at Horta Baixa and old Sonapur (old localities in South Bombay).

Reasons for the Goan Exodus

The Goan exodus was continuous, but not planned. Goan emigration was due to high (population) density, geographic factors, the social and intellectual evolution of the people, the poverty of the country and the ease with which goan emigrants by reason of their culture and assimilation of European civilization, even though superficial, were absorbed in British India, East Africa and the Persian Gulf.[8]

The opening of village schools in Goa and the subsequent spread of primary education provided a fresh impetus and set loose a train of aspirations. It may also have been responsible for a distaste for manual labour.[9]

The oppression of the *mundacares* by the *Battcaras*,[10] the breakdown of village economy and self-sufficiency of the community were also contributory factors. The Catholic population cultivated new habits, experienced new wants.

It underwent a complete social revolution. But, the social changes had foundations of sand.[11]

Economic necessity played a large part in the drain of human resources from Goa. The economy of Goa has, from Puranic times, been mainly agricultural. The *Gomantak* of ancient literature, 'full of cows', as it has been rendered, suggests a verdant, prosperous country, while Golden Goa of a much later period conjures up dazzling visions of glittering abundance. Whence then this state of economic insufficiency?

Not a small part of the blame has been put down by Goan writers to the Portuguese *hidalgo* (nobleman or gentleman of leisure) and his apathetic attitude to the economic welfare of the country which has led to a slow but sure deterioration of economic resources. Indigenous products and cottage industries-the cashew and areca nuts, coir, cabinet-making, gold and silver-ware-it is asserted, could have been the basis of a stable economy. Goa until recently years, was little industrialized, except for copper and manganese mines.[12] In the recent past, Goa has been marketed extensively as tourist attraction.

In addition, the returning 'heroes', painted glamorous pictures of easy money and made ostentatious displays of this at village feasts. These factors all combined to entice more and more Goans away from Goa.

Finally, the two World Wars and the widening market for human labour increased the tide of Goan emigration to a flight.

Immigration to India was fostered by the rapid industrialization of growing cities in the vicinity of Goa. On 26 December 1878, the Anglo-Portuguese Treaty was signed opening up the port of Mormugoa to rail traffic with India and the railway line was started on 18 April 1881. This increased trade and emigration as Goans began to emigrate in large numbers to Bombay, Karachi, Poona, Calcutta and towards the end of the last century, to East Africa.[13]

Out of a total of approximately 370 clubs (in 1958)[14] in Bombay from Colaba to Mahim, 341 were Goan clubs, 120 being predominantly seamens' clubs.[15] Out of these, 318 were men's clubs, the remaining 23 were women's and mixed clubs. Applied to the latter, the term 'club' is a misnomer, they being made up really of families sharing a room or rooms under a *ghorwalli* or landlady who charged them a monthly rent and laid down the law to suit her own personal needs. It had none of the co-operative organization of the original pattern.

The pattern of life in the club in the early days varied very little from the rural life they were used to 'back home'. The difference lay in the type of occupation and change of scenery. Each morning, they would go to work, return in the evening, go for walks or merely sit around in the clubs, smoking, chatting with fellow-members, till it was time for Rosary and bed. They observed the same village feasts, celebrating these occasions as far as the new surroundings would permit, in the same way, with Church services, and in the evening, the Rosary, the litany or *ladainha*, followed by light refreshment and the traditional *mando.*[16]

Contact with other groups or outside communities was practically nil. In fact, there was a tendency among the better class of immigrants to look down upon the *coors* and their inhabitants. *Coors*, though housed in the same building would not be on visiting terms with one another, 'outsiders' were regarded with suspicion, as often *coor* members had been swindled by outsiders claiming to provide services to them.

The Cudd System in General

The concentration of Goan men's clubs in the Bhobi Talao, Grant Road, Mazagaon and Byculla areas could have been a result of the following factors: (a) These were the lower rent areas (b) They were the centres of Catholic life (c) They were the areas in which the Goan population, generally speaking, was concentrated.

At the entrance to the *cudd* was a name-plate giving its name and date of establishment. Above the door, was another board reading "No Admission without Permission."

Cudd premises could consist of just one room to a whole building of 16 rooms, including kitchens and godowns. The centre of *cudd* life was the 'hall'. It was the parlour, dining-room (where there was no separate one), recreation room, study room, meeting-hall, (in some cases even the bedroom) and when the need arises, a reception-hall for the wedding of a member. *Cudds* ranged from 100 to 1,000 sq. yds.

The centre-piece of the 'hall' was the altar, dedicated to the Patron Saint of the *cudd*. A wooden structure, it was a matter of great pride and sometimes the handiwork of the members of the *cudd* themselves. A lamp burned before it, candlesticks and flower vases decorated it. Around the altar, members collected for prayers. Where space permitted, out of respect, no clothes were hung in the 'hall' and no sleeping was allowed there.

Arranged in a row, around the four walls of the *cudd* were the boxes of the members, as many as could fit in, the rest being stacked in other rooms. Apart from one or two chairs and a table, the boxes were the only furniture in the hall.

The safe or 'treasury', in keeping with the importance of its function, occupied a place of prominence too. The safe was a modern innovation from "the old days" when surplus *cudd* funds were stored in earthenware jars and concealed in a safe place. The safe also contained important documents and sometimes personal valuables of members.

Every *cudd* had a notice-board on which was displayed the list of resident members and their turn for household duties, members' mail, notices pertaining to the *cudd* and its affairs, complaints, or suggestions, in fact, any matter of relevance to the *cudd*. Only the manager or members of the Managing Committee were allowed to touch the notice board.

The bell too, was only touched by the manager, *jalador* or anyone authorized by them. In an emergency, any member could ring the bell, but had to pay a few paise for the privilege. The bell was usually used to inform members of a general body meeting or an emergency such as an accident, sudden illness or fight. All members were required to answer the bell in default of which a penalty was imposed.

Alongside the notice board was hung a framed set of rules. This was done in *cudds* where the rulers were not printed in book form.

.Female Emigration and Goan Women's and Mixed Clubs

Says one Goan writer,[17] "...the early Goan emigrants who left Goa for Bombay had neither Eves nor angels for company. The voyage from Goa to Bombay which occupies about twenty hours now, took as many days or more then, and it was uncomfortable as it was long. I am not quite certain whether any female emigrant travelled by *patmaris*..." He puts down the earliest female emigration to the beginning of this century when steamships or *hajikasamwallahs*, began playing between Bombay and Goa. The women came in driblets and belonged to that category which most needed employment to maintain themselves. They were mostly widows, relatives of the uneducated middle class emigrants, in fact, relatives of the residents of the *cudds*. The majority found work in European and Parsi homes, while few opened eating houses in the Dhobi Talao area (at Horta Baixa and Old Sonapur) and in Mazagoan (at Bandarvada), and these catered principally to the comforts of the Filipino sailors who worked on board the ships that touched Bombay. These men, it appeared, were free with money and "except that they indulged occasionally in knife-play among themselves, specially after a cock-fight, treated the women considerately and well. These women were happy in their way, and some of them married the Phillipinos".[18]

"The women with the Parsis", Slug continues in the same article, "were equally happy. They created such a favourable impression on the Parsis, that when the first batch of women of the lower classes arrived, they were promptly engaged..." They were, it appears, well treated, "less like a servant and more like an equal", they had very little to do and were well paid.

Like their male counterparts, these women must have returned to Goa with rose-coloured pictures of their lives in Bombay, till "every mother was naturally anxious to send her grown-up daughter to Bombay. But they came only in tens and twenties...It is an indisputable fact that immorality prevails more among domestic servants than among others, due to the conditions of service itself which have a baneful influence on a normal girl. What therefore happened to

Goan servants was that which be falls domestics the world over. Some sinned, some were sinned against. This however, did not check the influx of this class of females into Bombay, on the contrary, it increased to an extent that was truly appalling....they were glutting the labour market.[19]

These women needed some place to stay when they were out of a job or when they first arrived in the city. Accordingly women's *cudds* came into being. Goan women's and mixed clubs together numbered 23 in 1958, there were Mangalorean women's clubs too, but I was unable to trace them. On inquiry, I found that there were only about half a dozen women's *cudds*, i.e. *cudds* that had only women residents. The rest, accommodated families and so fall into the category of 'mixed' clubs. The residents of the women's *cudds* were generally *ayahs* (domestic servants) and factory hands.

The only point in common that these *cudds* share with men's *cudds* was that the residents shared a room. Otherwise it was just a one-man (rather a one-woman show, since the proprietors were all female) show run entirely on a profit-making basis, as a means of livelihood.

The landlady, usually hired a room and took in lodgers. Female members of a *cudd* were not restricted to any particular village, but came from all over Goa and entered a *cudd* on the recommendation of a friend. One such club was started by a couple who took in boarders to supplement the husband's income as a compounder. After his death, his widow turned it into a *cudd*.

Membership was open to Catholic Goans, a prospective lodger usually came to the club on the recommendation of a friend or acquaintance. Conditions for membership were few: The rent was to be paid regularly and even during absence from the clubs; a fixed curfew hour had to be maintained. In short, the landlady's word was law. Daily prayers were said in common, but not enforced. Rent for single individuals was about Rs. 2 (in women's and mixed clubs) and varied from Rs. 12 to Rs.15 for married couples, extra rent being charged per grown-up child.

Cooking arrangements were made individually and it was not uncommon to see whole rows of *sigrees* (stoves) and pots and pans in the kitchen of a woman's or mixed club. Each individual or family took turns in cleaning the premises and everyone joined in the monthly cleaning.

Over-crowding was common as the landladies wanted the most they could get out of the arrangements. For example, in the mixed *cudd* covered, the accommodation provided was two rooms and a kitchen, two bathrooms and two W.C.s, while the residents totalled 41 individuals-among them, six married couples, eight widows, ten unattached men and women, ten children and the *ghorwalli* (landlady) herself.

The lodgers appeared to get the worst of the bargain and conversations with some of them revealed that they only stayed on in the *cudd* out of sheer necessity, as their incomes were small and they lacked other accomodation. For them the *cudd* was just a roof over their heads.

One Goan welfare workers commented that over-crowding, besides being physically restricting, also led to "a deterioration in morals..."

Unscrupulous landladies, often gave unemployed girls a roof and shelter and used the obligation created as a means of inducting the girls into prostitution. In mixed clubs Advocate hoto a Goan lawyer involved in welfare work in the late 1950s observed that "in these small holes, men and women, boys and girls, live in countless numbers. They dress before one another, they undress before one another, they sleep next to one another as if they were not human beings nor animals, but mere males and females according to the dictionary meaning of the words. The outcome of such a life is rather serious and unbecoming."

Conclusion

The *cudds* provided both Goan catholic men and women with little money and few contacts in the alien city of Bombay, a roof over their heads and a reasonably secure environment. It so helped the unprepared migrant integrate into their new city of residence and in many cases, members helped each other find employment. Women who lived in *cudds* experienced the worst aspects of the system unless they were landladies. Nevertheless, the *cudds* provided many destitute women, with few or no skills a home base in an alien environment. It enabled them to live in the security of their own community, reinforcing practices they were used to while they struggled to find work and adapt themselves to city living.

Later, from the early 1960s onwards, Church organizations such as Regina Pacis (an organisation for domestics run by nuns) set up resource centres for Christian servant girls. Many of these girls acquired simple sewing skills, some learned English or Hindi and became literate, they were also made aware of their rights and were taught basic bank procedures and where and how to save their income. As a result, many 'girls' became self sufficient. The organizations also function as employment exchanges, which prospective employers approach domestic servants and the negotiation process is often mediated by the nuns who constantly try to get the best possible deal for the girls.

The 'Gulf Boom' which lasted from the late 1960s to the early 1980s, gave several hundred unskilled Goans an employment opportunity and *cudds* still served as stopover places where people rested in between the buds or ship journey from Goa and the flight to the Persian Gulf. Many expatriates spent their incomes on acquiring property in Goa and Bombay and on educating their children. On the return journey to Goa, several could afford to and opted to live in hotels rather than *cudds* and the role of *cudds* began to become increasingly irrelevant. They still function as homes for domestic servants in between jobs and for low-income earners, but several *cudds* have been discontinued since the late 1980s.

Children of *cudd* members of the late 1950s, are often educated to graduate level and beyond. Many still work in the hospitality industry as chiefs and service personnel and some are marine engineers and seamen, and most are better educated and more affluent than their parents were at their age. Several ex-*cudd* members have migrated from the Persian Gulf to Canada, Australia and the United States, though many of this category will not admit to having lived in *cudds* because of the stigma attached to these places.

Cudds evolved as a response to the needs and situation of low-income Goan Catholic migrants. Despite their limitations and disadvantages, they provided a safety net for the migrant and facilitated this or her integration into the city of their adoption. They enabled the migrant to develop coping mechanisms and acquire skills that appear to be transferable when these migrants re-settle in new homelands overseas.

Notes

1. Atropos, 'Random Jottings', *The Anglo-Lusitano* 31-1-1931.
2. Slug, 'Charivari' *Ibid*, 14-3-1931.
3. A comment by Archbishop Porter (1886), quoted by Earnest Hull S.J., Vol. II, p. 236.
4. C.F. Saldanha S.J. (1952) *A Short History of Goa*, Bombay, p. 22, 124.
5. Slug, *Ibid.*, 11-4-1931.
6. Slug, *Ibid*, 28-3-1931.
7. Eating houses
8. Prof. Avertano Correia-Fernandes *The Anglo-Lusitano*, 6-2-1932.
9. *Emigration Commission Report* (1931).
10. *Battcaras* were feudal overlords in Goa and *mundacares*, corresponded to the English 'villein' of the Middle Ages.
11. Atropos, 'Random Jottings' *The Anglo-Lusitano* 31-1-1931.
12. This had been suggested by Prof. J.A. Fernandes of the University of Bombay, in a discussion I had with him on the subject.
13. C.F. Saldanha S.J. (1952) *A Short History of Goa*, Bombay, p. 148-9.
14. In his report of the Catholic Clubs' Welfare Organisation, 1948-49, the Club Chaplain gives his figures as 370. The figures quoted in this study have been complied from a printed list provided by him. The Legion of Mary who also took up club welfare work in the mid-1950s, found these figures to be more or less constant.
15. From old manuscripts, the authorship of which cannot be verified: "In 1926 when the National Seamen's Union was founded, a survey of clubs was made and they found that there were only 120 clubs where only seamen were staying."
16. Goan folk songs.
17. Slug *The Anglo-Lusitano*, March, 28, 1931.
18. Slug *Ibid.*
19. Slug, *Ibid.*

East Indian, Goan, and Mangalorean Women in Melbourne-Who They Are and Who They Think They Are

Gillian Castellino

The act of migration implies the rejection of a past and the synthesis of future. It involves the remaking of an identity. What are the significant elements of this identity for East Indian, Goan and Mangalorean women migrants to Australia?

East Indians, Goans and Mangaloreans are part of the Indian Catholic community.[1] The 1986 Australian Census revealed that Catholics account for 30 per cent of both migrants and people born in Australia who claim Indian ancestry. The 1981 Indian census revealed that only 1.5 per cent of the Indian population was Christian.[2] This community is culturally hybrid and distinct from other Indian communities with respect to origin, colonial experience, historical, attitudes, religion and language.

East Indians, Goans and Mangaloreans were converted from Hinduism and in some cases Islam by the Portuguese around or after 1543 and their original homes are along the west coast of India in Bombay and Thane, Goa and Mangalore respectively.[3]

The East Indians

This community originated in and around Greater Bombay. They appear to be descendants of Hindu families who migrated to Mahim (now a part of Bombay) in the thirteenth century with Raja Bhimdev of Gujarat. After 1543 they were converted to Christianity by the Portuguese and forced to abandon their original names and adopt Portugese ones.

Their language was a dialect of Marathi, but after conversion they were introduced to Portuguese as a written and spoken language and Latin as their language of worship.

In 1662, Bombay became a British acquisition in the dowry of Catherine de Braganaca (the sister of the Portuguese king who married Charles II of England). After 1672 these people were recruited in clerical positions by the East Indian company because of their familiarity with the Roman script. By the 1830s they began referring to themselves as East Indians to distinguish themselves from Goans who began migrating to Bombay around this time in search of work.[4] East Indian Company employees in Bengal also referred to themselves as East Indians, but this study will not focus on that group.

The Goans

These people were descendants of mainly Hindu families from Goa who were converted to Christianity after was captured from Raja Adil Shah by the Portuguese between 1510 and 1543. Despite conversion, the Hindu caste system and the practice of giving and receiving dowry remained. The initial religious tolerance of the Portuguese ended in 1542 with the arrival of St Francis Xavier. In 1567 the Church Council of Goa rules that all Hindu temples by destroyed and Hindu orphans be raised by converts to Catholicism.[5] Portuguese became the official language and Konka, the local language, was written in the Western script. Latin became the language of worship.

In the 1830s, when regular shipping services were started between Bombay and Goa, Goans began migrating to Bombay in search of jobs.[6] They also migrated to Portuguese colonies in Africa and other parts of the world. In December 1961 the Indian army invaded Goa and liberated it from the Portuguese. Since then it has become part of India.

The Mangaloreans

Mangaloreans are Catholic converts who fled to Goa and the westernizing practices insisted upon by the Portuguese and settled in Kanara where they were allowed to do so by the Bednore kings (1565-1760), These people retained Hindu dress patterns and languages. In the last quarter of the eighteenth century, Tippu Sultan of Mysore, suspecting that the Catholics had supported the British against him, rounded up 60,000 to 80,000 of them and held them captive at Seringapatnam. In 1792 they were freed and some of them returned to Kanara to settle. They were seen by the British as 'a valuable connecting link' between Hindus and Europeans.[7] From the late eighteenth century onwards, some Mangaloreans migrated to Bombay in search of jobs and later to other cities around the world.

Descendants of Goans and Mangaloreans who migrated to Portuguese and British colonies in the nineteenth and early twentieth centuries developed loyalties to their adopted homelands. When these places were decolonized in the 1960s and 1970s, some elected to settle in the west rather than return to Goa which was by then a part of India. East Indians did not usually migrate, as Bombay developed into a thriving metropolis which provided them adequate employment opportunities until recently.

From the 1950s some East Indians, Goans and Mangaloreans went to the UK and Portugal for higher studies and stayed on. From the 1960s to the 1980s these communities joined the exodus of migrants Indian workers to the Persian Gulf.

After Indian Independence in 1947 East Indians, Goans and Mangaloreans along with Anglo-Indians, Punjabi, Keralite, Adivasi and other Christians in India came to be designated as Indian Christians. When immigration opportunities opened up in the West, some decided to leave India and settle in the UK, US, Canada, Australia, Portugal and in smaller numbers in other parts o the world. The group which migrated to Australia did so after the White Australia Policy was discontinued in 1966.

Perceptions of Identity among the women of this community.

When I began to comb the available literature for writings by or representations of these women, except for an article by Lariane Fonseca and a magazine called Link which were produced for private circulation by Laxmi Fonseca, I was confronted by a vast silence. Women of this community do not appear to write about themselves. So who are they are why are they silent?[8]

Like most Indian women, women of this community did not have the opportunity nor encouragement to develop a strong personal identity, a sense of 'self', an awareness of and capacity to express the uniqueness that differentiated one individual from the next and is free of role and relationship determinants. Their concept of identity was, and in many cases, is still bound up with their social identity, that is, a self-concept derived from group memberships, interpersonal relationships, social position and status.[9]

An important aspect of social identity is 'basic group identity', derived from what is loosely called an 'ethnic group'. It is an identity made up of what a person is born with or acquires as birth, such as a name, a particular body and a concept of a place as 'home',[10] By this reasoning, East Indians, Goans and Mangaloreans have an ethnic identity unique from other Indian ethnic groups.

The name given to a child reflects the history and origins of the group into which he or she is born, his or her nationality, language, religion and value system-his or her group identity. With this legacy comes not only the shaping circumstances of the past but those of the present and these determine how an individual's personality will be shaped-how he or she will measure h is or her own power or powerlessness.[11] East Indians, Goans and Mangaloreans have Portuguese surnames as expression and affirmation of their colonial experience and conversion in Christianity. Some members of this community in India have reverted to their original caste names, but this is not true of migrants to Asutralia. With respect to first names, which are usually an expression of the individual's parents' preferences, older members of the community often have Portuguese names, younger members have Anglicized versions, Indian names, or, in many cases, names that happen to be popular for that time.

The body is the most palpable element of which identity is made. A person can change his or her name, origins, language, nationality, ideologies and even rewrite his or her history, but there is not much he or she can do to change his or her body.[12] Many East Indians, Goans and Mangaloreans families were merely converted by the Portuguese. But the Portuguese sometimes intermarried and more often took mistresses from these communities. Of the group of racially mixed people who resulted from such unions, some, taking advantage of their European features, claimed to be Anglo-Indians during the Raj. It is for this reason that many Anglo-Indians (Eurasians) have Portuguese surnames. However, most families after conversion either abandoned their native tongues in favour of European languages or adopted European languages in addition to their native ones, as a means of upward social mobility.

The physical element in basic group identity has not to do only with the body but also with placc-thc land and soil to which the group is attached literally, historically and mythically-the real and imagined homelands.[13] Most East Indians, when asked to identify their 'home', tend to name it as Bombay, India. This is because migration is a recent phenomenon among them, and most are first-generation migrants. Most Mangaloreans, because of their traditional adherence to the Hindu elements in their culture, will identify their home as Mangalore, India. Goans vary: most will claim Goan ancestry, but differ when asked to name their nationality. Some of the older generation identify themselves as Indians, other as Portuguese, Pakistani, Kenyan of even as 'British subjects', depending on their family history and country they grew up in. Response patterns are similar among the younger generation. Many who grew up in Australia claim to be Australian. Others qualify the response, saying that they call themselves 'Indians' or 'Goans' when speaking to Australians and 'Australians' when speaking to Indians.

The observations mentioned are based on a pilot study I conducted on identity perceptions among women of the community in Melbourne. I interviewed eleven women from the ages of 22 to late seventies. Three women were in their twenties, three in their thirties, one in her forties, one in her fifties, tow in their sixties and one in her seventies. Of these two were solicitors, two teachers, three secretaries and an accountant, pathologist and a social worker. All, except for the two secretaries were educated up to tertairy levels. Six came to Australia from India (some having lived elsewhere before arriving here); four from Pakistan; one from the UK (but had lived most of her life in Kenya). Their length of residence in Australia varied from their one to twenty-five years. Their ages at the time of entry ranged from their early teens to the early fifties.

The women interviewed almost uniformly associated 'Indianness' with Hindu culture, which some of them acknowledged to be part of their own history, and institutions peculiar to Indian society such as the extended family, caste and emphasis on religion. They associate Goan, East Indian or Mangalorean identity with the family, languages (such as Konkani, Portuguese, Marathi and Tulu), cuisine, customs, dress (particular styles of wearing the sari) and folksongs.

The decision to migrate to Australia was prompted almost uniformly by economic considerations (usually the belief that opportunities for their children would be better in the West) and in some cases by a feeling of alienation in the home country 9 of being an outsider because of having a name, religion and lifestyle outside the mainstream culture) or because of insecurity caused by rising religious fundamentalism. With only one person, the oldest interviewed, was religion a consideration.

Many of the older women defined themselves in terms of their roles as wives, mothers, workers and churchgoers. This is understandable as until recently these women were not encouraged to define themselves beyond these roles, though the roles of a freira (nun) or beata (spinster) was an option to marriage for young women in the past. In fact, several wealthy Goan families actively encouraged their daughters to take on these roles, in order to keep their wealth within the family (as daughters were traditionally given a dowry at the time of marriage).[14] Many poor Christian women worked in British and postcolonial India as maids, but it is unlikely that any of these women met the qualifying criteria for immigration to Australia.

For many younger women, w hose idea of individual identity was well developed, the privacy, anonymity and choices presented by western society were especially attractive. To some of these women, their ethnic background and the traditions and history they represented, was something to be discarded or even denied as it was seen to confer to survival advantage, but in fact to impede acceptance by mainstream Australian society. The women who rejected their ethnicity were those who knew the least about their history and background. Their responses suggested an unquestioning acceptance of western stereotypes with respect to 'Indianness' which they had somehow come to see as other and distinct from themselves.

The rejection of the Indian component of self was common among urban, middle-class East indians, Goans and Mangaloreans during colonization. It was an attitude fostered by their colonial masters as part of the divide and rule policy.[15] It led these people to believe that they were saved from the degeneracy of their 'heathen' (non-Christian) countrymen and because of their westernized speech and customs were more educated and sophisticated. It resulted in these communities keeping aloof from other Indian communities, while simultaneously remaining subservient to and believing themselves less than the colonizers. It resulted in the formation of a community that was superficially westernized, but which retained many of the attitudes and traditions of their Hindu ancestors. It also resulted in a community that rejected their Hindu past in favour of a subordinate but relatively comfortable present. This rejection was, in most cases, unquestioning because until recently the church was seen to be the ultimate authority and its teachings sanctioned by God.

In this context, it is relevant to mention that colonization had a profound psychological impact upon Indian society. The nature of personal identity in traditional India differed markedly from its nature in the west. In the

Indian concept, personal identity was dependent on the fulfilment family and social roles and the development of the transcendent self. In the west the emphasis is on the individual and self-creation.[16] The formation of partial western selfhood in Indian personalities generated personal conflicts that were resolved through mixtures of three ideal outcomes: identification with the colonizer, rejection of the colonizer in favour of the Indian and incorporation of western elements into a new Indian synthesis.[17]

Whichever strategy East Indians, Goans and Mangaloreans in Australia adopted the act of migration has forced them to redefine their own identities in ways that diverge from members of their communities still in India.

In India today, the Catholic church, influenced by liberation theology and other social movements in becoming increasingly 'Indianized'. Moreover Christians in India, like their counterparts in other Indian communities, are more aware of and increasingly seek to reclaim their pre-colonial past. Women of the Goan, East Indian and Mangalorean communities in India are actively involved in this process. There foes not seem to be any comparable activity among the groups in Australia. This could be partially explained by the fact that the social world in Australia is very different from that in India, and the other countries these groups have come from. Also, as these three groups are relatively new in Australia, most of the women are preoccupied with establishing their families financially and professionally. Also those aspects of Indian culture which previous generations retained and integrated into their lifestyles may be increasingly irrelevant in Australia today.

However, in the context of identity, one's current identity includes both one's idea of who one was in the past and who one aspires to be in the future. As migration involves a transition, it demands a resynthesis of identity.[18] East Indian, Goan and Mangalorean women in Australia appear to have no real interest in and acceptance of their own history. In fact some indicated that they wanted to dissociate themselves from it. Their strategy was to ignore the experience of colonialism and its fallout.

Two major socio-psychological factors affect the migrant.

One is the nature of the relationship between the dominant group and the migrant group, including discrimination. The second is the clash of cultural values. The literature suggests that those experiencing discrimination internalize the derogatory images of themselves projected by the discriminators.[19] East Indians, Goans and Mangaloreans appear to contradict this. They can be categorized into two groups with respect to their reactions.

Some second-generation migrants appear to have internalized these images with respect to the group which they reject as insignificant and irrelevant to their lives. However, they do not appear to suffer from low self-esteem these women assert that ethnicity is not a salient aspect of their self-concept.

Older members of the group and recent migrations from India seem to contradict this assumption, presumably because they have been socialized in a non-western society. However, the experience of being a migrant does cause them to redefine their ethnicity, though the nature of the redefinition depends on their individual circumstances. A patterns does seem to exist: in the years soon after migration, most women exhibit some degree of reactive ethnicity, that is, a heightened awareness of their origins and previous national history.[20] This may persist, but it appears that between the fifth and twentieth year after migration, it is reshaped into a new ethnic coherence, that is a redefinition of ethnic identity incorporating elements of the new culture. It implies new self conceptions. It entails a realization that this emergent identity is a subclass among South Asian-Australian identities and will be subject to change. Many settled migrants are at this stage.

Notes

1. The term Indian is used top designate the ethnic identity of a group of people whose ancestral, cultural and linguistic roots are planted in or traced back to the pre-colonial South Asian subcontinent. See Purusottama Bilimoria, *Hinduism in Australia: Mandala for the Gods*, Melbourne, Spectrum Publications, 1988, p. 41.
2. Ian Castles, 'Religion', *Multicultural Australia*, ABS, cat. no. 2505.o, 1991, p. 44.

3. Gazetter of the Bombay Presidency, Thane, as quoted in Olga valladares, 'The East Indians', in *International Seminar on Indo-Portuguese History Souvenir*, 29 September 1978.
4. Olga Valladares, *Bombay and Goa*, Bombay, Allied Publishers, 1987, pp. 12; 18-21; Gloria Jean Moore, *The Anglo-Indian Vision*, Melbourne, A.E. Press, 1986, p. 21.
5. Jean Luc Camiller, *An Indo-Portuguese Territory on the Pepper Route: Goa, Cabiers de sociologie economique et culturelle ethnopsychologie*, 10 December 1988, pp. 13-28.
6. Valladares, p. 41.
7. Report by Commissioner J. Stokes to the Government of Madras as quoted in John Monteiro, 'Focus of Mangalorean Christians', *in The Mangalorean Golden Jubilee souvenir* 1933-83, Bombay, 1831, pp. 13-17.
8. Lariance Fonseca, 'Hustling Pool', in Jocelyn Scutt (ed.) *Breaking through Women, Work and Careers*, Melbourne, Artemis Publishing, 1992, p. 150.
9. See Glynis M. Breakwell (ed.), *Threatened Identities*, Chichester, John Wiley and Sons, pp. 3-28.
10. Harold Isaacs, 'Basis Group Identity: The Idols of the Tribe', in Narthan Glazer and Daniel P. Moynihan (eds), *Ethnicity-Theory and Experience*, Harvard University Press, 1975, pp. 29-36.
11. *Ibid.*, pp. 3-28.
12. *Ibid.*
13. *Ibid.*
14. Fatima da Silva Gracias, 'Women in Indo-Portuguese Literature-The many faces of *Sundorem*', 1994, paper presented at the Indo-Portuguese Seminar, Goa.
15. See Ranajit Guha, 'The Authority of Vernacular Pasts', *Meanjin*, 51.2 (1992), pp. 299-302; Percival Spear, *India, Pakistan and the West*, Oxford University Press, 1949; Benedict Anderson, *Imagined Communities: Reflections of the Spread of Nationalism*, Verso, 1983, pp. 80-104.
16. See Sudhir Kakar, *The Inner World: A Psychoanalytic Study of Childhood and Society in India*, Oxford, 1978, pp. 15-51.
17. Alan Roland, 'Identity, Contextualization and Individuation', *Comparative Civilization Review*, 8 (1992), pp. 59-69.
18. Peter Weinreich, 'Emerging from Threatened Identities: Ethnicity and Gender and Redefinitions of Ethnic Identity', in Glynis M. Breakwell (ed.), *Threatened Identities*, New York, John Wiley and Sons, 1983, p. 151.
19. See note 3.
20. See note 18.

Section IV
Self Representation and Identity Politics

Gender, Identity and the Politics of Subjectivity

Renuka Sharma

Only later I grew to look for the blade-edge difference between hurt, pain, grief, sorrow, loss, even the presence of absence...The melody of memory is now cacaphonic and the present is soldered to a past that must remain silent.' Vayu Naidu in 'Cultures of Silence.' in *Flaming Spirit.* Stories from the Asian Women's Writers' Collective. ed. Rukshana Ahmad and Rhila Gupta. Virago. 1994.

"In the figure of the witness of a postcolonial modernity we have another wisdom: it comes from those who have seen the nightmare of racism and oppression in the banal daylight of the everyday. They represent an idea of action and agency more complex than either the nihilism of despair or the Utopia of progress. They speak of the reality of survival and negotiation that constitutes the moment of resistance, its sorrow and salvation, but is rarely spoken in the heroisms or the horrors of history."

Homi. K. Bhabha. *in the location of culture.* Routledge. London. 1994.

The definition of individual identity is difficult within most narrative discourses. Within analytic western philosophy, self is broadly defined as a collection of logical premises or aligned to the notion of a transcendent *self or soul in Cartesian metaphysics. The Kantian self* remains an apriori and immune from the shaping of history and culture. Western psychology, based on western metaphysics has not shied away from formulating the notion of an essentialist self which can be understood and classified regardless of gender, class or culture concepts except for Hume. The focus of psychiatry has been the definition and treatment of psychopathology and as such concerned with quantitative descriptions and measurements with the notion of norms being overly prevalent. Psychoanalysis while not overtly essentialist has reduced the concepts of gender and subjectivity to a number of phrases such as lack, phenomenon of difference be it in the form of gender, class or culture is neatly labelled as the 'other,' beyond detailed phenomenological stock in trade descriptions of mainstream discourse.

A Foucouldean analysis, situating gender within the sociohistorical time frame, is one that may be frustrating; in that it removes the domain of the intrasubjective from narrow confines without substituting in its place a knowable object for study. It seems that the construction of knowable subject has to be individually constituted, given socio-historical individual variations and closures. Against the frustration of incommesurability and breaks in dialogue the creation of common spaces can be difficult not just between individuals but also between genres e.g. common spaces between first, second or third world feminists on the issues of authenticity, legitimacy and speaking positions that denote a presumed original political correct identity. Perhaps as Germaine Greer points out the,

"the very paradigm of first, second, and third worlds, of developed and undeveloped countries, is based on unquestioning arrogance".[1]

The politics of identity is well discussed in feminist literature utilizing often Foucault's theory of identity as contextual, constituted by the epistemic frameworks in which the individual is shaped and therefore open ended rather than being one that is essentialist. Thus difference, while it can be viewed with suspicion and fear of the unknowable 'other' within essentialist frameworks, as McNay points out it can also it can also be the basis of a healthy respect for difference both at an individual and political level. In the Foucouldian critique of essentialism, prioritizing the definition of self and identity can lead to a political exclusion, or worse of those that differs resulting in hierarchical power structures of oppression and colonialization. It could be argued that identity is preferentially situated in an open-ended space linked in concept to the fight against definition by institutions and governments as agents of colonialization and oppression. However, the Foucouldean self concept maintains in structure a coherence of identity and possibilities for action over time unlike the schizophrenia of the post-modern self posited by the breakdown of language, such that there is no sense of a continuing coherent self and no ego-centeredness for the initiation of action. Nihilism replaces the possibilities for meaning and agency. Nihilism replaces the possibilities for meaning and agency. This notion of self is explored for instance in the works of Baudrillard, Lyotard, Gilles and Gutteri.[2]

The notion of the isolated individual in the modernist theories of Marx, Hegel and Freud is however different from the nonessentialist notion of the constructed self aesthetic in Foucault. Foucault rejects the idea of a presocial nature, self is seen as constructed through the interpersonal realm of engagement. Self as active and other as passive remain dichotomised as distinct to Habermas's notion of intersubjectivity where the other is active and central to the construction of identity and communication. Thus Foucault's exclusive subjectivism can raise difficulties towards a greater self definition and engagement with the 'other'. Interesting parallels can be drawn to the work of Harry Stack Sullivan, founder of the Interpersonal school of psychoanalysis. Sullivan postulated a need for interpersonal relations as the prerequisite for the structuring of experience. His formulation of a 'tenderness theorem, a given intentionality towards the Mother/Other is complex, however postulates a socially constructed self.

Wittgenstein's emphasis appears to be on the instrumental and irreducibly social character of language i.e. we speak in order to do things, as in the case of the child learning his/her mother tongue, in order to instrumentalise and act. The emphasis is on the role the cultural context has on the development of language and knowledge acquisition. Identity is an expression of social contexts and patterns as well as an act of speaking from a presocial position. The paradox culture. Language is thus always contextual, and enclosed in this is the notion of the social basis of the construction of 'language games.' The bedrock of intentionality towards the other as the basis of identity for self.[3]

In subverting traditional Freudian frameworks of biological intentionality, drives and apriori motivational structures the hegemonic notions of self are open to further analysis. It is this project of questioning the solidity of psychoanalytic semantics towards the construction of self that points to a better understanding of self in the context of the historical Other. The vacuum of structuralism may possibly be contextualised as a democratic layering by the political 'Other'. The Foucaldian wariness of hierarchical structures may be 'Resisted' with a history of the political other.

This radical departure from traditional notions of self and society was what struck me most at the NGO/UN Women's conference in Beijing. At a workshop on Women and Mental Health at Hairou and subsequently at the mental health caucus at the UN conference at Beijing the discussion on these themes in simple ways for me led to these preliminary reflections on the growth in interest in mental health and identity as women recount the experience of loss grief, losing individuals from the vicissitudes of fascist regimes that possible new directions for the definitions of democracy will arise. At heart the simple exchange of experiences by women tear apart perceived notions of power and domination. In the simple recounting sharing of experiences of grief that new levels of analysis emerges. The Other revolution of feminism as it is joined by clear voices from the third- 'other' world women in challenging the hegemony of western norms of selfhood. The candlelight meeting by the 'Women in Black' drew crowds of thousands and spoke eloquently and symbolically of notions of sharing.

> "It struck me that, at the root of tooth's twitching nerve, the choice of an immigrant's distinction is often predetermined by he currency of language...To listen to the models of Foucault's understanding of power while studying the

> structure of prisons and monastic orders...The speaker concluded with `de-individualization,' in the case of the latter, `is the renounced power that gives power'."
>
> Vayu Naidu in 'Cultures of Silence.' in 'Flaming Spirit.' Stories from the Asian Women's Writers' Collective.
>
> ed. Rukshana Ahmad and Rhila Gupta. Virago. 1994.

Western feminist notions of difference, while creating space for gender differences did not often go far enough to include differences created by culture and class. The espousal of a psychoanalytic feminist self is equally problematic. In the postulation of a deeply gendered male or female self formulated in childhood and constant in certain biologically essential ways thereafter, across cultures, proves closed to the intersubjective impact of class, cultural communication systems and worse still to the sociohistorical differences across cultures. The feminist articulation of the politics of identity rejects the humanist construction of subjectivity yet stayed tethered to white middle class notions of selfhood and achievements. The language of enlightenment values of humanism was laden with sexist and racist tones. Charity carried with it notions of condescendence and hierarchy. Lauraine Code suggests a praxis of subjectivity typified by,

> "ambivalence and ambiguity....open places for developing interpretations that at once build on and depart from textual starting points...Postessential subjectivity refuses the coherence of humanistic labelling to affirm a multiple subjectivity liberated from the constraints of the old dogmas and political processes they inform."[4]

This paper was written initially, for the 'Woman in Asia' conference, in Melbourne in 1993 and has been subsequently expanded as ideas have developed and emerged from it. It was for me a very difficult paper to write as at that time the constraints of working with a psychoanalytic language within the Asian diaspora community as a therapist did not always sit well with my life as an activist or with my interests in philosophy or women's studies. During a year in which I founded the South Asian Women's Studies and Support Group (SAWSSG), teamed up with the International Feminist Bookfair Committee to plan the 4th International Conference held in 1994 as well as subsequently travel to Beijing for the Women's/UN Conference and launch the formation of the journal *Gender, Culture and Society* a considerable amount of attention by myself and others was devoted to the notions of identity being thrown up by he accelerated preparations for the Beijing conferences and the phenomenon of this 'other' revolution. Now after beijing, as I sit to edit and revive this article, it is to revisit a formative space that feels outworn by subsequent activities and yet the seeds of inspiration for those activities are retrospectively visible.

The endeavour of finding a language that allows growth in a space which is yet a potential space, a liminal space is reminiscent of the work of playing with children. Winnicot in 'Playing with Reality' explores the development of language between mother and child. Perhaps it is churlish to stick with the provisions of space that the object relations theorists, in particular, that the British Independent School enlarge upon. Yet in speaking as a Foucouldean structuralist would, the sweet krasa of a child's emergent speech is lost in epistemes of understanding. Macaulays' comment of the 'babblings of an infant race' in relation to his incomprehension of finding himself a colonialist in British India is perhaps the attempt to understand and colonise the 'other' with meaning derived from a particular point of reference. Postcolonial and post-modern studies have provided provisional maps of some spaces, yet it seems that the use of psychoanalytic language is yet open to some contextualization within its own history and the history of how it has framed others. Postmodern psychoanalysis or the contemporary trends within psychoanalysis has often provided a cultural language of possible understandings. The notions of 'identification with the aggressor' and 'internalised orientalism' are examples of some psychoanalytic notions of the impact of colonialisation on subjective spaces. Yet without critique of the 'language game' of psychoanalysis, self and other remain dichotomised and accepted as knowable only from within psychoanalytic frameworks. The uncertain spaces thus remain occluded. This paper then for me must remain a potential paper, a no-paper, an unthought of how is it possible to live, think and act in the present times within the present language structures of globalization, fundamentalism and oppression of the other within our midst. A post-modern cultural identity, is yet not discussed and yet the reality for the vast and growing numbers of global immigrants. The pastiche of culture, heritage and the past neatly packed in suitcases may be oppressive or liberating of new thought forms and is certainly formative of the individual cultures that each carries.

Mental health presumes a personal coherence and identity. Yet what defines mental and health? The structures of definition are as much culture-bound as any other. In asserting the need for health in our lives, bell hooks speaks clearly, that the purview for reflections on subjectivity should now no longer be class, race, culture, age or the privilege of any particular discursive field :

> "this is also related to what I was talking about earlier, about holocaust experience, about ongoing genocide, because a lot of my critical thinking right now is focused on black experience of oppression and how it damages and wounds us. And I am particularly concerned with what we do to heal ourselves, to recover a sense of wholeness. Here in the US self recovery is a term that is used most often in therapy related to substance abuse, addiction. That's not where I encountered the term; it came into my thinking when I was reading the work of the Buddhist monk Thich Nhat Hahn who talks about it in relation to ways people who are oppressed, dominated or otherwise politically victimised recover themselves, the way colonised people work to resist and throw of the coloniser

mentality, for example. Lately I say often that mental health is the important field right now, a central revolutionary frontier for black folk." bell hooks. An Interview With Bell Hooks by Gloria Watkins no, not talking back, just talking to myself., January 1989, in Yarning, race, gender and cultural politics, South End Press, Boston, 1990.

Women and the Framing of Cultural-Historical Subjectivity

The debates around the construction of self broadly speaking, falls in between the division between a biologically essentialist and socio-cultural relativist position. Critiques of relativism maintain that objectification of knowledge about self is rendered meaningless, humanistic and enlightenment notions of caring and connectedness based on individualistic essentialism are downplayed. Whilst in reverse critiques of essentialism call attention to the closures towards the social historical construction of self, be it in the form of language or action that incorporates racism, sexism and other means of oppression inherent in the language of stereotypes. Stereotypes point to accumulated cultural lores about reality that can be exclusive of differences and heterogeneity. The resulting pastiche of knowledge about the Orient for instances serves to make knowable the foreign be that by the use of feminist ideology, philosophy or psychoanalysis. The European gaze on the Orient well explored by said is on the realm of the mysterious other. The land, nation, people and concepts are framed by the powerful language of the conqueror, oppressor, coloniser professing enlightenment values.[5]

This dichotomy reflects very different notions of democracy, nationalisms, subjectivities as well as the actions inherent in these constructs. The question of multinational aid funding to the third world has many implications in the global context of the nineties. While the inherent political humanism may be objectionable, the issue of the dearth of health and other grassroots services cannot be avoided. In discussions at beijing on the issue of funding by the World Bank of women's health services in Mongolia it became apparent that negotiation with this politically incorrect funding source was essential. The total health budget for Mongolia, being $27,000. In order for the yurt based health network to stay viable the provisions of expertise and funding by the World Bank were not to be taken or rejected lightly. In the era of postcold war strategising, the humanism of imperialistic funding needs to be accompanied by continued political as well as a feminist understanding. Of the 3% women employed by the world bank, even the beginning of some analysis from within of power structures while not providing utopian alternatives may lead to more appropriate ways of engagement by the world bank on issues of third world debt. The euphoria of globalization may obscure the sinister implications of multinational investments in world economies. Humanistic charity may reflect a drop in the ocean in terms of the budgetary structures of the multinationals. However, if there is to be analysis of the new superpowers, as well as the structures of the GATT from women's grass roots perspectives then analysis can not be shirked. The implications for selves, nation-states and democracy are profound and at the present time being descripted. To claim economic nationhood in the context of fragile economies, rising religious fundamentalisms is as contentious as claiming a selfhood based on biological premises. The analysis of self it seems cannot be an either/ or but rather open to both forms of analysis. Perhaps this open-ended space, ludicrous as it may seem is the promise of the new democracies or the co existence of multiplicities of meaning for self and other.

The analysis of gender in relation to culture is fraught with epistemological difficulties. Readings of poetry written by 12th and 16th century Indian women convey some of the fiestyness of 'women writing in pre nineteenth century literature. Historically the nineteenth century focus became concerned with the deadly serious business of colonialization, nationalization, the freedom struggle and the emancipation of women from the travails of *sati*, dowry deaths. etc. This at a cursory reading provides a gory description of repression and self immolation among the primitive hoard as against the order of British rule. However the context and the elevation to prominence events devoid of a historiographic analysis belies the cultural fabric of a colonised society easily ridiculed for 'arcane' practices against its women. This dynamic is easily discerned in the frenzy of the freedom fighters efforts at the upliftment of the conditions for women during the nineteenth century. The interface between nationalism and feminism in most colonised societies is complex given the every pervasive presence of the master-slave power relationship thus shaping for posterity the trajectories of development of nationalism and feminisms. The self then broadly speaking arises historically in this mix of tradition and cultural mores; in the context of colonization; the placement of the feminist and nationalist movements; the moment of partition and independence determines notions of citizenship, democracy, the constitution in an overwhelming mix of parts that do and do not add up to an individual person. The confusions and contradictions are perhaps best captured by the poets and novelists.

> "This is an intervention. A message from that space in the margin that is a site of creativity and power, that inclusive space where we recover ourselves, where we move in solidarity to erase the category colonized/colonizer. Marginality as site of resistance. Enter that space. Let us meet there. Enter that space. We greet you as liberators".
> bell hooks. Ibid.

"Skin stretched tightly over cheekbones or falling in folds, it is important to note what seeps through the pores. It is the training of the mind behind the eye, like instinctively knowing the meaning between desire, lust, love and joy, that teaches you technique".

Vayu Naidu in 'Cultures of Silence.' in 'Flaming Spirit'. Stories from the Asian Women's Writers' Collective. ed. Rukshana Ahmad and Rhila Gupta. Virago. 1994.

Within psychologisms of various sorts the contention that personality, self and identity are largely socially and culturally created is still an anomaly especially in relation to 'Asian identities. Truth as an absolute essential is still very much part of the gist of psychology. However the proponents of cultural relativism and the interpersonalists who do not reduce human nature to biological givens are slow to explore the differences constructed by culture. At a time when the paradigms of knowledge construction are under assault from the deconstructionists, post -modern epistemologists, feminist theologians and feminist epistemologists arcane notions of psychologians and feminist epistemologists arcane notions of psychological identity formation grounded on the tenants of Newtonian principles of psychology are still touted a kind of psychological imperialism in which the native savage is endowed with primitive emotions or inappropriate kinds of emotional structures or worse still the idealisation of the erotic or social analysis. Personality constructs within mainstream psychology have been by and large white middle class male constructions. Freud, Jung, Ericksen paid little attention to the notion of gener in orthodox treatments. The notions of lack, castration and desire seemed to sum up the deficiencies. The feminist discourse has pointed to some of the closures from the vision of mainstream discourse. However cultural psychological critiques have been slow to emerge.

In addressing some of the flaws in the psychological constructions on 'indianess' I have had to examine the difficulties towards this enterprise. The variety of individual formative influences, the difficulties of rereading historical texts, the influence of the vedic period, the ferment of writing in the eighteenth century and the profound implications of anglicization and colonialization in the nineteenth century. Nationalism, the freedom movement and the impact of freedom fighters such as Gandhi in the shaping of public culture and attitudes to women played a role in the creation of expectations of the 'ideal woman.' The emergence of the womens' movement shaped by the forces of this century have implications for the contextualization of partition and communal violence in one of the largest democracies of the world. The attitudes of women towards themselves and their role in culture and society is shaped by these forces.

The subaltern enterprise has attempted to create a space in which new readings of history may emerge. In surveying the psychological fields in relation to India, the mammoth works of Sudhir Kakir come to one's gaze. In explicating the inner world of the Hindu child he appears blissfully unaware of the maelstrom of the century as it shaped a character such as Gandhi. Rather we see a reduction to anal retentiveness, maternal symbiosis and other personal psychopathology of his whole political enterprise, non violence movement and freedom struggle. Gandhi's attitudes rather than reduce these to psychoanalytic universals of repression and displacement better analysis may be achieved by examination of the realm of the political, social and historical realities of his time which would have formed his internal symbol systems. I shall attempt to locate some of the important historical markers that form the historical collective within which individual identity is formed. The construction of private spaces is always in contrast to other spaces. Mark C. Taylor in writing on the subject of altarity examines the questions posed by

> "difference and otherness....the issue of difference is undeniably political .....Are those who are different to be converted, integrated, dominated, excluded or repressed? the problem of the other, however is not only political; it is also an issue of considerable artistic, philosophical, psychological, and theological importance."[6]

The concerns of postmodernism appears at base level to be concerned with these issues. If indeed humanism with its attendant search for a universal psyche or notion of self, is to be equated with modernism then the language of modernism presumes a speaking self speaking in the language of modernist presumes a speaking self speaking in the language of modernist philosophy. To presume to speak of a cultural self, then must by a tautology be framed within the language of modernism with its notion of self framed by the discourse by western philosophy and psychology? Would it be better not to attempt a definition of a cultural self as the very language of definition buys in to irreconcilable idioms? is Spivak denying a knowledge or a language in her work or simply,

> "vigilant against simple notions of identity which neatly overlap with language or location....determinist or positivist definition of identity.....Indianess is not a thing that exists ...not moved by arguments for homogenisation on both sides". Thus in an attempted extrapolation of her work a new voice constantly vigilant of "her position as questioning subject aware of the pitfall of narrativisation and institutionalisation of the subject position".[7]

The preoccupation of psychology with differences and development as they present in relation to individuality, gender and socio-cultural differences can be approached from differing theoretical perspectives a growing concern with the epistemological flaws inherent in a number of frameworks leads top a certain staidness in the number of frameworks leads to a certain staidness in the way in which difference and development are characterised. Feminists have began the task of examining the construction of female subjectivity within existing theoretical frameworks such as psychoanalysis and philosophy (4). However the place of culture in the creation of difference often lays behind for a complex range of reasons.[8]

In attempting to understand gender in the context of a socio-historical framing it is important to examine the representation of women of colour in mainstream literature, the arts and other forms of representation. The power differential to many points of reference such as maleness, class, ethnicity reveal oppressive stereotypes. The dangers of internalization are increasingly discussed in 'marginal' literature by the subject speaking self. The representation of oriental women in western literature is explored by said.[9] Flaubert's encounter with the Egyptian courtesan Kuchuk Hanem formed a prototype of western perception of the oriental exotic;

> "never spoke of herself, never represented her emotions, presence, or history. He spoke for and represented her. He was foreign, comparatively wealthy male, and these were historical facts of domination that not only allowed him to possess ....but to speak for her and tell his readers in what way she was `typically Oriental.

Kuchuk was a famous dancing girl (ironically, alemah in arabic also means a learned women.) The imposition of a descriptive language of the west's structured learning, quantifies in to a hard copy of legitimacy, the image of the mystery of the other in the gaze of the west. Thus what is represented is in the realm of the imaginary rather than the real. In relation to Wittgenstein's 'language games', the social and cultural mores of a culture have prescribed the nature of the 'Other'. This text is then prescriptive of and for the quantification of concepts of culture, womenness and other. In this regards dominion is by the process of inscription on the silent other with the language of tradition and modernity. Thus the power of the dominant culture with its means of inscription produces texts which cannot be apolitical with hierarchical assigning positions of subordination and powerlessness. To enter in to the genre means participation in the language of subordination, sexism, racism of which critiques such as said, spivak, Foucault, Derrida are critical of.[10]

Foucault's analysis of culture is placed in the context of a number of disciplines linked to power under the guise of knowledge. This placement of power within the socio-political history of knowledge has enormous implications for the understanding of how marginality and identity are framed be it in the form of racism, sexism of history is careful to point out the power inequities in a framing of the often the closures are conscious and unconscious. The subjectivity of the historian is as much part of the process as the events themselves. (ii) on review of the subaltern literature this then becomes problematic. The subaltern on writing the method of subaltern studies becomes a tool of inscription as powerful as that inscripted under British rule unless like Foucault theirs is a move away from speaking for the oppressed subject towards barthes a move towards autobiography.

Subalternisam then places itself as an academic hegemony where the means of legitimating its activity is to speak to the underclass and interpret its anger to the receding elite, thus stepping in to the power vacuum of history and returning simply as anothers' text. Thus it is not the subjectivity and identity of the subaltern observer or the observation position being mapped but the oppositional identity of the subaltern to the powers of oppression. In times of historical revisionism areas such as subaltern studies and ethnoarcheology, (an interaction between the models of anthropology and archaeology) are new disciplines which challenge previous levels of semiotic understandings. The discipline of history is increasingly preoccupied with the process of interpretation utilizing multidisciplinary tools for the analysis of previously thought factual snapshots of historical periods of time.[12] The difficulties are compounded by the framing of truths from one culture to the language and concepts of another. In this liminal space no end point can be visualised. No final assessment is yet possible.

The Nineteenth Century Framing Of an Ego Ideal For Indian Women

Gandhi in fighting against the ills of Hinduism in the form of child marriage, discrimination of widows and the social status of women attempted to put in place a new ideal of woman that would help counteract imperial condescension of bramanicalism and the ruling British. The womens' struggle was closely connected with the political freedom struggle. The active participation of women in the freedom movement has stayed embedded in the memory of the middle classes. From the position of being the objects of social and religious reform to being active participants in the political and social sphere during the nineteenth and twentieth century. Maria Mias describes these changes as happening under the banners of education, legislation and politics.[13]

One of the first reformers was Raja Ram Mohan Roy who in 1828 founded the Hindu reform movement, 'Brahma Samaj', based on monothestistic principles and fought against the social evils of purdha, sati etc., along with other Hindu revival movements like the Arya Samaj, the Ramakrishan Mission, and the Theosophical society. Others more radical were fighting without debatable the role of english education in the social reform movement. The likes of Vidyasagar, Jyotiba Phooley, Lokhitavadi Gopal, Hari Deshmuk who attacked the links between high caste brahmanism, patriarchialism and the use of religious mythology to support the submissive Sita like position of women.

Mias lists some of the important legislative measures to have direct impact on the status of woman. In 1795 and 1802 female infanticide was prohibited in Bengal and in 1829 the Prohibition of sati was passed. This was achieved against the strengths of hindu orthodoxy and the problematic position of non interference by the British in issues deeded religious. In 1856 The Hindu Remarriage Act abolishing the celibacy of widows along with the introduction of laws on polygamy restricting polandric practices thought to be besmirching of national honour was also achieved. This was later also the case with the Indian Divorce Act of 1869 providing for dissolution of polygamic practices. The Hindu succession act (1865) and the special marriage act (1872) and various Nayar acts of the twentieth century were in a similar vein.

In 1860 the practice of child marriages was changed with the Indian Penal Code declaring cohabitation with a minor under the age of ten illegal. This was followed by the subsequent Age of Consent Act in 1891. In 1904 a further modification of child marriage legislature was in the form of the Early Marriage Prevention Act which laid down the minimum age of marriage at twelve. In 1929 the Child Marriage Restraint Act raised this to 14 for girls and 18 for men. In the forties and fifties and finally 1955 the Hindu Marriage Act and Hindu Succession Act sanctioned the rights to divorce and women's right to inheritance. Thus lifting at the level of legislature the issue of human rights for women and the subsequent creation of opportunities for legal redress.

However, conversely, at the level of the mass unconscious propaganda by the nationalist movements led to the identification of state with mother. The merger of feelings for woman, goddess, mother and state was a potent anti-colonial brew leading to a fervor for the honor of Mother India wronged, despoiled by colonial rule. This mobilization of a feeling of resistance over the body corpus of woman wronged became merged and flowed in to that Of the body of a state wronged. Thus the corporeality of state and woman became merged and formed an essential element of the 'language game' of the freedom movement lead by men leaders of the freedom movements. An essential corollary of this was the prescription of positions for the women within this movement. Thus also allowing for a sanctioned mobilization of women in their role in the freedom movement and in to the public sphere of resistance. Figures such as Pundita Ramabai remain resistance. figures such as Pundita Ramabai remain enigmatic and problematic because of their multiply converted speaking positions which seems to elude this definition of woman in and by the freedom movement.

The modernist women's movement in India was thus berthed in this proscriptive Machiavellian manner, shaped by the emerging ideal of womanhood and the purview of its aspirations shaped by the leaders of the emerging resistance movements funnelled in to the great Gandhian revolution and experiment with nonviolent reform at a national level. For this to occur guidelines for the conduct of one's individual life were carefully articulated. Thus in mobilising the energies of women both symbolically and literally the position of subversion was however carefully defined as to not besmirch the honour of woman-state at personal or national level in the eyes of the oppressor. It is no wonder that the ideal image was based on Western Victorian lines with an added component of moral superiority in the form of an aesthetic ago ideal derived from traditional Indian mythological models of purity. The polygamous Draupadi cults having been previously curbed by legislature aimed at improving the image of woman and also as distinct to the perception of the western woman as being amoral. This imago of ideal woman aspired to western education. western virtues of British standards and yet was more auspicious and pure so not to birsmirch nationhood or its masculine defenders. Thus the female position was sharply defined and constrained as virtue of a particular kind and identified with sanctioned traditional models of purity. The modern women's movement was from the beginning defined in tertiary opposition to men, the British and 'western women' which may account for the present women's movement having difficulties in facing the other of nationalism and finding correspondences to western feminism. At the present time there are echoes of this past wherein the fundamentalist reform movements again promulgate literary ideals to define masculinity (Rama like) as saviour of woman in the context of the other of Islam.

In Gandhi's appreciation of women's quality to suffer quietly he saw qualities that supplemented his principle of 'ahimsa' which was a central tenant of his non-violent freedom movement. Thus the principles of compassion and empathy he felt, were exemplified by women who he felt, were at a higher development than men, "If non-violence is the law of our being, the future is with women."[14] He viewed the conjunction of marriage as sacred and within which the purposes of spiritual maturity were attained together with a humanitarian orientation of service, on which basis the considerations of family and social order were constructed. Love, mutual attraction and sex were to be sublimated to the ideals of spiritual maturity and social service. Thus the Hindu family in this construction can be seen as a social unit with an outward looking perspective. His own experiments with sex, abstinence (bramacharya) and love are as well documented as Freud's that other proponent of libido theory. Ram and Sita are seem as the archtype of love and marriage wherein the relationship is placed within the context of a spiritual crucible. Mias explains the relative downplaying of woman as mother in Gandhi as distinct from the philosophies of Aurobindo and Vivekananda, based on regional differences, such as, Gujarat being more influenced by Jainism rather than Devi worship in Bengal. The puritan Victorian ideal of the ruling British may have been a further influence towards the choice of Sita above that of a figure like the polyandric Draupadi.

Historically the nineteenth century plays a decisive role in shaping the modernist womens movement. Together with the nationalist movement a Hindu-Aryan identity was forged. The collusion between nationalism and c`lonialism over a period of a hundred and fifty years left a deep imprint in the consciousness of the collective and individual psyche.[15] Gender deconstructions in the particular context can only be retrospective with all the 'pitfalls of narrativisation.'

More recently with the publication of a compilation of writings by Indian women from 600 BC to present times, a more through appreciation of the overall socio, economic, psycho-political consciousness of the placing of Indian women within the Indian tradition can be traced. The construction of gendered identity and how this is internalised through symbolic and linguistic processes can only be understood given a premodern tradition.[16] The labelling of premodern and modern spaces presupposes a discontinuity and yet this is not so. The nongendered postmodern self is itself a construct of western epistemes. The application of this epistemic structure to the work of women writing in 600 BC seems a contentious issues. In the words of Atukuri Molla a 16th writer and translator of the Ramayana in Telugu there seems to be a certain holism that defies fragmentation and holds immediate meaning in its bold style.

> 'I am no scholar Distinguishing the loan words from the native stock. I know no rules of combination no large vocabulary. I am no expert in composition and allocution, semantics and style. Nor do I know phonetics, case relations, roots of verbs and figures of speech, meter and prosody, either. Untrained though, in composing poems and epics in mastering lexicons and rules I do write poems.'

Emergent themes of oppression and violence both covert and overt are endemic as are notions of intimacy, *sorg* and capacity for inter relatedness in this prenineteenth century literature. Thus the notion of the 'beaten down third world women' fighting within the confines of definition by modernity belies the strength of a different notion of subjectivity. This in itself could be a form of psychological imperialism whereby the impact of culture on social psychological developments are underplayed or marginalised.

Uma Chakravarti explores with precision the development of the notion of the Aryan superwoman based on braminical, kshatriya values. Through the nineteenth century this was bolstered by the Orientalists, Anglicists and Evangelists e.g. Max Muller works on the babblings of Indians akin to infants gives no place for the contextualization of women in this 'infant' race. This kind of textualization is continued today in some of the psychoanalytic interpretations of mythology perpetrated in the west by western feminists borrowings from Indian mythology to signify immanent powerful feminine spirituality. This coupled with a particular reading of myths reinforces the notion of women as superspiritual, suffering, learned in fairly abstract ways i.e. divine women. By means of idealization the subject is rendered speechless. In fact writings of women such as Ramabai at the same time speak of a pragmatic concern with the tribulations of purdah, child brides and forewarn of the inroads of nationalism on a separatist feminist movement.

Thus this early (and present) forms of orientalism merged well with the writings of some of the cultural nationalists such as Dyananda, R.C. Dutt, Bankim Chandra Chatterji putting firmly in place the alignment of feminist, nationalist and religious concerns sanctioned by the strictures of a colonial era bent on constructing and perverting the course of history to reflect on the glorious past and present of British rule. With the rise of literacy for the middle classes schooling into an anglised reading of tradition of initiation into European sensibility further heightened the notion of the rarefied ideal superwoman.

The paternal colonial presence gave rise to a peculiar psych-cultural presence. Indian intellectuals in identifying with the oppressor felt at pains to prove their humanism in culturally sanctioned ways. Thus in reacting against the oppressor the language of oppression was internalised and gave rise to the aesthetic ideals of the time. Gandhi's famous parody on 'brown boys,' perhaps reflects this internalization of orientalism at both gross and subtle levels. In his struggles with his sexuality and indeed masculinity the internalised feminine ego ideal and feminine aesthetic was as much shaped by his socio historical placement in a particular time period. Kakar's Ericksonian reading of Gandhiji's'anal retentiveness and maternal symbiosis' may be as much open to critique and placement within a Foucouldean analysis of power structures and strictures. The framing of sexuality is as much subject to epistemic shaping as is the problematization of pleasures in the context of colonial rule. The use of seemingly a historical psychoanalytic strategies is a problematic within Kakar's works on Indian identity. Contemporary psychoanalysis seems as concerned with historical realities, as for instance postmodernism.

Socio-political studies examining the status of women in India have exposed the problems associated with dowry murders, custodial deaths, infanticide or infanticide by selective sex preferences and renewal of interest in *sati* practices.[17] An examination of the move by middle class women from a definition by caste to that based on class through the portals of education into those professional areas deemed respectable by notions of gender appropriateness. This new freedom is defined by patriarchal notions of class. Resistance to this has been in the form of a growing interest in feminist studies. The pitfalls of drawing from cultural mythology to bolster images of strength are that these are only too readily aligned by those espoused by the nationalist movement. Thus it seems that without awareness of a proper historiography the process of change remains embedded in the confusion between state, nationalism, religion and idealism. Class and economic analysis, while essential remain essentialist in their outlook.

Notions of sexism and racism remain embedded in the very language of modernism. Similar accounts are also seen in literature on class, culture and politics in the third world.[18]

In describing the sacred and religious shaping of feminine subjectivity McKibber gives voice to the need for a balance between an understanding of women's religious experience as well the sociopolitical and economic realities.[19] The reading of 'prakriti' as multifold essences of being and 'purusha' the masculine as the impersonal structure of consciousness constitutes the gendered identity framework of the pantheon of gods and archtypes in many readings. In turn these transpersonal selves are seen as the signatures for understanding the bisexuality/androgenous nature of human identity. Gendered human spirituality plays out some sort of polarity. The divine play as template for the personal endeavour and struggles on the one hand of a model of submission, purity, chastity and domesticity and on the other of a wild woman of unbridled passion, strength and knowledge seems to typify the readings of Indian iconography into the dichotomy between stereotypes of renunciation and exuberance, virginality and whoredom. Again a reading of the Gandhian superwoman, Max Mullers reading of dangerous sexuality and Flaherty's idealization of Jungian archtypes within the Indian pantheon seems a limited dichotomization of a multitude of positions and indeed realities.[20]

Perhaps historicity can not so easily be separated from personal symbol systems and experiences. It may be tendentious to suggest that the notion of the divine and numinisity are open to cultural, historical analysis. The lure of the rich symbolism of the Indian goddesses holds potent meanings for analysis and exploration but I am not sure whether a Jungian or Freudian/Ericksonian libido theory are necessarily the only tools of analysis. Perhaps the personal numinous experiences of womens' spirituality needs to come under the gaze of a sociopolitical and economic analysis. The construction of the notion of the notion of the divine as explored by McKibben highlights many of the difficulties. These difficulties in understanding become further accentuated by the regional differences and heterogeneity, such as in the considerably enlightened position of women in the Virasaivism sect; the polyandrous Nayars and Draupadi sects of southern India and the reasonably enlightened approach to education within Kerala.

Postscript

Traditionally, ethnographic constructions of personality often drew a personality theorities to formulate field observations. White and Kirpatrick[21] in their analysis point out the limitations of this approach whereby cultural data are analysed as macro-personality structures. Kakars work in relation to India specifically Gandhi reflects his particular Ericksonian understandings as for instance, of the preoedipal prolongation of the sons relationship to the mother in the development of subjectivity.[22] Such an oversimplification of the links between tradition, culture, complexity of the processes of person formation or to allow sufficient ethnographic analysis of the processes of inference, condensation, metaphor, symbolic interactionism and cross cultural interpersonal interactions, just some of the elliptical psychological processes of personhood formation and interpretation. Kakir and O'Flaherty nee Doniger in using strictly Freudian on Ericksonian models of interpretation of culture place themselves in the position of knowing observes from frameworks that have become themselves more critical of their own practices such as the interpersonal, object-relations and post Freudian frameworks.

The relationship between culture, self and affect are necessarily complex. The definition of personhood and interpersonal variation involves the understanding of early childhood developments, the handling of emotional conflict as well as the abstract principles structuring a common world view between mother/caretaker of the human infant in relation, to social culture and historical shaping of epistemes within and without that culture. Mother as the primary repository and transmitter of language and culture is as much shaped by culture. Mother as the first 'other' in the gaze of the newborn self is the agent of empathic, intersubjective, transgenerational transmission of the Mothercultrue or Mothertongue, in what is a complex, time related phenomenon, yet one that seems open to a socio-historical analysis along Foucouldean lines rather that reduction to essentialism of sorts. White and Krkpatrick take ethnopsychologies to be, "cultural understandings of personal identity, action and experience," based on a principal of self/other awareness as a human universal or Kantian category. Interpersonal relating is as necessary a corollary of this concept of self awareness and construction. The 'other' as self then opens up the possibility of a historical collective notion of self, a democratic self, accessible to historical-social analysis. A Husserlian intentionality towards the 'other' on the horizon of perception, history and culture results in an internal representation of this complex, multiple other. Conversely in a structuralist framework if personal identity is seen to be shaped by culture formulations of personhood, action and transgressions a dynamic interplay between a notion of self and culture emerges. Neither of which can be analysed in isolation and have wide-reaching implications for new notions of self and society.

Stern[23] in the 'Interpersonal World of the Human Infant', revolutionized the psychological perception of this process. The human infant as an actively engaging intentional subject orientated quite sensitively towards the external world, the mother or caretaker as mediator of the child's immediate and socio-historical contextualization. Biological epistemes of human nature and truly antiquated within contemporary psychoanalytic paradigms. Naming and labeling may aid towards a superficial classification of normal and psychopathological boundaries but do little in explicating the phenomena of meaning and the understanding of everyday life and range of human emotions. The issues are compounded by the unclear field of signification and semiotics. Assumptions of a common mother-tongue with which to understand human nature, symbolization, psyche and cognitive processes ellipses a vast range of heterogeneous processes.

Notes

1. Germaine Greer. Sex and Destiny. The Politics of Human Fertility. Harper Colophon Books, Sydney 1985.
2. Lois McNay, 'Foucault and Feminism. Power, Gender and the Self.' Polity Press. Cambridge 1992. Also numerous works examining the difficulties in definition of the concept of identity within philosophical, feminist and psychoanalytic practices. i.e. Linda Nicholsen. Feminism/Postmordernism. Routledge. New York London 1990. Mark Kruppnick 'Displacement Derida and After.' Indiana University Press Bloomington 1983. Derek Parfit. Reasons and Persons. Clarendon Press Oxford. 1984. This is an account of the difficulties within western analytic philosophy of the definition of identity. An attempt at unnraveling the framing of psychoanalytic epistemology and the concept of the 'Other' in Renuka Sharma. Understanding the Concept of Empathy and It's Foundations in Psychoanalysis. Edwin Mellon Press. NY. 1993.
3. Sorri. M., Gill. H.G. 'A Post Modern Epistemology. Language and Body.' The Edwin Mellen Press. Lewiston. 1990.
4. Lorraine Code. 'What Can She Know.' Cornell University Press. Ithaca and London. 1991. Also Corinne Suire. Significant Differences-Feminism in Psychology. London and New York. Routledge. 1989.
5. See Said. E. 'Orientalism and World Text and Critiqe' also Laura Donaldson, 'Decolonizing Feminism Race Gender and Empire Building.' Routledge. London. 1993.
6. Taylor. M.C. Alterity. The University of Chicago Press. Chicago and London. 1987.
7. Harasym. S. The Post Colonial Critic. Interviews, Strategies and Dialogues. Gayatri Chakravorty Spivak. Routledge. New York and London. 1990.
8. Kalpana Ram. 'Modernist Anthropology and the Construction of Indian Identity.' Meanjin. Culture Policy and Beyond. Volume 3/1993. Spring.
9. Said. E. Orientalism. Roiutledge and Kegan Paul. London and Henley. 1978.
10. Said. 'The Word, The Text, The Critic.' Harvard University Press. Cambridge Massachusetts 1983.
11. Historical examination of the subaltern enterprise over a decade of its inception, maturing and critique of established historigraphical procedures in Jim Masselos "The Dis/Appearance of Subalterns: A Reading of a Decade of Subaltern Studies. South Asia Volume XV, no 1 (1992), pp105-125. Also Kalpana Ram's critique of the subaltern enterprise and the postmodern rejection of humanism. However, there seems a flaw inherent in this argument, in that, in accepting a humanist language and concern for the oppressed there is an acceptance of implicit notions of gender, race and subjectivity. In rejecting categorically the anthropological, postmodern feminist, "Third World women watching" postmodernist discourses, the position of challenge is seriously hampered by a lack of methodological analysis of power and substituting an anbarchic position of knowledge construction. This proposition of 'incomplete modernism' as a possible paradigm for the third world holds to the language of modernism. See also Ram for

a critique of Spivak and Gunew 'Too Traditional Once Again : Some Post Structuralists on the Aspirations of the Immigrant Third World Subject'. Australian Feminist Studies, 17 (Autumn 1993), pp. 5-28.

12. For discussion of this see editorial inaugural volume Cultural Dynamics. An International Journal for the Study of Processes and Temporality of Culture. Volume 1. 1 1988. E.J. Brill. especially S.N. Balagangadhara. 'Comparative Anthropology and Moral domains. An Essay on Selfless Morality and the Moral Self.' Cultural Dynamics above. Also John McGuire. Quantification and South Asian History : Counting What. South Asia Vol XV no 1 1992 pp. 1-16.
13. Maria Mias. 'Indian Women and Patriarchy. Conflicts and Dilemmas of Students and Working Women.' Concept Publishing., New Delhi. 1980. See detailed discussion of this in Kumkum Sangari and Sudesh Vaid 'Recasting Women. Essays in Colonial History.' Kali for Women 1989. New Delhi. Also addressed by Flavia Agnes. 'Redefining the Agenda of the Womens Movement Within a Secular Framework. In this volume. Notes on domestic violence and need for relief networks-Anannya Bhattacharjee 'The Habit of Ex-Nomination : Nation, Woman and the Indian Migrant Bourgeoisie' Public Culture. Bulletin of The Society for Transactional Cultural Studies. Volume 5, Number 1. Fall 1992.
14. Gandhi quoted by Kakar. S., in Intimate Relations. Exploring Indian Sexuality. University of Chicago Press. Chicago. 1976.
15. Uma Chakravarti. 'Whatever Happened to the Vedic Dasi. Orientalism, Nationalism, and a Script for the Past.' In Sangari and Vaid (ed.). A good account of the formation of historical consciousness over this time period.
16. Latlitha. K., Tharu. S., 'Women Writing in India. 600 B.C. to the Early Twentieth Century.' Tracing Savitri's pedigree, Victorian racism and the image of women in Indo-anglian literature. An account of the construction of Savitri in the mode of Victorian sensibility-a reasonably idealised masculine freedom together with victorian ethos of sexual purity akin to the notion of the divine. The notion of 'divine' in Kristava as unknowable and mysterious has come under increasing scrutiny as having origins in a form of covert Catholicism however drawing on a form of orientalism.

    Also this conflation of imagery is present to some degree in religious writings largely seen as proscriptive in some religious traditions e.g. Great Women of India ed. Swami Madhavananda and Ramesh Chandra Majumdar. Advaita Ashrama Mayavati, Almora, Himalayas.
17. Detailed studies and exposes by a number of writers looking at gender and class biases along Marxist guidelines. Joanna Liddle and Rama Joshi 'Daughters of independence. Gender, caste and class in India.' Kali for Women. 1986. New Delhi; Krishna Raj Maithreyi. 'Womens Studies in India.' Popular Prakshan. Bombay. 1986.
18. Haleh Afshar. 'Women, Development and Survival in the Third World. Longman. London and New York. 1991; Emile Bergman et al Women Culture and Politics in Latin America. University of California Press. Los Angeles 1990.
19. Penelope. McKibben The Personalities of Prakriti-Keys to Feminist Perspective in Religions and Comparative Thought. Essays in Honour

of the late Dr. Ian Kersacodi Watson. Bilimoria. P., Fenner P. Indian Book Centre. New Delhi 1988.

20. Paul. D.M. The Buddhist Feminine Ideal. Queen Srimala and the Tathagatagarbha. American Academy of Religion. Dissertation Series Number 30. Scholars Press 1980. Also see Fredrique Apffel Marglin 'Female Sexuality in The Hindu World' in Immaculate and Powerful. The Fe male in Sacred Image and Social Reality ed Atkinson et al. The Harvard Womens Studies in Religion Series. Beacon Press. 1985. Also analysis of auspiciouness in Veena Das, Structure and Cognition. Aspects of Hindu Caste and Ritual. Delhi Oxford University Press 1982. Leela Mullatti. The Bhakti Movement and the Status of Women. A Case Study of Virasaivism. Abhinnav Publications. 1989. Robin Jefferies. Politics Women and Well Being. How Kerala Became a Model. Macmillan Press Cambridge Commonwealth Series 1992.
21. White and Kirkpatrick. Person, Self and Experience. Exploring Pacific Ethnographies. University of California Press. Los Angeles. 1985.
22. Kakar. S., The Inner World. A Psychoanalytic Study of Childhood and Society in India. Delhi. Oxford University Press. 1978.
23. Stern. D., The Interpersonal World of the Infant. A View from Psychoychoanalysis and Developmental Psychology. Basic Books. New York. 1985. Numerous developmentalists are now engaged in a analysis of the preoedipal years of the culture specific differences that contribute to the process of identity formation. See the works of Emde. R., Takeo Doi. Roland. R. The findings throw some light on epitemological difficulties within narrow classical psychoanalytic constructions on personality. The works of Kardinar on the narcisstic aspects of the Black American psyche-See account of this in, Sarah Lawrence Lightfoot. Balm in Gilead Biography. Journey of a Healer. This is a Biography of the first Black woman psychoanalyst and psychiatrist in Harlem who effectively concealed her religious experiences during her analysis for fear of misconception within the psychoanalytic frameworks. Her sociopolitical status within the analytic discourse of the time included her disagreement of Kardiner's (an establishment figure) ahistorical constructions about psyche and culture.

Gender and Difference : Towards A Re-Articulation

Seemanthini Niranjana

Chancing upon an observation made by Simone de Beauvoir (1972:38) several years ago-that "...the body is a situation..." is like rediscovering a forgotten latch to the sluice gates of a discourse dammed by oppositional structures of thought and identity. Never mind that the gates themselves have to be refashioned, perhaps even dispensed with. And again, never mind that the latch, or the observation itself, cannot be worked upon entirely or exclusively here; what we seek at this stage can only be a point of entry in to a theoretico-conceptual realm: of gender and difference.

In a sense, de Beauvoir's phrase is richly suggestive, especially in being emblematic of the terms along which the gender debate has been reconstructed. In particular; it opens up a space through which to re-view (or perhaps, even re-pose) questions within the gender realm, questions which have either been buried or only partially resolved over the years-issue (or questions) such as those regarding the presumed tangibility of body, an assumption which has sometimes moved the body beyond the reach of discursive appropriations; or, conversely, the perception of the body as an indeterminate field, open to contextual or situational elaboration; or, again, the tendency of conceptualizing the body as subject, as a 'lived body', presenting the interface between the body as a materiality and as set of representations. While some of these issues flow from the sex-gender distinction basic to feminist theory, they have also served as useful sounding boards in re-addressing another question which is becoming increasingly central to contemporary feminist debates - that of 'difference'. The term 'difference' itself has been subject to varying interpretation, ranging from its beginnings in sexual difference debates to an approach in terms of gendered subjectivities (Bock and James ed., 1992). But across these interpretations, what has been constant is the tendency to tie up gender difference with inequality and/or with oppositional structures of dominance and subordination. Could there be other avenues of conceptualizing gender and difference? To what extent can the 'hierarchical' principle animating (if Dumont is to be a guide) our context, be of use in analyzing gender difference? These are some of the questions which will be raised in the course of this paper. But before beginning to indicate the terms of such a conceptual re-articulation, we will first turn to a brief scrutiny of the gender concept itself, and the meanings attached to it. This is a pressing task, since gender has increasingly become a flaccid category, too loosely conceived to be conceptually effective. In the course of taking stock of its moves, we can also initiate a questioning which may change the very depths of our comprehension and the very morphology of our analytical conventions. Beginning such a task is my main purpose here.

A Reconnaissance

It is possible today, aided of course by the strength of hindsight. To trace the trajectory of the gender concept. But a comprehensive mapping of its development is not my intention here; rather, I propose to offer a reading of (what have now become) mainstream usages of 'gender' and then interrogate that reading in the light of meanings generated from an ethnographic context- the 'field'. This is not to posit a hiatus between the context and concept (or field and text, as it has conventionally been articulated), but to strive to collapse the two in to a singular gender narrative, one marked by certain continuing cadences.

Though it may be impossible to locate the exact moment at which gender realities emerged, it is clear that the emergence of 'gender' as a discursive tool is a recent phenomenon. The former has had a long and convoluted history, but gender as a concept is a specifically modern one, and has given rise to a relatively new field of research, what may be broadly described as 'gender studies'. This is not to negate the prior existence of a number of empirical and descriptive women-centred studies, indeed, studies which were largely instrumental in instituting 'women' as a field for analysis. Rather, in focusing on gender as a concept, what one is drawing attention to is the analytical confusion perpetrated by earlier usages such as 'status of women', or even 'sociology of women', where the social variability of 'women' as field for analysis. Rather, in focusing on gender as a concept, what one is drawing attention to is the analytical confusion perpetrated by earlier usages such as 'status of women', or even 'sociology of women', where the social variability of 'women' as a category is reduced to 'woman' as a biological category. Such a conflation inevitably entailed obscuring the cultural and contextual heterogeneity of the category of 'women', whose attributes and activities have varied in relation to the diverse intersections of caste, class, age, kinship, religion, region, and so on.

The study of gender primarily began by inserting itself in to the cracks revealed by the recognition that 'woman' was an inadequate sociological category for analysis. The propelling impulse behind the concept of gender was the challenge of formulating new categories which could better encounter the operation of gendering processes, the different spheres of activity of the sexes, the nature of male-female relations, as well as the diffusion of gender definitions. Perhaps inevitably, this resulted in a proliferation-not of answers-but, of questions questions as to what gender signified, its relation to the body, to sexuality, and so on: do bodies exist prior to gender? Or, are they always already gendered? Is one a gender, does one belong to a gender, or does one become a gender? If the last, what is the 'moment' of this becoming? Put more specifically, what does 'being female' signify? Is it a natural fact, derived from the female body? Or is it a cultural expression-something external, but acquired? If this posing of questions is any indication, the discourse one/of gender, inspite of its radical starting point. Appears to be mired in a very conventional farming of oppositions, between, for instance, gender as 'essential' trait and gender as 'constructed'. To move beyond these frames, it would be necessary to understand not just how gender is defined, structured and experienced within a culture, but also to be sensitive to the variations in the cultural content of gender attributions across and within cultures.[1]

In part, the troubled nature of gender as a concept derives from an early distinction made between 'sex' where the later term sought to forestall a naturalistic reduction of the gender question and to go beyond a reference to merely the sexual or biological difference between the male and female. The idea of sexual difference-which suggested that biology lay behind the differential capacities of women and men in the social or public domain-seems to have been an important point in relation to which the 'equality'/'difference' debate, central to Western feminism, was organized. Feminist theory during the 1970s subscribed to the equality position, denying differences between women and men and arguing that women must be equal to men in all respects (thus calling an end to inequality based on biological difference.) In the 1980s, trends within feminist theory veered round to an essentialist position, affirming and celebrating women's bodies and recreative capacities arguing that these be given equal social recognition (Rhode, ed., 1990). Clearly, irrespective of their varying stances toward sexual difference, the equality principle appears to underlay both the above positions.

In recent years, the perception of difference in terms of equality-inequality has increasingly been subject to clarification, based on a recognition of the need to differentiate between 'difference' as a biological fact and 'equality' as a socio-political one. And from within feminist practice itself, another notion of difference has emerged following a renewed feminist practice itself, another notion of difference has emerged following a renewed attentiveness to differences among women themselves. The earlier argument of sexual difference is seen as constraining in that it makes it impossible to articulate the differences obtaining among women themselves, in terms of their caste and class membership, as well as age and kinship positions. Also, this move emphasizes that the biological basis is overlaid with the cultural evaluations which affect not only the formation of subject identities, but also the manner in which subjects experience their own gender attributions. This recognition- that gendered meanings, or the cultural notions of femaleness and maleness, alongside their physiological dimension, are largely social and psychological products- paved the way for a perception of gender as a social construct; as a social category imposed on a sexed body" (Scott, 1988:32). Such a conceptualization of gender as a differential construction- produced across a range of socio-cultural practices, institutional discourses and practices of daily life- a facilitated a move beyond the theoretical closures inherent in preceding explanations.

A Re-appraisal

While it is true that privileging this understanding of gender as construction certainly takes us beyond the inadequacies of preceding categories (whether it be those of 'sexual difference' or 'women'), one should also alive to the pitfalls inherent in this very project of refurbishing concepts. In interrogating the old and, consequently, striving to open up new possibilities, the (re) formulation of gender (and/or difference) is also marked by certain closures built in to the logic of those very possibilities. For instance, at one level, the positing of gender (as construction) performs a critical function by highlighting the impossibility of raising certain kinds of questions- in particular, the question of difference- within the earlier frames. Yet, simultaneously, the increasing consolidation of gender as a major analytical category has today resulted in an interpretive hegemony where, again, only some questions can be raised (and only in certain ways): I refer in particular to the fact that the gender question has always been explicated in terms of inequality (which conceives of difference in unequal, oppositional terms), almost to the exclusion of other perspectives. It is this sense that a field of possibilities could begin to impose, or enforce, a closure at another level, but we must return to the point just made about the explication of gener in terms of inequality.

This association of gender with arrangements related to the organization of social inequality has favoured an analytical framework which one may characterize as, broadly, stratificational. Such a framework, in attempting to order a range of social differences in terms of a common underlying principle, has consisted in systematically reducing the complexities of phenomena such as caste, class and now gender, to the manifestation of inequality alone. With reference to the gender domain, the preoccupation with inequality is evident at many levels. The overwhelming tendency to cast the analysis in terms of gender exploitation, for instance, is merely a reflection of its imbrication in a series of dichotomous schemes such as equality-inequality, which set up male dominance and female subordination as opposite poles of relation. These relations, often perceived as a monolithic system of domination, and explicated under the overarching category of patriarchy, have tended to endorse the view of a universal oppression of women, at the hands of a determinate group of men. This scheme has invariably influenced the structure and perception of gender relations, often in advance of a knowledge of the specificities of local contexts, forgetting in the process, that such power relations are not homogeneous, but variable. Conceiving of gender as identity, that is, as referring to the definite set of roles and identities assumed by women and men would only serve to further entrench this reasoning.

But by far the key idea anchoring the equality-inequality axis is the notion of the 'individual'. As a distinctly modern conception, the term "individual" is inseparable from a western ideology of liberty and equality, with its accompanying doctrine of rights. It suggests an autonomous or free empirical agent, the individual as sovereign: as one who possesses a core identity or selfhood, which is the source of speech, thought and action. The question remains, however, as to whether this centrality of the individual can be transported unproblematically across cultures. Concepts of person in India, as strands of anthropological reasoning (for instance, Marriott, 1976) have opined, do not derive from a 'core' individual with a sovereign, unitary identity, but is revealed as an identity that is other-directed. This perception of, the self as a fluid entity, where there are no individuals, but 'dividual' or divisible selves, places the latter referring to the ways in which social relations between persons, or the nature of social action itself, is constituted. Such an understanding of the person as composed of multiple layers of meaning and relation becomes important in that it prompts a shift from the view of gender as 'identity' to a perception of gender as animating 'sociality' itself. This would allow an exploration of gender ideas, not as confined to the organization of relations between the sexes, but as also signifying the values and practices of a community, organizing its ideas about social space, work, sexuality, ritual, etc. Such a shift facilitates a view of gender as an irradiating concept, through which to understand processes within the social formation itself.

A Re-articulation

Though the diverse factors impinging on gender definitions and relations have often been recognized, there have not been many concerted efforts to theorize the implications of this heterogeneity. while this might hint at a certain degree of 'universalism' present in the concept of gender, our response can neither be to privilege a particularistic understanding, nor to suggest that we replace 'gender' with a more culturally resonant indigenous category. Rather, the attempt is to demonstrate that the concept, by being invested with a greater degree of tension, can be made more responsive to the refractions of meaning within local contexts. I will here offer the outlines of such a possible reworking, drawing on suggestions generated within a definite field, viz., a rural community in South India[2]. The workings of gender here exhibited several layers of meaning, resisting a reduction to any common ordering principle such as inequality.

An exposure to how ideas of gender, 'difference; and inequality are handled across local, everyday contexts appears to call for a questioning of the almost axiomatic assumption of an a symmetrical/antagonistic relation between the sexes. Verbalizations from the field, and its contrast with actual situations of a symmetry, highlight the need to attend to the modes by which these domains are negotiated daily. The fact that gender difference, rather than reflecting clear-cut alignments such as superiority-inferiority or dominance-submission, functions according to another 'logic' - one which will be thematized presently - brings to the fore the inadequacies of adopting a strictly stratificational perspective on gender. Could the concept of 'hierarchy' especially Louis Dumont's explication of it, yield an alternative? Would it be capable of conveying the nuances of meaning underlying gender relations in the field? Engaging with these questions will perhaps allow us to further open up the frames of gender for critical reflection.

The overall set of dispositions[3] which orient the perceptions, activities and relationships of people[4] within a community both constitutes, and derives from, a coherent (in the sense of a working or workable) universe of meaning which underlies their practice. Capturing the logic immanent in their practices, however, would require highlighting the key schema or principle organizing it. The Dumontian elucidation of 'hierarchy' as that principle "by which elements of a whole are ranked in relation to the whole" (1980:66) seems significant for our purposes. In Dumont's endeavour to explain parts of a society with reference to the whole, heterogeneous parts are seen as subsumed within, or determined by the whole, the process being characterized by the term 'encompassment'. He maintains that the whole hinges on the hierarchical co-existence of two opposites where "that which encompasses is more important than that which is encompassed" (1980:76). However, though the enveloping ideology of purity and impurity is central to his understanding of the hierarchical nature of caste society, there are other, secondary elements (such as power and territory in his model) which cannot be fitted in to the former. Such contrary factors are described as separate from, yet encompassed within (i.e. subordinate to) the whole. This almost complementary relation between an encompassing principle and the encompassed entities appears inextricably linked to a holistic vision of the hierarchical whole.

What could it mean to suggest a harnessing of this model to understand the patterning of gender relations in a specific context? To what extent would the latter lend itself to such an appropriation? Before elaborating on these questions, it should perhaps be clarified that what is being used here is the Dumontian model of encompassed and encompassing, which offers a way of speaking about relations between diverse entities, rather than seeking an engagement with the substantive elements in the model. As it stands, within Dumont's framework, it seems almost impossible to theorize the women's realm except as encompassed, subordinate, and receiving. In order to articulate the independent rhythms of this realm, it would be necessary to modify, even recast, the relations posited within the model, especially that between the encompassed and the encompassing, or more precisely, to refocus on and enhance the schema from the point of view of the encompassed. These possibilities may be elaborated.

Across varied realms such as ritual, work, marriage, familial life and so on, people across castes articulate a normative grid emphasizing one can say, 'mutuality', where the activities of one sex postulates, calls in to being, and completes the other. This is expressed, for instance, in observations which maintain that both male and female contributions together serve to perpetuate a household, or the economy. Likewise, in the symbolization of women as conduits of 'auspiciousness', where well-being and good fortune flow to the family through the woman, the mutuality of gender relations is stressed. While the grounds of similar 'reciprocal' activity or 'reciprocity' have, at times, been seen as representing an other-directed intentionality (Strathern, 1988), or even a 'complementary dualism' (Hoskins, 1987), it is imperative to spell out the terms of this relationship, especially the conditionality underlying each and every set of actions. This would perhaps expose a grammar which is not quite that of complementarity or a simple reciprocity.

Focusing on the realm of work alone, one can hint at the complexity of issues buried herein. Within the domestic realm, the arduous tasks of replenishing the subsistence base of the household take up much of the labour energies of women, whereas men increasingly seek work outside sphere. In addition, a significant number of women too work outside for wages, in order to meet the basic resource requirements of the household and its members. However, their work outside the home appears to be structured in particular ways, with not all economic opportunities being open to them. More specifically, the place of work and the nature of work (whether a skilled job, or unskilled labour at construction sites) are major factors influencing the economic participation of women. Their place of work is invariably near and familiar; travelling distances to work not only carries the fear of the alien or unknown, but also the stigma of moral suspicion. Articulations from the field reveal how maintaining the honour of women and family are the considerations uppermost in the minds of people. Apart from this underlying normative grade, a series of cultural evaluations intermesh with the sexual division of labour to dictate which jobs are done by women and men. However, while there is a clear-cut delineation of tasks between men and women in both agricultural and household domains, the nature of women's work across households is by no means uniform, being influenced by various socio-economic factors like poverty, caste, access to land and family structure. Across all these levels, whether it be the earning of a subsistence livelihood or subsistence agricultural production, the division of tasks between women and men is perceived as 'supplementing' one another, rather than as oppositional, and as 'necessary' for a proper running of the household.

This ideological emphasis on the cooperation of the sexes appears to present a contrast with the customary conflation of gender relations with inequality. Yet, it surely cannot be accepted uncritically as an alternative construct, since palpable instances of material asymmetry between the sexes do continue to exist. It has been observed within various ethnographies (Devereaux, 1987; Josephides, 1985) that the overt relations of complementarity which present male and female interests as inseparable could still hide inequalities in social practice. These pertain largely to the economic realm, where men and women neither have uniform access to and control over resources, nor equal availability of subsistence opportunities. As Strathern (1988:149) puts it:

> The notion of reciprocity in the division of labour between husband and wife..serves to hide inequalities in their access to productive resources... A wife's control over the fruits of her labour is restricted by her obligation to feed her family, and her claims to land depend on her marriage to her husband.

The control over economic and political resources, which determines the power available to a person, is an effect of prevailing structural arrangements in the community. Seen in these terms, it is clear that women neither have access to land, nor complete control over the products of their labour; and are asymmetrically positioned vis-a-vis men. While it is one thing to begin analysis from these unequal institutional arrangements, it is quite another to begin by asking how these arrangements work, or what mechanisms ensure their reproduction. It would be equality significant to see how women strive to work this unequal system to their relative advantage by placing an emphasis, for instance, on reciprocal obligations within the household. A woman can be seen as directing her actions toward that of her husband family (for example, processing food and carrying out other domestic chores) only in the anticipation (or, on the implicit condition), that the man will contribute his share to the maintenance of the household (for instance, by providing foodgrains). Undeniably, when one of the actors fails to respond or reciprocate, relations could revert to the asymmetrical. The modes in which agents negotiate unequal arrangements on a daily basis, as well as the terms of the negotiation, are so innumerable, veiled and complex that they can be explained neither in terms of a pure and simple asymmetry, nor with the idea of a harmonious complementarity. Rather it demands an alternative construct which can shift gears between these different levels with less effort, one capable of voicing the resonances of both meaning and materiality.

The term 'supplement', or better, the 'logic of supplementarity' can perhaps bear the burden of these demands more effectively than 'complementarity' or 'asymmetry'. These later two concepts work with distinctive understandings of difference or gender differentiation, both of which diverge from the former. While in the inequality/ asymmetry axis the difference between genders is oppositional, in the complementarity axis, gender differentiation is expressed in terms of pairs, which together form a consensual whole. The logic of supplementarity departs from the oppositional/consensual echoes of the above and offers a way of speaking about gender differentiation within communities in terms that are, yet, 'relational'. It seems to suggest a relationship between male-female spheres that is neither unequal (i.e. defined in terms of dominance-submission), nor one where the female sphere is encompassed within the male one (and thereby subsumed in the whole'). Theorizing the supplement draws attention, instead, to an entirely new relationship between two entities, which, while giving voice to the part, indicates that the whole is not defined in terms of the parts, but is incomplete without it. Resisting the Dumontian tendency of encompassing the female domain in the service of the whole, the notion of 'supplementarity' in gender relations can highlight the significance of the part, or more importantly, its indeterminancy, thus opening out terms of a conceptual engagement with gender difference.

To pursue this line of thought for a bit, the term 'supplement' may be seen as suggesting two aspects. One, it tells us about itself, indicating that it is marginal to, not a pre-existing part of, a whole, being what is added on. in order to complete; and that, despite its marginal status, it has an important contribution to make to the maintenance of the whole. Two, it signals something about the nature of the 'whole' itself, indicating that what exists as seemingly whole is incomplete without it; that the whole, by being in a constant process of flux, anticipates, requires, and calls in to being, the existence of the supplement. As such, the whole is not a unitary, seamless entity, but a composite of fragments, containing tensions, contradictions and oppositional pressures within it. In a way, the significance of the supplement derives from its ability to highlight the tensions within a hierarchical whole.

The implications of conceptualizing gender difference in these terms (the supplemental, the hierarchical) is suggestive on several counts. It is facilitative of a view of gender difference not in terms of an excluding definition, that is, one guided by a dualistic or oppositional logic, but rather, in terms of an encompassing definition, one emphasizing 'alongside' rather than (as in the former) 'against'. Further, and this is perhaps more crucial, this is not to reinforce consensualism nor to fall back upon the complementarity axis where the parts are invariably subordinated to the whole; rather, it is to initiate a redefinition of the relations between part and whole. With reference to the realm of gender, this offers a mode of conceptualizing women and their lives in society, where their alleged marginal contribution is belied by their actual centrality in the conduct of social life. Besides, by bringing in to play the tensions between the whole and the part (or the marginal), the terms of the suggested re-articulation could yield a perspective on the axes of power across male and female worlds, drawing attention, in particular, to the fissures within a dominant worldview. While it does not endorse a view of gender as predicated on inequality, it does offer a perspective on the gender domain as a whole, as embodying contestations at different levels between and within its constituent entities. By primarily exploring and highlighting the status of the encompassed realm, the notion of the supplement enables a re-reading of the gendered hierarchical domain. It enables a perspective on the encompassed, not as predetermined by a hierarchical whole, but as constantly restating/renegotiating its relations with the whole; a view of the encompassed realm as that without which the whole itself would not exist.

A Postscript

The paper could have ended at this juncture, but perhaps I should suggest more, eliminating, simultaneously, a possible ground for misunderstanding, and gesturing toward a problem that needs a great deal of investigation.

The notion of supplementarity is conceptually important also because it draws attention to the various levels at which gender operates. Though these levels are firmly intermeshed in the practices and discourses of everyday life, it may be necessary to separate them, if only analytically, to see how gender actually works. The two main grounds of gender which can be highlighted here are materiality (the substantive and asymmetrical institutional arrangements) and metaphoricity (an insightful and ideological expression of gender relations), both of which must enter in to characterizations of gender in a specific context. Yet, the pervasiveness of the inequality framework in explicating gender leads to an exclusive focus on the material realm, almost negating, as irrelevant, the metaphoricity of the gender idiom. The understanding which results is at best a partial one, which cannot grasp the fundamental continuities between the two, for the metaphorical is but a transformation, or a transcoding at another level, of the material. The metaphoricity of gender plays a doubly crucial role in the attempt to reformulate the concept of gender, primarily because it is not confined to representing gender relations between men and women alone, but can also be read as signifying the relations and principles animating the larger socio-cultural context in which it is embedded.

A single instance from the field-that of the ordering of gender relations in the economic sphere-can demonstrate this density at the heart of the gender concept, a density which necessitates a constant rephrasing of its terms, in accordance with the shifts it undergoes from one level of expression to another. In an economic realm characterized by subsistence production, the respective contributions of men and women are represented by the participants themselves as ideally and necessarily complementary in nature. This perception and representation of gender relations as reciprocal, however, cannot be translated in to a vocabulary of materiality, for it is obvious that despite the functionality of both male and female labour for running an economic unit, their access to, and control over, the means of production are different and asymmetrical. The gap between these two perspectives is not a matter of mere emphasis, but a matter of their very starting points being different. Their modes of being are also diverse, with one inhabiting a substantive space and the other embodying a metaphoricity which spills over its material reference. Each comes to transgress the terms of constitution of the other, giving way to another level (whether material or metaphorical) of representing gender(ing) practices. For example, the unequal economic arrangements between men and women is sought to be explained by drawing gender along another tangent of metaphoricity, such as the argument of 'natural capabilities;. Within each culture, the sexual division of labour defines the work done by men and women, often typifying certain tasks as 'naturally' left to women, who are seen as 'not capable' of undertaking other tasks. This naturalization of the division of labour, which actually has a cultural bias rather than a physical one, strives to present a harmonious picture of the social whole, while simultaneously serving to cement relations of asymmetry within it. An effective characterization of gender and/or gendering practices within a community must include an understanding of all these diverse levels and modes of expression. To focus on one moment or expressive mode alone, to the exclusion of others, is to be left with a distorted picture of the totality since the accretions of signification with each transformation of the gender concept- say, from a metaphorical (read, 'ideal', 'complementary') mode, through the real ('material', 'asymmetrical'), to another metaphorical (read, 'natural') expression is not adequately conveyed. For though the 'ideal' and 'natural' perceptions of gender are both representing and displacing the terms of the 'real', they are doing so in widely divergent ways and represent definite shifts within the metaphorical mode itself.

At each moment of transformation, then, the lodging of gender is different. In other words, the grounds inhabited by the concept of gender must be provisional, ever shifting. With each shift, the previous terms of the discourse would, or must, change. Accompanying each shifts is a distorting of the previous terms of the discourse. As we have seen, the emergence of the inequality question creates a distortive wave within a complementary metaphor of gender, since the latter defined 'difference' in terms of interdependence and mutuality, rather than in oppositional terms. To tackle inequality requires a shift to a new register altogether, wherein identities are conceived as units, where the categories of female/male are defined in opposition to one another. However, the basis of this opposition gets further distorted when difference comes to be seen in 'natural' (almost biological) terms, i.e. when the gender idiom gets re-converted to a new level of metaphor. To say, then, that the 'lodging' of gender varies from one context to another is to argue that the same set of gender practices can offer different meanings when seen through different schemes of thought. They can enter in to different relations from different points of view, all without apparent contradiction, primarily because of the 'indeterminate' quality of gender relations. This indeterminacy (used in the sense of a denial of determinism), which acquires a distinct form and colour when represented in terms of its links with the whole (through, for instance, a material or metaphoric idiom), is what is underlined by the idea of the supplement. Engaging with the notion of the supplement, in critical conjunction with the concept of hierarchy, can perhaps suggest an alternative axis along which to ask the question of gender difference. This could not only register references to both the metaphoric and material forms of gender, but could also, in giving voice to the part, constitute the seeds of a re-working of the concept of hierarchy itself.

Notes

1. The idea that there is a common experience and perception of feminine gender across the world - in short, a universal concept of womanhood

- has been acknowledged by scholars and feminists as increasingly problematic today. Yet, not many attempts have been made to address the implications of such a recognition for our conceptual frameworks. Recent anthropological studies (in particular Marilyn Strathern's The Gender of the Gift', whose suggestions I draw upon in this paper) have sought to engage with these issues, opening new avenues to the gender question in terms of the diversity of overall thought systems in different societies.

2. Fieldwork was conducted in a cluster of villages in Karnataka; ethnographic and other details can be had from my doctoral dissertation, 'Symbolic Meaning and Rural Social Structure: A Sociological Study in the Construction of Femininity' submitted to Bangalore University (1994). These details are not elaborated here, as my primary purpose is to offer an analysis at the level of concepts while drawing on insights from the field. To thus abstract from the field and suggest, in that basis, a generalized logic underlying gender relations, does raise the problem of specificity, of articulating the particular within the general, and in that process, effecting a transformation in our concepts of the latter.
3. Such a formulation feeds off Bourdieu's idea of dispositions as structured, what he formulates as the 'habitus'. "The habitus, as the system of dispositions to a certain practice, is an objective basis for regular modes of behaviour, and thus for the regularity of modes of practice, and if practices can be predicted, this is because the effect of the habitus is that agents who are equipped with it will behave in a because the effect of the habitus is that agents who are equipped with it will behave in a certain way in certain circumstances". This 'regularity'. however, Bourdieu maintains", do(es) not have the fine regularity of the modes of behaviour deduced from a legislative principle"; that is to say, "the habitus goes hand in above with vagueness and indeterminacy" (1990: 77). This also marks the standpoint from which we have come to ask never questions of our fieldwork materials. But see what follows: Dumont's civilizational frame might yet provide an axis within which to moderate Bourdieu's praxeological model.
4. Our usage "people", or even "community" might suggest too homogeneous a reference, obscuring the intricacies of operations within caste society. It remains a moot question, of course, whether the notion we work upon here, namely. The 'supplement', can be combined with caste phenomena. Indeed, to the extent that the 'supplemental' will be seen to issue from the 'relational' dimension of phenomena, the notion partakes of a basic characteristic of caste society, viz., relationality. As Louis Dumont avers; "In the caste society, nothing is true by nature and everything by situation, there are no essences, but only relations" (1970:29). In this light, one must reiterate that our usage "people" draws attention to agents within caste society, though admittedly, a fuller treatment than that presented here is called for.

Visualising Difference: A Feminist Perspective

Bernadette Joseph

What do we mean by 'difference'? The Webster's English Dictionary states that 'difference' means 'unlikeness; dissimilarity; distinguishing characteristics; disagreement; contention; the amount by which one thing exceeds another in weight or number' (W.E.D. 1991, p. 107). In Derridean analysis 'difference' or 'differance' (spelt with an 'a') is that which is signified through the presence of one signifier and the absence of the others. The interplay between presence and absence that produces meaning is posited as one of 'deferral'. What we have can only be understood, i.e. given meaning to, through that which we do not have, i.e. through difference. Meaning is produced through binary oppositions, such as, masculine/feminine, day/night, black/white.

Our world operates in a patriarchal system and it gives meaning to life through a patriarchal discourse. The binary oppositions are patriarchal in their essence which favours the 'male'. Everything is caught up in this endless game of patriarchal binary oppositions which ultimately boils down to the fundamental 'couple of male/female' (Sexual Textual Politics, p. 104). Hélène Cixous provides a list of binary oppositions in which she looks for the woman's place:

Activity/Passivity
Sun/Moon
Culture/Nature
Day/Night
Father/Mother
Head/Emotions
Intelligible/Sensitive
Logos/Pathos

Each of the oppositions can be analysed as a hierarchy where the male is powerful, assertive and positive while the female is categorized as weak, silent and negative.

Feminists are trying to understand this system and redefine their position in it. This dichotomy of the male/female and its consequence in our life is the basis of the feminist discourse. Feminists like Hélène Cixous attempts to break up the patriarchal system of producing meaning. To accomplish this, i.e. changing the meaning producing mechanism feminists are investigating the visual and the textual. Cixous believes that through feminine writing one can achieve the goal of producing a new way, a different way of looking at the world. Cixous argues that the sex of the author has nothing to do with the sex of the text. A text can be feminine or masculine independent of the sex of the author. What she ultimately wishes to achieve is a complete integration of the male and the female, to even abolish such terms as masculine and feminine.

If this hypothesis is applied to the film world then we can say that the film too will have either femininity or masculinity ascribed to it. Most films can be analysed according to this above argument. Feminist critics agree that by and large women have not been allowed to dominate the silver screen either in being depicted or in creating them. However, there are a few that can be analysed by their virtue of being made by males or by females. Alice Walker's inspirational novel *The Color Purple* is a case in point. This novel has been made into a major Hollywood movie by the highly acclaimed film director Steven Spielberg. We have a story written by a female, a black feminist writer, about the struggle of a black slave girl called Celie. Celie's struggle involves losing her sister, her own children, putting up with a drunk husband and his children and all the suffering that comes with slavery and being a negro. The book is not all about pain, there are happy events and uplifting situations and one of the positive presence in Celie's life was Shug, a liberated black female. Steven Spielberg successfully portrayed many of the difficult aspects of the novel which is written in format of letters, but he failed to be faithful to the relationship of Celie and Shug who become lovers in the course of their relationship. The 'femininity' of the whole text centered around the relationships of all the women in the novel which was not portrayed in their true essence. Spielberg sympathises with the story, with the situation, with the struggle but fails in handling the lesbianism and the bonding of the women. The 'femininity' of the text that is *The Color Purple* is lost in the film as it is interpreted in a masculine way.

Two other films that may illustrate the argument further are *Parama*, directed by Aparna Sen, and *Charulata* directed by Sattyajit Ray. Both the films deal with two Indian women who are in situations that are not under their control. Sen's film portrays her protagonist, Parama, a middle-aged housewife with very good-looks that nobody takes notice of until an American-trained award-winning photographer comes into her life. Aparna Sen makes very feminine statements throughout the film through her usage of symbols and signs and through silence. She uses a 'male medium', photography, (in a very symbolic manner as well as in a practical way) to convey her feminist stance as a film-maker. On the other hand, Ray portrays Charulata, a young housewife with a lot of time on her hands who sees the world around her through opera glasses. This is typical male interpretation of how women see the world, from inside out. Women are enclosed, unassertive, weak and without a voice. Though *Charulata* is an expression of Ray's sympathy with women and to a certain extent his film has a thin layer of femininity in his usage of silence and sound, he is still very masculine in his interpretation of the characters.

Feminists take their cue from the notion of the women being the 'other'. This notion of otherness is a 'fundamental category of human thought' (Feminism and Philosophy, p. 51). Feminists are asking 'Why must women be the perpetual Other and the object and man occupy the position of absolute subject?' Luce Irigaray, a French feminist uses Freud's 'penis envy theory' as her springboard to redefine the position of women and her sexuality. In her essay *Another 'Cause' - Castration*, Irigaray looks at the castration theory and argues that women have no reason to have any 'penis envy'. She believes that it is imposed upon women by the male who is in fear of losing his own, therefore he must project this fear in order to have a sense of security himself. The 'logic of the gaze' is at the centre of the 'penis envy' theory that Irigaray takes to task. The Freudian theory of sexual difference is based on the visibility of difference: it is the eye that decides what is clearly true and what is not. (Toril Moi, *Sexual Textual Politics*). It is the sight of the penis that the little girl realizes that she has not got one and therefore 'feels seriously wronged' (*Castration*, p. 405). The woman has nothing that can be castrated and therefore the woman, being in fear of castration or envious of a penis is according to Irigaray 'displaced castration'. Freud's theory is based on his speculation of the little girl as the little boy. According to the feminist critique he is putting the 'same desire' on the female.

The logic of the gaze is more aptly drawn in an Islamic society where the woman is kept behind a veil. She is not to be seen. Her sexuality must never emerge. She is denied the pleasure of expressing her sexuality in any form and the male must not be allowed to gaze, unlike Freud, but the logic is the same. Freud looks and does not see anything and the Muslim male can only see a veil. What is interesting to observe is that while the males are denied the visibility, the females have the full view of them. Ray's Charulata is denied access to the outer world but she does see everything through her opera glasses. That is the situation of the woman, as far as her physical situation is concerned. However her psyche and her sexuality (which are very much in tune with each other) have a better stance than the male. According to Irigaray,

> ...woman has sex organs more or less everywhere. She finds pleasure almost anywhere. Even if we refrain from invoking the hystericization of her entire body, the geography of her pleasure is far more diversified, more multiple in its differences, more complex, more subtle, than is commonly imagined - in an imaginary rather too narrowly focused on sameness. (*This Sex Which is Not One*)

A woman does not need the 'other' as the male does to affirm his sex, rather she is one and the other in herself. Irigaray's explanation of female sexuality follows too much idealogical discourse. It hardly touches the 'multiplicity of women' who are situated at many different levels of social and cultural experience. Feminists like Hélène Cixous, Kate Millet and Monique Plaza are very critical of idealogical discourse that is separated from the everyday material existence of life. Cixous argues that feminists who are involved in the thematic and theoretical analysis are turning away from the present to the past and they will be caught up in the oppressive network, of 'hierarchical binary oppositions propagated by patriarchal idealogy'. Monique Plaza believes that feminists like Irigaray are playing the same game of power politics as their 'fathers'. She criticizes Irigaray for excluding the material conditions of women's oppression. Toril Moi in her criticism says that Irigaray lacks historical orientation but defends her by acknowledging the fact that in the Western World there are recurrent patriarchal strategies that are played against women.

But what is happening in the East? In terms of Freud's penis envy theory let us take a look at the Hindu festival of the 'Shiva Linga' (Penis of Shiva, the god of power and might and love and fertility, one can find a slight similarity with Bacchus, the Greek god of wine and fertility). During this festival (*puja*) Hindu women pay homage to a statue of the penis which they decorate and paint and put garlands around it hoping to have a good husband and healthy children. The Shiva Linga is the symbol of power and fertility and women of all creed and caste, of different background are deeply faithful to their belief. The question is whether this is a mode of oppression or a mode of expression? What will these Indian women say to the idea of the 'penis envy' theory? What do other women of different ethnic backgrounds think of their sexuality? What are the differences or the similarities? Can these differences be analysed in a Derridian fashion or in terms of the notion of the 'other'?

We understand what we have in relation to what we do

not have. 'A' is what 'B' or 'C' or 'Y' is not. To know us we need to look at others. Anthropologists and cultural theorists have gone out into other worlds and studied other cultures to have a better understanding of their own culture. Asian and African cultures have been the dominant sources of cultural studies. The time has come when the voices are now coming from these very sources redefining their existence and opening up vistas of new studies. They too need their 'other' to give meaning to their existence. These voices from the margin are marked as a game of 'political identity'. The centre of intellectual seat, the West hardly acknowledges them or considers them to be 'original'. It is a crisis in cultural studies as to how to incorporate these voices from the margin along with the centre. There is a similar crisis in the feminist movement. Apart from the idealogical and functional differences of the feminist movement, there are race and class differences. We are faced with Black Feminism, Black Lesbian Feminism, Third World Feminism and feminisms in England, France, West Germany, Italy and Latin America that can be termed as 'International Feminism' if brought under a single category.

Gayatri Chakravorty Spivak in her *In Other Worlds* tries to answer the question: 'What is the constituency of an international feminism?' As a Bengali woman from Calcutta and educated in the West, her position in the feminist discourse is not without its complicities that involves 'reversing and displacing the ironclad opposition of West and East' (Spivak, *In Other Worlds*, p. 135).

As an Asian woman myself I was critical of Susan Faludi's (author of *The Backlash*), comment during an interview on Australian Television. When she asked the female audience at the show whether they believed in equal pay and equal rise and when the answer came in the affirmative, she declared them as feminists. I asked myself what would a mother who stays home (by choice) to look after home and children have to say? What would a black lesbian feminist say to that simple analysis of Feminism? What would Alice Walker say who in her book *In Search of Our Mothers' Garden* said that is never possible for a white gentile woman to understand the pain and agony of a

Jewish or a Black woman. The differences gain depth and life becomes more complex and yet a lot more meaningful when we take these differences into the feminist discourse.

When Toni Morrison's novel *Beloved* was reviewed, critiques, both male and female applauded her style and language but continuously failed to offer a criticism of the content: A young slave girl who escapes and gives birth while fleeing and finally killing her own baby daughter (whom she names Beloved) and the ghostly presence of the baby throughout the novel and the black community that survives insufferable pain is written in a language as one critique has put it 'like thick menstrual blood' is full of symbols that need to be decoded in order to be understood. Barbara Smith in her essay *The Truth That Never Hurts* says that 'Black feminist literature has a unique set of characteristics and emphasis which distinquishes it from other work' (*Feminism, An Anthology*, p. 692). The critiques of Toni Morrison's novel found it difficult to accept much of those characteristics, the sexual vioilence, black women's relationship with each other or women bonding and black lesbianism and in Morrison's case, her usage of symbols and signs. We must remember that we are heavily coded by the patriarchal signs of language and therefore fail to interpret a feminist text that seeks a very different kind of a reading. The process may not be simple or rational and at times can be totally unacceptable but feminists are seeking for a language that would be accessible to the women.

The quest for a new language, according to Elaine Showalter must be founded on idealogical and cultural determinants of expression. The reason behind that is 'women have been denied the full resources of language and have been forced into silence, euphemism and circumlocation'. (Showalter, 'Feminist criticism in the wilderness', *Critical Inquiry* 8, no.2, 1981, p. 193).

The femininity or the masculinity of the text can be analysed through a close reading of the text, decoding the codes and hearing what is not being said. The differences lie in our interpretation of the text. When a woman says 'pain' it may not be the same 'pain' to a man. This is a very simplistic analysis but that is the basis of all our discourse of visualising differences. It only becomes lucid when it is applied to the dichotomy of male/female, black/white and east/west.

Bibliography

Irigaray, Luce *This Sex Which is Not One*, Trans. Catherine Porter, Ithaca: Cornell University Press, 1985.

Gatens, Moira, *Feminism and French Philosophy Perspective on Difference and Equality*, Indiana University Press, Bloomington and Indianapolis, 1991.

Moi, Toril, *Sexual Textual Politics: Feminist Literary Theory*, Routledge, London, New York, 1985.

Showalter, Elaine, 'Feminist Criticism in the Wilderness', *Critical Inquiry 8*, No.2, 1981.

Spivak, Gayatri Chakravorty, *In Other Worlds: Essays in Cultural Politics*, London: Routledge, 1988.

Warhol, Robyn, R. and Herndle, Diane Price (eds), *Feminisms: An Anthology of Literary Theory and Criticism*; Rutgers University Press, New Brunswick, New Jersey, 1991.

Walker, Alice, *The Color Purple*, Women's Press Limited, 1983.

In Search of Our Mothers' Garden: Womanist Prose, New York; Harcourt Brace, Jovanovich, 1984.

Morrison, Toni, *Beloved*, Picador, 1988.

Films:

The Color Purple, Directed by Steven Spielberg, A Steven Spielberg Film.

Parama, Directed by Aparna Sen, Usha Enterprise Film, 1985.

Charulata, Directed by Sattayajit Ray, Produced by R. D. Bonshal, 1964.

Gandhi, Women and Identity

Videsha Bagchi

Whether the writing of biographies of political figures might benefit from the teachings of psychoanalysis has been considered by various commentators. Falk (1985) contends that political biography differs from literary biography in that the political biographer deals not with the products of creative fantasy but with reality-oriented actions. Furthermore, because it is equally possible for political action to be influenced by unconscious conflict or fantasy as it is for literary creation, the skilled political biographer must be able to recognise the existence of these fantasies and conflicts in abstract political entities. Finally, Edel (1985) contends that providing the biographer has sufficient psychological skills and does not allow his unconscious identifications with the subject to intrude too deeply, the biographer will have succeeded in conveying his subject's deepest political motives.

The way in which a psychobiography differs from an orthodox biography is well illustrated in the case of Gandhi. Louis Fischer's biography of Gandhi, *The Life of Mahatma Gandhi*, is concerned primarily with providing a factual account of Gandhi's life and his role in the achievement of India's independence from Britain. All material used, particularly Gandhi's own writings, is taken at face value, with no attempt at further interpretation. Fischer is as uninterested in Gandhi's unconscious motivations as he is in his own for choosing Gandhi. There is no introduction in which Fischer discusses his reasons for his choice of subject and the work is essentially hagiographic. Gandhi is always attributed the most generous of motives.

There are advantages of this orthodox approach to writing a biography. Most importantly, it provides the requisite data without which a psychobiography cannot proceed. Fischer's work is loaded with facts, the essential ingredients to the real story of Gandhi's life.

However, as I shall outline, there is evidence that Fischer has failed to disentangle himself from his subject. Given Fischer's treatment of Gandhi's wife, Kasturba, and his portrayal of her as a rather weak and slow witted creature, it is not implausible that he felt an unconscious identification with Gandhi. There is further evidence of this in the way in which Fischer interprets Gandhi's acts of violence towards women with regard to their hair, jewellery and clothing. Finally, there is evidence that in what is ostensibly an objective recounting of the facts, Fischer allows his own prejudices to emerge. A striking example of this is when he describes Hinduism as an insidious religion.

In contrast to Fischer, Erik Erikson in *Gandhi's Truth* has not written a biography in the conventional sense. He is more concerned with the psychological origins of Gandhi's main weapon, Satyagraha or militant non-violence. The work concentrates on one event, a mill strike at Ahmedabad as the prototype for Gandhi's future political actions. Erikson is interested in revealing the inner sources of Gandhi's power and does not portray him as a self sacrificing saint. He conducts a psychological examination of Gandhi's motives which seeks to uncover the deeper reasons for his actions. He does not baldly assume altruistic ones. Furthermore Erikson's work is prefaced with an introduction in which he attempts to convey his own initial motives for writing about Gandhi, and his subsequent ambivalence towards his subject.

However, Erikson, despite the psychological orientation of his approach, does not escape the danger of allowing his unconscious identification with Gandhi to emerge. This is evident in his wholly inappropriate references to Gandhi by various pet names used by his family. The use of these names conveys an entirely false sense of familiarity which suggests that Erikson, in part, had an unconscious desire to be close to his subject.

The original intention of this paper was to make a comparison of two biographies of Gandhi, an orthodox one and a psychobiography, and to demonstrate how the latter, by Erikson, provides insight not accessible using orthodox biographical techniques, which are more concerned with providing the facts than with their interpretation. Although Erikson claims to penetrate the psychological origins of Gandhi's philosophy, I shall argue that Erikson's biography seriously lacks in this regard. It appears Erikson is aware of Edel's (1985) contention that a successful psychobiography must convey the notion that all personal feelings and experiences are re-enacted unconsciously on the public stage. Therefore, the problem with Erikson lies not in the method in itself. As a psychoanalyst, Erikson is equipped with the requisite tools, but fails to use them to their full advantage. There is ample evidence to suggest that Gandhi had a fear of women and children which was acted out on his political stage. Erikson does hint at this in a number of places. However, when Erikson confronts Gandhi's attitude toward his parents, like Fischer, he accepts Gandhi at his own word that he was afraid of his mother but loved his father.

Erikson's magnification of Gandhi's ambivalent relationship with his father is similar to the way in which Kafka inverted his problematic relationship with his mother, displacing it onto his father. (Carroll, 1985) Kafka blamed his own father entirely for his own misery; the evidence from his creative writings suggests that it was his mother who was the problem. This is particularly evident in *Letter to his Father* where Kafka is openly hostile:

> You asked me recently why I am afraid of you. As usual I was unable to think of my answer to your question, partly for the very reason that I am very afraid of you.(30)

Later in the *Letter* he accuses his father of the crime of indifference when he writes:

> But since there was nothing at all I was certain of, since I needed to be provided at every instant with a new confirmation off my existence..- in sober truth a disinherited son.(61)

Although this is what Kafka writes explicitly, it is in what is ostensibly a piece of fiction, that he reveals unconsciously his feelings towards his mother. *The Little Woman* is only one of numerous examples.

> Her objection to me, as I am now aware, is a fundamental one; nothing can remove it, not even removal of myself, if she heard that I had committed suicide she would fall into transports of rage.(162)

It is the intention of this paper to demonstrate, using the evidence provided by both Erikson and Fischer, that Gandhi's political actions where powerfully motivated by his fear of women and children. This will be undertaken by focusing on a number of events described in both biographies, in particular his relieving women of their jewels, the hair cutting incident at Tolstoy Farm and a mill strike at Ahmedabad. Aspects of Gandhi's philosophy, most notably his extreme asceticism will be used as further evidence for this claim. Finally, it will be contended that Gandhi's fear of women and children fostered in him a powerful desire to establish a new order in which he would be both mother and father to the nation, a desire which despite his protests to the contrary, culminated in what was Gandhi's unconscious ambition- the partition of India into India and Pakistan. The result of this was India symbolically representing a new child to which Gandhi could regard himself as both parents.

In order to achieve a clearer understanding of Gandhi's personality, and the political motivations which arose from it, it is useful to employ Kierkegaard's distinction between the religious, ethical and aesthetic spheres. Kierkegaard considered the three spheres to be quite separate from one another, with the religious belonging to the realm of faith, the ethical belonging to the realm of morality and law and the aesthetic as the domain of psychology under the predominance of the pleasure principle. The spheres form a hierarchy: the collapse of the religious leads to the collapse of the ethical which then results in life solely reduced to the pursuit of pleasure.

One becomes suspicious of Gandhi's religious faith,

when the fact of its over-assertion is considered. It was necessary for him to assert publicly at every turn that he was acting on the behalf of God, which suggests that because his religious faith was weak, a public avowal of it would somehow strengthen it. Furthermore, his desire to establish a new order, which will be elaborated upon later, suggests that because Gandhi himself lacked faith, his only chance of proximity to the religious lay in his assuming the status of a God with a band of devotees.

With regard to the ethical, the means Gandhi employed to achieve his ends were often dubious and manipulative, particularly in his treatment of his wife and family. (I shall return to examples later.) He must have had an awareness that much of his glory rested upon the sacrifice of others.

Thus, it may be argued that because he failed in both the religious and the ethical, his subsequent actions were motivated by his descent into the aesthetic. This manifested itself in various obsessional neuroses such as the preoccupation with cleanliness, which characterised his extreme asceticism. Gandhi did not apply his asceticism only to himself, but subtly employed whatever means necessary to coerce others to act in accordance with his own compulsions.

Jewels

One of the most striking examples of Gandhi's obsessions is the case of Gandhi relieving women of their jewels in order to raise funds for his cause. It will be argued here that Gandhi's motives for doing so in reality had very little to do with the jewels' pecuniary value but was in fact a recognition of their profound symbolic value. Jewels are worn by women as a symbol of feminine strength and power. They are worn by queens who represent the most powerful of women. As they are a female adornment, jewels also represent the temptress who will use her charms to lure a man to his downfall. There are also references in folklore to jewels in caves in which case the obvious association is of the jewels in the womb. The story of Ali Baba robbing the cave of its jewels represents an unconscious fantasy of a man robbing a woman of her strength. Finally, in the Indian context, jewellery represents concrete financial security and is given to the bride by her father, not only for adornment, but also as an asset. Thus in relieving women of their jewellery, Gandhi was removing their power, strength and security. Gandhi's use of his cause to coerce women to relinquish their jewels was in fact a case of him acting out his own unconscious fantasies on the public stage.

The way in which Gandhi did this was also particularly devious. Although Fischer writes ' He found special relish in stripping women of their jewellery' (p.289), he doesn't even consider the implications and certainly sees nothing untoward as having occurred here. Gandhi himself recounts how he taunted a ten-year-old girl into giving up her bangles. He says that he gently explained that the bangles were too heavy for her small wrists. Her grandfather then encouraged her to give the bangles to Gandhi. He then went on to say that he was embarrassed. He was only joking with the young girl, as he was wont to do, so as to create in her a distaste for ornamentation. Then because he was only joking, he tried to return the bangles. The girl's grandfather refused saying that her mother would consider it a bad omen to take the bangles back. Gandhi then agreed to take them on the condition that the girl was not to ask for new ones. The same day he addressed a ladies' meeting in the town, recounted the story of the young girl, and stripped some more women of their jewels (290).

It is extraordinary that Fischer takes Gandhi at his own word that he was merely joking with the young girl. Gandhi manipulated the event masterfully, not only relieving the young girl of her bangles, but in addition, ensuring that she would have none to replace them. His extraordinary manipulative powers are also evident in this incident as he twisted the situation in such a way that he was able to dictate the conditions under which he would take the bangles, thus making the young girl and her grandfather feel that they should be honoured that Gandhi would deign to take her bangles. The fact that Gandhi had no regard for the age of those whom he was prepared to strip of their ornaments reveals the extreme nature of his fear. It is as if by capturing the girls at a young age, he would then be able to prevent them from developing into the adult women he feared.

On another occasion in a different town, Gandhi began the address to a ladies' meeting with various criticisms of their jewellery. He expressed the opinion that they must find such heavy ornamentation oppressive and that it did nothing to add to the beauty of their person. He ended the address by remarking that the jewellery in any case could lead to disease, being a repository for dirt. Fischer then writes that Gandhi feared that he may have offended the ladies, but when he had finished speaking, many of the ladies handed him their ornaments. (Fischer, 1951:290)

The incident above is another of example of Gandhi's manipulative powers. He began the address feigning concern that the women must find their jewellery oppressive and ended it suggesting that it would cause disease. This reveals one of Gandhi's main obsessions, that of cleanliness. His association of jewels with dirt and disease suggests that he considered femininity to be dangerous and polluting.

The final episode concerning jewels to be considered here demonstrates not only Gandhi's fear of women, but also his lack of any ethical standards regarding his wife, Kasturba. On the eve of Gandhi's departure for India from South Africa he was presented with many ornaments, including a necklace for Kasturba from the Indian community. Gandhi wished to use the gifts in order to establish a community fund but realised that his wife would object. He then sent his sons to convince their mother of his plan. The sons reasoned that as they had no desire for the jewels, neither should their mother. The boys were unable to convince her and when Gandhi himself went to see her she shouted that the ornaments were to be kept. Finally she argued that if nothing else the necklace had been given specifically to her. Gandhi retorted that the necklace had been given to her for *his* labours, to which she replied that she toiled for him day and night. None of the jewels were kept. (84) Fischer's assessment of the incident is that Gandhi was justified in asserting his male authority.

Fischer condemns what he regards as the two equally primitive female desires, for security and adornment. He acknowledges no injustice towards Kasturba which suggests that his judgement may have been clouded by his own unconscious projections of his fear of women.

There is further evidence to illustrate that Gandhi harboured a fear of women. In keeping with the theme of Gandhi stripping women of the jewels is the hair cutting episode at Tolstoy farm in South Africa. The incident is recounted by both Fischer and Erikson though in very different ways.

Erikson tells the story in some detail in a chapter titled 'A Personal Word'. He quotes Gandhi's own version of his experiment of sending 'boys reputed to be mischievous and innocent young girls' to the same place to bathe together. Gandhi then questions the wisdom of expecting the children to remain innocent after this and writes that he was usually at the spring at the same time. One day it came to his attention that some of the young men had 'made fun' of two of the girls. After this he wished to 'sterilise the sinners' eyes in order to give the girls a sense of security. In the morning he 'gently suggested' that he cut off the girls' 'fine long hair'. At first the girls resisted but finally they submitted after he had convinced the older women at the farm of his plan. (Erikson, 1969:238)

The tone which predominates in Erikson's recounting of the incident is one of outrage. The section is written by Erikson in the form of a personal letter in which he accuses Gandhi of violence and intolerance towards the young girls. Erikson reproaches Gandhi for justifying his arbitrary idiosyncrasies in the name of Satyagraha- militant non-violence. Thus he demonstrates a recognition of Gandhi acting out his unconscious fantasies on the political stage. He further accuses Gandhi of setting up the scenario in the hope that 'they *would* show some of the interest which had aroused the guardian's all too hungry curiosity.' (Erikson, 1969:239). With respect to Gandhi's disregard for the feelings of the parents of tne girls, Erikson accuses Gandhi of a combination of dictatorial maternalism and paternalism. However he does not explore the implications for Gandhi's 'usurpation of motherhood' (241), a theme which will be returned to later.

Erikson in his contention that the word 'sterilise' has connotations of preventing offspring demonstrates some awareness of what cutting off the girls' hair represented. However, he writes that the cutting off of women's hair is an age-old ritual used for punishment. What Erikson does not do is explore *why* it is such an effective punishment, though he does write that it was an abortive monastic ritual.

In cutting off the girls' hair, Erikson is correct to assert that it was an act of deliberate violence, the reason being that it was yet another move by Gandhi to rob women of their strength. The symbolic value of hair as strength is represented in the story of Samson and Delilah. Samson tells Delilah that the secret of his strength lies in his hair after which she cuts it off. In women, hair is even more potent, being in addition a symbol of fertility, and an adornment. Gandhi wished not only to sterilise the eyes of the boys but to sterilise the girls so that they would present no temptation. Gandhi was stripping the women of one of their natural jewels.

Fischer's account of the episode is considerably different. He gives it only cursory attention. In response to Gandhi writing that his eyes followed the bathing girls with the eyes of a mother, Fischer suggests that the boys' eyes followed the girls also, though undoubtedly far less innocently. Thus Fischer is unquestioning of Gandhi's motives and implies that Gandhi's measure was justified. Fischer writes that although the girls were shocked at the suggestion that Gandhi cut their hair, '. . . he had an irresistible way and they finally consented. He himself did the cutting.'(137) The way in which Fischer writes the last sentence suggests that Fischer himself would liked to have done the cutting.

A final point which further illustrates the theme of Gandhi's unconscious desire to strip women of their jewels is his relentless promotion of homespun cloth. He urged the whole nation, men and women, to wear this cloth which was non-descript in colour and coarse in texture. Gandhi's official reason for this was that a restoration of the spinning wheel was essential for the maintenance of India's cultural and spiritual identity. As Erikson points out, there was some truth in this, as the weaving tradition was embedded in a system which made guild, caste and religion interdependent. (Erikson, 1969:260)

However, there were unconscious psychological motives at play. India produces fine silks and brocades in an array of beautiful colours to be worn by women. In contrast, men traditionally dress very simply in white or brown cotton. Thus Gandhi's exhortations that men and women alike dress in homespun cloth was yet another attempt by him to strip women of their adornment.

Erikson recounts the case of Saraladevi, a woman who was to become one of Gandhi's close associates. At a prayer meeting she sat down next to him on the ground. He remarked smilingly 'You will make your beautiful sari dirty.' (Erikson,1969:299) She, along with her sister and eldest daughter, is said to have worn homespun cloth ever since. Again Gandhi, managed to achieve his ends whilst maintaining an appearance of concern.

Further support for the notion that Gandhi's political actions were motivated by an unconscious fear of women and children may be drawn from one of his most well known characteristics-his asceticism. The three main manifestations of this which will be discussed here are his spartan eating habits, his obsession with cleanliness and his celibacy.

One of the most effective weapons Gandhi employed to achieve his ends was the hunger strike. His first successful use of this was in the mill strike at Ahmedabad in 1918. The leader of the mill owners, Amabalal Sarabhai, one of the first to give Gandhi generous financial support, was Gandhi's adversary in this matter. However it was Sarabhai's sister, Anasuya, who had enlisted Gandhi's support for the mill hands. The implications of Gandhi's involvement in the battle between brother and sister, which despite conflicting interests always remained respectful, will be returned to later. Throughout the strike Gandhi maintained cordial relations with Sarabhai, as Sarabhai considered the strike to be quite separate from Gandhi's nationalist activities.

The mill hands encouraged by Gandhi were striking for a 35 percent wage increase. The mill owners were adamant that they would not be granted this. Gandhi's equally strong resolve that the workers would settle for nothing less resulted in the situation of the workers becoming desperate to the point that a number of them were on the brink of starvation. Gandhi's hold on the workers began to subside and finally Gandhi undertook the first of seventeen 'fasts to the death' (Erikson,1969,p.352) It was because of Sarabhai's regard for Gandhi that he consented to the figure of 35 per cent on the condition that Gandhi would stay out of Ahmedabad labour disputes forever, '*this* time' and '*only* for you'. (Erikson, 196:353) This was unacceptable to Gandhi:

> If I had done anything of the kind, I would have felt that I was breaking my fast by swallowing something most repulsive. (Erikson, 1969:359)

Eventually an elaborate compromise designed to preserve the honour of both the owners and workers was reached.

In subsequent years Gandhi was lyrical about the virtues of fasting as a cure for an array of ailments: amongst them, constipation, anaemia, gout and depression. (Fischer, 1951:295) During what was the most serious illness of his life, acute dysentery, (he had been living on a diet of peanut butter and lemons Gandhi's own cure was to fast). His own cure failed and as his situation became desperate, the doctors advised milk. Gandhi refused on the grounds of a vow he had taken never to drink milk because of the cruel manner of milking cows and buffaloes. Elsewhere he had proclaimed milk as a 'dangerous substance.' It was his wife Kasturba who found an ingenious solution to the problem. He had not vowed not to drink goat's milk. It seems clear that the obvious maternal association with milk had some bearing on Gandhi's attitude. This was then manifested in an aversion to all intake of food. Gandhi asserted:

> The process of eating is as unclean as evacuation, the only difference being that, while evacuation ends in relief, eating, if one's tongue is not held in

> control, brings discomfort. Just as we attend to evacuation etc. in private, we should likewise perform other actions common to animals in private. (Erikson, 1969:289)

Gandhi once conducted a twenty-one day fast from which he said he lost nothing physically. Indeed he broke the fast half-an-hour later than he needed to. (Fischer, 1951:296) This brings to mind similarities between Gandhi's attitude towards food and eating and the central character in Kafka's short story *The Hunger Artist*- subtitled in a way rather applicable to Gandhi as 'The Fasting Showman'. He is a showman, sometimes stretching an arm out through the bars of his cage so that his audience may feel how thin he is. He resents the fact that he is not permitted to fast for more than forty days and feels cheated out of the fame he would get for fasting longer. The very thought of a meal gives him nausea. Of the ladies who were to take the Hunger Artist to his meal following his fast, Kafka writes: 'And he looked up into the eyes of the ladies who were apparently so friendly and in reality so cruel.'(168)

The Hunger Artist finds eating just as distasteful as Gandhi did. The artist compensates for early maternal neglect by winning the admiration of an audience for making a vocation out of his hostility toward his mother, manifested in his rejection of nourishment. The Hunger Artist is admired for fasting, something which he finds easy. The truth being, that had he found any food he liked, he would have eaten with relish. Just as Gandhi associated eating with something as profane as evacuation, and causing discomfort, the Hunger Artist found it nauseating.

On the seventh day of Gandhi's twenty-one day fast he wrote an article which furnished nine rules for fasting. Rule number five was 'Take an enema regularly during fast. You will be surprised at the impurities you will expel daily.', (Fischer, 1951:296) Gandhi wished to ensure that no pollutants would remain in his body. By fasting, nothing would enter, and anything that may have slipped through despite his precautions could be removed with an enema. There is more than a hint of paranoia in this and the plausible explanation of Gandhi's enthusiasm for the enema is its obvious abortive connotations. Since his advice was equally intended for women, it appears that Gandhi was urging women to expel the dangerous objects they harboured inside them. Not only the contents of their wombs, but ultimately the wombs themselves. In this way Gandhi could purge the nation of the two things that threatened him - women and children.

The most compelling evidence which suggests that Gandhi had a fear of children is his celibacy. He even declared 'My main object was to escape having more children.' (Fischer,1951:96) Fischer briefly explores the motives for his celibacy. He considers Kasturba's ill health and the guilt Gandhi had felt when it turned out that he had been lying in bed with his wife when his father died. However, ultimately Fischer accepts Gandhi's at his word that his renunciation of sex reinforced his passion and determination to work for the common good. (Fischer, 1951:97) It is in this aspect of Gandhi's life that Erikson's work is perhaps the most insightful. He acknowledges that Gandhi's celibacy was in part motivated by his vindictiveness towards woman as temptress and that he regarded a loss of semen as a drain on vitality. The presence of his children served Gandhi as a constant reminder of his incontinence.

Erikson also makes a somewhat speculative but not uninteresting point about Gandhi's public speaking. Usually quite an accomplished speaker, Gandhi however faltered on two occasions. Both times the theme was conception. The first time occurred when Gandhi tried to give a speech in support of a doctor who advocated birth control. Undoubtedly the only method of birth control Gandhi supported was abstinence. The second incident occurred at a party Gandhi gave at a fashionable restaurant before leaving England. He attempted to open the speech with the story of the politician Addison, who in his maiden speech in the House of Commons began with the words, 'I conceive.' He became flustered and repeated the words twice to which a colleague replied 'The gentleman has conceived thrice but has produced nothing.' The laughter however was directed at Gandhi, who could not finish the story. (Erikson, 1969:150)

Erikson provides possibly the clearest insight into Gandhi's fear of children in his recounting of a dream which Gandhi wrote in a letter to his youngest son, Devadas. In the letter, Gandhi writes that he dreamed that Devadas stole some currency notes from his safe and spent them on vice. He then writes how relieved he was upon waking to find out that it was not true. When Gandhi himself was young, he pilfered a piece of gold from his brother and spent it on vice. Thus Erikson asserts that Gandhi, himself the youngest son, associated what was worst in him with his son.(Erikson, 1969:320) The precise cause of Gandhi's fear of children is unclear. It was, however, motivated at least in part by Gandhi's projection of the basest elements of his character onto his children. In doing so he could disown anything which he found distasteful.

The final part of this paper will be devoted to an examination of the ultimate political manifestation of Gandhi's fear of women and children- the partition of India into India and Pakistan. There is evidence apart from the hair cutting incident in which Gandhi did not consult the girls' parents, which suggests Gandhi's zeal for what Erikson refers to as his usurpation of motherhood.

The death of Gandhi's father provides a telling example. His father was bedridden with a fistula and Gandhi used to massage his legs every night. Gandhi recalled he loved to do this service. (Fischer, 1951:29) One evening Gandhi wished to go to his wife's bed and his uncle relieved him of the massaging. A few minutes later a servant informed Gandhi that his father had died. He wrote of the incident forty years later:

> If passion had not blinded me, I should have been spared the torture of separation from my father during his last moments. I should have been massaging him and he would have died in my arms. But now it was my uncle who had this privilege. (Fischer, 1951:29)

The guilt suffered by Gandhi was different to that suffered by Max Weber over the death of his father. Weber, following a fierce argument with his father threw him out of his house. This was the last Weber saw of his father who died a few months later. Weber then suffered a breakdown from which it took him twenty years to recover. (Carroll, 1985) Gandhi's problem was not one of Oedipal guilt, but that he failed to perform what was in essence maternal service to his father. The incident suggests that it was Gandhi's desire to be a mother, and not a son to his father.

Further evidence of Gandhi's desire to usurp the role of motherhood is in his assertion regarding the children at Tolstoy Farm. He said that the young folks knew he loved them with a 'mother's love'.(Fischer, 1951:137) Of the episode where he sent the young boys and girls to bathe together he wrote—'My eyes followed the girls as a mother's eyes follows a daughter.' (Fischer, 1951:137)

Finally there is Gandhi's renaming of Untouchables, the lowest of Hindu castes, as Harijans, meaning literally, 'children of God'. The appellation is suggestive of a desire on Gandhi's part to remove their parents and for him to acquire their parenthood.

That it was children of God also appears not to be accidental. Just as Christ demanded that his disciples be prepared to hate mother, father and all kin if they were to follow him, (Luke 14:26), Gandhi wrote to a lapsed follower:

> Your duty lay in honouring it, even if your entire family were to starve in consequence. Only persons of that stamp can mould a nation. Others are just not to be reckoned as men. (Erikson, 1969:318)

Thus Gandhi regarded familial loyalties as subordinate to his cause. This is also evident in his absorption in the mill strike. Gandhi did not see anything untoward in his involvement in a conflict involving brother and sister. Indeed, he appeared to thrive on the testing of loyalties by creation of the division.

Conclusion

The final division created by Gandhi was the division of India into India and Pakistan. Despite Gandhi's protests to the contrary, the only outcome of India's independence from Britain could be its division. Thus Gandhi achieved the ultimate division- that of the nation. In doing so, symbolically he created a new child- one that would not pose a threat to him. To this child of his creation he was both mother and father. It is therefore ironic that Gandhi's assassin was a Hindu. The child to which Gandhi's political endeavours were devoted creating murdered him. This does appear to suggest that perhaps Gandhi's fears regarding children *were* justified.

References

Carroll, John, *Guilt*, London, Routledge & Kegan Paul, 1980.

Edel, Leon, *Writing Lives: Principa Biographica*, New York, Norton, 1984.

Erikson, Erik, *Gandhi's Truth*, New York, Norton, 1969.

Falk, Avner, 'Aspects of Political Psychobiography' *Political Psychology*, Vol 6, No. 4, 1985.

Fischer, Louis, *The Life of Mahatma Gandhi*, Great Britain, Jonathon Cape Ltd., 1951.

Geertz, Clifford, 'Gandhi: Non Violence as Therapy', *New York Review of Books*, November 20, 1969.

Kafka, Franz, *Wedding Preparations in the Country and Other Stories*, Harmondsworth, Penguin, 1978.

Kierkegaard, Soren, *Fear and Trembling*, Princeton, Princeton University Press, 1983.

Lasch, Christopher, 'Gandhi's Truth', *The New York Times Book Review*, September 14, 1969.

Identifications, Gender and Racial Difference: Moving Beyond the Limits of a Psychoanalytical Account of Subjectivity

Sara Ahmed

The question of subjectivity has become significant precisely at the moment when it is in crisis, where available conceptions of the subject seem inadequate to explain the complications of identity that structure everyday negotiations in this so-called postmodern, late capitalist and multi-cultural world. This crisis seems to mark out or signal the overwhelming dominance of psychanalysis in recent Western critical theory in a double sense: firstly, the crisis of the Cartesian subject is already announced by the arrival of psychoanalysis and the 'discovery' of the unconscious, and secondly, a crisis that returns to psychoanalysis in the form of its apparent complicity in failing to deal with the problematic of the subject within the uncertainly of historical contexts. A feminist reading may want to remind psychoanalysis of a blurring that troubles the notion of the passage of the subject into being, regardless of whether psychoanalysis is itself a theory of the difficulty, or indeed the impossibility, of that passage being fully or successfully resolved. A feminist reading, rather than simply suggesting that the singular passage of the subject into being cannot take place in any ideal sense, may rather dispute the very singularity of the terms in which the problematic of the subject is originally framed. The subject *as such* may not be a question for feminism, as the subject of feminism seems inseparable from the issues of cultural location, gender and, in my interpretation, race and ethnicity. The unavailability of 'a subject' abstracted from points of implication in historicaly forged power relations, is precisely from where a feminist critique may proceed.

What I want to address in this paper is the way in which this troubling of the frames in which certain psychoanalytically derived questions of subjectivity takes place within a feminist and anti-racist reading. Here, such a reading will inhabit and displace the terms of psychoanalysis in order to conceptualise subject identifications which deal with the complications and intersections of regimes of sexual and racial difference. Psychoanalysis will be displaced by an 'interior' reading which locates points of contraction within its own terms, and by being brought into collision with the pragmatic and historicist demands of a feminist and anti-racist politics of reading. I will proceed by discussing identification as it operates within Lacan and Althusser, and then by reading from an auto-biographical example which involved a confrontation between the police and myself in Adelaide, 1984. Auto-biographical modes of writing may help convey how the construction and stabilisation of the "I" (the phantasy of identity) cannot fully abolish the distance or otherness that haunts the "I", rendering impossible any realisation of a proper or true identity. Auto-biography does not function to halt the narrative in the "truth" or "real" of the subject which writes or speaks it. Rather, the (re)turn of the narrative to the "I" may function precisely to convey its rhetorical limits, by providing a "brake on rhetorical spinning" (Miller, 1991, xiii). These limits-partially understood in terms of the opening out of an-other which is repudiated in the construction of an "I"-will be associated here with the absent signifiers in may personalised narrative: "Pakistan" and "Black Woman".

Now, it seems to me that one of the great values of feminist research and methodology is the awareness of self-reflexivity as a problem which has potential for theory itself. Through the impact of various kinds of feminist theory, we have been made aware that the 'I' as such cannot be escaped or avoided, but neither can it be simply located to stabilise any text or to guarantee its meaning.[1] The feminist 'I' may be simultaneously *there* and *opaque*, at once declared through a politics of location, as it is complicated *vis a vis* the very complications of location. In keeping with this tradition within feminist research, I feel that is important to locate my own position to the extent that this is possible, and to remind others that this does not render me either a representative, insofar as I cannot speak for (or on behalf of) others.

I am a product of a 'mixed race' marriage, and an immigrant to Australia from England where I was born in 1969. My father, who is from Lahore, Pakistan, lost much of his own cultural heritage when marrying my English mother: he did quite literally marry (into) the West. So although as a young person I was very aware of not being white, not being like 'the others', I was never aware of actually what I might be, never able to positively address what my difference really was. I was not simply in between identities, for my upbringing was 'fully Western' (although infrequent trips to Pakistan did effect my own sense of another culture being there, it simply wasn't there *for* me). Rather, the presence of my father and the colour of my skin was there as a constant reminder that I didn't fully belong to the only cultural identity that I was really aware existed.

I do not want, of course, to extrapolate wildly from my own personal experiences. However much knowledge and experience are implicated in each other (in the very impossibility of detaching the subject from the cognitive process) I do not think experience can or should be given the status of a ground or foundation which would act as a guarantee or authority for any writing or speech. I re-present myself here merely for the purposes of defining what or whom I *cannot* speak for: I cannot speak for either white European women, or for South Asian women, or, really for any particular or clearly demarcated group of women at all. But perhaps my inability to speak on behalf of any group of women may not be an *exception* of biography or place, but a *trace of a dynamic that troubles the very intersection of race and gender in structures of identification.*

It will be this *symptomatic nature of the failure of my own person address* that my passage into psychoanalysis will attempt to explore: the way in which the impossibility of adequately naming myself for the demands of representation is symptomatic of the impossibility of the racially marked and gendered subject being addressed through a singular name.[2]

1. Theorising the Limits of A Psychoanalytical Model of Identification

The child's accession into the realm of subjectivity within Lacanian psychoanalysis in predicated on a structure of identification. In Lacan's 'The Mirror Stage as Formative of the Function of the I', the child sees itself in the mirror, and misrecognizes the images as itself.[3] This act 'rebounds in the case of the child in a series of gestures in which he experiences in play the relation between the movements assumed in the image and the reflected environment — the child's own body, and the persons and things' (1977, 1). This play with an image structures the relation of the child to its body and to others, in the form of an identification, that is, in 'the transformation that takes place in the subject when he assumes an image' (1977, 2). Such an identification is imaginary and phantasmatic, projecting from the fragmentation of the bodily state a specular and Ideal-I, understood as the agency of the ego (1977, 2).

The importance and value of the Lacanian notion of the mirror stage, is precisely that it 'leads us to oppose any philosophy directly issuing from the *Cogito* ' — 'I think therefore I am' (1977, 1). The unity and Ideality of the I is a misrecognition which, while structuring the relation of the I to others (in the forms of the projection of the ego onto others), conceals the lack that inflects its own coming into being, returning to disrupt the self-presence of the imago in the discordance and alienation of the fractured body. The notion of misrecognition helps us to investigate the passage of the subject into an identity as entailing phantasy, projection and the concealment of otherness, in the irreducibility of the body to its specular imago. As Lacan summarises:

> The *mirror stage* is a drama whose internal thrust is precipitated from insufficiency to anticipation —and which manufactures for the subject, caught up in the lure of spatialidentification, the succession of phantasies that extends from a fragmented body-image to a form of its totality that I shall call orthopaedic — and, lastly, to the assumption of the armour of an alienating identity, which will mark with its rigid structure the subject's entire mental development. (1977, 4).

Identification hence performs the fundamental split that structures the subject's relation to language, whereby the 'I' which is the subject of an enunciation is divided from the 'I' who speaks. The split constitutes the emergence of the unconscious. The disruption of the *Cogito* is, indeed, centrally performed through the formulation of a theory of the unconscious. Shoshana Felman provides us with an excellent reading of the unconscious as determined by Lacan's rereading of Freud:

> The unconscious is henceforth no longer as it has been traditionally conceived — the simple outside of the conscious, but rather a division, *Spaltung* , cleft within consciousness itself; the unconscious is no longer the difference between consciousness and the unconscious, but rather the inherent, irreducible difference between consciousness and itself. (1987, 57).

The problem with the notion of 'having an unconscious' is precisely, the implication that it is a place, and in this sense, a totality, a supplementing identity to the conscious self, but an identity nevertheless. Lacan in contrast argues in 'The Agency of the Letter in the Unconscious' that the unconscious is structured like a language which, of course, begs the question of what he means by language. Lacan explicitly defines the limits of Saussure's model of language as the limits of the sign, understood as 'the illusion that the signifier answers to the function of representing the signified' (1977, 150) — leading to a linear and closed model. He elaborates: 'There is no effect in the signifying chain that does not have, as if attached to the punctuation of it units, *a whole articulation of contexts* suspended 'vertically', as it were, from that point' (1977, 154, emphasis mine). Here, the polyphonic nature of the agency of the signifier, which is inseparable from, if irreducible to, the contexts which surround it (both linguistic and otherwise), can be read in terms of the function of metaphor or condensation and metonymy or displacement (1977, 157-8). it is this agency of the letter which Freud' called his discovery of the unconscious' (1977, 159).

To say that the unconscious is structured like a language in the Lacanian schema, is to outline the function of the linguistic process of condensation and displacement as the dynamics of desire, whereby the contextualized play of the signifier prevents the fixing of meaning (or the signified) as presence, and the subject as self-presence. The sliding of the signifier divides the moment of interiority that invests the Cartesian subject with self-mastery and mastery over others (both the other in transference or inter-relations, as well as the Other). Meaning is not where it is literally supposed, but remains elsewhere, not in a singular place or repository, but in the divisions and relations of language, and the instability of the desire for presence it necessarily deflects as lack of being.

It may be on the issue of the relation between Lacan's theory of language and his theory of subjectivity or desire that our reading may expose certain problems. Jean Luc Nancy and Phillipe Lacoue-Labarthe in *The Title of the Letter: A Reading of Lacan* examine the way in which the logic of the signifiers *settles* into a theory of the subject. They argue that, if the subject is simply 'the locus of the signifier' then it follows literally that it is in 'a theory of the subject that the logic of the signifier settles' (1992, 65). Indeed, Lacan's very definition of the signifier as 'that which represents a subject for another signifier' seems to presuppose the there-ness of the subject, as that what the signifier represents, and as unable to represent anything but for another signifier. The subject is instituted then, in and by a signifier. This returns the theory of the letter to a theory of the subject, coming into a full circle, *in which the maintenance of the name 'subject' stops the letter on its travels.* Nancy and Lacoue-Labarthe argue that the return of the letter to the subject reinstates a metaphysics of the subject — albeit a negative one. The subject is de-centered, disrupted and subverted *but only through the pre-supposition that the letter returns to it in the first place.*[4]

What Nancy and Lacoue-Labarthe's philosophical and deconstructive reading of Lacan may serve to reveal, is perhaps not simply the metaphysics which may pervade the Lacanian narrative, but also the irreducibility of the gap between the theory of the signifier and the theory of the subject (and its desire). This irreducibility may be decisive upon considering the role or dynamics of desire. Returning to the axis of metonymy, it can be noted that the shift from signifier to signifier with its contiguity and fluidity, renders that the signified is constantly deferred, is always already lacking. Lacan locates the axis of metonymy as one of desire. Indeed, 'The Agency of the Letter in the Unconscious' ends by declaring 'desire *is* a metonymy, however funny people may find the idea' (1977, 175). The linguistic trope of metonymy becomes reducible to the dynamic of the subject's desire, *vis a vis* an analogy: both shift from signifier to signifier without halting that signifier into a signified or object. But I think their relation is stronger than mere likeness. In the Lacanian narrative, desire and metonymy form an identity, it is a copula which divides them (desire is metonymy). What divides metonymy and desire is, then, a metaphor, word-for-word, and as such a symptom (1977, 175). The division between metonymy and desire, between the theory of subjectivity as the axis of desire and the theory of language as the axis of metonymic, meets its limit precisely through metaphor, through the substitutions of language which are symptomatic of the bar that frustrates the realization of the identification forged between the subject and signifier.

By focusing on the division that prevents Lacan's narrative being instituted into Law as the foundation of a 'true' theory of subjectivity, my reading may dislodge its apparent role as Master (of the other), which has frustrated the possibility that psychoanalysis could deal with the demands and concerns of a feminist and anti-racist politics. The Lacanian narrative is structured by its own suturing operation, in which the gap between its theory of the signifier and its model of the subject and of desire, is covered over through a metaphoric elision. This does not lead us to reject the text, although perhaps it helps us to question its status as Law or as a universal theory. Rather, an analysis of the gaps and divisions which structure Lacanian psychoanalysis may enable us to renegotiate its movements as a textual and performative operation which is governed by certain limits.

If, as we have discovered, the Lacanian narrative settles into the singularity of the signifier of the subject, then we can establish the limits of identification as defined in 'The Mirror Phase'. For here, the act of the child seeing itself in the mirror and misrecognizing the image as itself is a singular process, however much that act is taken figuratively to signify that which structures the impossibility of 'becoming' a subject, in the sense of *being* an image. What is the significance of a theory which takes its *figure* of subjectivity in such a singular act? I use 'figured' here deliberately. I am not claiming that this figuring exhausts the terms of psychoanalysis (which complicates the discreteness of the subject again and again) but rather that the reliance on the 'mirror phase' and the figure of the child's encounter and projection of an image, is over-determined by the status of the subject as *signifier*. In this sense, the narrative reliance on the figure enables the return of the letter to the subject whose singularity as signifier is already assured (the complication of identification is hence contained by the outlines established by this metaphoric reliance). That *figure* is certainly associated with the whole question of the *nature* of the subject, for the child's misrecognition of its image which comes to *stand for* 'the assumption of an alienating identity, which will mark with its rigid structure the child's entire mental development' (1977, 4). Is this very metaphoric reliance that situates the psychoanalytical refusal of a complication of the discreteness of the signifier 'subject' by markings such as colour, ethnicity and even, ironicaly, sex? The limitations of the Lacanian model which sutures the divisions it recognizes in the relations of language and the unconscious by centering on the subject (and its lack) may establish the limitations of a theory of identification itself, which can no longer be *figured* in terms of a singular (visual or otherwise) encounter with an image.

To shift towards a model which differentiates between various structures of identification according to regimes such as gender and race, I will discuss briefly Althusser's Marxist appropriation of Lacan's concept of misrecognition. Althusser writes:

> idealogy 'acts' or 'functions' in such a way that it 'recruits' subjects among the individuals (it recruits them all), or 'transforms' the individuals into subjects (it transforms them all) by that very precise operation which I have called interpellation or hailing, and which can be imagined along the lines of the most commonplace everyday police (or other) hailing: 'Hey, you there!' (1971, 162-3)

Althusser argues that the individual's 'recognition' that he or she is being addressed, represents the point of entrance into subjectivity, and perhaps, into the authority of Law, where the potential for the subject to be *suspected* is inscribed by the possibility that the police is hailing. This links accession into subjectivity with the maintenance of a system of prohibitions and regulations. I want to stress two issues raised by Althusser's thesis that are often neglected. Firstly, the act of interpellation is a relation between subjects (or, to be more precise, the act of becoming a subject involves a relationship with another — equally imaginary — subject whose speech authorises this instant of becoming). It entails an addresser and addressee: it is necessarily inter-subjective. This clearly takes us away from the implications of the Lacanian narrative or metaphor whereby identification names the process of a subject's relation to itself - in the form of a projection of itself (or its lack of self) onto an image. Secondly, Althusser argues that hailing hardly ever misses its mark, 'the one hailed always recognizes that it is really him who is being hailed' (1971, 163). We may need to rethink the implications of *the structural possibility that hailing may miss its mark* , and that the subject, sexed or otherwise, may think he or she is being hailed or addressed (when they are not) or think they are not being hailed or addressed (when they are). This may suggest that the process of becoming a subject is more fractured and potentially unsuccessful than Athusser's schema may seem on the surface to suggest, and that this fracturing and failure is a way of theorising differences between subject identifications, according to regimes such as gender and race.[5]

Rather then locating the difficulties of 'becoming' a subject in the discordance between the fragmented body and the specular imago, this approach may investigate how specific structures of address (including signifiers such as names, as well as the metonymic association between names and values) fail to grasp or fix their object. I will discuss the way in which the subject is identified (and hence stabilised) by structures of address whose values are partially fixed in the very process of systematization.[6] This inter-subjective structure of address is hence stabilised by its location within institutional limits that assign or partially fix meanings to signifiers and subjects (in the form of power relations). But I will also focus on the way in which that identification does not fully or adequately name the subject, or divides the subject by naming it in contradictory and conflicting ways. The excess of the names for the subject as signifier is one way of re-introducing a notion of the contingency of the signifiers as the dynamic of the unconscious, without pre-supposing the subject as lack.

Given this, the subject as such is never the subject as such, because its point of excess to the very name or signifier of 'the subject' locates it precisely as marked or named by colliding regimes of address which attach (asymmetrical) value and meaning to specific subject positions. A feminist and anti-racist reading also exposes the phantasmatic nature of identifications and their consequent implication in otherness.[7] But such a reading would necessarily pluralise forms of identification to include 'woman', 'man', 'black', 'white'. Importantly, this does not simply *add on* certain features to the Lacanian subject, supplementing its singularity.[8] For the act of pluralising the subject necessarily divides it, dividing what is already the subject of division, so it is no longer even nameable in, or through, this singular signifier.

2. An Alternative and Auto-Biographical Reading of Identification

I want here to discuss an auto-biographical example as a text which negotiates these various structures of identification. This example relates back to an incident when I was 14 years old, walking around the streets of Adelaide without any shoes on (I was in a 'scruffy' phase). I was stopped and addressed by two policemen in a car. They called me over, asked me what I was doing (I said I was walking) and then asked me why I wasn't wearing shoes (I can't remember my reply, but I was indignant about my rights). The policeman closest to me asked me if I was Aboriginal. Again I was indignant, replying 'no'. The other policeman interrupted, gave me a wink, and said 'it's a sun tan, isn't it?' I smiled, but did not reply. They asked me where I lived and I told them, and mentioned which school I went to (a private girl's school). They said that was fine, but to wear shoes. I asked them why they stopped me. They said there had been some break-ins in the area recently, and that they were checking it out. When I arrived home and told my mother and sister, my sister suggested that if I lost weight I wouldn't be 'suspected' of being an Aboriginal. Needless to say, this incident ended in tears, and left me angry and resistant.[9]

Looking back, there were a number of complex identifications and dis-identifications going on, often unconscious, in the sense of forming contexts that were not obvious at the time, or upon a literal reading of the event. I will read the event chronologically, and in the next section, re-interpret my own reading for its sets of narrative investments and elisions that may give us further insight into the concept of auto-biography and the construction of the gendered and racially marked subject.

It seems to me now that the policemen addressed me, in the first instance, as working class (from dress), and Aboriginal (from colour). This identification *read* me as a subject, *by rendering me a suspect* , as a danger to the Law (of property), a potential robber. Here, the absence of shoes becomes fetishized as an object which signifies not simply a lack of proper dress, but an improper status as somebody who does not belong to this middle class and respectable suburb, somebody whose presence can only have the function and effect of a threat. Indeed, the address shifts immediately from the absence of shoes to a query about race. The address of the policemen in the first instance, their positioning of me as a suspect, somebody to be queried and interrogated, was on the mistaken assumption I was Aboriginal. Their question demanded to know the extent of my threat by demanding to know whether my racial origin was Aboriginal. In this sense, Aboriginality becomes figured as the most threatening or disruptive presence. But the error of their address gave me a space to address them, through denial and disavowal.

To returning their address a shift occurred which forced a dis-identification from my identity as suspect. Not an Aboriginal (but perhaps only sun tanned), not working class (in fact quite well off). My denial of being Aboriginal and my failure to name or declare my race (which of course was unnoticed or invisible to them) implicated me in their structure of address, by rendering Aborginality something to be disavowed. The gesture of smiling can here be figured as a collusion, a desire in some sense to be figured as white, as respectable, as somebody who has a legitimate right to walk in these leafy suburbs. My disavowal thus suggests an implicit desire for 'whiteness'. That desire creates an imaginary (and impossible) conception of a purified and ideal self, as well as a coherent social order (to which I could 'fit in'), by assigning certain values to 'whiteness'. Such an assignment entails a disavowal and repudiation of the other, of 'blackness', or Aboriginality. As such, desire itself projects an imaginary presence through a process of exclusion. The temporality of the act of disavowal stages the impossibility of desire's fulfilment generally, but also the racialist logic that demands the purification of colour, as a reminder of an-other that refuses to inhabit these terms and returns (to walk the streets) only as a threat.[10]

This disavowal was also structured by a class dynamic whereby legitimacy was restored to my presence through naming my school (a private girl's school). This information was not asked for - but projected by me onto them as a sign that I was 'with them', that they were policing for me, rather than against me, as an owner rather than a taker of property. The disavowal and repudiation of Aboriginality hence structured a desire to be taken as inhabiting the policing demand, as somebody worthy of protection, as white and middle class: a tax payer not dole bludger or a waster.

The structure of identification which involved the exchange of a wink and the quip about being sun tanned caused me the most discomfort. Although inspired by my dis-identification as Aboriginal (which was implicated in the assigning of certain values to Aboriginality, as something to be disavowed) and my refusal to identify my race, this quip both made light of their mistake (their hailing of the wrong person, their error of reading) while positioning me as woman, a recipient of a wink (and of a gaze), and as someone who sun bathes, who tans her body. The entrance of the body into the exchange, while apparently undoing the identifications of race and class, shifted me from being suspect to object, from a threat to property, to property itself. While defining the body in terms of leisure, where colour is a sign of a 'higher' class, the quip shifted my attention from the social relation of policeman to suspect, to the sexual relation of man to woman. The colour of my body was evoked as an adornment rather than a stain, as 'a paying attention to the body', in the form of the sexualization of colour. Here, colour is literally a detachable signifier, inessential to the subject, and hence acceptable. By rendering colour inessential rather than essential, the exchange rendered by body something to be valued, adorned, protected. Colour becomes inscribed as a detachable signifier, positioned me as essentailly white, as truly and properly white underneath the luxury of a brown veil. Inscribed as a white woman I was the legitimate object of the policeman's protective gaze.

I dealt with the uncertainty and anxiety over my body and colour by addressing the policeman, in the structure of a demand: a demand that they explained their presence, their interruption of my walk. That demand, gave me a point of entry into identifying them as racist (although, of course, I would not have been able to return their address in the form of a demand unless I'd already dis-identified myself as Aboriginal, as I would not have had the inscribed agency to speak lawfully, to speak with legitimacy). Their explanation linked their project (fighting street crime) to their identification of me as Aboriginal, which made me a suspect. Through identifying the racism that constituted their identification, I withdrew from the situation very angry, and ashamed that I had disavowed being Aboriginal, and had so been implicated in a structure of racial identification which (despite my own desire for whiteness and legitimacy) I sensed was wrong. By returning their address in the structure of a demand, I hence read the policemen and assigned them to a place in my own self-identification as non-white and non-racist.

It was this role in identification (which I still think made its mark) that, when walking away from the police car, shifted me from the anxiety over my sex and body, to a sense of being a subject. That sense, again, was only to be shattered by my sister's evocation of 'fatness' as a sign of Aboriginality and hence of error. Read/the text implicit here: laziness, indulgence, excess. Fatness not only inscribes certain negative values to Aboriginality it also positions me as a woman who has failed, who has failed to police and discipline her body into acceptable 'feminine' contours. Within this structure of address the fat woman is (like) an Aboriginal, in excess of the norms and values inscribed by a proper social and sexual order. Again, identified in this way, I was returned to a feeling of anger, to not being a (legitimate) subject.

What this example may evoke is the complexity of the identification process. The very temporality of identifications renders not only that they can miss its mark, but that always already does miss its mark, by enacting the divisions that frustrate the identification of the subject by a singular name. The over-lapping of the issues of race and gender in this 'recalled event', suggests that the relation of power to identification is constitutive but divisive, where the position of the subject is perpetually assigned and threatened by their designation in related, but distinct, regimes of difference. The relation between the social relation of law to subject (who may be suspect, who may be black), and the sexual relation of man to woman is, here, over-determined. My identification as a woman, and as a recipient to both a quip and a wink produced my identity as property, returning my attention to my body, while evoking the body as already sexed, as adorned. That identity was always already threatened by the potential to return the address in the form of both denial and demand. The constant negotiation of identifications temporarily assign the subject to a fixed identity (both racial, class and gendered) which are open to contestation in the negotiation of everyday encounters with the Law, family and others.

3. Colliding and Dividing Race and Gender

This auto-biographical account is necessarily a reading and interpretation which, in recalling an event, constructs it, excluding certain details as it attends to others. The constructive nature of an auto-biography is one way of theorising the way in which the subject is temporarily and partially fixed through the very discourses on the subject: discourses which decide what and who counts as legitimate, as legitimate subjects for a subject. Auto-biography may itself be a process of phantasmatic identification which locates its subject, only to find that subject already other to its own frames. But the question of an auto-biography may have particular pertinence for women, especially coloured and black women, given the way in which traditional auto-biography has been constructed around individualism, around the heroic identity of the individual agent. As Susan Freedman puts it, ' The emphasis on individualism as the necessary pre-condition for auto-biography is thus a reflection of the privilege, one that excludes from the canon of auto-biography those that have been denied by history the illusion of individualism' (1988, 35). Given that the individual has been constructed around a masculine set of experiential limits (see Pateman, 1989, 223), strange things may happen when women, especially black women, write auto-biographically. In light of this, I want here to return to my reading of this event (while maintaining a distance from it, hence the change of an 'I' into 'the subject', a distance from the 'I' which is of course already marked by the event of writing), before I make some tentative gestures towards theorising the inter-relation of gender and racial differences.

How then do race and gender intersect in my interpretation? Firstly, it can be pointed out that the shift in the interpretation was from a racial identification and dis-identification to a sexual identification. This entailed a temporal shift from a disavowal of Aboriginality by the subject, to being positioned as a white woman whose colour was an adornment and therefore sexual. Such a shift was organized by a desire for whiteness, a desire to be the recipient of an admiring rather than defiling gaze. Desire *constructed* this slippage from race to sex. This slippage takes place both at the level of event and at the level of narrative. The narrative, that is, accepts the terms of the explicit police interrogation with its shift from race to sex. It does not complicate that interrogation by opening up how the address concerning race suspends the question of sex only temporarily and partially: indeed, it actively keeps race and sex as forms of address apart.[11] The query about racial origin does not abolish the implication of the original gaze in a sexual regime that found (finds) the subject walking the street. The hailing and address of the policeman was surely then an address to an Aboriginal woman.

What happens to this narrative, if we complicate the scene and assume that sex and race collide (at least unconsciously) right from the start? For the original act of hailing situated the subject as suspect and threat, and so positions the subject's sexuality as well as race as suspect and threatening. A white woman walking the streets is a potential victim, requiring a protective gaze. Is this to say that the Aboriginal woman inscribed here is positioned differentially in relation to male violence: that her threat to the harmony of the suburb is precisely the threat of a sex which is uncontained by the proper social and racial order? Theorist such as Jan Pettman in Living in the Margins have argued the Aboriginal woman is always already sexualised in White Australian colonial narratives (Pettman 1992, 27). So if the original address (are you an Aboriginal?) positioned my colour as a stain, as a sign of a natural criminality determined by the fact of my skin, then how does this criminalisation of colour link with the gendering of the address? It may suggest that the Black woman is defined in terms of the physicality of her skin, as a stain which confirms her over-sexed being, her threat to the proper social and sexual order of the domesticated suburb. She is constructed in this sense as a social and sexual danger. Such a reading connects with Vron Ware's work in *Beyond the Pale* . Here, she discusses the way in which vulnerability is both sexed as woman, and racially marked as white: such that the dominant media construction of sexual violence is 'a white woman threatened by the aggression of black men' (1992,7). This leaves the black woman hanging precariously in the site of a division, where the 'vulnerability' of her sex is divided from the threat to the sexual relation already imposed by the strength of her colour. This also connects with Abena P. A. Busia's work on the way in which the black woman is constructed as *morally unrapable* , as lacking the appropriate feminine virtues which would make the concept of race and violation make sense (1993, 228). The position of black women in relation to sexual violence is hence differential and divided: at once a site of violence, they are also removed from the conceptualization of woman as victim. The collision of race and sex in the original act of hailing (however absent from the surface of both event and text) is one that positions the black woman as a symptom (with a doubling of cause and effect) of the sexual threat of blackness. Needless to say, if it was a 'Aboriginal' man that had been hailed in this scene, the threat to the proper order of the suburb may have been perceived differently, and the address may have been less a question (are you Aboriginal, are you a threat) than a demand.

But the slippage whereby the subject became inscribed

as a white woman prevented a meeting or collision of the regimes of race and sex at a conscious level, where the subject would have been addressed as 'a black woman'. The black woman (whether Aboriginal or Asian)[12] is an absent signifier in this narrative, which can explicitly address the subject as woman only by disavowing her colour, or sexualizing her colour in the reception of a gaze. The possibility of the inscriptions colliding is negated by the structure of her desire, which temporarily resolved the trauma of otherness through acts and gestures of collusion.

The absence of the signifier of 'black woman' (where 'black' and 'woman' are separated by a telling gap, an unspeakable blank space) is also already the absence of the figure of Pakistan, the unacknowledged invisible trace of a racial otherness. The refusal to name Pakistan in her desire to be inscribed as white enabled the signifiers of colour and sex to stay apart, leading from one stable identification to another: from the violence to exclusion to a violence of inclusion. The signifier 'Pakistan' however cannot in itself be excluded. The desire to keep Pakistan out rendered that Pakistan was always there in the violence of her own identification, her hailing of herself as white. The return of Pakistan, as the return of the other, in her recognition and refusal of the policemen's racialist regime splits the narrative: at once desiring whiteness and legitimacy, and yet also refusing the terms and violence of the laws that govern the equation between white and legitimate. Pakistan was to return as a structure of feeling, in guilt and anger, as a rem(a)inder, a point of excess, that prevented the subject taking on or 'fully assuming' the place and position of a white woman. In some sense it is Pakistan and her own self-identification as a non-white woman, a black woman, that has led me here to write this paper, to write this event, to refuse its gestures, to refuse the names that have circulated and caught her in the violence of their repudiation.

Forcing a collision then between the signifiers of woman and black within the context of the narrative may be to enact a radical de-stabilization of its terms. The contradiction between the sexual and racial inscriptions, between being positioned simultaneously as a threat to the proper *and* as property, is enacted in the profound ambivalence of the signifier and position 'black woman'. Brought together these signifiers are at once inside and outside, marking woman both as adorned and as stained by colour, as gazed and objectified in an act of both defilement and protection. Although it is not the case that a white woman is simply included, for to be the object or property of a gaze, is surely to be made other to the rational economy of 'looking' upon which so much of Western culture is predicated. But the position of woman is never free from an implication in a racial logic, and a woman is gazed or addressed in ways that already position her as racially unmarked or marked, and so value (or devalue) her in differential ways. The violence of the absence of the black woman, as a signifier in this own narrative re-enacts the violence of her otherness, her invisibility in dominant narratives of both sexuality and race.[13] The violence that takes place when colour meets woman in the peculiarity of its many manifestations and contexts can only be remembered here in what the narrative itself forgot, the name that it refused to name.

This notion of a double otherness represented by an absence in narrative may repeat Gayatgri Spivak's notion of the doubly muted subaltern woman, whose silence a post-colonial feminism must learn to speak to (1988, 287). This woman is not subsumable under a postmodern 'figure' of woman as a name for otherness. The collision with race or colour halts the event of figuring and the singularity it shapes through the re-tracing of a signifier. This parallel may be especially interesting in light of Benita Parry's critique of Spivak for over-estimating the silencing of the subaltern woman and hence writes out evidence of the 'native agency' recorded in India's 200 year struggle against British conquest (1987, 35). Parry writes: 'since the native woman is constructed within multiple social relationships and positioned as the product of different class, casts and cultural specificities it should be possible to locate traces and testimony of women's voices, those sites where women inscribed as healers, ascetics, singers of the sacred songs, artizans and artists, and by this modify Spivak's model of the silent subaltern' (1987, 35).[14]

I cite these two theorists as they help convey the important tension and doubleness that a theory of a sexed and racially marked subjectivity carries with it. Like Spivak, my reading has shown the way in which the coloured or subaltern woman is doubly silenced by the structures of racial and sexual identification which divide her both as threat and victim. Her name becomes a site of division and collision, whereby the contradictions in gaze and address leave her inarticulate. But my reading has also exposed that, by being irreducible to, and in excess of, these structures of address, this woman who is not a figure, or one figure, may radically undermine and re-negotiate her silencing. That woman, at least metaphorically, may write back, by opening out the signifiers from their contexts, dividing subjects from the phantasy of an 'I', opening out an otherness whose repudiation is impossible. That otherness is not the glorious space of a postmodern heterogeneity as it is necessarily a relation implicated in violence: it exists only in relation to the structures of address which violates her with a name, and is hence de-limited, bound and marked by a system of violence which is far from heterogeneous. But this otherness may open out the very process of *dis-identification* determined by a (necessarily) auto-biographical gesture of a feminist and anti-racist politics of reading. Such an auto-biographical dis-identification occupies the sites of division and absence in its own narrativization of sexual and racial difference.

This model I am tentatively offering here, in which the phantasmatic nature of identifications are perpetually re-negotiated in an inter-subjective context, entailing the temporary fixing of values to sliding signifiers (such as colour, Aboriginality, woman, class), both pre-supposes and displaces the narratives offered by Lacanian psychoanalysis. This model of identifying subjects assumes, following Lacan, that identity is phantasmatic and perpetually under threat by the sliding of signifiers along vertical plains, enacting the division and the repression which institutes the unconscious elements of subjectivity. But it displaces the Lacanian theory of the subject as locus of the signifier, by arguing that the process of identification and dis-identification is one of division between as well as within structures of address. My model does not suture the gap between language and the subject: the status of the subject as signifier may, in itself, become *suspect* . The model of phantasmatic identifications which temporarily assigns the subject as sexed and racially marked, but is threatened by the divisions and contexts which structure the collision of these identifications, is hence not simply psychoanalytical. Rather, it situates the specificity of a feminist and anti-racist politics of reading for the complications of sexual and racial differences. These complications open out the double othering of the black woman as an absence which returns to narrative, and which shifts and expands its terms, allowing for the very dis-identification entailed by the (auto-biographical) politics of anti-sexism and anti-racism.

Notes

1. Such feminisms reminds us that 'universal' knowledge is in fact located within a masculine set of experiential limits. Dorothy Smith examines the way in which the conceptual modes of sociology are organized by a 'male universal universe' (1987, 86), Susan Bordo discusses the way in which knowledge is always located and suggests postmodernism entails a fantasy of escape from the limits of embodied location (1990, 136), Catherine Mackinnon examines the way in which the 'universal' perspective assumed by traditional jurisprudence represents a male investment suggesting the importance of situation to a feminist methodology (1983, 636), Nancy Holland looks at the way in which philosophy itself has been defined through a male perspective on personhood, leading to the importance of conceptualizing experience within philosophy (1990, 4) and, within the context of post-colonial feminism, Rajeswari Suder Rajan reminds us that location is not simply an address, but the effect of multiple, contingent and contradictory affiliations (1993, 8). The emphasis on knowledge as situated and interested is here a critical gesture which dislodges past universalisms that have supported a specifically patriarchal investment, and an affirmative gesture which writes women into structures of knowledge through a re-evaluation of embodiment and place.
   Abena P. A. Busia poetically describes the difficulty of naming within post-colonial contexts: 'The indeterminate aspects of 'identity' that slide between the concept of 'hybridity' and the concept of 'translation' suggest, though, like the refracted image in a mirror, they cannot contain the issues at stake for those of us — migrants, exiles and other

kinds of homeless — troubled by the anxiety of trying to name ourselves in different tongues and voices, and place ourselves in or out of the manifold places from which we speak' (1993, 204).

3. This, is needless to say, not necessarily an empirical or literal event. Rather it links the construction of identity to the dominance of the visual sense, a dominance which is later evident in forms of conceptualization.
4. This notion of the travel (or agency) of the letter being halted at the signifier of the subject (and its lack) may be expanded to enable us to deal with the problem of the phallus. Derrida's reading of Lacan as phallocentric, for example, focusses on the way in which the travels of the letter in Lacan's reading of Edgar Allen Poe's 'The Purloined Letter' halt at the privileged point of the phallus, in that the letter always returns to the phallus as its proper destination (1987, 41). Extending from this, it could be argued that Lacan manages only to sustain the notion of Phallus as privileged signifier (1990, 79) by protecting the signifier of the phallus from the contingency identified in the form of the (unconscious) vertical contexts surrounding the signifier. To expose the phallus as signifier contingent upon other such signifying contexts (and hence itself open to being dis-placed), would constitute a feminist refusal of the topology of phallogocentrism.
5. This of course returns us to the link between identification and a theory of the unconscious. The imaginary nature of an identification (which nevertheless sustains material effects) renders that it cannot hold or fix the relation of subject to image. Within the context of my use of identification, the unconscious helps us to address that which is 'left out' by the identification of subjects between specific modes of address: the divisions are not integral to the subject (as the subject of lack) but the relation of the subject to specific and conflicting modes of address. The impossibility of an identity being fixed (and so excluding the play of the unconscious) here opens out the structures of division through which subjects are partially named.
6. We could relate this notion of partial fixation to Lacan's theory of the *point de capitons* (quilting) where there is a partial though mythic fixing of the signified under the sliding of the signifier (1993, 267-8). This is taken up in an interesting fashion by Ernesto Laciou and Chantal Mouffe in *Hegemony and Socialist Strategy* , where they develop the idea that the intelligibility of the social is sustained by a partial and temporary fixing of the signified constituted by an impossible desire to halt the sliding of the signifier (1985, 112).
7. I am sympathetic with Judith Butler's project of establishing how phantasmatic identification involves a logic of repudiation, where the other is violently repudiated: rendered abject. My project of complicating identification differs from hers, however, in that I am attempting to locate the divisions between specific structures of identification (both sexual and otherwise) as they operate contextually (1993, 3).
8. As Rose M. Brewer (1993, 16) argues we must eschew 'additive analyses' which simply place specific power regimes (gender, race, class) alongside each other (gender + race + class). Such additions prevents a more complex analysis of how power regimes inter-relate and conflict in the production of subjectivists.

9. Already we have a context for this event: the encounters of a non-White immigrant within 'multi-cultural' Australia. As such, the confusions of identification I discuss locate, or at least emerge from, the specific dynamics of this post-colonial encounter. As Trinh. T, Minh-Ha puts it, 'In the complex reality of post coloniality it is therefore vital to assume one's radical 'impurity' and to recognize the necessity of speaking from a hybrid place, hence of saying at least two, three things at a time' (1992, 139-40).
10. This connects with Drucilla Cornell's recent work on how 'whiteness' and 'blackness' gain significance through a psycho-sexual dynamics of desire (1993, 9).
11. Elizabeth Spelma discusses the problem of the way in which race and sex are *kept apart* as distinct components of subjectivity and calls for an approach which examines points of intersection and collision (1990, 114-5).
12. I want to stress here the dilemma I have had over how to name racial difference within the context of this reading. The word 'colour' is problematic, in that it implies that 'white' is 'a lack of colour' and by this that 'white' is 'a lack of race', as the norm from which race deviates. The word 'black' is far more empowering and can help positively define what non-white women share through the violence of colonial history. But in using black I do not want to equate the experience of Aboriginal and South Asian women in Australia. I do not want to silence the difference of these positions within an Australian context, and commit another violence against Aboriginal people, for the extent of their oppression within Australia is incomparable, and I am fully aware of the history of suspicion and racism between Aboriginals and 'black immigrants'. To trace the difference and division within the signifier 'black woman' would further open out the conflicting contexts for the inter-section of race and gender. See Alistair Bennet for an examination of some of the cross-cultural differences in the use of the term 'Black' (1993, 6).
13. As Glorio T. Hull, Patricia Bell-Scott and Barbara Smith address this issue on terms of the twin inadequacy of 'Women's Studies' and 'Black Studies'. They write: 'Women's Studies courses . . .focused almost exclusively upon the lives of white women. Black studies, which was much too often male-dominated, also ignored black women . . . Because of white women's racism and black men's sexism, there was no room in either area for the consideration of lives of Black women; (1982, xx, xxi).
14. Parry's call for a recognition of agency is paralleled by Rajeswari Sander Rajan, who theorises a post-colonial resisting subject, in part through exploring the 'historically victimized' subject as the site for the constitution of 'alternative' subjectivities (1993, 11). In defence of Spivak, she does write elsewhere that we should divide the name woman, so that woman can name as well as be named, opening out the potential for an agency (1989, 211).

References

Althusser, Louis (1971), *Lenin and Philosophy and Other Essays* (London, NLB)

Bennett, Alastair (1993), *Radicalism, Anti-Racism and Representation* (London and New York, Routledge).

Bordo, Susan (1990), 'Feminism, Postmodernism and Gender Scepticism', in Linda Nicholson (ed.), *Feminism/Postmodernism* (New York and London, Routledge), 133-56.

Brewer, Rose M. (1993), ' Theorizing Race, Class and Gender: The New Scholarship of Black Feminist Intellectuals and Black Women's Labour', in Stanlie M. James and Abena P. A. Busia (eds), *Theorising Black Feminisms: The Visionary Pragmatism of Black Women* (London and New York, Routledge), 13-30.

Busia, Abena P. A, (1993), 'Performance, Transcription and the Languages of the Self: Interrogating Identity as a Post-Colonial Poet' Stanlie M. James and Abena P. A. Busia (eds), *Theorising Black Feminisms: The Visionary Pragmatism of Black Women* (London and New York, Routledge), 203-14.

Busia, Abena P. A. (1993), 'AFTER/WORDS'...' and this is what we've decided to tell you after everything we've shared', in Stanlie M. James and Abena P. A. Busia (eds), *Theorising Black Feminisms, The Visionary Pragmatism of Black Women* (London and New York, Routledge), 283-92.

Butler, Judith (1993), *Bodies That Matter: On the Discursive Limits of "Sex"* (New York and London, Routledge).

Cornell, Drucilla (1993), *Transformations: Recollective Imagination and Sexual Difference* (New York and London, Routledge).

Derrida, Jacques (1987), *The Post Card: From Socrates to Freud and Beyond* (Chicago and London, University of Chicago Press).

Felman, Shoshabna (1987), *Jacques Lacan and the Adventures of Insight: Psychoanalysis in Contemporary Culture* (Cambridge, Massachusetts and London, England, Harvard University Press).

Holland, Nancy J. (1990), *Is Women's Philosophy Possible?* (Maryland, Rowman and Littlefield Pub. Inc.).

Hull, Gloria T., Patricia Bell-Scott and Barbara Smith (eds) (1982), *All the Women are White, All the Blacks are Men* (Old Westbury and New York, Feminist Press).

Lacan, Jacques (1977), *Ecrits: A Selection* (London, Tavistock Publications).

Lacan, Jacques (1990), *Feminine Sexuality: Jacques Lacan and the 'ecole freudienne'* , Juliet Mitchell and Jacqueline Rose (eds) (Houndmills and London, Macmillan).

Lacan, Jacques (1993), *The Psychoses: The Seminar of Jacques Lacan Book III 1955-56*, Jacques-Alain Miller (ed.), Russell Grig (trans.), (London, Routledge).

Laclou, Ernesto and Chantal Mouffe (1985), *Hegemony and Socialist Strategy: Towards a Radical Democratic Politics* (London, Verso).

Mackinnon, Catherine (1983), 'Feminism, Marxism, Method and the State: Towards Feminist Jurisprudence; *Signs* 8, 4, 635-58.

Minh-Ha, Trinh T. (1992), *Framer Framed* (New York and London, Routledge),

Nancy, Jean-Luc and Phillipe Lacoue-Labarthe (1992), *The Title of the Letter: A Reading of Lacan*, Trans. Francois Raffoul and David Pettigrew (Albany, State University of New York Press).

Parry, Benita (1987), 'Problems in Current Theories of Colonial Discourse', in *Oxford Literary Review*, 9: 27-58.

Pateman, Carole (1989), *The Sexual Contract* (Cambridge, Polity Press).

Rajan, Rajeswari Sander (1993), *Real and Imagined Women: Gender, Culture and Post-Colonialism* (New York and London, Routledge).

Smith, Dorothy (1987), 'Women's Perspective as Radical Critique of Sociology', in Sandra Harding (ed.), *Feminism and Methodology* (Bloomington and Indianapolis, Indiana University Press), 84-97.

Spelman, Elizabeth V. (1992), *Inessential Woman: Problems of Exclusion in Feminist Thought* (London, The Women's Press).

Spivak, Gayatri Chakravorty (1988), 'Can the Subaltern Speak?' in Lawrence Grossberg and Cary Nelson (eds), *Marxism and the Interpretation of Culture* (Urbano and Chicago, University of Illinois Press), 271-314.

Spivak, Gayatri Chakravorty (1989), ' Feminism and Deconstruction Again: Negotiating with Unacknowledged Masculinism, in *Between Feminism and Psychoanalysis* , ed. Teresa Brennan (London and New York, Routledge), 206-23.

Stanford Freidman, Susan (1988), 'Women's Auto-Biographical Self: Theory and Practice', in Benstock, Shari (ed.), *The Private Self* (Chapel Hill, University of North Carolina Press).

Ware, Vron (1992), *Beyond the Pale: White Women, Racism and History* (London and New York, Verso).

Section V
Postscript

Three Women Leaders — Agents of Change in the Village

Nalini Kasynathan

I wish to present today the stories of three women from different parts of the sub continent — from Orissa in North-East India, Kanyakumary in South India and from Chenkalady in Eastern Srilanka. These three women and the organizations to which they belong are instruments of change transforming the lives of both men and women in their communities. As a development worker, I am very impressed by them and the kind of leadership roles they have taken in their respective communities. I would like to share these stories with you and we may perhaps be able to make some observations about the conditions which have shaped their emergence in their present roles. Though the circumstances of these women and their communities are in many ways different, there are also, naturally, many similarities.

Konarack is a fishing village in the district of Gopalpur in Orissa. It has now a strong women's organization with a membership of 300 women. Karallemma is the president of the women's organization as well as of the regional organization which is a co-ordinating body for the women's and men's organizations in the Gopalpur district. She is about 35 years old, illiterate and earns her living as a fish vendor. She was elected president by the women of her society and during her tenure as president, her village and the 700 fishing families there have made many gains. Karallemma organized the fisherwomen to refuse to sell prawns to the middlemen who had hitherto controlled the price of prawns. Initially the women incurred a loss. They however then proceeded to sell directly at the market instead of handing over the catch to the middlemen who came to the beach.

Now the women set the prices not only in Knorack but in the district of Gopalpur as well. After the success of Karallemma's group in fighting the power of the middlemen who had controlled the prawn trade for so long, the men in the village have accepted the existence of the women's organization. The Fisheries Co-operative Council in the district which hitherto serviced only rich fishermen was reconstituted with women holding 50 per cent of the membership.

When I spoke to Karallemma, she said that even some of the disputes among the men in the village are now brought to her for arbitration. The women and the youth of her village have worked together to prevent the sale of illicit liquor within their village. The stores that were selling alcohol were destroyed with the approval of the police. Men who were found drunk and openly misbehaving have on occasions been tied to a tree and disgraced in public as deterrent punishment.

Karallemma was elected recently to represent the village in the municipal council along with 12 others, all of whom were educated and from the high caste in the village. Karallemma's community which is a depressed group in the village has never had direct representation in the MC in the past. Karallemma was thus the first representative of a depressed community that has never been represented before. In the council Karallemma was elected to be the vice-chairperson because she was found to have the support of the largest number of members in the constituency. The recognition of Karallemma as a leader with a firm base of voter support behind her has now won land rights to 300 fisher families who were been living on state land and had been threatened with frequent eviction notices. She has also organized women and men in her region to support other groups in protests against trawler fishing, commercial logging, etc. She is now a role model in the village.

In Kanyakumary, Santhi Dan has mobilized over 300 members and a hundred women's groups (sangams) have been formed. They have also elected an executive body that governs all the sangams. Anthoniyamma is the president of a cluster of ten villages in the project area and is also a member of the executive council of Santhi Dan. She is illiterate. After having taken on the responsibility of representing her community at the cluster and at the national level, she sees her illiteracy as a drawback and promotes night schools for the women and young girls in the area. With the assistance of her Sangam she has brought light, water and bus transport into her village and has led the march against trawler fishing and once sat in front of the collectors office for more than 48 hours demanding drinking water for her village. The credit society of her Sangam has a 100 per cent repayment rate and she is in the process of organizing a pension scheme for the old, disabled and widowed women who otherwise have no support.

The weekly meetings organized by her within her cluster (attendance at which meetings is a condition for the grant of loans) have among the women led to increased awareness of many issues affecting them — the role of tradition and its impact on the place of women, the role of religion, dowry, middlemen, accessing Government funding, etc. At these meetings the women are given the space to discuss without inhibitions and to feel free to share with others the issues that concern all of them. The meetings are recorded and a monthly news letter is circulated to the membership.

A dowry death in the neighbourhood was given publicity and many meetings were organized in the project area to examine this issue. As a positive step to discourage the demanding of dowries, households which accepted brides without a dowry were commended as leaders of the community. Anthoniyamma has proposed that the members of her Sangam should refrain from accepting dowries and has led by example by not asking for a dowry when her son got married recently. Every meeting which she chairs starts with a formal vow by the members that they would work to end the dowry system.

Thilaka is the president of the credit society in her village and is also the president of the co-ordinating council for 40 societies in the Chenkalady region in Eastern Srilanka with a total of approximately 1200 members. She is a widow with three daughters. Two of her sons-in-law have been killed during the last two years due to the ongoing conflict in the region. Her society is located in the war zone and she routinely needs to negotiate with the militants and the members of the armed forces to be permitted to carry out the activities of the society — to deposit the daily collection in the bank or to purchase seeds and inputs from the town for cultivation of vegetables.

The death of large numbers of fathers and husbands and the disruption by war of established structures, guidelines and taboos has made room for the women to move into functions from which they were previously excluded. Even the men who are left are vulnerable to attack or harassment. The women therefore find themselves having to take on public roles and decisions. They feel less endgangered than the men in negotiating with the army, officials and with the militants.

Despite the fact that Srilanka elected a widow some years ago as the prime minister of the country, traditional prejudices die hard and widows are yet considered by many to be inauspicious and a bad omen. There was a reluctance at first to accept Thilaka as the president of the society but her efficiency has now earned for her the support of most members.

1 These women do not come from the upper strata of their communities from which leaders have traditionally come. Nor do they have other prestigious qualifications or status which comes from attainment in education or membership of a profession. The three women whom I have spoken about come from the lowest strata in the village. They are in most ways ordinary women who were available to do jobs which needed to be done. There is no rush to pick up these leadership positions among them. One woman was chosen because her children were grown up and she was considered to have the time for this kind of extra work; another was chosen because she knew how to read and write. In another case two very traumatised women — one who was a rape victim and the other whose husband had

disappeared during the war — were given leadership roles because the group thought that it would be good for them to inter act with others in ways which would make them feel useful.

2 These women did not become leaders with the motivation at any stage of empowering themselves in relation to the men in their families or in their communities. They have worked to solve problems which were common to all of them in the community and their success has led to recognition and respect from all including the men. In seeking to solve these problems they have moved into areas which are well outside the roles which were traditionally considered theirs. A public role and stature leads to empowerment within the household too. When I asked Karallemma how her husband treated her she said that the had not really changed but that she had changed. He no longer dares to be violent with her. As she put it, she is not merely his woman now; others know her, are aware of what happens to her and are concerned about her.

3 The emergence of these leaders is very much connected to their identification of the problems which face them and the attainment to an understanding of the ways of working towards remedies to those problems. This has brought them a freedom to act and to move away from an occult idea of leadership and from the dependence on others who may do things for them. The understanding fostered by these groups has given to these women purposes and roles which are authentic and not bound by tradition or prejudice about their gender. The groups and their regular discussions are thus powerful instruments of change in these rural communities.

The groups are small, informal, democratic, co-operative and issues based. They often use strategies which involve resistance. The women in these areas were more suitable as agents of change not only because they felt more keenly the destitution in their villages but also because they were not bound as much as their husbands and fathers were, by the hierarchical and feudal power arrangements in their communities. In the meetings and discussions of the group there is a greater sense of equality among them than was possible among the men. They were all equally deprived. This sense of equality insofar as it is a function of their disempowerment may not last. However, it now gives them a courage and forthrightness which eludes their men who are locked into their subordination. Not only do we find Thilaka feeling less fearful than her husband in going up to the army but Karallemma too is willing to take on officials and structures which are more overwhelming to her menfolk. One may call this the courage of innocence. Or, one may see that the wife of a slave is not entirely a slave.

Scholar, Fighter, Mother
The life of Ratnamayi Devi as Narrated to Madhu Kishwar

Madhu Kishwar

Most of the women who were politically active in the freedom movement came into it through the prior involvement of male members of their families and, after independence, some of them rose to positions of prominence. Ratnamayi Devi is one of the very few women who was drawn into the movement on her own, through her search for a livelihood and the wherewithal to educate her children. After independence, the compulsions that had brought her into political activity drew her out of it. Her life is remarkable for the tremendous courage and endurance with which she raised her large family of real and adopted children. A crucial factor in the family's achievement of upward mobility were the strong bonds of continuing support between mothers and daughters, who sustained each other's attempts to get an education and become self reliant.

I was born in 1909 in Pachallur, a village four miles from Trivandrum, Kerala. I belong to a family of landowners. We are Naris. In the highest Nair families in Kerala, generally, women marry Brahmans, not other Naris. The woman stays in her own house and the husband comes and visits her there. She does not shift to his house. The children are the responsibility of the mother's family, not the father's. This was the custom till the first quarter of the twentieth century. The matrilineal system was prevalent. If there is no girl, the lineage will be destroyed. So when I say "my family" I am referring not to my father's but to my mother's, grandmother's great grandmother's family.

My grandmother had several brothers and sisters. But she had only one surviving child, my mother. And I also happened to be an only child. In a joint family the brothers and sisters lived together. The eldest brother and sister together managed the family affairs.

In our family, my grandmother's eldest brother managed all the family property-we had big compounds with many trees, fields, house. He had 40 wives. When he saw a woman he liked, he would talk to her uncle or brother and say he would like to make her his wife. His being a noble family, they would not refuse. He would go to her every night, as long as he liked. Then, he would give her some property without telling other family members. This was illegal. But my grandmother was illiterate and never questioned his doings, so he carried on like that. We had so many cousins in surrounding villages.

My grandmother, Gouriamma, was married at the age of nine to a Tamil Brahman scholar. It so happened that each time she had a child, and conceived again, the first child died as soon as the second one was born. In this way, she lost four daughters. When my mother, Parvatiamma, was born and her elder sister died, my grandmother got very upset, and told her husband : "I must have committed some sin. Maybe I am not serving you properly. I want this daughter to survive so you please leave me." She thought there was some fault in her service of him, because wives in those days thought the husband was god. In this case the feeling was stronger because he was a Brahman.

My grandfather took my mother in his lap and said: "I swear, the day this child dies I will divorce you. But let me take care of her." And he took my mother to his house.

First Educated Woman

She was brought up there, by his second wife, a Tamilian. My grandfather was careful that she should get a good basic education. That was the first time for hundreds of years a girl in our family was educated. Men used to be educated in Sanskrit and Malayalam but women only learnt to sing and dance within the four walls of the house.

My grandmother sometimes used to go and stay with her husband and he too came to stay in her house. When my mother was 10 years old, her father died, and she returned to our house. My grandmother was 35 years old at that time. By then, almost all the property, except the house, had been given away to others by my mother's uncle.

My mother insisted that she would continue her studies. When her uncle heard it, he came with the ceremonial sword and said: "I will cut you to pieces if you try to study." She said: "Cut me if you like but I will study." He said: "I will see how you go. I will burn the house down." She said: "Burn the house. We will manage somehow."

So she started going to school with her mother's support and with the help of a friend of her father's. In those days, the government used to give a scholarship of Rs. 5 to every girl who went to school. So she completed her education. She was the only educated woman in the whole area. Other girls would not dare disobey their uncles or brothers. But she had great courage and self confidence. She was also very beautiful.

After she passed the required examination, she was appointed as the headmistress of a vernacular girls' school, on a salary of Rs 10 a month. The lifestyle at home was no longer luxurious. They needed the extra income. My mother took a separate house near the school and lived there with her mother.

When she was 20 years old, my mother got married. My father was a classmate and friend of hers. He used to visit the house and my grandmother also was very fond of him. The marriage created an uproar because he was also a Nair. Her uncle continually threatened to burn the house down and to kill all concerned. But my mother was undeterred. She said: "I will do what I think is right." For three years, they had no child. My grandmother was worried because the family name would continue only if my mother had children. Even though a girl was considered the mainstay of the family, when I was born, my grandmother's sister exclaimed in disappointment "Oh, it's a girl!" My grandmother said: "But she's gold for me." And she was the one who brought me up.

My father too was a teacher one grade lower than my mother. She used to get transferred to various places within Travancore state. My father would take leave and accompany her, or ask for transfer to the same place. But was never the other way around my mother never did this.

There was a great contrast between them. My mother was a terrible disciplinarian. My father was very soft by nature. He could not scold anyone or get angry. My mother's word was law for him. He loved her so much. He had lost his parents in early childhood and had been brought up by his sister. He treated my grandmother as his own mother.

Now they were in great financial difficulties due to the loss of the land. So my mother field a suit against her uncle, claiming the property he had illegally transferred to his wives. She had to face a lot of criticism for this. I was born when she was 24 years old, and soon after, she won the case and all the property became legally hers. Naturally, they thought it was my luck! Anyway, they were now well off. My grandmother told my mother there was no need for her to continue working. But she refused to leave her job.

My mother got all the property whereas her cousins and their children got nothing. They were just poor relations. Some of them worked in our house. They were not educated. My mother was very charitable and generous but when I grew up I felt the division was unjust. But no one dared tell my mother that. She was very dominating.

All Work, No Play

She was a headmistress and she brought school discipline into the house too. I was admitted in her school at the age of two and a half. I was supposed to stand first in class on my own merit, without the slightest favouritism, and if I did not, I would be punished.

From the age of five, the routine was—get up at 4 a.m., have a bath, join my parents' worship of the goddess, take a lesson from the music master at 5 a.m., go to school from 10 to 4, then after a quick wash and a meal, do my homework with my tutor, study for an hour and go to bed at 8 p.m. This routine continued till I matriculated at the age of 14.

I had to go to school with my mother and return with her. As soon as the bell rang for recess I had to reach her room or I would be scolded or beaten. I was not to talk to anyone or go out. Well, yes, I did play with my father sometimes. I was also a voracious reader. And one game I played with my parents was *antyakshri* in malayalam poetry. That way I learnt a lot of poems. My daughter and I still enjoy doing this.

That was a particularly rich period for Malayalam literature. I read the works of Bankim, Tagore and others in translation. My mother encouraged me to participate in extracurricular activities at school—drama, debates, writing for magazines. She was very ambitious for me.

Till the age of 15, I did not know what sorrow was. I was afraid only of my mother. If she came to know I had told an untruth or even lost a pencil, she would speak not with words but with a stick.

In 1925, a new law was passed in Travancore that all joint family property amongst Naris should be split up equally amongst all members of the family. So our family property had to be divided among 60 people—my mother's distant relatives, nephews, nieces and others. Naturally, our share was very small and our standard of living suddenly declined.

At this time, I was studying in an English school. My mother was determined that I should be a doctor and take the medical exams in England. My Malayalam teacher Munshi K.R. Parameshwaran Pillai was attracted to me because I was a good student. I never thought of him as anything but my teacher. I was 15 years old and he was 33.

Marriage at Fifteen

He belonged to a rich Nair family of Adoor. He proposed that I marry his younger brother whom he was educating to be a lawyer. My father happened to find out that this brother was having an affair with a lady student at Trivandrum, whom he later married.

Then my teacher proposed on his own behalf and made Ma accept. My father was against it—he did not like the family. My grandmother too was not happy. She did not like the idea of a daughter going faraway from the house after marriage as, according to the prevalent custom, the daughter belonged to the house and should stay there. But my mother liked him. To this day, I have not understood what made her arrange my marriage so early, when she had earlier been so determined on my becoming a doctor.

I was not very happy. I wanted to study, and my husband said I could continue studying after marriage. I was not unwilling either—I enjoyed the pomp and show of the wedding. We were married in June 1924.

The funniest part of it was that on the first night, the first thing he had to tell me was: "Don't think I believe any woman. I know what all women are. Nobody is indispensable for me. Don't think I will trust any woman." I was shocked. I was only 15. I didn't know what he meant.

Later, I came to know he was already married and had a son, and was already a disillusioned person. He wanted to forget that marriage. I came to know this through others. I asked him. He said: "Yes, so what?" By that time I was also disillusioned.

In Trivandrum, monogamy was practised but in the place where his family lived, polyandry was the custom—like Draupadi. It is the right of all the brothers to share the eldest brother's wife. We in South Travancore didn't know this.

I was sent to Trivandrum for my medical studies. My husband did not want me to stay in a hostel so we took a house. But I was not happy there and I fell ill so we wound up the house and I came back to my home. In June, I joined college, and in August I left.

My husband was very nice to me. But he was of a suspicious nature. If I talked to somebody he would interpret it in a different way. So I gave up talking to people. He was also suspicious of my mother. She had many friends. She was a social worker and a headmistress. She was a very independent person.

My husband did not like my father's friends visiting our house. He even insulted one of them and told him to get out of the house. That hurt me. I asked : "Do you mean to say our friends cannot visit us?" He said : "No, nobody will come." I told my mother and she agreed with him, for my sake. But I was very upset. Also, he did not show proper respect to my mother. Slowly, his attitude to her had changed.

My husband used to ask my mother for money to educate his brother. My father objected to this. But my mother insisted on giving it. Property was sold, money was borrowed. Her reason for giving in to my husband in everything was: "Otherwise, my daughter will suffer."

Trying to be an Ideal Wife

But, slowly, I was getting estranged from him. He used to drink heavily which we did not know earlier. He used to stay out for one or two nights at a time. But I thought I should remember the stories in the *Puratnas* and win him over by my loyalty and love. But there came a point when my father and husband clashed. My husband succeeded in estranging my father from my mother. My mother began to wrongly suspect my father of having other relationships and, one day, she shaved her head, wore a white *sari*, and said she had taken *sanyas*.

In 1926, my daughter was born, in our own house. My grandmother was about 75 years old but quite healthy, managing everything, as I am doing now. My daughter was named Sharada, and called Omana (which means "darling") at home, or Om for short.

When she was three months old, I went to stay at my in-laws' house at Adoor. In my parents' house, I had never done any housework. I did not know how to cook. My in-laws' house was a huge feudal set up with labourers living and eating at the house. Food was cooked for more than 40 people daily. I tried to learn the work. But everyone there criticised and taunted me, thinking I was proud because I was an educated girl from the city. My ways were strange to them, for instance, women there did not wear blouses and were used to bathing in the open whereas I was brought up with urban ways, always bathing in the house and wearing blouses. I was also the first woman in that family who refused to live with her husband's brothers. This may be one reason they did not like me although they could not state it openly. That custom has died out now.

My mother kept sending clothes and other things for me and Om. But they used to disappear from my room because everything was treated as common property. Nor did my husband provide these things for us. My mother had given me gold jewellery—four thick bracelets, two chains, a belt and anklets. My husband took them to keep in the bank. When I next asked for them he said: "They have been sold." Twice more, my mother bought me jewellery and it went the same way.

Often, he used to come very late at night. I would be waiting for him. I would not eat. He would say: "Why do you wait?" But I believed that a wife should eat the husband's leftovers. I was a vegetarian and if he was eating fish or meat, I could not bear to eat the leftovers. So I would go without eating for three to four days at a time. I would drink tea or have some rice and salt. I dared not complain because I was afraid people would say I was proud of my education. This was my greatest fear.

My husband's widowed sister was also staying in the house with her two daughters, Thangam and Sarasam. She told me that everyone ill treated and neglected them. So I adopted the two girls, even though I had to face opposition from other relatives.

As a student, I used to write for various magazines and had become quite a well known writer. But all my literary activities had to stop once I came to Adoor. I had written one novelette *Venugopalan* about a boy who goes from a village to a city to study. My husband got it published. He too was a writer so he had contacts. But he gave the copyright of my book to a friend of his. That book became a prescribed text in schools, and sold in thousands. It is still an approved text. All the money went to that man. I got only Rs 100. My husband would do anything for his friends.

I was discontented by my condition in Adoor but I was determined to do my duty—to serve my husband. And he never insulted me or tried to hit me. He always showed me great respect in the presence of others. He showed love and respect in words but not so much in actions. We did not have the closeness a husband and wife should have. I could not bear his drinking and going to other women. I could not stand the smell of drink. And he never brought his salary home—he spent it in drinking or gave it away to his friends. It was the same with his income from his writing.

When I became pregnant again, my husband refused to send me to my mother for delivery. I was not keeping well. So my mother took leave on half pay, and came to Adoor. We took a separate house near my in-laws' house, and we began to live separately. My husband sometimes came and gave some money but for months together, he would not give any. My son Viresh was born in May 1929.

I was now very worried. How would I bring up and educate the children properly? I was not qualified enough to stand on my own feet. At this time, an exclassmate, Ponnamma, came to see me. She had become a doctor in these four years. I much regretted having given up my studies and decided that I must resume my studies. But where would the money come from?

Education Resumed

Anyway, I took a chance and sent an application to Trivandrum Women's College. Fortunately, I was admitted. There was terrible opposition from my in-laws. My mother encouraged me, and promised to look after the children. When I asked my husband, he said: "I will not help you with a single pice, but you can do as you like:" He did not stop me. That was a blessing to me. So I decided to go. I felt if it was god's will, a way would be opened.

When I left, my son, Viresh, was 40 days old. My husband's brother and I went to Trivandrum. We reached at 7 p.m. and the hostel warden refused to admit me, saying the hostel was only for unmarried women. She would not let me stay even one night. My husband had said that if I could not get into the hostel, I should return home. I just sat on the verandah and cried. Then, the Sanskrit lecturer in the college, who was acquainted with my brother-in-law, took me to her house. Her name was V.K. Kartyayaniamma.

She was a great support to me. Soon, the principal admitted me into the hostel.

In the beginning, I had great difficulty in English because I was out of touch with it for four years. I was the oldest girl in the class. The first day, the English teacher made very sarcastic remarks about my English essay. I cried and cried. I did not want to attend class. But my English teacher called me, apologised, and then took the responsibility of improving my English. She worked so hard with me that I stood first in English in the first year exam. Such were the teachers I had. So I had a good time in the college and hostel.

In this year, my mother and the children were thrown out of the house by my husband, so they went to the place where my mother was posted and she reported to duty. I was meeting my expenses by giving tuition to two small children. I copied out most of my textbooks by hand. I used to go to my mother in the vacations.

Just before the selection exams in the second year, my mother suddenly came to see me. I was surprised. Then she told me that my son and died of diphtheria. She had informed my husband but he didn't come. She came herself to tell me instead of writing.

In the final exam, I got very good marks in all subjects but I failed in British history which I had never liked. So I failed. Every one except my mother laughed at me and taunted me. It was a very dark period for me. I even stopped praying to god. But my teachers insisted that I should take the supplementary exam in September. Their affection compelled me to agree.

In July, my mother suddenly was struck by paralysis. She was a rheumatism patient. We had no money. My husband used to just come, talk sarcastically and go back. Then, fortunately, I was appointed in my mother's place in her school. It was easy for me to teach because I had observed my mother's teaching. I appeared for the exam and passed with distinction marks. When my mother recovered, I also taught in another school and saved some money.

My Sanskrit teacher advised me to join BA Sanskrit honours in the Presidency College, Madras University. In those days, Madras University had a system—one could get a BA degree in two years. But if one continued for another year, one would get a BA honours degree and after one year, also an MA degree automatically. But if one failed the exam one would get no degree at all-not even BA. It was a risk.

I wanted to join. I thought now that god had brought me so far, he would definitely show me a way. My mother sold the little gold she had and gave me Rs 200. She had retired and was getting a pension of Rs 25 a month. She stayed alone with my children, in a house belonging to my in-laws, at Adoor. My husband came and stayed there off and on. I went to Madras and stayed in the Queen Mary's hostel.

I joined in 1932. That year, the Sanskrit Academy had started some competitions such as writing a critical study of a Sanskrit drama, recitation from the *Gita* and writing the message of the *Gita* in any language. My professor, Kuppuswami Shastri, knew I needed financial help. He told me to enter these competitions. I was hesitant because I knew even MA students were competing for the first one. I did not want to be laughed at. But on my teacher's insistence, I entered. I got all three scholarships—a total of about Rs 85 a month.

This was a very difficult time for me. I had to support four people—mother, Om, Thangam, and myself. Also, my husband was constantly asking my mother for money; often, she had to feed him and his friends. So I had to keep sending money. Of course, I was not forced to do so. But I felt I had to do my duty. I used to borrow from friends and classmates. I got into so much debt.

I used to go home for vacations. I would take sets of clothes for Om. Her father would often present them to his nieces or his friends' daughters. The poor child would not dare tell him not to give them. Nor could I. Because my mother was living in his house. And I had to keep a calm and peaceful picture of our home life, otherwise people would blame the woman, whatever be the truth.

Anyway, three years passed and I passed BA honours with a first class. In 1935, I joined the Madras University as a PhD student working on the topic "The technique of

Sanskrit drama in theory and practice" on a scholarship of Rs 75 a month.

But now another problem arose. While studying for BA, from 1929 to 1935, I did not have any physical relations with my husband. But in 1935 we had relations and immediately I conceived. My son, 10 years younger to Om, was born His name is Jotindranath (called Mani at home). Then, I came to Madras with my mother and children and rented a house there. I got my husband's older niece, Thangam, married off. I had brought her up as my daughter. She now has four sons. Most people still know her as my eldest daughter. At that time, I got a small job in Queen Mary's College, distributing the mail, on a salary of Rs 20. This added to my income.

I admitted Om in a convent school. She was very good in Malayalam and Sanskrit, but she didn't know English. She did not know Tamil either. So she couldn't mix with the other girls. Most students in that school were from rich families, whereas I couldn't afford to give her even good skirts and blouses. She had to wash and wear the same sets again and again. She was miserable there at first but she didn't let me know. Other girls used to come well dressed for school functions. Om wouldn't attend. She would say: "It's a holiday." Then sometimes I saw her in tears, and I knew. I couldn't do anything about it.

But I kept her in that school because my one and only ambition was to give the children the best education. I wanted her to study and get a good job. Slowly, by reading novels, she picked up English and made a few friends with whom she still maintains contact.

During this time, I also did my MA in Malayalam privately. Madras University did not have any provision for private examinations but I applied for special permission. I did not get it. Then I went through all the regulations of the university and I found a small clause saying that a person who has an MA degree in one language can appear privately for MA in another language. Om and I typed 24 copies of this clause and sent it to all the authorities. In February 1939, I got permission to appear and the exam was in March! Anyway, I passed and topped the list-first class first.

Simultaneously, I also passed MA in English privately. I also started learning Urdu. I got a temporary job teaching Malayalam in Madras Christian College. I was the first woman teacher there.

But my research guide found my thesis unsatisfactory and asked me to rewrite it. He did not like my having a child during the search period and thought I was not serious. I could not afford to rewrite and submit it again as I had no job, and so no income. I had to borrow money from moneylenders, at 10 percent interest per month, to feed my children.

My husband used to come and stay with me off and on. He had become a good playwright but I never asked him for money because it was another principle of mine not to ask for money. My son Shrish was born in 1940.

Another Mother

There was another development in my life at this time. I came very close to the Ramakrishna Mission. Both my parents had been attached to the Mission for a long time. After shifting to Madras, I used to go to the Math every Sunday. My mother used to get injections from their free dispensary. Both my sons were named by the Swami who was the president of the Math. The second son was named Narendra Nath, after Swami Vivekananda. He is called Shrish at home. Om too was named Shardamani Devi, after the Holy Mother. In 1940, the Holy Mother's birthday was celebrated as usual. I was asked to speak in English at the public meeting about her life and message. When my speech was over, an old. Foreign lady wearing a *sari* came to me and asked: "What is your name, child?" In the south, we don't have Mr and Mrs. So I told my name: "Ratnamayi Devi." She asked what I was doing. I said I was teaching in a college. She said: "Then you are a lady." I said: "No, I am not a lady."

There was a reason for my answer. In 1935, when I was in BA final year, Sarojini Naidu had come to our college. One student got up and requested her for a message for the "lady students." She replied: "Lady students? Are you ashamed to call yourself a woman?" She continued that "lady" is an anglicised word whereas "woman" is more dignified; it is the confidence and will power of women which keeps the nation going forward; Bapu has called women to come to the forefront. These words were fixed in my heart.

Umadevi was a polish lady who came to India in 1933 and got converted to Hinduism. She had a friend, Mr Maurice Friedman, working in Mysore as an engineer, who was like a brother to her. She was visiting different places, doing social work. She visited my house. I prepared boiled vegetables for her. She was a pure vegetarian. Then she said: "You are my first daughter in India." She said it with so much love that I accepted her as my mother. I invited her to come and stay with me. She stayed in our house for one and a half months. We grew very close to each other. She came to know all about me. She asked Mr Friedman to pay up my debt of Rs 400. I was hesitant to take it but he insisted, saying he had given it to Uma and she was giving it to me.

Now, my term in the college was coming to an end and I was wondering how to manage. Then, Umadevi wrote to Bapu. Mr Friedman was a constant visitor to the Wardha Ashram. Later, Umadevi settled in Dharamsala and opened an Ashram there, where Tibetan refuges also stayed. She died only a few years ago. Till the end, she considered me her daughter.

In 1941, I got a letter from Wardha, asking me to go and see the Ashram. Umadevi gavc me Rs 30 for the fare and I went to Sewagram. I had read about the freedom movement, but I was not involved. I had no intention of joining it. My one aim at that time was to get a job and educate my children. That was all I wanted to achieve, nothing else.

I came to Mahila Ashram, Wardha. At that time, it was an asylum for women-daughters, sisters, wives, mothers-of men who had joined the movement, gone to jail or died, and could not support them. Shri Jamnalal Bajaj had started this institution. The building belonged to one Shantabai Raniwala who had donated it for this purpose, and was the chief donor.

In Search of A Living

When I reached, Mr Friedman told me: "Bapu wants you to stay here. What do you say?" He had already told Bapu about me. I said: "If I get a suitable job I will come. I need a livelihood and I have to educate my children."

Then I met Bapu. He asked me : "Do you want to come here?" I said : "Yes." "Why?" "Mr Friedman said I can get a job here." "What about your political ideas?" I had no political ideas so I kept quiet. When he repeated the question, I said: "I don't have any political ideas. I am just living for the sake of educating my children." He had a good laugh and said: "No, no, if you come here you must have some political ideas." I was very nervous, talking to such a big person. Then he said :"If you want to come, there are two conditions. You must believe in *swavalamban* (self reliance) and you must learn to speak and write Hindi well, because in Mahila Ashram, all correspondence is in Hindi. It is December now and you have to join in June. Must learn Hindi before you join."

I saw the place, stayed there two days and liked it. But I felt this was not the right place for me. Because the principle there was : most work, least pay. And my first aim was to educate my children. I believed and still believed that once I had become a mother, my first duty was to my family. If I wanted to do public service, I should not have married.

So when I returned to Madras, I hoped to continue as a lecturer somewhere and I forgot all about Hindi. Some of my friends did say that I should go to Wardha because it was a good opportunity, but I did not take their opinion seriously. Then, my college job, which was temporary, ended, and I was in the wilderness again. At that time, another letter came from Mahila Ashram, asking me to join as the Sanskrit and English teacher, and slowly learn to the job to take the position of the principal.

I decided to go. Om was admitted to Queen Mary's College, getting a scholarship, studying science. My mother stayed in Madras with Om and Mani. I took Saras and the baby Shrish with me to Wardha. There was a small house for me, and I settled in.

The next day I had to go to meet Bapu. Bapu was in

Sewagram and the Ashram was in Wardha, four and a half miles away. When I reached, Bapu asked in Hindi : "How are you? and how did you come?" I replied in English that I had come in a *tonga*. Then he said in English : "I told you to learn Hindi. Now you will go back to the Ashram and will not come to see me till you are able to talk to me in Hindi. Secondly, you came in a *tonga*. How many Indians would be able to take a *tonga*? You have come to serve the people. If you want to see me, you must walk and come here." I was almost in tears and thought I would go back to Madras. He said: "You are not going back, you are going to the Ashram. Join duty and learn Hindi as soon as possible and then come and see me."

New Way of Life

So I came and joined duty in the Mahila Ashram. At that time there were about 300 women and girls living there, aged between 12 and 40. All the work was done by the inmates. There were no servants at all. We were divided into groups and rotated the different kinds of work between us—cooking, washing, cleaning the rooms, cleaning toilets, filling water. In the morning, one group would have classes and the other group would work; in the afternoon, in reverse order. Hindi and spinning was compulsory for everyone. We had to wear *khadi* which we had spun ourselves. We were not allowed to have more than three sets of clothes each. The maximum pay for any worker was Rs 75 and the minimum Rs 50.

We got three meals a day—free. This was paid for by the founder. The meals were-wheat porridge and milk in the morning, lentils, vegetables and rice and *roti* in the afternoon, curds every alternate day, and lentils, vegetables and rice in the evening at 7 p.m. At festivals, we prepared Maharastrian sweets.

Our routine was like this. In the morning we would get up at 4.30 and have prayers on the terrace. Then, the groups would begin their work and the classes according to the shifts. After lunch, one hour rest and then the second shift. English started in class six. We also laid stress on physical training and exercises because Bapu insisted that women should be trained in self defence, so that to save their honour even if they had to fight and kill they should be able to do it. We had drills with dumbells and lezium. At that time, most of the teachers there were married couples.

I started studying Hindi. I read novels. The first novel I read was Premchand's *Godan*. I found the gender system difficult. In Hindi every object is either masculine or feminine, whereas in Malayalam, like English, all inanimate objects are neuter gender. For several months, I had to struggle to fit in. The other teachers were political workers who had worked for years in the movement, giving up everything. They felt it was favouritism for me to be brought in and placed above them. Apart from willingness to work, I had no other qualification. I was sympathetic but had no political background. Most of the women could not speak to me because they didn't know English. When I spoke my broken Hindi, they would laugh. But anyway I picked up the work, and learnt to spin.

Another problem arose-my mother fell very ill in Madras. Om had a very difficult time going to college, and looking after her and the house and Mani too. And my mother had a very bad temper. Om was afraid of her. My children always had complete faith in me, Om particularly. There have never been any secrets between us. Once, when she was about seven years old, my mother told her something and asked her not to tell me. She replied: "If mother is not to be told. Don't tell me because I tell mother everything." This shows what our relationship always was. I did not hide anything from her. Once, when she was small she asked me what is the difference between a boy and girl. I told her to observe her brother and herself and find out. When she said : "This is the difference" I said: "Yes, that is it and that is for producing children when one is grown up."

So Om wrote and told me that it was becoming very difficult for her to look after my mother. It would be better for me to take mother with me to Wardha. Then Om could stay in the hostel and she could get a fee concession. I would not have to send her any money. I brought my mother and Mani also to Wardha. But my mother was more or less paralysed. It was very difficult for me to manage with her and the two children and the Ashram work. Also, I felt I should not take advantage of the older workers, and I was not of much use to them. So I should leave and return to Madras. I had to take Bapu's permission. But he had made a condition that I must speak to him in Hindi.

Finally, I plucked up my courage and wrote a letter to him in my broken Hindi. He sent a reply saying that he went for a walk every day at 6 am. I could go and walk with him and discuss whatever I wanted with him during the walk. No other time was available. He always took two girls with him as his walking sticks. He would keep me as one of them. I was very nervous, first because I was not sure of my Hindi, and second, to speak Hindi while walking—he used to walk very fast and I was not used to walking at all. As it is, I had to walk to Sewagram to meet him. Anyway, I went. When I bowed to him, he slapped my back and said: "So, you have come." We set out, Manu on one side and I on the other. Bapu said : "Now tell me." I tried my best to explain in Hindi. He saw it was difficult so he said : "If you want, speak in English." But I said : "No, I will speak in Hindi." He laughed : "You are obstinate!"

Then he spoke in English and asked how I would find a job in Madras. He advised me to wait till Jammalalji came out of prison, in a month's time. He said : "We will consult him and then we will decide. You have put up with so much, you have come all the way from Madras, now I think you should stay here." When we returned, Bapu asked : "How did you come?" I said : "I came walking." He laughed : "so, you have learnt. All right, now you can go." It was 7 a.m. I touched his feet and he went for his bath. I had expected he would at least ask me to have breakfast. I was wondering how I would walk back.

Just then, Ba sent someone to call me. She smiled and asked me to sit, and gave me breakfast. This was the difference between a father and a mother! I walked back and by the time I reached Sewagram I had 104 degrees fever. I was not used to walking and I had walked about 11 miles at a stretch. That was the only illness I had all my life, except for my asthma.

The Ashram Is Yours

Then I decided to send my mother back and she agreed. In November, Jamnalalji came out of prison. He called me and we had a long talk. I told him that the other Ashram workers did not much like me and perhaps I should leave rather than annoy them. I was also worried about my debts and my mother's illness.

He listened and then said : "You can send your mother back as you have decided. If you need money, we do have the treasury. You need not worry. All I have to tell you is that you belong to the Ashram and the Ashram is yours. If some people say something about me, will I leave the Ashram and go? Where you are thinking of going, will people never say anything against you? Would you then leave that place too? You cannot run away from everywhere. You are to stay here. You are not to leave. I am sure your problems will gradually get resolved." He advised me to keep the children with me and put them in the Bal Bhavan, Wardha. I decided to obey Jamnalalji.

My husband at this time never wrote to me and as usual never bothered to help look after my mother or the children.

In February 1942, Jamnalal Bajaj died suddenly of a heart attack. By that time, the people of the Ashram had changed their behaviour towards me. Our work was going on well. Things became smooth for me. By then, I had become friendly with the Dixit family. Dixitiji was the secretary of the Ashram. Vyasji was the Hindi teacher. Everyone advised me to take lessons from them. At first, I took a dislike to Dixitji and tried to stay away from him because he was a widower who had married again. He was living with his second wife and his two children by the first wife. His second wife, Dayabehen, was also unwell-she had been mentally ill for some time and was recently cured. I became friendly with her. She had to bring up two children-Kusum, aged 10, and Satish, about six. These children became very friendly with my children and close to me.

When Dayabehen's first child, Lalli, was born in 1942, I went with her to the hospital. Dixitji's brother's wife was there. She exclaimed : "Oh, it's a girl!" I said : "So what if it is a girl. I am also a female. I have daughters. If you find it difficult, give me the baby, I'll bring her up." At that time, I was nursing Shrish. So I began to nurse Lalli too.

Quit India

Three months later, in August 1942, the Quit India movement started. It was a very big crisis AICC meetings used to be held at Wardha and we were the hostesses to delegates from all over India. We women were in the arrangement side, not in the discussion. Men went for discussions also.

The last meeting was in August 1942. We were told that most probably Bapu and other leaders would be arrested immediately after the announcement of Quit India. We knew we should not yield the Ashram to the government. We were afraid they would confiscate it. As soon as we heard the arrests had taken place, we held a meeting of all the inmates and decided to close the Ashram. The students were to return to their homes.

The teachers had to decide whether they would disperse or would continue the movement. We discussed and decided that we would not go home. We would close the Ashram, stay elsewhere, and continue propaganda work. Women would go house to house and men would join the main programme, underground, carrying messages from place to place, and trying to prevent violence from breaking out. Dixitji went to Nagpur and then to Chhindwara. He was arrested on August 22. On August 9 Bapu was arrested; the next day we closed the Ashram. Dayabehen and her children were sent to Bilaspur to her parents home.

On the 14th, Om left college and came to me. She on her own had decided to going the movement. I had written a letter to the president of the students' union of Presidency College, Madras, as an older student, saying it was the duty of the students who thought India needed freedom to leave their studies, come out and court arrest in a nonviolent way as Bapu had shown. I didn't think it would have much effect. But recently I found this letter quoted in a book *Quit India.* All the students had read this letter and many had left college, inspired by it. Om also confirmed this, as she knew about it before she left college.

The grown up girls, about 75 of them, refused to go home. They insisted on remaining with us teachers and joining the movement. So, our programme started. The men used to bring pamphlets. At night, we would sit and copy them by hand. In the morning, we would go out in groups of five, singing nationalist songs like "*Jhanda uncha rahe hamara*" and "*Uth jag musafr bhor bhayi*" and distribute pamphlets. Om, Saras and I were involved. I sent Mani and Shrish with the maidservant back to my mother at Adoor.

Om had an idea that on Rakhi day we should tie *rakhis* on the wrists of all the officials and policemen of the area. So we made *rakhis* of *khadi*, dyed them yellow, and after the *prabhat pheri* that day, the girls went to the policemen's houses. They did not allow us to tie *rakhis*. Very politely, they said : "Sisters, forgive us. We cannot honour this *rakhi* so please don't tie it." The constables who saw us coming, disappeared. Some women managed to forcibly tie *rakhi* on the police inspector. A few days later, he get himself transferred because he knew he could not do his duty as a brother to them. But most of the police were sympathetic to us. Soon after, all of them were transferred and new men came.

In Prison

That time, nothing mattered except that we must do all that could be done to get the British out. Everyone was in that mood. I was no exception.

On August 27, Om, I and 10 other girls aged between 14 and 17 were arrested. The first 20 days were very difficult. All of us were locked into a space meant for eight persons. There were already eight women there. It was dark and rats were running about. We were given horrible food—hard maize *roti* and *dal* which looked like black water. The numbers arrested and pushed into this room increased every day, until it became impossible to lie down and difficult even to sit. The lack of hygiene was incredible. They confiscated our spinning wheels, but finally, on our insistence, gave them back. We used them as weapons to scare away the rats. Soon, several of the girls fell sick with upset stomachs and fever.

One day, when we were let into the courtyard, we flatly refused to return to the cell. They threatened to beat us but we still refused. Finally, they brought a van and took us to Nagpur jail.

The conditions there were much better. The jail superintendent there, Radhabai, was a very nice woman. She looked upon us as her younger sisters. She was a widow. The criminal women simply worshipped her. At first, we were C class prisoners but in a few days we were given B class privileges because we were detenus. There were no charges against us. This meant that we got better food-bread, butter and milk for breakfast and books to read. Our friends outside could send us things. We began to live there like one family. Om, Saras and I took responsibility for anyone who fell sick. If the jail authorities treated us unreasonably, we thought we would go on fast to protest. But they did not trouble us much—a kind of adjustment took place.

The criminal women were very nice to us. We started classes for them in literacy and spinning. Every day, we used to have prayers—reading the *Bible*, the *Quran* and the *Gita*. Most of the criminal women were there on charges of murder. Some of them had been falsely implicated. One woman had killed her brother-in-law who was trying to rape her. Another had killed her illegitimate child. But they were such nice women, one could never think they were capable of killing anyone.

More Than Sisters

For one and a half years, we lived together like this. There were two women to whom I became very close while in jail. One was Sarojbehen, the other was Raihanabehen. We three were like daughters to Kakasaheb Kalelkar. These two were very good friends, in fact, more than sisters. But they were very different from each other in temperament. Sarojbehen was calm, affectionate, unable to find fault with anyone. Raihanabehen had a short temper and a great sense of humour. She was a Muslim, the daughter of Abbas Tyebjee, a former president of the Congress. She was a great devotee of Sri Krishna. She used to compose poems and songs, and sing them. She had a beautiful voice.

Kakasaheb was a widower and he had two sons. He stayed next to the Mahila Ashram and was devoted to Bapu. He was doing very good work—he wrote prolifically in Hindi, Marathi, Gujarati, English, even though his mother tongue was Marathi. Sarojbehen was introduced to him by Raihanabehen and she became his secretary. Raihanabehen also lived in the same house, as his daughter.

Raihanabehen was very rich and being a muslim, had inheritance rights in her father's property. She used to constantly help people. She helped me very often. It was in jail that we became very close. We disagreed on many things. But she was very straightforward and never hesitated to say what she thought. But if she realised she was in the wrong, she did not hesitate to apologise either.

In February 1943 we came to know that Bapu was going on a fast the Aga Khan palace, in protest against the violence that had broken out in the movement. We did not get newspapers but we heard the male prisoners talking loudly about it in their ward. I decided to fast along with Bapu. I didn't tell anyone. Raihanabehen noticed that I was not eating and she tried her best to dissuade me. When nothing worked, she said. "You are doing a lot of work, serving those who are ill here. If you become weak, you will not be able to do this work. Is your obstinacy more important or your service?" Then I promised her that the day I felt too weak to continue my routine I would break the fast. But by god's grace, I was able to fast till Bapu broke his fast, after 21 days. I continued doing all the work, and just having the juice of one lemon and water every day. Of course, I was already used to fasting, as I was in the habit of keeping *nirjala* (fast without water) three times a week and eating only one meal on Sunday.

In October 1943 I was released Saras and Om were released in March 1943 and had gone home. Sarojbehen, Raihanabehen, and I were the last to be released. I was released one week before them. I was anxious to return to Kerala. I had learnt from my children's letters, censored though they were, that they were being neglected, treated like orphans, even though staying with their father. When I reached the station, there was no one to receive me. I got into a bus to go home, and as the bus was passing the local school suddenly a shout was heard : "Stop, stop." The bus stopped and the next moment, my son Mani had climbed in and was in my lap, crying. "Ma! Never leave me again, never leave me." You can imagine how it affected me.

When my husband came home after a few days, he behaved as if I had never been away. He did not ask me anything about my jail experience. I also didn't bother. I was now wondering what to do. He didn't ask whether I was staying or going. I wanted to stay because my mother was sick and my children needed me. But how to survive on her pension of Rs 25?

About three weeks passed. Then I got a letter from Wardha, saying that since everyone had been released and Bapu was to be released soon, the Ashram was being reopened and I should go. My salary would be Rs 75. If I went and took the children, they would be fed and educated, and we could manage somehow. My mother could manage on her pension. I told my husband and said : "If you want me to stay, say so now. Once I go, I won't be able to return." He said : "No, no, you should go. You will do well." I asked him if he would help me get a job in Kerala. He was a well known literary figure by now. But he did not try for me. So I left and went back to Wardha.

The Ashram opened and the routine went on normally. Many men who had joined the movement had died in the interim and their womenfolk had come to the Ashram. Bapu too had arrived. I renewed my practice of going for a walk with him every Sunday morning and talking to him about the Ashram. He was interested in every small detail. For example, once, some yarn was stolen. I announced that I would be on fast till it was returned. We were not interested in catching the thief. We just wanted the yarn back. On the second day, it was quietly returned. Bapu told me : "You handled it rightly."

I also discussed my personal problems with him. He would give his opinion but never force it on anyone. One example of this was before I went to jail. One day, Bapu said to me : "You are allowing your daughter to study in a government college on a scholarship. This is not right. You should practise what you preach. How can you ask others to do what you cannot ask your daughter to do?" I said : "Then the only alternative is for me to leave the Ashram."

"Why?"

"I cannot call her here because my one aim is that she should be educated and enabled to stand on her own feet. To make my daughter independent is my first aim which I cannot forget or abandon." He asked : "Is it necessary that she study English for this?" I said : "Yes, it is necessary to find a job, today. Without a degree she cannot find a job. How will she live? Will the Ashram feed her for ever?"

He laughed and said : "No."

I said : "Bapu, let me ask you one question. Why did you call me here? I had no background of political work. My family is an agricultural family but my parents were teachers. I studied in an English medium school and college and became a lecturer in a city. You called me to be trained as the principal here because I was an MA, nearly a PhD, with research experience, and you thought I was more capable than the others here who had a political background. If an MA degree is valuable in the institution, how much more will it be in the outside world. That is why I cannot discontinue her education."

He listened quietly and said : "If that is what you think, let her continue."

But a year later, Om herself flung away the scholarship and came to the Ashram to join the movement. Afterwards, she could not get into any college because she had a jail record. So she studied privately. She did not take any financial help from me. She worked in the Ashram and studied. Today, she is 62 years old. She has been my mainstay in life, never dependent as girls are supposed to be, always my companion in every crisis.

In 1945 Saras marriage was arranged with a Congress leader, Sukumar Pagare. He had been with Dixitji in jail and Dixitji arranged the match. When I told Bapu, he said : "It is all right. But you have found a Brahman for your daughter. I would have attended the marriage if he had been a Harijan." I said : "I didn't look for a Brahman, Bapu. He just happened to be a Brahman. To tell the truth I didn't look for a Harijan either. I accepted the person whom we came across and who seems suitable."

But I said : "I have another daughter. I will marry her to a Harijan only you will have to find the groom. He should have similar ideas and way of thinking as my daughter has." He said : "Yes, I will find a boy." I said : "She will be married when you find the boy."

Well, neither did Bapu find the boy nor did Om marry. She did not want to marry and I did not insist. I never insisted that any of my children should marry. My sons found partners for themselves and I accepted them.

So Saras was married. We spent a total of Rs 500 on the marriage. She wore a beautiful *khadi* sari for Rs 10. A few days later, her husband won the elections in Madhya Pradesh and became an MLA.

In those days, Bapu was disturbed because the Hindu-Muslim riots had started and famine had broken out in Calcutta. I remember one incident. He was to visit the Ashram. We prepared a big map of India on the floor with different coloured foodgrains and lentils. When he saw it, he looked grave and called me aside. He asked : "What will you do with these grains?" Before I could answer, Malatitai of the Ashram said : "We will make *khichdi* of it and eat it."

Bapu was satisfied and said : "Nothing should be wasted. People are starving. Food is the only thing that can satisfy human beings and keep them alive. I was pained to think these grains might be wasted."

We used to put up small cultural programmes to entertain Bapu. On Rakhi day, 1944, we put up a Hindi play in which the gods gather to discuss how to end the famine earth. One suggested that they call the greatest leader on earth and give him their powers. But Indrani objects saying that war cannot be ended by war. She recounts the origin of

Raksha Bandhan, saying that the war between the gods and demons ended only when she tied a *rakhi*, the emblem of women's strength, on Indra's wrist and endowed him with her power. So they decide to tie a *rakhi* on the wrist of the leader who can bring about peace. They call world leaders one by one, Churchill, Roosevelt, Hilter, the Japanese emperor. Each one says that he will establish peace by defeating all the others in war. Then Narad comes and suggests that Mahatma Gandhi be called. The play ends with the *rakhi* being tied on Bapu's wrist.

When the play was staged, I was standing behind Bapu. He kept joking with me throughout. When Narad suggested his name, Bapu thought the actors would ask him to enter the play. He took up his *lathi* and was ready. But then an actor (Om) dressed as Bapu came on stage. Bapu said : "Oh, you have found another Bapu. Now you do not need me." And he laughed heartily.

We used to join Bapu for prayers when we could. His presence would not make any difference to our way of conducting the prayers. We used to sing *bhajans*—by Meera, Kabir, Surdas or by Raihanabehen. Bapu would give a short message sometimes or answer questions.

In November 1944, my mother died. Om looked after her in the last days. She sent me a wire when mother became seriously ill but by the time I reached, she had died. My husband came only after the cremation. Those days, he used to come home only once a fortnight or so. After this, he and I had hardly any contact.

In 1945 Dayabehen had her second child. We were like sisters by this time. She was ailing after the childbirth. Her child came into my lap. His name was Suresh.

Somewhat Disillusioned

At this time, Bapu was busy, trying to quell the Hindu-Muslim violence in various places. The situation in the Ashram was deteriorating. New people had come who did not live by the principles of the institution. They were more interested in pushing themselves forward. Some of them did not like Babuji (Mr Dixit) and wanted him to leave. In the meantime Dayabehen had developed TB so she could not stay in the Ashram. Ultimately, he had to resign. I was very upset at his being insulted like this. WE had worked together—we used to go for Sunday walks together with Bapu.

In fact, the women of the Ashram were not better or purer than other women outside. They were like any other women in their behaviour, capable of quarrelling, jealousy, gossipping, Raihanabehen, Sarojbehen and I felt that many of the criminal women were far better human beings then many of the Ashram inmates.

In found that repression had negative effects at times, for instance in the Ashram, we used to eat plain boiled food but in jail some of the inmates used to quietly steal spices and eat them. Similarly, Ashram inmates were to observe *brahmacharya* and many married couples took the celibacy vow but were not able to observe it. Most of the followers were there because they were deeply attached to Bapu. But some women were there because their menfolk had joined the movement, leaving them no other place to go. The men decide to follow Bapu's ideals and the women of the family had no other choice.

Most of the followers came not so much to implement Bapu's ideals as due to love and reverence for Bapu. They worshipped him like a god. Even Jawaharlal Nehru could not implement all Bapu's ideals, let along others. Of course, some followers were completely dedicated to the ideals, for example, Mahadevohai and Manubehen.

Bapu walked alone on his path and placed complete faith in those who came to him. He disregarded any accusations against them. I don't know whether he couldn't always judge character right or he didn't want to, but those he though were very good did not always turn out to be so good. There was no other reason for his failure. So I became somewhat disillusioned by Bapu's followers.

Once Babuji (Mr Dixit) resigned all the responsibility for the children fell on me. Bapu was in Koakhali. I wrote and told him everything. He suggested it would be good if I went to the Kasturba Harijan Balika Ashram at Okhla, Delhi, and took charge as its principal. I agreed, and came to Delhi with all the children except Om and Satish. As Dayabehen was very ill brought her to Delhi and admitted her to the TB hospital here.

Now I had to bring up five small children—Shrish aged six, Lalli aged our, Suresh aged two, Mani and Kusum. Om was in Wardha, studying and working at the Ashram. It was hard to manage on my small salary. In 1946, Dayabehen died. Her children refused to go with their uncle and aunt who offered to like them. The children insisted on staying with me. So the full responsibility was now mine. I had brought up Suresh since his birth and Lalli too.

Mother to Many

While I was in prison, I had organised the care of many girls who were political prisoners. They started calling me "Amma" as my daughters did. By the time I was released, not only all the inmates but even the authorities had started addressing me as Amma. When I met Bapu after his release in 1944, he met me with laughter and a slap on the back, saying : "I am sure you can talk in Hindi very well now." Before I could reply, one of the Ashram women, Kanchanbehen, said : "Bapu, she talks only in Hindi now. And do you know who she is ? She has become Amma to all of us who were in jail with her and to all in the Ashram too." Bapu looked at me gravely and said : "Do you know the meaning of being called Amma. It brings many responsibilities with it. Do not allow anyone to call you Amma lightly. Now you see, you cannot be Amma to me, you are my daughter. If it is impossible to stop others calling you mother, then try to become really Amma to them." And, Madhu, from that day, I have tried my best to follow his words. Wherever I went, this title followed me. And I have tried to do justice to it. Any I have tried to do justice to it. Any child for whom I took responsibility became mine.

In April 1947, my adopted son Suresh died of diphtheria. This upset me and I was not keeping well. So I took leave without pay from Kasturba Ashram. At that time, Babuji was working in *The Hindustan Times*, Delhi. For a while in this year, I and the children lived with different friends—in Udaipur, in Vellore. Because I did not like the idea of Babuji and I living in the same house. So I went to Wardha and stayed a week with Raihanabehen. She was the only one who could give me practical advice. She said : "Either you completely cut yourself off from Babuji, which is not possible because of the children. Otherwise, you become one family. Because you have to live in this society. The best solution is to get married. He will like it, I know, but what do you say?"

I asked my daughters what they thought. Kusum said: "Whether you marry or not, you are my mother"; Saras was not very happy; Om had already suggested that we should marry. So I wrote to Bapu, he gave his blessings, and in December 1947 we got married. I had already broken off from my first husband. He was very upset. But the funniest part was that he had already re-married much earlier. Om maintained correspondence with him up to his last days. He died in 1961.

The children were the main reason for my getting married again. I was not averse to the idea but neither was I keen on it. If not for the children, I would not have remarried, but lived alone and looked after myself. At this time, Babuji was getting Rs 200 a month. I got a job in a school at Rs 125 a month. In 1950, my youngest son, Sharad, was born and in 1951 Kusum was married to one Surendranath Tripathi, a lecturer in Aligarh University.

Babuji and I divided the work of looking after Sharad between us. Still, it was hard. I had to cook for a dozen people and we always had some others staying with as—like when Om came in 1951, she brought one of her students who was very attached to her and there was one boy from Nagpur who looked up to me as his mother and he was looking for a job in Delhi, and Babuji's and the children's friends.

I revived my literary career at this time. I have written several books in english, Malayalam, Sanskrit and Hindi. I used to sit up late at night and write. Babuji encouraged and helped me greatly in my writing.

Babuji changed his job many times. He used to get restless and change his job. In between he was unemployed for two years. It was very hard to manage things then. All the responsibility was mine. Maybe it was my temperament to take on responsibility In 1963 Babuji resigned from "The Collected Works of Mahatma Gandhi" where he worked the last eight years and after that, only wrote articles for newspapers. He never bothered about household expenses or how the house was run.

Through all this, Raihanabehen helped me a lot. Whenever I needed something, she would anticipate my need and send me money. Never once did I have to ask for it. She did it on her own—must be altogether not less than Rs 20,000 or so. There was no limit for her. She never made me feel I was begging. If not for her, I would not have been able to do what I did.

New Pastures

I also registered for PhD in Sanskrit at Delhi University on the topic "Women in Sanskrit Drama." By this time, Mani graduated and joined the diplomatic service. He got married to a Tamilian girl. I said : "Anyone you bring is mine." Because I have always believed that if you love someone, you must love those whom they love. But I had a very hard time convincing Babuji because she was a Tamilian. Also, she was her parents' only daughter and they wanted to give a lot of dowry. But I refused and said neither would we give anything nor should they. Our house is literally a symbol of national integration. My daughters-in-law are from Tamil Nadu, Bengal, Andhra Pradesh and the youngest, the daughter of a Gujarat father and Nagaland mother. My sons-in-law belong to Madhya Pradesh, UP, and Punjab.

In 1959, Kakasaheb Kalelkar, who was a father figure to me, and was vicepresident of the Indian Council of Cultural Relations, asked me to go to British Guyana as India's cultural representative. After I accepted, one Swami Purnananda of Guyana wrote a letter to Kakasaheb, asking him not to send a woman as she wouldn't be able to manage the work. When Kakasaheb told my husband, he said that I should not go in that case. Anyway, he did not much like my going for such a long time. Kakasaheb laughed and said : "I wrote a long reply to the letter, saying that woman is the mainstay of Indian culture, and if a woman cannot do the job, nobody can do it. So I went to Guyana, taking eight year old Sharad with me.

There, I stayed in the capital Georgetown, but I travelled a lot in the interior. My predecessor had stayed only in the capital and run Hindi classes there. But when I received invitations to visit other places, I decided I must go. The first year, on Janmashtami day, I visited a total of 32 places and spoke in schools and temples, in a mixture of English and Hindi, because the people did not know either language well.

Fifty two percent of the population of Guyana was of Indian origin. Their ancestors were shipped out there by the British to work as labourers on the plantations. After they were freed, the Indian community became the most prosperous, working their own land. They had a vision of India as their homeland, a paradise. But they were feeling isolated.

My speaking in temples created a sensation—crowds came—and after that, I received a spate of invitations to go and speak in different institutions. So I used to travel at weekends, taking Sharad with me, and, during the week, I took Hindi classes in Georgetown. I also organised staging of Hindi plays which were so successful that we raised enough money through tickets and donations to build a cultural centre in the capital. A big plot of land was donated by a Guyanese Indian, Mr Hariprasad. My Hindi students joined together and we made 10,000 cement bricks to build the centre. Indrani Rehman and her troupe came to Guyana and performed to raise money. The governor presided over the ceremony of laying the foundation stone, performed by the oldest living Indian migrant, then 108 years old.

All the Indians in Guyana whom I met—Hindus, Muslims and others—were very friendly and helpful to me in the two years that I lived there. Others too-Chinese, Africans—participated in the Hindi plays and other activities. We used to celebrate all Indian festivals, Muslim and Hindu, and national holidays, together.

Even today, 25 years later, many people in Guyana keep in touch with me. One whom I remember particularly is Beni Singh, then 23 years old, who was my right hand in all the work I did there. Although we were together only two years, he became a son to me. He looked after me and carried on the work even when I was hospitalised with asthma. Now, he is in London, doing good work among his people there.

After one year there, my husband started writing to me asking me to come back. But I kept quiet. In June 1959, Om came home from England where she had gone on a fellowship and found the house in Delhi a shambles. No one to cook, no one to look after anything. She took charge of the house and wrote to me not to worry.

After two years, even though the ICCR as well as the people in Guyana pressed me to stay on, I had to come back. I took my successors around to every place which I had visited and where I had set up Hindi classes, but later, they stayed only in Georgetown and just gave big parties for the rich and the diplomats. So that was the last the others outside Georgetown saw of any Indian cultural committee. When I left Guyana, there were $4,000 in the bank, the land and the bricks for the centre. I do not know what became of all this.

During this period, I completed my PhD with the help of my husband and Om. I would write each chapter and send it to them, they would finalise the footnotes, type it, take it to my guide and get his approval which he gave without any difficulty. In 1960, the degree was granted without any viva, and the judges recommended it for publication immediately.

In 1961 I joined Miranda House as a lecturer in Sanskrit. To begin with, I was not much liked there because I was quite old and I was selected in preference to one of their old students. But, gradually, when they saw that I did my work and did not interfere with anyone, all the problems were solved. I directed the first Sanskrit plays in the college which won many prizes.

By the time I retired in 1974, all my responsibilities were complete. All the children were well settled. Mani is now Indian ambassador in Sri Lanka, Satish regional manager in Kelvinators, Shrish in with PTI, Sharad is an air force squadon leader, Om was a lecturer at the Central Institute of Education, Delhi, and has now retired.

In 1976, Babuji died suddenly of cerebral thrombosis while I was away in Kathmandu, visiting Shrish. I used to go to Kerala every two years to visit my father also until his death in 1972.

Greatest Blessing

Throughout life, I have felt that my first responsibility is to my children. If not for them, probably I would not even have come out of the situation in my first husband's family. There would have been no interest in life. It was Om who saved me from that life when I even contemplated suicide. She was just two years old, my only child at that time.

She is not only my daughter, she is my mother. She has put up with everything, cheerfully. Can you imagine a 17 year old girl accepting her mother's second marriage and taking on three grown up children as her own responsibility? From the age of 17 she has been independent. She has really kept this house together. All the sisters and brothers, and their children—25 of them now-and grandchildren really adore her. No one will say a word against her. My greatest blessing is my daughter.